To Dad
with love Sue
Christmas 1973

Ex Libris

R. J. Unstead

ALDOUS HUXLEY

A BIOGRAPHY

Volume One: 1894-1939

ALDOUS HUXLEY

A BIOGRAPHY

Volume One: 1894-1939

SYBILLE BEDFORD

CHATTO & WINDUS

in association with

COLLINS·LONDON

Published jointly by

William Collins Sons & Co. Ltd
London · Glasgow · Sydney · Auckland
Toronto · Johannesburg

and

Chatto & Windus Ltd
London

ISBN 00 216006 4

© Sybille Bedford 1973

Printed in Great Britain by
T. & A. Constable Ltd
Edinburgh

To
MATTHEW

I am not concerned here with Aldous Huxley's literary fame; whether future literary historians will rank him with Thomas Love Peacock or with Dean Swift. My concern is his heritage to those who really care about the future of the human race, and in this respect I hope that he will be remembered. . . .

DENNIS GABOR

. . with that special sensibility to the contours of the future [he] stood on the edge of, and peered beyond, the present frontiers of our self-knowledge . . . There is a sense in which he knew that he stood on the frontier of the old astrology that was passing and the new astronomy that was beginning in the science of man. . . .

SIR ISAIAH BERLIN

. . Biography is to give a man some kind of shape after his death.

VIRGINIA WOOLF

CONTENTS

vii

CONTENTS

CONTENTS

PART SEVEN: CAESURA 1937-1939

ILLUSTRATIONS

x

PREFACE

The object of this book is to give a truthful and coherent account of the life of Aldous Huxley and of Aldous Huxley as a man. Although it is no way intended as a work of literary criticism or an evaluation of his thought, such a book must—quite inevitably—contain a good deal of his writing and his thought. Naturally I feel presumptuous in attempting the biography of a man of his moral and intellectual quality. I was persuaded by the nearest members of his family, his widow, his brother, his son; I finally accepted because my own fondness for Aldous made me want to do it. (There was perhaps, as well, some element of personal logic: because when I was young and everything seemed easy, I had lightly thought that one day I might do precisely this.) If the work was a labour of love, it was also work done in a spirit of detachment. I have been entirely candid—to the best of my knowledge and ability—about everything concerning Aldous Huxley's character and actions. And although this principle had to be moderated—very occasionally—when writing about people now living, the rule which, throughout, I set before me was a dictum of the late Desmond MacCarthy's: A biographer is an artist upon oath.

Because of the particular circumstances—the destruction of the Huxley papers by fire—a perhaps unusually large proportion of the sources of this biography is verbal. I should like to divide all sources into five categories: published sources, documentary, oral-documentary, oral and personal sources.

Published Sources: Of these the main ones are of course the works of Aldous Huxley *in toto* and his *Letters* in the admirable collection edited by Professor Grover Smith. Another major source is Laura Archera Huxley's *This Eternal Moment*. Other works, such as the A. H. Memorial Volume edited by Sir Julian Huxley, Sir Julian's own *Memories*, some letters of D. H. Lawrence, etc, etc, will be acknowledged in their place. (I have—purposely—omitted to read books and theses on A. H.'s work.)

Documentary Sources: Some of the most relevant original material is found in the letters of Maria Huxley. The three main (extant) collections of these are (roughly chronologically) her letters to the late Lord Sackville, to her sister Jeanne (Mme George Neveux), and the letters to her son.

Much of the material for Maria's own youth and background,

for the Huxleys' early married years, travels and some of their California life is derived from a memoir of some 30,000 words written originally for the purpose of this biography by Maria's second sister Suzanne (Mme Joep Nicolas)—a most charming work, in French, which, I hope, will see publication in its own right.

Other documentary sources are the letters of the late Robert Nichols, the poet; the journal of George Neveux; the diary of Beth (Mrs Sanford) Wendel; Professor Roy Lamson's working copy of Aldous Huxley's lectures at the Massachusetts Institute of Technology; the letters of Aldous's mother-in-law, the late Marguérite Nys; transcripts of B.B.C. Radio and Television interviews; and a large number of letters and memoirs addressed to me which will be individually acknowledged in the text.

Oral-Documentary Sources: Five gramophone records made from the original tape of an interview with Aldous Huxley by John Chandos in London in June 1961 commissioned by Record Supervision Ltd. Some tape-recordings in the possession of the University of California at Los Angeles (UCLA); and some tape-recordings made by Laura Huxley.

Oral Sources: The first-hand recollections of friends, relations, acquaintances, colleagues—some of whom knew Aldous long and well, others who had had some brief, incisive glimpse—communicated to me in conversations and interviews.

The fifth and personal source is what I saw, heard, learned—and perhaps learned to understand—in the course of forty years friendship with Aldous and friendship with some members of his family and his circle. Such insight as I may have come to about Aldous's character and development is very much due to foundations early laid by Maria Huxley.

The book owes a great deal to the generous, intelligent and devoted co-operation of Aldous's family and friends. This has made the research an extraordinary experience for which I find it hard to express anything like adequate gratitude.

I want to thank Laura Archera (Mrs Aldous) Huxley, Sir Julian Huxley and Matthew Huxley for their endless goodwill and help of many kinds as well as for their permission to quote from their own works or letters in their possession.

I want to thank the late Gervas Huxley—Aldous's cousin and exact contemporary—for his first-hand account of Aldous's schoolboy years and his first year at Oxford. I want to thank Juliette (Lady) Huxley who provided much of the material for the young Aldous at Garsington and many touches about other episodes in later years, and has been unfailingly kind and resourceful. I want to thank Jeanne Neveux, whose inside knowledge of the Huxleys' life from the 1920s to 1955 makes her one of the mainstays of the biography, and who, step by step, has given me constant help—answering questions, verifying facts, undertaking journeys, over the last five years.

I want to thank the following for supplying essential material: Suzanne Nicolas; Rina Rontini (Mme Marcel) Eustration; Aldous's niece Sophie (Mme Willem) Welling; Roy Fenton; Beth (Mrs Sanford) Wendel; Roy Lamson of M.I.T. and Peggy Lamson; Dr Humphrey Osmond.

I want to thank Professor Grover Smith, whose published collection of Aldous Huxley's *Letters* provides of course so much of the basic biographical material, for his great personal courtesy and kindness in answering any question I put to him.

I want to thank the following for help or contributions—often considerable—of various kinds:

Madge (Lady) Ashton, Mrs Barbara Bagenal, Enid Bagnold, Sir Isaiah Berlin, Constance Bessie, Denys Blakelock, The Hon. Dorothy Brett, Dr Barbara B. Brown, Miss Olive Brown, Moura (Baroness) Budberg, Joan Collier (Mrs F. A.) Buzzard, Cass and Mrs Cass Canfield, John Chandos, Sir George Clark, Kenneth Clark (Lord Clark of Saltwood), Sir Lawrence Collier, Cyril Connolly, Jeff (Mrs Douglas) Corner, Robert Craft, Dr Max Cutler, Denis D. David, Leonard K. Elmhirst, Eugene Exman, Miss Victoire Fairtlough, The Rev. R. A. L. Fell, Miss Bernadine Fritz, Professor Dennis Gabor, the late Eileen Garrett, the late Sylvester Gates, Ellen (Mrs Adam) Giffard, Mrs Arthur Goldschmid, Russell Green, Gillian (Mrs Anthony) Greenwood, Ena (Mrs F. Duglas) Curry Grundy, Major Leonard Handley, Yvonne (Mrs Hamish) Hamilton, Miss Patience Hardcastle, Professor Garrett Hardin, the late Lord Harman, Allanah Harper, L. P. Hartley, Rose de Haulleville, Eva Herrmann, Mrs Faith Hiles, Grace (Mrs Edwin) Hubble, Professor Robert M. Hutchins, Jeremy Hutchinson Q.C., Mary (Mrs St-John) Hutchinson, David Huxley, Francis Huxley, Judith (Mrs Matthew) Huxley, Miss Margaret Huxley, Rosalind (Mrs Leonard) Huxley, Christopher Isherwood, Miss Margaret Isherwood, Lionel Jardine, C.I.E., Professor and Mrs Frank Pierce Jones, Paul C. Jones, Peggy (Mrs William) Kiskadden, Franklin Lacey, Nadine (Mrs G.W.) Lambert, Rosamund Lehmann, Peter Leslie, Frances Lindley, Yolanda (Mrs) Loeffler, Anita Loos, Sir Alan Lubbock, Edward Maisel, Dr Felix Mann, Miss M. Marshall, C. E. Menor Jr, Yehudi and Diana Menuhin, Professor Andrew Greer Meyer, Naomi (Lady) Mitchison, Ivan Moffat, Professor Ashley Montagu, Sybil Morrison, Raymond Mortimer, Percy Muir, John Murray, Alan Napier, Georges Neveux, Noële Neveux, Mariana Newton, Vicomte Charles de

Noailles, Dr Elmer Noble, Liam O'-Gallagher, Sylvia Nicolas (Mrs Luke) O'Neill, Arthur Ormont, Katherine Peak, Eric Petrie and the late Maria Petrie, the late Virginia Pfeiffer, Lawrence Clark Powell, Swami Prabhavananda, Marie le Put, Rosalind Rajagopal, Mr and Mrs Harold Raymond, Professor J. B. Rhine, Professor Mason Rose, Henry Walter Rowan, Sir Steven Runciman, Elizabeth Salter, Dr William H. Sheldon, James and Radha Sloss, Professor Houston Smith, Vera (Mrs Igor) Stravinsky, H. G. C. Streatfeild, Professor Dauwe Sturman, Professor J. M. Tanner, Theo Townshend, Francis Thompson, Renée (Mrs Jerrard) Tickell, Miss Jane Turner, Professor Patrick D. Wall, Professor Howard Warshaw, Goodwin Weisberg, Sanford Wendel, Claire Nicolas (Mrs Robert Winthrop) White, Sebastian White, Professor George Wickes, Professor Jack Wilkinson, Miss Helen Witt, Dr Charlotte Wolff, the late Leonard Woolf, the late Marjorie Worthington, Jacob Israel Zeitlin and Maurice Zuserano.

I want to thank my friends Evelyn Gendel, Eda Lord and Richard Ollard for having sustained me, each from their side of the Atlantic, with their indispensable interest, criticism and advice.

Author's Note
[Re Quotations and Sources]

A number of quotations in this book are not entirely accurate: none are without full authority. In quoting from Aldous Huxley's books and letters I have freely extracted, eliminated, juxtaposed, conflated as best suited my immediate purpose. I have never put words into his mouth.

From the many sources whose help I have gratefully acknowledged I have often supplemented the printed sources (Gervas Huxley, Lady Huxley, Enid Bagnold come immediately to mind) by the private correspondence and conversation with which particular passages may have been fused or even substantially modified.

Note

The author and publishers wish to thank the following for permission to reprint excerpts from copyright material:

Sir Isaiah Berlin for his contribution to the *Aldous Huxley Memorial Volume*.

Harcourt Brace Tovanovich, Inc. for *The Strange World of Willie Seabrook* by Marjorie Worthington.

Anne Charleton for Robert Nicols' letters to Dr and Mrs Henry Head.

The Harvard University Library for Miss Dorothy Ward's letter to Miss Jewett.

The editors of *The Kenyon Review*, Gambier, Ohio for Gerald Heard's article "Poignant Prophet". (© 1965 Kenyon College)

Longmans Ltd for Lord Annan's contribution to *Studies in Social History: A Tribute to G. M. Trevelyan*, edited by J. H. Plumb, entitled "The Intellectual Aristocracy".

Laurence Pollinger Ltd., William Heinemann Ltd. and the Estate of the late Mrs Frieda Lawrence for *The Collected Letters of D. H. Lawrence*.

Denis Preston and Record Supervision Ltd. for taped interviews with Aldous Huxley.

PART ONE

The Young Boy: 1894-1908

"What are you thinking about,
Aldous dear?"

Aldous, aged four, turning his head
from the window, "*Skin*."

SIR JULIAN HUXLEY

His descent both on his father's and
his mother's side brought down on him
a weight of intellectual authority and
a momentum of moral obligations.

GERALD HEARD

Oh, what fun we had walking over
to Prior's Field. A walk with Aldous
was sheer joy. . . .

GERVAS HUXLEY

Chapter One

Laleham, Surrey, England

ALDOUS LEONARD HUXLEY was born on 26th July 1894 at Laleham near Godalming in Surrey, the third son of Leonard Huxley and Julia Frances Arnold.

Leonard Huxley at the time was an assistant master at Charterhouse, thirty-four years old, the son, we need hardly be reminded of Thomas Henry Huxley who was still living and survived Aldous's birth by a short year. Julia Huxley—granddaughter of Dr Arnold of Rugby, niece of Matthew Arnold, daughter of the Rev. Thomas Arnold who twice left the Anglican Church for the Church of Rome, sister of Mrs Humphry Ward, the novelist—was thirty-two. She had been educated at Somerville, Oxford (a first in English in 1882). Aldous's two brothers Julian and Trevenen were aged seven and five.

Laleham (still standing) is a pleasant, middle-sized, late Victorian house with about half an acre of garden. Family life was a very happy one; although standards of behaviour were high, the atmosphere of Aldous's first home was affectionate and gay. His mother, described by those who knew her as a remarkable, an admirable, a formidable woman, is remembered nevertheless with immense affection rather than with awe—*"How she could laugh"*, and she certainly gave her own affection to her children. Leonard Huxley enjoyed life, was gentle, even-tempered, "jolly, kindly, full of jokes." Baby Aldous was looked after by the family servants and a young girl from Königsberg, Fräulein Ella Salkowski (whom *he* sent for, in due course, for his infant son); he was treated with love by his parents; his brothers indulged him. Occasionally he was teased.

What we know about him as a young child is the usual residue of anecdote and snapshot. During his first years his head was proportionally enormous, so that he could not walk till he was two because he was apt to topple over. "We put father's hat on him and it fitted." In another country, at a great distance in time and place, when he lay ill and near his end in Southern California, a friend, wanting to distract him, said, "Aldous, didn't you ever have a nickname when you were small?" and Aldous who hardly ever talked about his childhood or indeed about himself (possibly because one did not ask) said promptly, "They called me Ogie. Short for Ogre."

The Ogre was a pretty little boy, the photographs—he sprawling in Bubble's costume in an armchair, leaning against his mother, leaning against his Aunt Mary Ward, in a tender stance—show the high forehead, the (then) clear gaze, the tremulous mouth and a sweetness of expression, an alertness beyond that of other angelic little boys looking into a camera. Aldous, his brother Julian tells us, sat quietly a good deal of the time "contemplating the strangeness of things.

> He showed some quality,[1] some innate superiority, which called for respect even in the nursery jungle. This recognition dawned when Aldous was five and I a prep school boy of twelve.

"I used to watch him with a pencil," said his cousin and contemporary, Gervas Huxley,[2] "you see, he was always drawing . . . My earliest memory of him is sitting—absorbed—to me it was magic, a little boy of my own age drawing so beautifully, drawing such wonderful things." "I was always told," (this comes from a much younger second cousin) "that when he was five or six, *everybody knew that Aldous was different.*"[3]

Different; at the same time a young child. "Not only, but also," as the later Aldous would have said. There are a few glimpses. He was delicate; he had mischievous moods; he could play. He carried his rag doll about with him for company until he was eight. He was fond of grumbling. They gave him a milk mug which bore the inscription,

> *Oh, isn't the world extremely flat*
> *With nothing whatever to grumble at.*

Aldous, they say, was mortified. Coming in from the shrubbery one day, he told them, "I was walking along when I saw a mouse —and I *fled*".[4] Then there was the rocking-horse, the great rocking-horse in the nursery at Laleham with flaring nostrils and with flowing mane, "Such a horse!" says Julian,[5] ". . real swing —we got on the five of us, myself, Trev, Aldous, the two Eckersley[6] boys, holding on to the belly and the mane—and then going—oh boy, oh boy. . . ."

And Aldous aged six being taken with all the Huxleys to the

[1] Sir Julian Huxley, *Aldous Huxley*, mainly from *A Memorial Volume*. Chatto & Windus, 1965. (Hereafter cited as *Mem. Vol.*)

[2] The late Gervas Huxley, C.M.G., M.C., son of Dr Henry Huxley (youngest son of T. H. Huxley) and of Sophy Wylde Stobart. Talking to S. B.

[3] Jill (Mrs Anthony) Greenwood. Talking to S. B.

[4] Sir Julian Huxley, *Memories*, Vol. I. George Allen & Unwin, 1970.

[5] Sir Julian Huxley, talking to S. B.

[6] First cousin—the sons of William Alfred Eckersley and Rachel Huxley, third daughter of T. H. Huxley.

unveiling of the statue of his grandfather at the Natural History Museum by the Prince of Wales, and his mother trying, in urgent whispers, to persuade Julian, then a young Etonian, to give up his top hat—a very young Etonian and a very new top hat—to Aldous, queazy, overcome, to be sick in.

In 1899 Mrs Huxley's fourth and last child, Margaret, was born. Aldous began his education by going to St Bruno's, a day school nearby for very small children. In 1900 Aldous with his brothers, his parents, aunts and uncles, Huxley and Collier cousins drove in four-wheelers—a stable family in a stable era— to the Christmas Pantomime at Drury Lane. The party occupied the dress circle. Aldous and his cousin Gervas lost in awe sat side by side.

Leonard Huxley's biography of his father, *Life and Letters of Thomas Henry Huxley*, which he had been working on for the last five years, was published in 1900 in London and New York with considerable success. ("Do you know the *Life and Letters* by my father?" Aldous wrote in his maturity, "It's a good book.") Leonard Huxley was able to leave Charterhouse after fifteen years of not entirely congenial school-mastering. Originally, he had planned to read for the Bar, but when the assistant mastership was offered to him in 1885 he accepted it in order to be able to marry. He now joined the publishing firm of Smith, Elder as reader and literary adviser, and at the same time became assistant editor of the *Cornhill*.

In 1901, late in the year in which Queen Victoria died, the family left Laleham. They did, however, not move to London but to another house two miles away called Prior's Field. There, as Aldous wrote sixty years later,[1] "My mother founded a girls' school which became very large and is still flourishing."[1]

---

[1] *Letters of Aldous Huxley*, edited by Professor Grover Smith. Chatto & Windus, 1969. All not otherwise attributed quotation from Aldous Huxley in this volume will be from this published collection. (Hereafter cited as *Letters*.)

Chapter Two

Prior's Field

MRS HUXLEY'S school opened on 23rd January 1902. There were seven pupils: one girl boarder who brought her dog, five day girls and Aldous. "The school building," Julia Huxley recorded in the School Magazine,

> consisted only of a moderate sized house [which also served as the family home] we had bought six months before together with all the land . . . We had just begun to build what is now the girls' hall.

The land was twenty-five acres of peaceful rural Surrey—a garden, a field, woods full of violets and bluebells in the spring. The house had been built by Voysey who also designed the school buildings and the book-plate—an owl, an olive tree and a heart encircled by the school motto WE LIVE BY ADMIRATION HOPE & LOVE. The teaching staff consisted of three.

> Miss English and Mademoiselle Bonnet . . . Miss English and I taught everything except French and music! . . . there was only one form, though the ages ranged between seven and sixteen.

As for games,

> We could not very well play hockey with only six girls, so we purchased a foot ball . . .

By next term there were new boarders, making fourteen pupils; Mrs Huxley divided them into two forms, the sixth and fifth. Aldous was in the fifth. "His beating me so easily was a source of humiliation to me," writes one of the older girls, Victoire Fairtlough, who did lessons with him. "I did not realize then that I would not be expected to excel the grandson of the great T. H. Huxley!

> I did get my revenge by beating him in the junior high jump at sports day at Lady Jekyll's house. Aldous and I reached the finals and after a great tussle I just managed to beat him which he took in very good part. He was rather a quiet little boy and never seemed at all bumptious in spite of his exceptional ability.[1]

[1] Miss Victoire Fairtlough in a letter to S. B.

5

Aldous used to go out beetle hunting with another little girl, Barbara Hiles,[1] and once at least he did show temper.

> We had made a beating net, a yard of cotton fixed to two long hazel sticks; you shoved it into the hedge, all sorts of caterpillars fell into it. We took turns to keep what fell in. One Sunday morning Julian came with us, looking for wild orchids. At one of my turns I got a fine tussock moth caterpillar; Aldous's turn got nothing exciting. Next beat I got another even finer tussock. For a moment Aldous was upset and was going to punch me, when Julian said, "Aldous, Aldous you can't behave like that to a lady."

After deceptively amateurish beginnings Prior's Field grew quickly. Julia Huxley, helped no doubt at first by the Arnold-Huxley aura, built up an unusual, for those days unconventional school. Art and literature, galleries, Shakespeare matinées in London, concerts at Haslemere; books—with the girls free to choose them; no compulsory church or games. At a time when most schools took their walks in crocodiles, they were allowed to go for walks and bicycle rides and sketching parties on their own.

> I want to tell you more about Prior's Field [Barbara Hiles Bagenal wrote to me]. It was a wonderful school—and for those days very modern. For instance, none of the staff lived in the school—they all had little houses round the estate. In non-school hours we were looked after by two matrons and by Mrs Huxley.
> To me it was heaven, I met civilized people for the first time; and I could go off into the woods alone and look for flowers and toadstools and birds.

Already in the first two years the number of girls had risen to fifty, then "in a flash there were a hundred".[2] They were able to play hockey, croquet and lacrosse. "We beat Heathfield four times in succession in all three games," Mrs Huxley recorded.

Mrs Huxley had a dogcart which she drove with a coachman sitting at the back in a top hat. She (with little Aldous) accompanied the team on away matches. Many of the Prior's Field girls were daughters of the intelligentsia or future intellectuals in their own right. Gilbert Murray's and Maurice Hewlett's daughters, Conan Doyle's daughter, Marjorie Huxley, Margaret Huxley, Joan Collier, Enid Bagnold, Barbara Hiles. The staff was

---

[1] The present Mrs Bagenal in a letter to S. B.
[2] Enid Bagnold.

"brilliant—two of them outstanding, Ethel Sidgwick and the half-Greek, Emma Neurotsos".[1]

The food was good; the house well-run, comfortable, well-furnished, "rather unschool-like", in various memories, "good prints on the walls," "chintzy rooms, modern with William Morris"; the Huxley family much in evidence. "I cannot think of the lovely gardens without the figure of Leonard Huxley hard at work looking after his alpines and roses."[2] The girls would help him weed "and get to know all the names—for he like his sons was a hand at imparting knowledge."[2] Julian and Trevenen were about when their Eton and Oxford holidays overlapped with the term. They went bird watching, exploring on their own but also joined in the games, the picnics . . .

Although only a small child [Victoire Fairtlough] I can well remember the atmosphere of goodness and kindness that prevailed throughout the school and the home life of the Huxleys.

On Saturday evenings they danced in the gymnasium; the girls (changed into white silk blouses and white serge skirts), the staff, Leonard, the elder boys, a mistress at the piano. "Mr Huxley loved dancing and was very good. He taught us to waltz and reverse. He was very jolly with us and occasionally joined in our games."[3]

He was very tall [Victoire Fairtlough] and I remember him tearing down the field at lacrosse and crashing into me whom he had not seen from his great height . . . I went over like a shot rabbit . . . How scared poor Mrs Huxley looked.

Mrs Huxley. "We all loved Mrs Huxley." "She was quite extraordinary." ". . A slender lady with a beautifully shaped small head, as clear as someone now standing by my side." "She made a lasting impression on all of us who were there." "Kind, yes; but away and above my understanding. Each time before she spoke she seemed to reflect."

Her own children loved her intensely, and Aldous even more passionately than the others.[4] Her early influence went very deep; so did her loss; both are keys to his character and development. He very rarely brought himself to speak of her. This is why I am recording here such living memories of Julia Huxley as are left. They are the memories of women looking back on what they

[1] Enid Bagnold.
[2] Miss Helen Witt, letter to S. B.
[3] Miss Helen Witt.
[4] Sir Julian Huxley; he used the word *passionately*.

experienced when they were schoolgirls half a century ago. We all reshape our memories; yet at times memory has a quality that separates it from our selves, and what we wish to serve as simply as we can is truth. And Aldous too, for his part, only knew his mother as a schoolboy.

We all loved Mrs Huxley and thought her word was law, none of us were ever in the least afraid of her. I never heard a joke made at her expense, or her authority even questioned let alone disregarded.[1]

One saw her every day. Either she spoke in the morning after breakfast, or she read aloud to us in the evening . . . She read [poetry] without stressing the sense: she let the rhyming wave by itself . . in her silvery even voice the words had their head.[2]

When Victoire Fairtlough lost her grandmother she

was deeply grieved. Mrs Huxley somehow knew this and as I was sitting at my desk scanning an examination paper I felt a comforting arm round my shoulders, "You will do your best, Victoire, won't you?" . . . .

And Barbara Hiles lamed at hockey. "Mrs Huxley sent for me and offered to send me home.

I ran across the room to her and said, "Please, please, don't send me home." She was touched and asked if I was unhappy at home? I said I was very happy at home but I am much happier here.

. . In the little room on the right of the front door as you came in she talked to me—I was twelve. I never knew before that grown-up women *could* speak to children like that—so fair, so reasonable. How grateful one was![3]

What had happened was this: Enid Bagnold in nights of full moon and spring flowers climbed out over the roof down the lavatory pipes to sleep in the woods among the bluebells. Once she was seen by the cook, another time she was caught by Mrs Huxley's sister, Mrs Humphry Ward. In the headmistress's study,

I wasn't scolded, hardly rebuked. Mrs Huxley seems to blush a little before explaining—one had to run a school, one was responsible for all of you to your parents—I didn't argue, though she would have let me . . . I was a child and she was soon to die, but the gap was bridged.[4]

Mrs Huxley tried to transfer to us her great knowledge of literature and the arts, sometimes at the expense of the more basic subjects,

---

[1] Victoire Fairtlough.   [2] Enid Bagnold, *Autobiography*.
[3] Enid Bagnold, talking to S. B.
[4] Enid Bagnold, *Autobiography*, and letter to S. B.

illustrated by the fact that most of us failed in arithmetic in the Lower Certificate exam.

And yet as a headmistress she was outstanding. She did not give the impression of a strong personality but of someone with great inner reserves, integrity & a refreshing lack of sentimentality. There was a strain of austerity & reticence about her which could raise a barrier between herself and a shy schoolgirl. Many would not agree with this. Personally, I felt her rather remote.[1]

"Remote?" in the view of another Prior's Field pupil,[2] "Perhaps a being of another order. She was extraordinary. Not at all the headmistress. Yet how good the school was! Her atmosphere, her influence have *lasted all one's life*. Thinking of her, one did not want to tell a lie." And now to that ever puzzling question of Arnold religiosity in the context of Huxleyan agnosticism. "I feel sure that she had a very deep faith, but perhaps no conventional religion."[2]

All her children had been baptized in the Church of England. Here she and Leonard had followed his father's precept and example.

As to the question[3] whether children should be brought up in entire disregard to the beliefs rejected by himself, but still current among the mass of his fellow-countrymen, he was of the opinion that they ought to know "the mythology of their time and country", otherwise one would at the best tend to make young prigs out of them; but as they grew up, their questions should be answered frankly.

So much for principle. As for practice,

. . My wife will have the youngsters christened, although I am always in a bad temper from the time it is talked about until the ceremony is over. . . .[4]

It was at Prior's Field, in that home, that atmosphere, that Aldous spent the first nine years of his life. We know more about his elders—naturally—than we know about the child himself. The handful of letters extant might have been written by any

[1] Miss Helen Witt.

[2] Nadine Noble, the present Mrs Lambert, talking to S. B.

[3] Leonard Huxley, *Life and Letters of Thomas Henry Huxley*, Vol. II. Macmillan & Co., 1900.

[4] Thomas Henry Huxley in a letter to Hooker of 3rd January 1861, op. cit. Vol. I.

reasonably well-disposed small boy enjoying a nice country child-hood. (Possibly, the punctuation is a bit beyond his years.) Here is a fair sample.

My dear Julian   7th December 1902
    It is very frosty weather: and I can stand on the pond. We have been giving crumbs to the birds; the pigeons can fly nicely now (we saw them drinking out of the pond just now). The staircase in the cottage has been put up. I and Kathleen found a mouse in the pig's bran and we chased it about till it escaped. One of the pigs has a cough. We went to Church. . . .
                                    Good by, your loving brother
                                                        Aldous

And here he is in another light.[1]

Aldous sat silent, inscrutable, antagonistic, rather green (all the Huxley boys looked green—they didn't eat; though Mrs Huxley's food was excellent), aged about eight. I was a fat girl of twelve? thirteen? Sitting on Sunday at Mrs Huxley's table—at which we took turns—knowing that I was supposed to make an effort and talk.
    Eventually (heavily bumping it out) "What have you been doing today, Aldous?"
    No answer.
    Rising indignation, and louder, "What have you been doing today, Aldous?"
    He raised his eyes, leant a little nearer, "I *heard* you the first time."

Aldous's cousin, Laurence Collier,[2] too, found him "aloof and secretly critical at the early age of nine. When Uncle Leonard held forth, as he was apt to, on the joys of mountaineering, '*Per ardua ad astra* . . .' Aldous said nothing, but . . gazed abstracted into the distance with a fixed and enigmatic smile."
    Sir Laurence Collier's sister Joan[3] gives us one *instantané* of the small boy with his mother. They used to go on vast family holidays in the summer. In 1903 they were in Switzerland.

    I must tell you the nicest story about Aldous [In Joan Collier's words]. We were all at Rosenlauie being dragged up mountains &

---

[1] This story was first told to me by Enid Bagnold in 1968; afterwards she also put it down in a letter to me; some years later I read it in print in her *Autobiography*. The wording of the present version is a composite of all three.
[2] Sir Laurence Collier, K.C.M.G., son of the Hon. John Collier and Ethel Huxley, youngest daughter of T. H. Huxley; thus a nephew of Leonard Huxley. From *North House*: A Memoir.
[3] Joan Collier, the present Mrs F. A. Buzzard, a first cousin of Aldous.

there was at our hotel one Canon Rawnsley, who considered himself an authority on the Lake poets. I & my mother and Aunt Judy [Julia Huxley] were waiting outside the hotel when another visitor came up to Aunt Judy and said, "It is so charming to see your little boy listening with such interest to the conversation between his father & dear Canon Rawnsley." At which moment Aldous came hurtling down the path, flung himself on Aunt Judy & said, "Mother! Do you know how many times Canon Rawnsley has said, 'NO Really!' "

Chapter Three

Hillside

IN the autumn of 1903 Aldous was sent away from home. He and his cousin Gervas entered Hillside, a preparatory school near Godalming run by Gidley Robinson. Huxley major (Gervas, the elder by three months) and Huxley minor: they were nine years old when they went, rising fourteen when they left. For five years the two boys lived side by side. Through Gervas Huxley we have a first hand account.

At the beginning of the term I had been deposited forlornly by my mother. Aldous' bed, next to mine in the big dormitory for the smaller fry, was empty. As was so often the case in his prep school days Aldous had been ill, and it was a week or more before he arrived. By that time I had begun to settle in . . and was able to offer what feeble protection I could . . in Hillside's strange, rough and often brutal world.[1]

"You see, it wasn't a good school, not any longer. Headmaster far too old . . . All small boys are nasty, I think; the only thing to do with small boys is to supervise them very closely. We weren't. And a lot of bad bullying went on."[2]

The food was abominable, as well as distressingly inadequate.

My stomach still turns at the thought of the breakfast porridge full of greenish, sour-tasting lumps . . . Between lunch and breakfast next morning, all we had was thick chunks of bread at tea, thinly buttered and with a scrape of jam.[3]

Aldous arrived. A new boy, late, rather homesick, looking delicate, perhaps green. They turned on him—Aldous didn't lose his temper; Aldous wasn't afraid. "Oh no, no."

That's very unusual?

G. H. "Very, very unusual."

They tried to bully him, they tried to rag him: it was no good. Aldous wasn't there. "He put on the cloak of invisibility and simply disappeared." Meanwhile the boys discovered that *they*

---

[1] Gervas Huxley, *Mem. Vol.*
[2] Gervas Huxley, talking to S. B.
[3] Gervas Huxley, *Both Hands, An Autobiography*. Chatto & Windus, 1970.

couldn't lose their tempers with him either. "Quite impossible to." So they let him be. "And that is why Aldous was happier I think than *anyone else* at Hillside.

"There was another thing, which seems to surprise people who knew him later, that Aldous was very very much the schoolboy. With all the liking for jokes and japes and pulling people's legs— he joined in all our nonsense, only it was more imaginative nonsense than anybody else's, I mean Aldous' jokes were better jokes .. and he was enormous *fun* to be with, and *very popular* for that reason."[1]

Gervas and Aldous, inseparable, acquired a mutual great friend, Lewis Gielgud (Sir John's eldest brother), a bright boy, hopeless at games, rather dandified. "He had a poor time at Hillside and needed a lot of protection; he depended more on Aldous than the other way round ... Aldous was tremendously loyal to his friends ..."

They played paper cricket, they played football, they played conkers—*cheesers* at Hillside—and Aldous became a champion; they collected puss moths and went bug hunting. Every Sunday afternoon they walked over to Prior's Field, "the main object of the exercise was getting a tremendous blow-out tea [Aldous did eat]. On the way out we'd sing ditties and discuss what we were going to have."

At that tea-table, Gervas, rather awed, first met Aldous' mother, his Aunt Judy. The awe dissolved:

She had a happy laugh, she understood young people. I soon realized why Aldous was so deeply devoted to her and what a key role she played in his life.

The teaching at Hillside was good:

Thanks to such masters as Mr Aston who took the senior boys in classics, Mr Taylor the mathematics master and [later on] Hugh Parr, an unusual and most inspiring young master (he was killed in the 1914 war) who encouraged in us a lively interest in English literature.[1]

There was also Mr Jacques, Jacko, who was unable to preserve discipline but gave interesting lessons in elementary science. Aldous brilliant at his work? "No, Not then. For one thing, his memory was not nearly as good as it became and being ill so often he missed quite a bit of school in the first two or three years (while less gifted boys bore off the prizes). At any rate, he was not

[1] Gervas Huxley, talking to S. B.

the kind of boy who is conventionally good at lessons. Lewis was, very much so; and I was, incidentally, much more so than Aldous who was not considered academically outstanding at Hillside." All the same, he was usually among the first two or three of his age. "He was willing and industrious, and never in trouble for idleness or inattention."[1]

Another Hillside boy (Mr Lionel Jardine) told me about a moment that baffled and impressed the form, still grappling with the conventional symbols of elementary geometry—Aldous standing by the blackboard, chalk in hand, at ease, blithely saying, "Let $D F T$ be a triangle."

If Aldous was untroubled at school, there were hints of pressures at home. "*So* much was expected." [Joan Collier, talking.] "His Aunt Mary . . . His health was delicate—all the boys were delicate—yet at one time when Aldous wasn't supposed to be strong enough to get up for breakfast there was displeasure over low marks."

In the summer of 1905 Aldous and Gervas "enjoyed a very happy holiday together up at the house we had in the Lakes—his and my parents rented the house together, Mirehouse on Bassenthwaite. We travelled up with Uncle Leonard, bringing our bicycles. Julian and Trev were there; Julian was in his last year at Eton and brought a very grand friend called Neville Bland.[2] Aldous and I shared a room together contentedly."[1]

They climbed Saddleback, a long tramp for eleven year old boys. In the evenings they played pen and paper games and those charades called Nebuchadnezzars, organized by Julian and Trev. "Aldous was a formidable player—Uncle Leonard had to win at all cost, he'd invent words which he said were in the dictionary, but which weren't; it would annoy my own father and mother, but Aldous took it lightly. "*Father—cheating* again?"

"Yes, Aldous was fond of him. Yes, in a way he was. But he thought he was silly. He *was* silly. He wasn't the kind of father one looked up to, or went to when one was in trouble; I wouldn't have dreamt of going to Uncle Leonard. I would go to Aunt Judy. On the other hand, he was invariably kind to us and I enjoyed his company, I enjoyed his puns and jokes and talk. But I think it was this lack of respect that troubled Aldous and marred his relationship with his father—in those days grown-ups were supposed to behave like grown-ups and not like fellow school-boys . . ."

In his later years at Hillside Aldous became physically much

1 Gervas Huxley, talking to S. B.
2 Who indeed became an Ambassador.

stronger. "By 1905 or 6 he was quite as strong as I was. He was never an athlete but enjoyed school games—he was scorer for our cricket eleven and in our last year he and I helped to make up a highly unprofessional halfback line in the soccer team—and he was a tremendous walker and climber, and very keen on it." He explored the Surrey countryside on foot as his brothers used to, and he was fond of bicycling (well into adult life) and rode down Devil's Punch Bowl into Milford at terrific speeds.

In the autumn term of 1905 a new headmaster took over, Jimmy Douglas, a comparatively young man and a first-class cricketer, "very much to the school's good". The bullying ceased, lessons became more interesting, the food improved; the school took to acting. "Lewis Gielgud, as a Terry, came into his own." In 1907 the boys did the *Merchant of Venice* on a platform raised at the end of the dining-hall. Aldous aged thirteen played Antonio and (writes his cousin Joan) "we were moved to tears". Gervas confirms this. "How good Aldous's acting was! He did convey emotion. And he was an extremely good speaker of verse. Then of course he always had this very, very beautiful speaking voice—an unhurried voice—it had got this lovely tone in it. . . ."

In the same year Lewis Gielgud, Gervas and Aldous, encouraged by Hugh Parr, the new young English master, got out a literary magazine, the *Doddite*. Two issues (three dozen copies each) appeared, produced on a jelligraph machine. Aldous's first appearance in print. He contributed a poem and a short story illustrated by himself. The poem, called *Sea Horses*, began with the dashing extravert lines,

> *At a gallop we charge up the shingle*
> *At a gallop we leap the sea-wall*
> *With mad exultation we tingle*
> *For we, we can overcome all.*

That summer, the family holiday was spent in Switzerland at Montana. There Aldous was observed by his Collier cousin, Lawrence, then between Bedales and Balliol. He saw Aldous as

a very young schoolboy, a pale and apparently fragile child with a big, high-browed head posed unsteadily on a very long, thin body . . . His brothers called him the Ogre, but they listened with interest to his talk, which was well worth listening to even then . . . He had already begun that flow of conversation, both instructive and amusing. . . .[1]

[1] Sir Laurence collier, op. cit.

By 1907, Gervas was head of the school. He over-exercised authority, he says, and was so unpopular that a rebellion was hatched. He was sent to Coventry, books were hurled at him whenever the masters' backs were turned; Aldous alone among the fifty boys stood by him.

> After lights went out that Saturday evening in the cubicles where the seniors slept, Aldous's shout of "You swine and curs" silenced the abuse against me. . . . Next day, on the school outing, Aldous walked with me while the rest of the school kept a hostile distance.

Lionel Jardine speaks of another—unselfconscious—act of courage, Aldous's talking away about Swiss wild flowers to the other boys. "You see, he had this curiosity,"[1] [Gervas once more] "the deeply interested curiosity with which he regarded the behaviour of the world." When he was given his first encyclopaedia, he wrote to Julian, "Thank you for the cyclopaedia. I now know everything from who invented dice to the normal temperature of the sea-cucumber."[2]

Between Gervas and Aldous there had "never even been the breath of a quarrel" during those five years of shared daily life. "This was in no way due to any virtue on my part—he was someone with whom you couldn't quarrel: he didn't give way to violent emotions as most of us did. He met ill-nature or spite with serene integrity and detached unselfishness—there was a shining goodness about Aldous. . . . There was that utter trust one had that he'd never say one nasty thing. He seems to have had a perspective, a sense of proportion, even at that age, and that must have helped him in dealing with the inevitable ups and downs of existence at school." Then Gervas added, "*And* he was such a gay character, *such* a gay character: never forget that."[1]

Lewis Gielgud had already left for Eton; Gervas left at Easter; Aldous succeeded him as head of the school for his own last term. In June 1908 he, too, left.

That summer there was another holiday in the mountains. Mrs Huxley had not been well, but was expected to join the family later on. Aldous wrote one of his happy, hearty letters.

> This is the most splendid place . . . . We had a vast walk yesterday up a loathsome mountain called le Buet . . . . The day before we went up the glacier and father pulled me about on a rope and we

---

[1] Gervas speaking.　　　　[2] Unpublished letter of June 1908.

had great fun. This place has a splendid air which makes me sleep and eat enormously. There is also a most beautiful view of MONG BLONG . . . there is also an American Bore! It's a great pity mother can't come out yet but I expect she comes in about 10 days,

Your loving,

Aldous[1]

[1] From a letter to Gervas Huxley, part published in *Mem. Vol.*, dated 12th August 1908 from Hotel du Col des Montets, Chamonix.

Chapter Four

The Inheritance

ALDOUS HUXLEY is now fourteen. The future will be shaped —up to a point—in terms of the present and the past. We are able to look at both (in fragments). Let us begin with the present, such as it appears: *Les jeux sont faits?* All is still wide open? We can see a boy, getting on for six foot four, slender-boned, congenitally thin, of delicate constitution, under life sentence, as he became so aware, to his own exposed and linear physique. (No wonder he was fascinated when he was able to recognize himself some thirty-five years later as an extreme example of the Third Sheldonian type, The Cerebrotonic Ectomorph.) We see a boy of equable temperament who does not give way to violent emotions, who may not be prone to violent emotions, who is capable already of detachment, capable also of judging, of not suffering fools gladly, of seeing elders plain. ("Cheating, Father?" "I *heard* you the first time", "NO Really!") A boy who shows courage, immense curiosity, is fond of words, jokes, drawing, learning ("Let *D F T* be a triangle"), who is able to inspire respect in young barbarians, whose talk is listened to by Balliol undergraduates and who can speak verse in a voice that moves adults to tears. An exceptional boy, in the judgement of his elders and contemporaries; exceptional not so much in intelligence— though of course he is intelligent, highly intelligent, but in the context of his brothers and his cousins, he is as yet simply conforming to a standard—the *otherness*, the sense that *Aldous is quite different* emanates from a moral quality, one might say a spiritual quality, they discern in him. *Une âme bien née.*

Now to the past. His ancestors, known and unknown; the genetic lottery. They are English: first heard of in the twelfth century (in Cheshire, at Hodesleia-Huxley). The known ones loom large. Aldous is the grandson (the litany once again) of Thomas Henry Huxley, biologist, man of letters, protagonist of Evolution, one of the most forceful minds England has produced —self-educated, a fighter, a formidable member of public bodies, formidable debater, lucid and light-handed essayist, family man, sufferer from poor health, prey to bouts of depression. Aldous is the grandson, on his mother's side, of that curious character the Rev. Thomas Arnold who kept hopping from one religion to another (who appears in *Robert Elsmere* and again in Rose Macaulay's *Told By An Idiot*); he is the great-grandson of that eminent Victorian, Dr Arnold of Rugby, educational reformer, creator of generations of Christian gentlemen. He is the great-nephew of Matthew Arnold (poet *and* educator); the nephew of the earnest, but oh so competent, novelist Mrs Humphry Ward. His mother, as we have seen, founded a school. All took something upon themselves, assumed duties; Aldous's descent, in the words of his friend, Gerald Heard, "brought down on him a weight of intellectual authority and a momentum of moral obligations".[1]

Descent. Also class. Aldous was born into a particular and self-conscious enclave, a class within a class, the governing upper middle—an elite, an intellectual aristocracy made up of a handful of families—Trevelyans, Macaulays, Arnolds, Wedgwoods, Darwins, Huxleys—who had produced a number of extra-ordinarily and diversely gifted individuals whose influence, although they never confused themselves with the actual nobility, upon nineteenth-century England had been tremendous. Their common denominator was an intense desire to acquire, to advance and to disseminate knowledge—all of them, it goes without saying were highly though not necessarily expensively educated men and women—a wish to improve the lot as well as the administration of mankind, an assumption of responsibility—*l'intelligence oblige*—and a passion, no tamer word will do, for truth. It was the values, the habits, the glory, and the limitations, of this aristocracy which informed the spiritual and material background of Aldous's youth.

"They lived in houses in which books were part of existence . . . Literature of course was in their bones," says Lord Annan in his admirable essay, "The Intellectual Aristocracy" to which I am greatly indebted.

> Their prose at its worst was lucid and free from scholarly jargon; and time and again they produced work of surpassing literary merit . . . they wrote not for a scholarly clique but for the intelligent public at large whom they addressed confident that they would be under-stood.[2]

In the 1860s and 70s they had worked for franchise reforms, women's education, university entrance irrespective of religious beliefs, a civil service open to the talents. (T. H. Huxley, though he only sat two years on the London School Board, "probably more than any man," the Britannica dixit, "left his mark on . . national elementary education".) Great as their influence was in the middle of the century,

[1] Gerald Heard, "The Poignant Prophet", article in *The Kenyon Review*, November 1965.

[2] *Studies in Social History*, A Tribute to G. M. Trevelyan, ed. J. H. Plumb. Longmans, 1955.

it was perhaps even more important at the end. For the restraints of religion and thrift and accepted class distinction started to crumble and English society to rock under the flood of money ... and a materialism of wealthy snobbery and aggressive philistinism arose far exceeding anything hitherto seen in England. The intellectual aristocracy were one of the few barriers which resisted these forces. They insisted that honesty and courtesy were valuable; and they continued to set before the young unworldly ideals. They suggested that if public life was inseparable from spiritual ignominy, another *life devoted to unravelling the mysteries of mind, matter and heart was to be desired* [My italics].[1]

They could be intimidating to meet. "Intellectuals often are. Perhaps they were a little too severe on inconsequential behaviour fully to understand human nature." And here is a passage about their children which concerns us.

. . As infants they had learnt by listening to their parents to extend their vocabulary and talk in grammatical sentences ... they developed inner resources for entertaining themselves ... Competitive examination at the schools and universities sharpened their minds, and if those children who did not inherit their parents' intellectual talents suffered unjustly by the feeling that they had failed, the successful children gained by acquiring the habit of thinking accurately in concepts at an early age. Nor was childhood dull: they were freer to read and play as they liked than most middle-class children.[2]

The successful children. Aldous's own childhood was a good one. Given his disposition, given the time (post-Victorian England), the inadequacies, then as now, of any education, it might be called a near perfect one. Intellectually he was fish in water; he had a country childhood with its freedom and resources as well as a discipline of work and purpose; he had encouragement and sympathy at home; he had fun and the stimulating presence of his brilliant elder brothers; he had safety, he had affection, he had love.

Much love. (One of the constants of Aldous's life was that he inspired in the men and women he met affection and protective tenderness.) There *were* pressures. *So* much was expected. Those competitive exams, for a start, had to be knuckled down to, passed, passed well. "Huxleys always get firsts." This may have been irksome but I do not think that it weighed unduly on his

1 N. F. Annan, op. cit.   2 Ibid.

spirit (whether the grind overtaxed his physical constitution is another question) and that the obligations put on him by his descent were felt by this boy not as a burden but as a momentum.

Aldous had left Hillside in June of 1908. In the autumn of the year he went to Eton as a scholar.

PART TWO

"Impaired": 1908-1914

"For a boy in his teens it was a liberal
education—but *liberal*."
"In what?"
"In Pure and Applied Pointlessness.
And a few weeks after my private course
in the subject came the grand opening
of the public curse. World War."

ALDOUS HUXLEY, *Island*, 1962

Chapter One

First Damage

ALDOUS is in his first Half at Eton—separated from Gervas who has gone to Rugby—finding his bearings. With ease it would seem and cheerfully. He lives in College, is in the Lower Fifth, will have to do some fagging, "poor little me", for three Halves. "I look so chic in tailcoats . . . M'tutor is a dear man", there's been the awful event of 400 lines of Vergil. There is a brief view of him at that carefree stage. Aldous went to Oxford on a visit, and met George Clark,[1] Trev's and Julian's undergraduate friend.

He came to us and talked; easily—a lively and intelligent schoolboy.

In the last week of November he writes to Gervas asking if he has done anything bad lately such as putting his fagmaster's tea in the bath or breaking two dozen eggs. He has only been whipped twice so far, "(1) in a general working off of the whole of college . . (2) for forgetting to take VI form cheese out of Hall". Next Monday is St Andrew's Day, the day of the Wall game—"Julian and Trev are coming I think".

Julian and Trev did not come. Julia Huxley died that Sunday, 29th November. She had not been well for only four months, known to be very ill for two. It was cancer. And almost in no time she was dead. The younger children, Aldous and Margaret, had had no real warning.

At the end one could really give thanks that she was released— even though on the other hand, one could feel nothing but bewildered rebellion that such a thing could be—such pouring out of a life still young—only 45—and so *wanted*, so ineffably *wanted*. . . .

So wrote Dorothy Ward, Julia Huxley's niece, in a long letter to her friend Miss Jewett.[2]

I cannot tell you what a nightmare of an autumn it has been . . . since the great doctor's final verdict at the end of September—"no operation possible" . . . and [to] watch her week by week . . .

---

[1] Sir George Clark, the historian.
[2] Dated, Stocks, Tring, Dec.13.08.

Mother [Mrs Humphry Ward] went down to see her, even if she could only be with her 5 minutes—slipping down the path of life and out gradually into the Great Unknown. The *pity* of it!

The day my aunt died . . . Mother brought the 2 youngest children back here—Margaret, the little 9-year-old girl . . and Aldous . . poor little fellow. . .

Leonard Huxley that evening read to the assembled school at Prior's Field a poem on his wife's death which he had written a few hours before.

The 2nd boy, a dear of 19, came the next day from Oxford (his first term at Balliol, where his older brother is—both with scholarships, oh! how proud & justly proud she was of them!)—and we tried our best to love and comfort them, and took them to the funeral from here . . .

We lay . . Julia Huxley to rest in the lovely little hillside cemetery in Surrey, whereof Watts designed and painted the little chapel.

It is the small churchyard at Compton—a few graves on a grassy slope in country peace under trees.

It was a funeral never to be forgotten by those who loved my aunt —for the outward and visible signs it brought us of the love in which our dear one was held. You know she had founded & *created* the great school. . . . All the older girls were there—40 of them—in their simple blue serge frocks & schoolhats, just as she would have liked— their young faces awed and hushed at first, and then all breaking down at the last sentence by the grave. ["It was my first terrible grief," said Enid Bagnold.] All the mistresses were there, and all the servants—and many, *many* friends. And her poor husband and boys! it was piteous to see them—and my mother's drawn face.

Joan Collier held Aldous's hand; he was shaking with sobs.

Afterwards they took the children back to Stocks—"The little Eton boy very sensitive and brooding and white, and feels it deeply—and dumbly." Presently he was sent back to Eton for the last fortnight of the Half; Trev and Margaret stayed on for the time being, as "of course it means the breaking-up of the home for my Uncle and the children and *their* plans are entirely unsettled at present". The break-up was complete indeed. "I lost my mother, my home, my school, living in the country and my governess all at one blow" wrote Aldous's sister Margaret sixty-one years after.[1]

---

[1] Miss Margaret Huxley in a letter to S. B. October 1969.

As for the school, Mrs Huxley two years earlier, finding the sheer practical work unmanageable, had taken on a partner, Mrs Burton-Brown, "a rather well-known classical lecturer", and that lady was going to carry on, so the continuation of Prior's Field at least was assured. "But the wonder," Enid Bagnold said, "went out of the school with Mrs Huxley."

As for Aldous, "There remained with him, latent at ordinary times but always ready to come to the surface, a haunting sense of the vanity, the transience, the hopeless precariousness of all merely human happiness."[1]

[1] Aldous Huxley on François Leclerc du Tremblay losing his father at the age of ten. *Grey Eminence*, 1941.

Chapter Two

Aldous at Eton

ALDOUS HUXLEY had gone to Eton as a King's Scholar in September 1908. Eleven new boys entered College at the same time, the beginning of the Michaelmas Half (Halves being what the three Eton terms are called), and five more in the course of the school year. Of these, six were killed in the 1914-18 war. Four or five are living today.

The scholars—seventy boys—live together in College. A fellow Etonian, contemporary of Aldous, the Rev. R. A. L. Fell, describes the physical conditions of their day,[1]

> The fifteen junior Collegers are housed in "Chamber", the remains of the Long Chamber, in which till about the middle of last century all the Scholars lived, and were locked in every night. In Chamber each boy has a "stall" containing a fold-up bed, desk and bookcase and a Windsor chair; also a fixed wash-basin with a cold tap, on a spring so that it cannot be left running, a saucer bath and can, marked with his name. [There were no bathrooms—long baths with taps, that luxurious dream—in College till about 1911, when showers were installed, their use being confined to the upper half of College.] Carrying cans of hot water formed an important part of a fag's duty. (In College a boy is a fag for his first year: I do not think the institution of fagging was resented, and I never heard any abuse of it.)
>
> The stalls reached nearly half way up to the ceiling, the bottom of the windows being about level with the top of the stalls; it is a high room so that you have to climb up (on the wash-stand) to open or shut a window. Every stall has a reading-lamp which has to be turned off some time before the Captain of Chamber calls "Good night all, stop talking"—10 pm, I think, 10.30 on Saturdays. A light in the ceiling stays on all night, but no-one could read by that. [Some boys, certainly Aldous, read under the bed-clothes with an electric torch.]

The headmaster at the time was Edward Lyttelton. The tradition still prevailed that the head should be a clergyman and a classic. Lyttelton had succeeded Dr Warre, who had been head-master for twenty years, in 1905

[1] All, needless to say, changed, in the recent reconstruction of College.

27

and was expected to be something of a "new broom';' but I fancy that he found it difficult to carry some of the older masters with him. He certainly wished to modify the old dominance of the Classics. The general public regarded Lyttelton as a crank . . . It was not realized in what respect and affection he was regarded by the boys . . . The Master in College was A. W. Whitworth, who was also Aldous's Tutor [m'tutor; and still living in 1973]. Every boy at Eton has a Tutor and is under his care for the whole of his school life.

We have three sources about Aldous at Eton. His letters—a dozen of them, mostly to Julian or Gervas, facetious, conformist, rather hearty, full of doggerel and doodles. The recollections of four of his contemporaries, the Rev. R. A. L. Fell, Lord Justice Harman, H. G. C. Streatfeild and Henry Rowan Walker (Lewis Gielgud, Aldous's greatest friend at Eton, is dead). Aldous's later comments in print and conversation.

Other men who were at Eton in his time and alive today were either a few years older or younger, a gap unmanageable in their circumstances then. Sir Alan Lubbock writes that he remembers Aldous well by sight, "I can see him now sitting with a toasting fork by the fire in College Kitchen, talking to Lewis Gielgud. But I never spoke to him, nor he to me."

Aldous at Eton was "a tall lanky youth with a thick shock of hair" (Lord Harman who says that he knew Aldous as well as anybody). Again there was no bullying—"No one ever dreamt of bullying Aldous!

From the word go, he was clearly going to be a superior being. He possessed a kind of effortless aristocratic approach to his work.[1]

What Aldous himself recorded[2] is that he did a high jump at 4 foot 3, is messing about the lab, finds cricket pretty boring (he was a dry-bob: cricket in the summer, not rowing). The weather is poor . . the provost has died . . . He is in a room of his own now in passages (the two long corridors in New Building where collegers live after their first spell in stalls) . . . By December he and Gielgud have accomplished forty recruit drills and Aldous is "very nearly a full-fledged territorial". Next Half he is fourth in trials which "hurls me forth from upper tea-room fag to

1 Henry Rowan Walker, letter to S. B.
2 In letters at the time.

captain of Lower Tea", a change he thinks for the better, "for to wield the fork is a superior pastime to carrying the kettle". He sends Julian two longish poems, one in the style of Noyes, the other of Browning, and thanks him for "a box of lush produce". He is beginning to paint.

As for work. "We did classics," (Lord Harman talking) "Aldous preferring Greek." (He must have been a fairly good classical scholar as the Scholarship Examination was mainly based on classics.) "A little modern history, some French which was taught by a man who had fought in the Franco-Prussian war. I think I was better in French than Aldous was at the time."

"Actually," Aldous said half a century later,[1] "the education at Eton was uncommonly good at that time . . . There were a few *very good teachers* . . . There were funny things about it, I mean it was in many respects still a *renaissance* education. We used to spend the whole of every Tuesday from 7 in the summer and 7.30 in winter till 10.30 at night composing Latin verses—we were given a piece of Tennyson or something and were told to turn it into elegiacs or hexameters or Alcaics or Sapphics, and if you were a little further advanced Greek iambics—[with great wonder and relish in his voice]—which was a sort of *immense* jig-saw puzzle game . . . it was the most *extraordinary* proceeding . . ."

Aldous's English work "struck us as a long way out of the ordinary", says H. G. C. Streatfeild (who became a master at Eton). "His potentialities were obvious to us all."

We often worked together (legitimately) . . . I used to read his essays and Sunday questions (an exercise in religious or semi-religious subjects intended to keep us employed on Sunday). My own efforts [he adds with charming unassumingness] were common-place, and I envied his facility and maturity.

One day when Aldous, aged fifteen, was in 5B, the Upper Fifth, the boys were up to a master called Macnaghten and were told to spend half an hour writing down what they knew about the Conquistadors. Everybody scribbled away. This is what Aldous produced.

> *It's my settled belief that Pissarro*
> *Must have been educated at Harro*
> *This alone would suffice*
> *To account for his vice*
> *And his morals so scroobious and narro.*

[1] In a long interview with John Chandos in July 1961, recorded by Lansdowne Studios, hereafter cited as London interview.

Lord Harman puts Aldous among the Eton Aesthetes. "These were Aldous, myself, Monroe, a man called Pemberton . . . We read Walter Pater, Oscar Wilde, Later G. B. Shaw, all fashionable authors then . . ." H. G. C. Streatfeild found Aldous "apart from his brilliance, ordinary in the best sense. He enjoyed his games . . I can see him now in a muddy wall-sack, wall-cap and corduroy trousers. . . ."

At any rate Aldous read a vast amount. "You were largely left to your own devices . . . Everybody had a room to themselves, [again the slow relish in his voice] which was an *immense luxury* . . This was a curious school, I think it was a very good school, and if one wanted to learn, one *could* learn, one could learn a *great deal*. It was very civilized in many ways."

His other main interest was science (how naturally Aldous's mind vaulted between the two cultures but then, "I suppose I always had a passion for knowledge, and a certain gift for co-ordinating different fields.") His master was M. H. Hill, the biologist (who kept a cage of lemurs in his garden), "One of the best masters in the place, and he was *very good*." Through most of 1910 Aldous was taking an intensive course in biology. He was sixteen and had decided—or it had been decided, the way such things *emerge* in families—that he would be a doctor, with a view to going in for medical research.

Aldous's father had moved to London in 1909, to a house in Bayswater (27, Westbourne Square)—a bachelor's establishment, though Sarah, Julia Huxley's old parlourmaid whom everybody relied on, had come with him and was doing her best to make it homelike. Aldous spent his holidays mostly at his Aunt Mary's house Stocks at Tring in the Chilterns, or with Gervas's parents, Dr Henry Huxley and his wife Sophy, round the corner in Porchester Terrace. For Easter 1910 they took him down to Devonshire with them. The Henry Huxleys, the Harries, were "very very devoted to Aldous. [Gervas speaking] I think after Aunt Judy died, my mother meant a great deal to him. . . ."

On the day of Edward VII's funeral—20th May 1910—Aldous stood in the ranks of the Eton C.O.T.C. lining the route of the procession. He could not see very much, he complained, as they kept reversing arms, and the heat was simply dreadful.

That summer he was still learning to paint and did a good deal of sketching out of doors "which is very nice". In July he writes to his Gran'Moo (T. H. Huxley's widow) from O.T.C. Camp at Farnborough by the "fitful radiance of a quarter candlepower candle". They have marched 8 miles on Wednesday and 16 on Thursday, "a rather boring proceeding" the Corps was to be inspected by the Duke of Connaught and kept waiting while "H.R.H. was considerably unpunctual,

> I calculated that the whole brigade together wasted 333 days, allowing each man to have wasted 2 hours and the brigade to consist of 4000 men.

Aldous will be glad to return to hot baths and other than straw mattresses to sleep on; but his tone is boisterous and he seems pleased with himself rather than put out. His last letter of the year is to Julian. Aldous is thinking of talking to his Tutor about specializing in biology; they have had an enormous beano at Fuller's and he has made up a first-rate riddle about a platypus and a cat.

Chapter Three

The Second Impairment

IN the winter of 1911, during the Easter Half at Eton, Aldous began having trouble with his eyes. One morning they were swollen and extremely red; Matron, who had no medical training in those days, believed that it was pink-eye and would clear in a week or so. Nobody appears to have been alarmed. Aldous himself was curious about his condition and would peer at his eyes with interest in the looking-glass.[1] Time passed and the trouble did not clear. Matron told him to stay in the dark; this he did most reluctantly, having seldom spent a waking moment by himself without a book. Charles Harman sat up with him for one whole night. "Next day he was gone."

He turned up at his Aunt Ethel Collier's house in Swiss Cottage while the family were at luncheon.[2] "What are you doing, Aldous? Why aren't you at Eton?" A touch of pink-eye, been sent up to see a doctor. Next time he came to the house he walked into a four-poster bed.

Within a number of days or weeks—memories of dates and sequence are uncertain, no medical records subsist—Aldous could not see. The diagnosis, ultimately, was *keratitis punctata*, an inflammation of the cornea, in a particularly violent form, and hope for recovery at the stage the disease had reached was regarded as slight. Dr Henry Huxley used to tell his son that by the time he had got hold of Aldous, well, the damage had been done.

What exactly had happened? For the second time in Aldous's life sudden illness struck. What was—whatever is—the cause? Ill-chance, a chain of circumstances? Gervas always believed from what he heard that Aldous had been run down or ill, had had a bout of influenza, then went out with the O.T.C. and got some infected dust into his eye. "Infected dust—that's what my father always told me."

A pinch of dust at a moment of low resistance. Aldous—essentially incommunicado since his mother's death two years ago—growing too tall too fast. (Now, at sixteen, he was nearly his full height of 6 foot 4½.) No one at school particularly anxious about him. He was probably over-worked. ("The boys *were* worked

---

[1] Told by Lord Harman.
[2] Told by Joan Collier Buzzard.

too hard at Eton," said his step-mother[1] later on—one would not
have deduced this from the leisurely chatty letters. "He didn't
get enough food, he certainly didn't have enough of the right
food. Eton was a curious place then—not very healthy.")

The damage had been done and there he was. The boy with
the immense curiosity about the world, the boy who wanted to
read all the books, was nearly blind. He could just distinguish
light from darkness; he was unable to go about by himself. He
could not read.

> We were appalled [Gervas speaking] The shock of it. *I* was shattered,
> but not Aldous. He faced it with fantastic courage; and a complete
> absence of self-pity.

In the immediate present, Aldous needed medical help and
looking after. His father being a single man spending his days in
editorial offices, Aldous stayed in turns with the Henry Huxleys,
the Colliers in London, with Mrs Humphry Ward and other
Arnold relations. He was treated first by his Uncle Henry in
consultation with various oculists, then by an eminent eye
surgeon, Ernest Clarke, who is believed to have made the diagnosis of *staphylococcus aureus* as the cause of the infection in December
1911. From then on Aldous was taken once a week to the Institute
of Tropical Medicine for injections. (Penicillin or cortisone, of
course, were not available at the time.) The actual inflammation
subsided gradually, leaving opacities in the corneas which grossly
impaired the sight.

There was never any question of Aldous being able to return
to Eton. He had left one morning in the middle of a school week
and did not come back. His things—the useless books—were
packed up and sent to his father's house. He had been in College
for just under two and a half years, not long enough to have
attained any distinction in work or games. Let H. G. C. Streatfeild
have the last word about Aldous at Eton. His simple memoir,
from which I have already quoted, ends:

> His books are known to the world, I will confine myself to my
> memories of him as an ordinary boy . . . We used to take walks on
> Sundays, and his conversation was never above my head, and now
> I realize what a gentle and simple companion he was, ready to
> share with me ordinary not high-brow subjects . . . In fact I cannot
> recall a single unattractive characteristic in him.

I cannot remember any more details, as our ways parted all too

---

[1] Rosalind (Mrs Leonard) Huxley.

soon, but I hope that even these inadequate notes will give some impression of Aldous as a boy, enjoying all our activities as a lovable companion, and without a trace of affectation, conceit, or superiority.

Aldous was now on his own; cut off from his friends, his pursuits, his education, at sixteen and a half. They were as good to him as he let them be—"he was not easy to help"—his father, the Huxley and Collier aunts, Aunt Mary Ward ("she would have done anything for him [Gervas] and she did *a lot, always*; and he was very fond of her"). Julian was tied up at Oxford with a demonstratorship and a lectureship at Balliol; Trevenen, still an undergraduate, came to look after his brother when he could. For any positive survival Aldous had to summon up his own resources.

With tough concentration, he taught himself to read Braille and to type on a small portable. He taught himself to play the piano—first with one hand on the Braille page and the other hand on the piano keys; then the other way round: reading with the right, learning to play with the left, until he knew both parts by heart. He trained himself, alone, in upstairs rooms, filling the hours with slow, tedious, constructive tasks. What he felt, what he feared, what he held on to, was not said; he never talked about it. In print, much later, he stated the facts, once, laconically. "At sixteen, I had a violent attack of *keratitis punctata* . . . eighteen months of near-blindness, during which I had to depend on Braille for my reading and guide for my walking."[1] (There is only one blind character in all of Aldous's fiction, a young man appearing briefly in the IIIrd act of *The World of Light*; and he is an embittered extravert sketched conventionally, at arm's length as it were.) A two-line note sent by Aldous at the time to his cousin Joan congratulating her on her engagement, begins,

Dearest Joan,
Scuse bad writing which same I can't see.[2]

For the adult family it was a tale of fortitude, pride, withdrawal; to his sister, a child of twelve, Aldous was disturbing, someone to shy away from when he came to stay with the connections in[3] Surrey she had been living with since her mother's death.

[1] *The Art of Seeing*, 1943.
[2] *Letters*. Dated by the editor July 1911.
[3] They were the Rev. E. Carus Selwyn and his wife Maud; his first wife had been Aldous's mother's sister Lucy who had died in 1894. The house was Undershaw at Hindhead and belonged to Conan Doyle.

He spent hours playing rather curiously on the piano, or shut in his room, typing, typing; or if not upstairs, concentrating on learning Braille and there were very few points of contact between us. I think I was rather frightened by his attempts at re-adjusting himself.[1]

As soon as Aldous had mastered the new techniques, he went on with his education. He got through the required reading, typed his written work and was taught by a succession of tutors. One was the present Sir George Clark, the seventeenth-century historian, and Aldous used to say he had learnt much from him.

He was a very remarkable man—he was a contemporary of my second brother—he had just come down from Oxford and he tutored me. I certainly got a good deal out of *him*. He was extremely well-read and a highly civilized young man . . .[2]

Aldous read a great amount himself at that period—with his finger-tips slowly, maddeningly slowly, off the thick Braille page. He spoke of the tedium of reading Macaulay, "You can't just glance over the page," of how intolerable the style became when spelt out letter by letter. Reading *anything* more than once must have been intolerable, and it was now that Aldous began to develop that extraordinary memory of his.

Never one to fritter away his time—I don't think that he was ever prone to the adolescent's—and the artist's!—commonplace equation: idleness = boredom = guilt = despair—it was actually during that year that Aldous started to write. He began, and finished, a novel on his little typewriter. A novel of about 80,000 words which, he said,

I never subsequently read. It disappeared. I rather regret that it *has* disappeared—I would be interested to know what it was like now.

It was sort of romantic—no it wasn't romantic—it was a rather *bitter* novel about a young man and his relationship to two different kind of women, as I remember it.[2]

By the spring of 1912, Aldous was able to walk about by himself and had hopes of being able to go to Oxford. His Eton contemporary Charles Harman met him again, after more than a year of separation, when they were both staying at Stocks with Mrs Humphry Ward. Aldous appeared unchanged.

[1] Miss Margaret Huxley, in a letter to S. B.
[2] London interview. 1961.

Mrs Humphry Ward's complete works—a set of them—were in every spare bedroom in the house. Aldous went about muddling them up, managing to put three *Robert Elsmere*'s in a row and so on. He loved mischief.[1]

But his sight and all that it entailed was never mentioned between them. Englishmen did not talk about such things.

For these Easter holidays Aldous went to Cornwall with the Henry Huxleys. Gervas talks of his determination to lead an absolutely normal life.

You did not take in how handicapped he was because he wouldn't let you think of him as handicapped. Incredibly, he insisted on bicycling. Although he really couldn't see—my mother would ride in front of him; but Aldous insisted on bicycling to the station on his own. It was terrific courage, it really was.

One bitter cold morning Gervas came into his room and Aldous said, "You know, Gerry, there's one great advantage in Braille, you can read in bed without getting your hands cold."

If there were moments of appalling discouragement and strain "he never showed it", Gervas said. "He never showed it."

[1] Lord Harman, talking.

Chapter Four

Pulling Through

ALDOUS'S sight was beginning to recover (to some extent). There is the fact that he was able to bicycle at all, that he was able to pick out *Robert Elsmere*'s from the shelves. Gervas thinks that it was sometime in the spring of 1912 that he first saw Aldous poring over print through an enormous magnifying glass. There is evidence also in a rather pathetic letter typed that May.

Dearest Father,
   Many thanks for your last letter, which, I regret to say was rather too small for me to read with any comfort. In fact I was only able to take the cream off each sentence by picking out one word in every four or so . . .

Leonard Huxley had married again in February 1912. He was only fifty-two and had been on his own for over three years. He married Rosalind Bruce, a young woman of twenty-two: they were very much in love, and their marriage turned out to be an extraordinarily happy one. A man marries according to his choice and instincts; his marriage and its timing is his own affair. But a second marriage, inevitably, also involves his children, and the situation for them, for the new wife, for the man himself, is seldom an entirely easy one. Here, the ground seems not to have been well enough prepared, the intended marriage (in Sir George Clark's words) was "casually announced to the boys"; there were undertones of shock and hurt. The bride was very young, younger, in fact, than Julian and Trev, very young to face those particular four step-children. It was late in the day to re-make a home for them, and Julia Huxley would have been hard to replace by *anyone*. Julian was then a brilliant and not particularly considerate young man in his first intellectual pride, steeped in his own conflicts and concerns; Margaret probably still child enough to show a child's feelings; Aldous enigmatic, docile and aloof; Trevenen alone gave warmth, came forward, tried to build the bridges. The second Mrs Huxley did her best. "Oh Lord, yes," Gervas said, "she was very good to them, she was very good to Aldous and Trev." She faced the formidably intellectual brood, and came to have a great affection for them all.
   Meanwhile she looked after Aldous—whose home base was now

37

Westbourne Square—as much as he would let her. As a matter
of fact she did one of the nicest things: giving him the use of the
piano, the wedding-present of her grandfather's.

In May Aldous went off to Germany for part of the summer.
It would seem that he made the railway journey, changes and
all, by himself. Whether he went mainly to consult an oculist or
to study music or to learn German is not clear. (He once told me
that as he never *saw* German his knowledge of the language was
purely oral.) He stayed at Marburg, lodging with a university
professor of geology called Kayser; his letters home were cheerful.

The Kaysers have the most delightful dog .. Professor K. took
them on an all-day geological expedition .. He went to a funeral
where everyone was in magnificent uniform and he wished he had
brought his Eton C.O.T.C. private's uniform to outshine at least
the railway porters .. He has made a new philosophy called
Space & Suet which is really immense and will satisfy everything
.. He has just polished off Beethoven's Funeral March and is
going to start on a Chopin Prelude .. in the German line they
are doing Schiller and Charybdis. (He regretfully adds that the
pun is not his own.) Once he reported on the state of his eyes.

> About the autumn: it all so very much depends on E Clarke's
> remarks. I don't know if it would be good to use the one eye for
> doing anything much. The right does not seem to alter much, but
> the left is certainly progressing well. [16th June 1912.]

Back in England Aldous was again with his contemporaries,
spending the end of the summer holiday with Gervas and Lewis
Gielgud in Surrey. For Christmas 1912 they were all in London.
"We very much tended to go about in threes then," Gervas said,
"and we did a great deal together. Later that winter he and
Aldous went to Montana with their uncle John Collier and a
party.

> Trev. Not Julian, Julian was too old, he was doing other things[1] ...
> There again, Aldous came with us when we all went skiing. He
> couldn't see very much but he skied as well as I did.

1913 began well. In January Aldous went on a walking tour
on the South Downs with Trev; in February he was definitely

[1] Julian Huxley was first in America, then Heidelberg in the autumn.

getting ready for Oxford Matriculation. Once more he struggled
with his bugbear.

My most valuable time [he writes to Julian] is taken up . . by
reading MacAulay, and ten chapters of him at that, for matriculatio
ad absurdum. Dreadful old man to write in Latin Prose style: still,
it must be.

That tough capacity for knuckling down may well have come
down to Aldous from his grandfather (himself a man far from
robust in health). This is how T. H. Huxley taught himself a
language (German at the age of sixteen): ". . go straight to the
book you want to read, translate the first ten lines with the aid
of a dictionary, and learn all the words. Do this day by day and
it will not be long before you only need to use the dictionary now
and then."[1]

Spring and early summer Aldous actually spent at Oxford, not
as yet a member of the university but staying with Trev in his
digs in the Banbury Road, reading, working, being read to and
tutored by Trev, going about in the afternoons, punting, walking,
seeing their friends. The brothers were devoted to each other and
these were happy days.

It is time to say something about Trevenen Huxley. He was
twenty-three years old then, in his last term at Balliol, and a
brilliant mathematician (which Aldous was not, and lightly
regretted). Trev had been educated, like his brothers, at Hillside
and Eton, had taken a first in Math Mods in 1911 and was now
reading for his final in Greats. He loved mountains and rock-
climbing and was outstanding at it, he had a mild stammer, and
he is remembered as a human being of rare quality. We can
only see him now through the wrong end of the opera glass—
an unforgotten figure, remote in time. His contemporaries
regarded him as the most out-going and human of the brothers.
Number Two, he called himself.

> *One Huxley Brother*
> *Is as good as another;*
> *This is the view*
> *Of Number Two.*

"Never, indeed," writes Sir Laurence Collier, "have I known a
man so widely liked."[2]

[1] C. Bibby op. cit.
[2] Sir Laurence Collier op cit.

Trev, "most radiant and beloved of his generation",[1] was affectionate, gay—sunny—of limitless kindness and great sweetness of nature; he was unselfish to an extreme degree, agonizingly sensitive, chiefly for others (and very much affected by the shock of Aldous's blindness); self-demanding, self-critical; a gay companion but also a conscientious worrier who drove himself too hard, who over-worked, over-exercised, did not bother about when or what he ate or take care of his own health. He had an ascetic streak, detesting jokes and boys' talk about sex, and an inclination to subdue his instincts by his principles. We have Aldous's re-creation of his brother as Brian Foxe in *Eyeless in Gaza* (perhaps his only fully intentional portrait of an actual person).

At Oxford, that May, Trev, Aldous and Lewis Gielgud were enjoying themselves rehearsing a play. The author was Naomi Haldane,[2] then a very young girl, who professes to have forgotten the title. It was a strawberry and gooseberry summer—the summer of 1913; there is a photograph of Aldous doubled up under a bush, eating gooseberries. He was getting on for nineteen, and all of a sudden one *sees* Aldous—he is no longer a boy, already he has become the ageless adult.

> He was long and dreadfully vulnerable looking, his long arms and legs dangling across the back of chairs or sofas.[3]

It is also one's first view of Aldous through the eyes of a pretty girl

> We were always having picnics up the Cherwell, making fires and boiling kettles . . We were always laughing and scrapping . . .

Aldous introduced Naomi to literature. He told her mother that of course she must read *Tom Jones*; Mrs Haldane gave in. He asked her general-personal questions. "Are you in love?" "Describe it to me." While all the time she was admiring his yellow tie and white socks and wished he would kiss her.

Oh yes, she says now, "Aldous was very much sought by the girls".

He did not kiss. But "he threw open a whole world to me. French books . . . made me read French poetry . . . Mallarmé . . .

---

[1] Leonard Huxley, letter to Gidley Robinson 1915.

[2] Naomi Mitchison (the present Lady Mitchison), the writer; daughter of Professor John Scott Haldane, sister of J. B. S. Haldane, the biologist.

[3] This and the following quotation are by Naomi Mitchison, *Mem. Vol.* and conversation with S.B.

He knew an amazing amount about all the arts and took them seriously in a way that was tremendously encouraging to me in our somewhat anti-art Oxford home.

Aldous still drew.

In some extraordinary way he did the most brilliant drawings, using a thick pencil . . . And he played on our schoolroom piano—was it Beethoven? was it Chopin? What I remember most is his long hands on the piano and his half-blind face reaching forward into the music. I only listened, but he was immersed.

Trev in his Oxford finals that summer got a second in Greats. It was a disappointment. It was due, the family think, to exhaustion, worry and overwork. Trev had been worked too hard since Eton (at one point Matron had advised withdrawing him for a time, but his father and mother decided to keep him on[1]). At a recent examination session at Oxford he had felt so ill that he handed in blank pages; and whenever he had a holiday "Leonard dragged him up a mountain"[2] (which *was* what Trev enjoyed). Whatever the cause, he took the relative failure as a blow.

In July Aldous went to Grenoble for two months to work at his French. He had lessons with an Abbé Lincelon, read Musset and Taine, "filling it up with the Oxford Book of French Verse," translated chunks of E. F. Benson with the aid of a dictionary $1\frac{1}{2}$ inch by 2, and explored the countryside. Again there are long filial letters, "Dearest Father," with sketches on the margin. The slopes of Savoy are full of the homeliest trees, just like the low valleys in Wales . . . the French at the pension are really much nicer than he thought . . . He has had four letters for his birthday, three on the day and one two days late . . . and would they send on the two shirts which were at the wash when he left . . .

Lewis Gielgud arrived. They went up on mules to the Grande Chartreuse. The maquis is thicker than anything he has seen before, "Oak, hazel, maple, wild cherry . . . but the thing is to start early, today we were off by 6.30 and it was delicious—the butterflies and flowers . . wonderful Apollos and Camberwell beauties and fritillaries, brand new and shining like new minted coins." (An instance of what Aldous could see at times—not always, not

---

[1] Rosalind (Mrs Leonard) Huxley.
[2] Joan Collier Buzzard.

consistently—*managed* to see, long before his Bates training, by his own desire and application.)

The letters often end with an affectionate enquiry about his eldest and peripatetic brother, "How, where, when and why is Julian?" (in Texas, actually, teaching biology). "I hope everyone flourishes, Julian in particular."

In September Aldous and Lewis Gielgud returned to England and joined Gervas in Yorkshire who says that Aldous came back with an extremely good French accent.

Chapter Five

"That One Glorious Year at Balliol"

AND in October Aldous was able to enter Balliol. He went, as it worked out, at the same time as Gervas who had not missed a day of school at Rugby. Aldous had done it, the tough concentration, the solitary disciplines had paid off.

His sight had reached a platform; it had recovered to the limited extent he described precisely in *The Art of Seeing:*

> I was left . . . with one eye just capable of light perception, and the other with enough vision to permit of my detecting the two-hundred foot letter on the Snellen chart at ten feet.

In practice this meant that he could read, though not with any ease. The pupil of his better eye had to be kept dilated with an atropine solution so that it might see round a heavy patch of opacity at the centre of the cornea; nor was he allowed the use of spectacles as yet, but had to do his reading through a powerful hand magnifying glass or—when the right books were available —in Braille. His other senses had sharpened: he used his long, tactile hands to sort out objects, crossed roads by hearing. He had come to terms with the slow process of Braille. True, one could not skim, he would say, but it made one absorb, it made one *remember*. Aldous actually had done rather more than catch up by the time he went to Oxford.

> We had just gone on at school [says Gervas], Aldous had read a great deal while he was blind—working on his own, he read a lot of things, like French, which we didn't know.

Aldous slid into his first Oxford term with ease. There was Trev, who had arranged to stay on doing post-graduate work, to be with his brother, there was Gervas, there was Lewis, the Haldanes; and then all at once there was that first full plunge into an adult world, a young man's first year at the university: new friends, ideas, freedoms, and time, time seemingly inexhaustible before him.

"Everybody adored Aldous—he fascinated them. He made a tremendous impression, [Gervas] and became the most popular person of the year." Raymond Mortimer—fellow freshman at

43

Balliol—called him "formidably sophisticated—he was dazzling, *dazzling* . . . The erudition: he had read everything."

The Dean of Balliol was Neville Talbot. Pre-eminence in scholarship, Gervas writes,

> was as great as ever, but the tone had changed in the last few years; rowdiness and drunkenness were no longer fashionable among the bloods, and the college had become a generally sober and serious place, with such eminent undergraduates as Godfrey Elton, Harold MacMillan and "God" Wedderburn, the rowing blue, setting the tone.
>
> As for the dons, "Sligger" Urquhart still kept open house in his rooms every evening, while distinguished scholars like A. L. Smith and Cyril Bailey were our friends as well as our tutors.

It was pre-wars Oxford, pre-industries, pre-motor cars; there were horse trams going up the High and everybody went on foot or bicycle. Aldous's room in college overlooked the Broad; he had a piano and a bright French poster over the fireplace.

> The room seemed always full of people talking and laughing . . . It was the centre where the elite of the year gathered.

It was Aldous who introduced them to Jazz (which he came to loathe so whole-heartedly ever after). Then he was fascinated by syncopation and he would strum with relish,

> *He'd have to get under, Get out or get under . . .*

"He was always picking up something new [Gervas]—and this was certainly brand new to us."

Aldous's allowance at Oxford was two hundred pounds a year. Gervas had two hundred and fifty.

> Money never seemed to mean very much to him—his wants were never extravagant—he managed all right, but couldn't indulge in the clothes or book buying that I could with my extra fifty a year; but I am sure that it never bothered him.

They were blissfully untroubled. There was as yet no thought of examinations—poor Trev sat for the Civil Service exam and again did not do well—for Aldous and Gervas there were only the ridiculous Divvers, Sacred History (which Aldous failed at his first go). They had time for a lot of acting. Naomi Haldane had written another play, performed in her parents' garden—"We

were immediately made completely free of Mrs Haldane's house"[1]
—and they also did scenes from Aristophanes' *Frogs*. Lewis
Gielgud acted and stage managed, Aldous played Charon. "I
was fierce about my plays," Naomi says, "but couldn't fault his
performance. Yes, he could see enough to get himself on and off
stage. How gay we all were!"

We—Naomi's brother Jack, Dick her fiancé,[2] Gervas, Lewis,
some girls in the cast ("a refreshing change"), Aldous, "always
a little apart .. with a book .. he was somehow brooding, not
unenjoyably, without".

As for work. He enjoyed his tutorials "I had a very able tutor,
Tiddy, R. J. E. Tiddy, lecturer in classics and English Literature . . ."[3] He went to few lectures. "I never attended more than,
at the outside, two lectures a week." He typed his essays and
wrote a good deal of verse. "Well, things flourish," he reported
to his father,

the only fly in the ointment being P. Mods—infernally stupid exam,
trod out by the feet of weeping boys from the wine-press of boredom.

All in all it was tremendous fun, as Gervas put it: "We had
that one glorious year. One year was wonderful for Aldous, it
really was. We took everything Oxford had to offer. And it was
an awful lot."

They broke off for the long vacation in June 1914.

1 Cherwell Edge in north Oxford, now Wolfson College.
2 The late Lord Mitchison.
3 London interview, 1961.

Chapter Six

Trevenen

IN August 1914 Aldous was in Scotland at Connel Ferry with his father and step-mother. Julian, temporarily home from Texas, was with them. Trev was not. Since the beginning of the year he had been in a state of depression. The strain over exams, the anxieties for others, the delicate constitution assaulted by fanatical exercising and underfeeding, the conflict between a young man's ordinary sexual impulses and high ideals—it all had become too much for him.

It was in that condition that he was faced by a crisis in his life. He fell in love, idealistically *and* sensually. He gave way to the sensuality. Fifty years ago, such things went very deep. The girl, who was charming and loving, and very unhappy herself, was a girl whom Trev could not have married in the social circumstances of their time without bringing much unhappiness upon them both. The family knew nothing; Trev wrote about it to at least one friend (abroad in the crucial months). Sarah knew, the Leonard Huxleys' old parlourmaid. (Aldous must have been told something because he made his brother's conflict the theme of his opening poem in *The Defeat of Youth*.) By summer Trev was at the end of his tether and had a severe, medically acknowledged breakdown: depression punctuated by fits of melancholia.

T. H. Huxley had suffered from long bouts of depression in his later life; Julian had had a nervous breakdown, or depression neurosis as we would say now (the first of a series), the year before when he had been treated, successfully as far as it went, by a rest cure in a nursing home. Earlier in the summer of 1914 he had returned, on leave from his American appointment, to that same nursing home for another brief spell of rest, and it was there (in Surrey) that Trev was now confined, on psychiatric advice. At the beginning of August he was said to be improving.

On 15th August, a Saturday, he set out for a walk on the downs by himself. He spoke to the nurse on leaving and had appeared to be cheerful and calm. (It is known that the treating London psychiatrist had given explicit orders that the patient must never be left out of sight.)

He failed to return from his walk. The police were told the same evening. A search began—his father came down from Scotland—there was no trace of Trevenen for seven days. It was thought that he might have gone and enlisted in the war. Then there was news that he had been seen earlier wandering about the neighbourhood.

The following Sunday, 23rd August, Trevenen was found in a wood only a few hundred yards away. He had hanged himself from a tree.

The news came to Julian and Aldous by telegraph.

Trevenen was not yet twenty-five. Aldous was twenty. A brother, a loved companion, had taken his life, returned his entrance ticket to God, in that phrase of Dostoevski's Aldous was to use again; a brother had hanged himself. Where does it leave one? Englishmen did not talk about such things.

To Gervas, Aldous wrote a few days after, a seven-line letter:

There is—apart from the sheer grief of the loss—an added pain in the cynicism of the situation. It is just the highest and best in Trev—his ideals—which have driven him to his death . . . Trev was not strong, but he had the courage to face life with ideals—and his ideals were too much for him.

Some weeks later, in a letter to Jelly d'Aranyi,[1] Aldous let go a little. He spoke of his father—he is better now. "he was most terribly broken for a time". He spoke of his sister—she is still so much of a child in some ways, "and I am glad for her sake, because it has saved her from fully realizing the whole tragedy". (Here Aldous did not know enough. When Julian went to America, Trev, in Margaret Huxley's own words,[2] became "the be-all and end-all of my life, and his death was far more shattering to me than my mother's, strange and even unnatural as that may sound . . . Trev was, I think, the hub of the family wheel . .") Aldous spoke of himself—"I . . am sitting . . here in the room that Trev and I used to share together,

where every book and every picture helps to keep alive the memories —which, though they bring a terrible sadness with them, are always of a past time that has been very happy.

It is of that one ought to think, of the past, and one ought to be grateful and thankful for all the years one has spent with one who was among the noblest and best of men—but Oh God, it's bitter sometimes to sit in this room reading before the fire—alone and to think of all the happy evenings we sat there together and all the hours I hoped to have again, when he was better. It's a selfish grief perhaps, but oh Jelly, you know what he was to me.

[1] The violinist; a great friend of the Huxley family, a girl then in her early twenties.
[2] Margaret Huxley, letter to S. B., 1969.

Chapter Seven

Return to Oxford

"WHEN we broke off for the long vacation, none of us took the slightest interest in world politics, none of us took the slightest thought . . imagined a future with a war."[1]

Aldous went back to Oxford in October 1914. *Everybody had gone.* Balliol was deserted. "One enlisted at once. We all did. We just disappeared . . ."[1]

Not only had we physically gone, we were mentally gone—one had to cut out Oxford completely in order to survive . . . start an entirely new life in the war. You had to make yourself forget about your friends, that was one of the awful things; we didn't dare to think, you had to train yourself to live wholly in the day.[1]

And there was Aldous, there he was left, his friends gone, the life gone. He was cut off abruptly, for the second time, became again a stranger to the world of contemporary experience. That second isolation must have been a very bitter thing.

"He told me quite a bit about it," Gervas said, "that day I went to France and he saw me off, December I think it was, December 1914 . . ."

Gervas was passing through London on his way to Grimsby to take a draft of his regiment to France. Unasked, Aldous was waiting for him at Paddington. They spent the day together.

"He was terribly anxious, you know, about practical matters—had I got enough warm clothes? He was thinking much more about me than about himself that day."

They bought a Shetland shawl together at the Army & Navy Stores. Aldous did say how much he missed his friends, how *awful* Balliol was now with *nobody* there. He still hoped, he said, not to get actually into the Army but into some kind of war work that he could do.

No, no, he didn't think of himself as lucky—far from it. I think he was feeling rather envious, in the way you do when all your friends are doing something and you can't.

[1] Gervas Huxley, talking.

48

They said goodbye on the platform at King's Cross. Gervas holding this thought in his mind: if one survived one would never need to bother about one's communications with Aldous—"there was something imperishable there".

And then, presumably, Aldous walked out of the station, crossed London, took another train and went back to Oxford.

I spoke to Sir George Clark, the man who had been Aldous's tutor and his friend, who had seen the gay intelligent schoolboy, as it were before the fall, talking at Oxford to his elders. I asked him if he could imagine an Aldous unmarked by the events of those six years. What had they done to him? Sir George used one word. "He was—impaired."

PART THREE

The Hard Years: 1914-1921

". . I must say I am amazed that I did get through as much as I did. It must obviously have been rather tiring this whole process—but I managed to do it."

ALDOUS HUXLEY

Chapter One

The Quiet Life of Anglo Saxon Lectures

THROUGHOUT his life we have sudden views, *momentanés* as it were, of Aldous imprinted at points in time on the minds of alert observers. At Oxford that winter a woman undergraduate saw him listening at lectures. He always stood; he took no notes.

> One day the then Prince of Wales was sitting in a row above me, and he did not write notes either; a student near him leant forward and offered him a pencil which was gratefully accepted. But behind me was Mr Huxley standing near a pillar by the doorway against the window just listening to the lecture.

"I have always remembered him standing against that pillar, alone and detached, neatly dressed."[1]

Aldous had not returned to his rooms in college and was living with the Haldanes in their house, Cherwell Edge, in north Oxford. "It is nicer, I think, being here than in an empty Balliol. They are very nice people I am staying with."

The Haldanes looked after him with some anxiety but Aldous, who turns out to have been the least neurotic of men, went his way mildly melancholy, resolutely cheerful, always contained.

He had a large room next to the schoolroom where he played the piano for long hours by himself. Again he was looking after Naomi's literary education. "And while I was learning," she said, "he was picking up science from my father." For the present he was making no new men friends; "The last able-bodied British undergraduates", wrote T. S. Eliot,

> were passing from the O.T.C. to the trenches, and beyond the Rhodes scholars from America and the Commonwealth there were hardly any left except those who like Aldous were wholly unfit for military service.[2]

"Practically speaking [Aldous to Julian] Sligger and myself are the only possibles left alive in Oxford; [Tiddy, his own tutor,

1 Miss M. Marshall in a letter to S. B.
2 T. S. Eliot, *Mem. Vol.*; T. S. E. and Aldous did not meet that term at Oxford.

is already in the war and soon to be killed] even the few possibilities of last term have now vanished . . . Meanwhile, the quiet life of Anglo-Saxon lectures amid a crowd of painful young women."

He tried to enlist himself but was of course rejected by every recruiting office. Aldous's attitude to the war at that particular time, that year in Rupert Brooke's England when one's friends "were going off to war with their noble young heads in the air", was neither original nor extreme. He easily spoke of Boches and Huns though never quite without his pinch of detachment.

It is, of course, axiomatic that the Germans are lying . . but still, it is for the historian of 2000 to settle that question, for us to extirpate the vipers.

And only a few months later, in April 1915,

This hustling of aliens is rather damnable—mob-law . . [the Government] betrays mere feeble-mindedness to drift on the stream of popular passion. We are losing our heads and our sense of humour.

Meanwhile he worked. Now on Milton—his special subject— now on "the mediaeval creatures—terrible people, who never wrote anything less than an epic". Oh yes, he writes to his old headmaster at Hillside, there *is* backbone to what is called the mere reading of literature.

"Back bone" here at Oxford is provided by the Anglo Saxon branch of the school . . . considerably more difficult than Greek . . . and the literature obscure and dull.

How bored poor Aldous was! All the same he persevered with the "nauseous diet of Anglo Saxon", went through the mass of excruciatingly dull—and for him painful and laborious—reading. And at the same time he read a great deal for his own pleasure and instruction.

Actually I think that the most exciting people I read as an undergraduate were French writers . . . I had my introduction to French literature at that time. I read Proust when he first came out in 1914, *Du Coté de chez Swann,* and I read the French poets then—Mallarmé made an *immense* impression upon me.

One should hear his voice—lingering over the word *immense*, giving every consonant its value.

And still *does*. I am still very fond of him. And Rimbaud made an *immense* impression on me then.[1]

How did he manage it?

"Well, every handicap is of course a challenge." In that long recorded interview Aldous gave in London to John Chandos forty years later on, he spoke about it. Lightly, in that serene, clear voice, he said,

I mean one is limited to what one can do. I was strictly limited in all kinds of otherwise normal activities; many things that I liked doing, like mountain climbing and so on, became difficult or impossible for me. I couldn't practise any kind of sport requiring a ball, because [and his voice rises in a characteristic curve] because I couldn't *see* the balls.

On the other hand .. if the handicap isn't too great and overwhelming, it can also stimulate one to do things which in other circumstances one wouldn't do . . .

I *did* read a great deal. And I am extremely astonished at how much I was able to read. Because .. for about two years after this thing came upon me .. I couldn't read at all. Well, little by little I was able to read again—but I did all my reading while I was at Oxford with a powerful magnifying glass—I must say I am amazed that I did get through as much as I did. It must obviously have been rather tiring this whole process: but *I managed to do it.*

[1] London interview, 1961.

Chapter Two

A Young Man on His Own

NOT only reading—writing. Typing away, bent over his small portable on his knees: "I discovered that I liked writing, and that I had a certain gift for it."

Aldous wrote mostly verse that second year at Oxford. He wrote and translated French verse and pastiche, he competed for the Newdigate Prize (which he failed to get) with a long Byronic poem on Glastonbury. He also tried his hand at prose, writing his first short stories, among them that curious "Eupompus Gave Splendour To Art By Numbers", and of course he wrote the required essays for his tutor.

I must say [the London interview again] I was interested not long ago in looking over old volumes . . They were on all sorts of literary subjects, I mean from Chaucer down to the present day, and I was interested and surprised to find that well, I mean I was writing quite well at the time—I had a certain feeling for style, there was even a certain elegance in what I was doing at the age of twenty.

Aldous added,

I had obviously some kind of natural gift for writing.

"Home-Sickness—From the Town" was published that year in *Oxford Poetry*. As it is Aldous's first (adult) poem in print and has, to my knowledge, never been re-published, it might be worth quoting here as it is typical of one side of early Aldous and of what he liked to do with words when he was young.

> *Frou-Frouery and faint patchouli smells,*
> *And debile virgins talking Keats,*
> *And the arch widow in accordion pleats,*
> *Artfully fringing with the tales she tells*
> *The giggling prurient.*
> *Life nauseous! Let the whole crowd be sent*
> *To the chosen limbos and appropriate hells*
> *Reserved in memory's blackest stagnancy.*
> *Back, back! No Social Contract! From the teats*
> *Of our old wolfish mother nature drink*
> *Sweet unrestraint and lust and savagery.*

55

Feel goat-hair growing thick and redolent
On loin and thigh; look back
And mark the cloven hoof-marks of the track
You leave, then forward eyes again; no wink,
Lest for an instant you should miss the sight
Of moony floating flanks and haunches white
Flashed by your fleeing nymph girl through the leaves.

Naomi still wanted kisses. Indeed, she wanted Aldous to become her lover and told him so. Aldous refused to do anything of the kind. "I think it was his principles."

What were his principles?

Aldous—according to Gervas, and one can well imagine it— was gaily outspoken as a boy and, unlike poor Trev, without prudishness. They used to rag each other about mythical attachments to smaller pretty boys and to Prior's Field girls; at Oxford Aldous joined in the singing of Jack Haldane's extremely bawdy songs. As to actual behaviour,

Aldous and I had the same code that while one might cherish a romantic love for somebody (I had one for Naomi in 1914!) it all remained purely platonic—no kissing or necking—one cherished from afar (pleasantly, too) but that one only declared one's love or attempted a closer attachment with a girl of one's own class if one proposed marriage and one only did this if one was in a position to marry.

So much for the temporal and explicit. On other levels there is the post-Victorian childhood (which, however, does not appear to have been troubled by the corrupt governesses of Aldous's fiction—Fräulein Ella was no Fräulein Lili[1]); there is Aldous's temperament and physique: the fastidiousness, the sensitiveness, the intense physiological response, the "almost frantic sensuality" of the extreme Sheldonian ectomorph. There is the effect of Trevenen's death and its immediate cause. There is the latent dichotomy between his indulgent, ironical, consciously *dix-huitième* taking to sensuality and his sense, stressed mostly in his writing, of Swiftian and Baudelairian horror.

On a non-verbal level Aldous was extremely susceptible to pretty women. If the girls sought him, it was not least because principles or no principles he was naturally responsive. ("Happily, as I fall in love with every woman I meet .. at any rate

[1] Fräulein Lili, a character in the fragment of an unfinished novel by A. H. published in Laura Archera Huxley's *This Timeless Moment*.

with the better women I meet . . ."[1]) Yet Gervas, who would
be the one man to know, thought that Aldous had no serious
love affair or attachment before the 1914 war. There was one
incident (again, only Gervas knew about it) which should be told
to lay the legend of Aldous Huxley the helpless, hopeless, tentative
young man who got it all out of books. It happened in the summer
of 1913, shortly before Aldous went to Grenoble. For some reason
he was alone in the Westbourne Square house. He went out for
a stroll and he picked up a girl (who was, he thought, an au pair
girl on her evening off) and took her home and made love to her
on the sofa. He told Gervas that what had most impressed,
excited and surprised him was the eagerness of the girl's approach
and embraces. ("You must remember that in those days one
imagined that the eagerness only came from the man.")

Aldous was reading Jacob Boehme then, and Blake. "Well, I
was always interested in the descriptions and philosophies of the
mystical life," he said in the London interview; "I read a fair
amount [about it] at the time—with a mixture of admiration and
hostility."
(John Chandos, his interviewer, then asked him, "Mr Huxley,
at that time you regarded mystical experience, I imagine, with
derision?" And Aldous replied mildly, "Not with *derision* but with
a good deal of scepticism. And with a good deal of fascinated
interest.")

During those war years, Aldous's letters were more outgoing
than they became. He was young, he was alone, he was not as
yet a professional writer who must monger words for his daily
bread. He often wrote to Jelly d'Aranyi, the young violinist,
young but slightly older, to whom he had been able to write
about Trevenen. Oxford that June was hot and damp; it was the
time of the long casualty lists, of bad news every day . . . At the
end of the Trinity terms Aldous escaped to his stepmother's house
on the west coast of Scotland . .

I know nothing more beautiful than this place, with its beautifully
shaped mountains, its great lochs . . and glimpses of broad seas . . .
These evenings are so wonderfully peaceful—
    Les lacs éperdus des longs couchants défunts . . .
It all helps to mellow the thought that one's friends are being killed,
into a quiet kind of resigned sadness.

[1] From a letter to Lewis Gielgud 29th September 1916.

It is a curious letter—so different in style and mood from his contemporary verse—with its intimations of his future quest.

> One does feel tremendously that one is part of a larger soul, which embraces everything . . . But then again . . when I get back among all the wretchedness of the town it is impossible to recognize this splendid unity.
>
> It looks as though the amount of good and evil were about the same in the world. I think the good will probably win in the end—though not necessarily, unless the most persistent and tremendous efforts are made . . . I'm not a pessimist, and I think it will be all right. I think we shall ultimately work all the disorder into a single principle, which will be an Absolute—but which at present exists only potentially and at the nature of which we can only very dimly guess.

A few weeks later, in London in his father's house, Aldous came of age. "Well, I'm twenty-one today—grown up." Later on he wrote again to Jelly d'Aranyi:

> . . This war impresses on me more than ever the fact that friendship, love, whatever you like to call it is the only reality . . . You never knew my mother—I wish you had because she was a very wonderful woman: Trev was most like her. I have just been reading again what she wrote to me just before she died. The last words of her letter were "Don't be too critical of other people and 'love much' "—and I have come to see more and more how wise that advice was. It's a warning against a rather conceited and selfish fault of my own and it's a whole philosophy of life.

Chapter Three

Starting Points

AFTER a family summer spent mostly at Westbourne Square and Prior's Field, Aldous went back to Oxford for his third and last year. Naomi Haldane was having scarlet fever and so he moved back into Balliol; "to a nice room in the new building—airy and light," and finds living in college again "very nice in some ways, but rather sad too".

Yet Oxford was brightening up. "It's a very curious place now," he writes to his father, "there are a good many (relatively) nice people, most of them oddities of one kind or another—aesthetic, exotically religious and the like."

He joined a small club which met once a week to read members' poems, where he met Eric Dodds, later Regius Professor of Greek; Roland Childe, Roy Campbell and above all Tommy Earp,[1] a rich and eccentric young man who like Aldous was fond of French poetry and strange stories about people. They became great friends. And there was Russell Green, another eccentric, the future author of the novel *Prophet Without Honour*. It was he who had won the Newdigate, for which Aldous had competed, with a poem on Venice. From that moment, Green maintains, Aldous developed an affectionate attitude towards him. He was a classical scholar at Queen's and had also won the Chancellor's English Essay prize of 1915. "Thus," he writes, "for a brief space Aldous and I ran neck and neck . . . Alas, how widely our paths diverged." By Green we have another of those *momentanés*.

Aldous was highly sensitive to the faintest hint of feminine allure . . . Once in Oxford we were lunching with Tommy Earp at a seat separated from the waitresses, who were dishing up food, by a screen of some soft material draped from a rail six feet high down to the floor. When, in my insatiable curiosity, I lifted it up with my left hand (what a memory I have!) Aldous sniggered, since it suggested to him the lifting of a skirt.

That term, L. P. Hartley fit for home service and waiting to be called up, had rooms on the same staircase. There he heard Aldous typing away, playing the piano, declaiming to himself

---

[1] The late T. W. Earp; his father was a Liberal M.P. for Newark and member of the firm of maltsters, Gilstrap, Earp & Co.

59

"To a Coy Mistress." "I loved his voice." Then Aldous asked him to cocoa—"quite a fashionable drink in those diminished days. Aldous talked of T. S. Eliot; the first time I had heard of him.

I had never known anyone like Aldous. His voice, his rangy height, his elegant clothes, his noble white brow, crowned with a patch of unruly black hair, his mysterious rather glaucous eyes . . peering through the oblong magnifying glass he used when he was reading —these left an ineffable impression. Culture had found a mortal envelope worthy of itself.[1]

"I had an amusing day on Sunday—going out to Garsington for luncheon to the Philip Morrells, who have bought the lovely Elizabethan manor there." So wrote Aldous casually to his father that December. When one is young, any encounter may be a starting, a turning point; we half expect this, yet run into it blindly. Aldous had been brought over to Garsington by Desmond MacCarthy and introduced as the grandson of T. H. Huxley.

Lady Ottoline, Philip's wife [he went on in that letter], is a quite incredible creature—arty beyond the dreams of avarice and a patroness of literature and the modernities. She is intelligent, but her affectation is overwhelming.

There is another record of that casual Sunday. Juliette Baillot's, as she was then, young and Swiss and living at Garsington as part-time student at Oxford and governess-companion to the Morrell's little girl, Julian. "Then Aldous came. Very silent, very young.

. . His six foot four seemed even taller because of the slenderness of his body and his slight stoop. Under the thick brown hair, his wide face was pale with full lips and blue eyes which had an inward look . . . He did not talk much at his first visit, but as soon as he was gone, everyone agreed about the deep impression of unique quality, of gentleness and depth.[2]

One of the immediate consequences was Lady Ottoline's writing to D. H. Lawrence to suggest that he should meet Aldous. D. H. L., who was living at Hampstead with Frieda, wrote a note asking Aldous to tea. Aldous went.

[1] L. P. Hartley talking on a BBC broadcast 17th August 1964.
[2] Juliette (Lady) Huxley, in *Mem. Vol.*

The place was London, the time 1915. But Lawrence's passionate talk was of the geographically remote and the personally very near. Of the horrors in the middle distance—war, winter, the town—he would not speak. For he was on the point, or so he imagined, of setting off to Florida—to Florida, where he was going to plant that colony of escape of which to the last he never ceased to dream . . . That wintry afternoon it was Florida. Before tea was over he asked me if I would join the colony, and though I was an intellectually cautious young man, not at all inclined to enthusiasms, though Lawrence had startled and embarrassed me with sincerities of a kind to which my upbringing had not accustomed me, I answered yes.[1]

So Aldous wrote fifteen years after the event. In that actual wintry month of 1915, he described the meeting to Julian with the same blend of recognition and aloofness.

. . One D. H. Lawrence, a novelist . . . whose recent work *The Rainbow* was regrettably burnt by the common hangman for obscenity . . . well, this good man, who impresses me as a good man more than most, proposes . . to go to the deserts of Florida with one Armenian [Michael Arlen], one German wife and, problematically, one young woman called Dorothy Warren . . to await a sort of Pentecostal inspiration of new life, which, whether it will come is another question. But Lawrence is a great man, and as he finds the world too destructive for his taste, he must, I suppose be allowed to get out of it . . .

D. H. L. himself, again in that same December, added a postscript of one line to a letter to Lady Ottoline Morrell.

I liked Huxley *very* much. He will come to Florida.

The scheme fell through. Cities of God, in Aldous's words, have always crumbled.

[1] A. H in the preface to *The Letters of D. H. Lawrence*. Heinemann, 1932.

Chapter Four

The Artificial Roses of Academic Distinction

ALDOUS'S last winter and spring at Oxford were full and strenuous. He had decided to compete for the Stanhope Historical Essay prize (theme, The Development of Political Satire in England from the Restoration to the Revolution), and was doing his reading in Bodley which they kept, he said, so hideously stuffy that it was hardly possible to stop going to sleep.

Meanwhile conscription had come in and he had to present himself to get classified. He was declared totally unfit.

He went over to Garsington quite often now and was meeting people. "The strange creature Lytton Strachey," and Barbara Hiles, his friend of the caterpillar hunts at Prior's Field, "delightfully cheerful and irresponsible as ever—with her hair still close-cut and curly and gold, gipsy-like rings in her ears." Juliette Baillot he asked to tea with him at Balliol; she came bringing little Julian Morrell.

> His room was long, rather dark, a curious room, almost like a corridor. He was very gentle with the child and talked more easily to her than he did to Ottoline.

Aldous gave them China tea and crumpets, and recited Carroll and Edward Lear.

Tommy Earp put up the money and he and Aldous were getting out their own literary review, the *Palatine*, and were drumming up subscriptions. (3/6d. a year, six numbers, and already thirty-six paid-up subscribers.) The first issue came out in February 1916 and contained Aldous's poem "Mole" and three other poems.

> *Tunnelled in solid blackness creeps*
> *The old mole-soul, and wakes or sleeps,*
> *He knows not which, but tunnels on*
> *Through ages of oblivion. . . .*

The editor of the *Nation*, H. W. Massingham, wrote to say how much he liked "Mole" and asked Aldous to send some poems to the new quarterly *Form*.

Aldous had mistakenly supposed that the Stanhope essay had to be in by 31st March. On 22nd February, late in the shortest month, he discovered that the date was 1st March—"and not a word written". On top of it he had neuralgia and a cold. "I never spent a more beastly week." He made the dead-line.

That exertion was followed almost at once by terminal exams in early March, "nightmarish collections in Anglo Saxon—that loathsome language is a nuisance beyond all words".

Julian Huxley was considering returning from America to England and the war. Aldous wrote him that he could not help thinking that it would be unwise to come home.

> There is very little to be done unless one means to fight—and in these days when one can't get commissions it is impossible to fight with that elegance and efficiency which in the old days, as an officer, were within one's reach. Work in munitions factories is intolerable [because of systematic overworking] . . Government departments are sometimes interesting but of a fearful strenuity.

For his own part he had thought of going into the Foreign Press department of the War Office last winter but had found that 12-14 hours work a day was normal so that it "would have been quite beyond my ocular abilities to stand the strain.

> The longer this war goes on, the more one loathes and detests it. At the beginning I should have liked very much to fight; but now if I could (having seen all the results), I think I'd be a conscientious objector, or nearly so.

In May Aldous went into training for his Oxford finals. "Three hours of strenuous writing this afternoon [doing papers under examination conditions] . . . I fear I have not the Bensonian faculty of writing 1500 words an hour—600 is about my exam rate."

And in June Finals are upon him. The papers were bad, he found, bad and stupid. An uninteresting paper on Chaucer, an uninteresting one on Shakespeare, and the history of literature one a disgrace to the University. As for himself:

> I am in the middle of Schools—which I find more tiring than any labour I have ever undertaken. Not only is the mental strain great, but the physical strain on the eyes—even using a typewriter . . . I stagger out . . feeling as if I had been bruised all over.

Meanwhile he heard that he had "picked off the Stanhope . . quite unexpectedly . . for it was a shoddy piece of work, my essay".

It was a comfort though, "even if one does badly in Schools". The prize was £20 in books. "Regrettably—one would have preferred the naked cash."

Aldous did not do badly in Schools. He got a first in English. "Well, Oxford is over," he wrote to Julian.

Crowned with the artificial roses of academic distinction, I stagger, magnificently drunk with youthful conceit, into the symposium, not of philosophers, but of apes and wolves and swine . . . No more of the sheltered, the academic life . . the life, which, I believe, when led by a man of high and independent spirit, is the fullest and the best of lives, though one of the most bedraggled and wretched as led by the ordinary crew of bovine intellectuals.

I should like to go on for ever learning. I lust for knowledge, as well theoretic as empirical. Comparing small things with great, I think I am rather like the incomparable John Donne.

Chapter Five

Prospects

"WHAT I'm going to do—God knows."
It was expected as a matter of course that Aldous must earn his living. Earn it at once, what's more, as his allowance ceased as soon as he was down from Oxford.

The scientific career he had wanted was out of the question, as he could not have used a microscope or done any of the laboratory work. As for writing, his poems and short stories were seeing the light of print in periodicals such as *Oxford Poetry* and the *Palatine* and he had a book of verse coming out in the autumn; yet writing as a profession, if he did have it in mind, was not an immediate prospect. "The solution of the HEIRESS presents itself," he wrote to Julian. ". . Of the more repulsive solutions two main ones appear. (*a*) To disseminate mendacity in our Great Modern Press. (*b*) To disseminate mendacity in our Great Modern Public Schools." And indeed in July, having hardly left Oxford ("a wrench, so personal has it become"), after only five pleasant days in London, Aldous found himself translated—"I am very much alone and at times depressed"—to Repton. His predecessor, he suspected, had been sacked, and the headmaster, G. F. Fisher,[1] had asked Aldous to fill the post till the end of term.

> I am in quite pleasant digs [he wrote to his father], the job—teaching Latin, history and English to the lower forms—is quite interesting. The boys know nil and so whatever I manage to teach them will be pure gain.

Rather a waste, he felt though, teaching on the strength of Pass Mods when one has a first in English. He must look for a university job. To his young friend Frances Petersen,[2] he admitted that though the boys are very well behaved, "the masters—what a set of Calibans . . . It really is too utterly bloody living alone. To bed, to bed! I have to get up at 6.30!" To Julian he wrote about his need for friends,

> How essential to one. I am utterly stranded and wretched without them.

[1] The future Archibshop of Canterbury.
[2] Frances Petersen, a granddaughter of P. W. Henderson, Warden of Wadham College, then a young girl at Oxford.

Term, however, will be over by the end of the month. And after Repton, *what*? He has quarrelled with Rugby, somewhat to his relief, and he doesn't want any of the other jobs he has been offered. But what to do? "I cannot even play the clarinet outside public houses." Perhaps he will go and hoe the ground somewhere. "I have a belief that it would be very good for one .. better than schoolmastering at any rate."

In August: summer holidays and return to civilization. First a week at Garsington—"hectically talking after the enforced silence of Repton . . . talking with intelligent people." The interlude has been even more amusing than usual; but he will not describe his adventures. "They are always peculiar." At least they make one forget the hollowness of existence, ". . a hollowness I find particularly reverberant when I come to regard my future prospects. Damn them!"

On to Prior's Field, boring but placid, where the days "slide away, as rapid and elusive as macaroni from the corners of an Englishman's mouth," but where he hopes to do some writing.

The *Nation* had published three of Aldous's poems, but by mistake over the signature of Leonard Huxley, who, Aldous says, received a letter from A. C. Benson congratulating him on the extreme beauty of his verse. "And now wherever my father goes showers of felicitations fall upon him." However, it is Aldous who is paid, gratifyingly, a guinea a piece—"I think I shall write an ode to money."

In September he is back in London and has made up his mind about the future. He will hoe the ground "or rather like G. Washington cut down .. trees, for it is, they seem to think, as a forester that I am going to function upon that curious and utterly unknown quantity, THE LAND". But it will be on the farm of his very dear friends the Morrells and the experience should be pleasing.

Aldous's first book came out in September. *The Burning Wheel*, a volume of poetry. "A tomelet of fifty pages and on every page a deceased personality," he wrote to Julian; "one changes, grows with the rapidity of one of those amorphophallic tropical fungi." These are a very young man's protestations, yet Aldous was to prove himself more capable of changing than most men; at the same time there was also a continuous thread and one may find it here already.

> *Wearied of its own turning,*
> *Distressed with its own busy restlessness,*

Yearning to draw the circumferent pain—
The rim that is dizzy with speed—
To the motionless centre, there to rest,
The wheel must strain through agony
On agony contracting, returning
Into the core of steel.
. . . .
. . . .
. . . . *the wheel that yearns—*
Sick with its speed—for the terrible stillness
Of the adamant core 1

The Burning Wheel is the verse of a young man who—after private tragedy—had to begin life in 1914, and is charged with a sense of the moral and physical suicide of the world.

The West has plucked its flowers and has thrown
Them fading on the night.2

A recurrent theme—as again in *The Defeat of Youth*, the second collection of Aldous's wartime poems—is the defeat of hope. The verse reflects scepticism, revulsion, longings. Much of it is clever, intricate, allusive, much is gruesome, deliberately appalling; there is also another and less well-remembered strain. I am transcribing "The Canal", one of his sonnets, for its lyrical and visual quality.

No dip and dart of swallows wakes the black
Slumber of the canal: —a mirror dead
For lack of loveliness remembered
From ancient azures and green trees, for lack
of some white beauty given and flung back,
Secret, to her that gave: no sun has bled
To wake an echo here of answering red;
The surface stirs to no leaf's wind-blown track.

Between unseeing walls the waters rest,
Lifeless and hushed, till suddenly a swan
Glides from some broader river blue as day,
And with the mirrored magic of his breast
Creates within that barren water-way
New life, new loveliness, and passes on.3

1 From *The Burning Wheel*, republished in *The Collected Poetry of Aldous Huxley*. Chatto & Windus, 1970.
2 Ibid.   3 Ibid.

At the time of publication Aldous wrote to Lewis Gielgud (back from the war and wounded) that he was so nauseated by the sight of his own poems that he had not had the strength to cut a copy.

Reviews appeared in due course. The one in *The Times* "pleasantly offensive", the one in the *Morning Post* quite pleasing. "They make me out very distinguished. Don't they?"

Chapter Six

"The Extraordinary Good Fortune"

ALDOUS'S statement that he was off to grapple with that unknown quantity the land was misleading. Garsington, his "dear friends' household", is now part of English social and literary history.

We have heard about and read about the moderate-sized Elizabethan manor house six miles from Oxford, we have read about Lady Ottoline Morrell, we have read about the house parties and the men and women who were the guests: Bertrand Russell, Asquith, Maynard Keynes, Lytton Strachey, D. H. Lawrence, Virginia Woolf, T. S. Eliot, Clive Bell and Roger Fry, Katherine Mansfield and John Middleton Murry, Duncan Grant, Mark Gertler, Siegfried Sassoon, Robert Graves . . . We have read their works and about their works, read their biographies and autobiographies, their diaries and their letters. We know that the severity of the intellectual atmosphere was lightened by the presence of young girls—Brett and Carrington, Mary Hutchinson, Juliette Baillot—and that in the early days there was a heady sense of freedom.

> . . Of nights [Aldous about one of his summer weeks at Garsington] I have been sleeping out on the roof in company with an artistic young woman in short hair and purple pyjamas . . . spending most of the night in conversation or in singing folk-songs and rag-time to the stars . . . while early in the morning we would be wakened by a gorgeous great peacock howling like a damned soul while he stalked about the tiles showing off his plumage to the sunrise.

In his maturity he spoke of Garsington as an education.

> I had the extraordinary fortune to meet a great many of the ablest people of my time. There were the Bloomsbury people . . . There was Virginia and Vanessa, there was Maynard Keynes . . *He* was always facinating—he had this immense range of knowledge, and he would come out with these *curiously* elliptical remarks about things: he was a very fascinating character . . . Russell I met then, and Roger Fry—from whom I learnt a *great deal* about art—well, he remains a very good art critic, I mean he had extraordinary sensibility and great knowledge, and enthusiasms; and he was a genuinely *good* man, as well as immensely charming and interesting.

69

He was very kind to me. And then Clive Bell—*he* was always extremely stimulating and very kind to me—from them, I learnt a great deal about art which I really didn't know anything about at all before. They introduced me to modern art, to Post-Impressionism, Cubism and so on . . .

The meeting of all these people was of capital importance to me.[1]

Lady Ottoline told him to read *War and Peace*; he met T. S. Eliot (what struck him was the contrast between the works and the man—"just an Europeanized American, overwhelmingly cultured, talking about French literature in the most uninspiring fashion imaginable[2]).

. . And all this happened at the house of Lady Ottoline Morrell. . . .[1]

Lady Ottoline. How much recognition she has had, and how much abuse. She did a great deal, for the young, the unorthodox, the talented (whose talents she did recognize: on her own, early on); she helped young men who were making a stand against the war; she tried to help Lawrence and Frieda; she took young Aldous under her wing. She inspired some love, less loyalty, little gratitude. Aldous described her (though only at first shock) as affected beyond wildest dreams; she was naturally, congenitally, aristocratic and eccentric to an outrageous degree. Her appearance, and her presentation of it, loomed large. No-one who has known her will forget it, nor the extraordinary voice, the modulated, entirely unselfconscious Boom. The Augustus John portrait reveals her admirably. One must recall that she was immensely tall with an elongated, huge Elizabethan face, Elizabethan with a touch of Aubrey Beardsley, heavily made up, sometimes in haste, topped with a great mass of high coiffure. She exaggerated her height by heels and elevators in her shoes—a towering figure with immense poise. Sometimes grotesque, she could be very beautiful in her strange grand way. Then there were the startling clothes, the enormous pearls, badly strung and kept.

Her dresses were made by her maid.[3] Ottoline went and had a look at fashion shows in London or Paris or Venice and then described what she thought she had seen. She deviated on purpose, she did not follow the fashions. She always wore longer dresses. And there were those wide hats with georgette veils in different colours flowing behind her.

Juliette Baillot had come to Garsington through an agency, meeting the Morrells by appointment in the first-class waiting-

---

[1] London interview.   [2] *Letters.*
[3] Juliette (Lady) Huxley, talking.

room at Oxford station. (They nearly missed meeting at all, one party having gone to the waiting-room on the Up platform, the other to the Down platform.) Philip Morrell said nothing at all, Lady Ottoline talked of the horrors of war. No one asked for credentials from the future governess. "They just took me on."

She arrived (by pony trap with her trunk)—and there was the perfect stone house and the forecourt flanked by immense yew hedges. She was shown straight into the big drawing-room, the red room:

> Well, it was a fantastic room. It was painted Chinese red—the little square Tudor panellings were all painted red, and the grooves were gilt. There were yellow and flame-coloured curtains framing the tall windows, gold and salmon Samarkand rugs, Chinese lacquer cabinets, black and gold, logs burning in the stone fireplace . . .[1]

The dining gallery and the smaller drawing-room were painted turquoise green; there was a pianola in the hall and an Italian cassone with dressing-up clothes, enormous armchairs in shiny chintz and a vague scent of incense and pot-pourri. The furniture was Philip's and inherited; the paint, the gilt, the colours were Lady Ottoline's. Her taste and most of her appreciations were her own. Many say that she was intelligent; she was generous and often very kind. She also gave a sense of some vicarious avidity —for art, for those who were able to produce it—that made people feel that she was not a happy woman. In the succinct wording of Brett,[2] "Lady Ottoline was a very strange woman with a heart of gold and a yen for men." Brett was evoked by Aldous in *Crome Yellow* in the character of Jenny, the disquietening secretive observer, who "sat apart looking down at the world through piercingly sharp eyes. What did she think of men and women and things?"

What Lady Ottoline's heart prompted was often resented rather than appreciated. For instance she was always crocheting for the Garsington poor—great counterpanes made up of bits of bright wools, which they were given for Christmas and which they hated. One year she made a counterpane for Lawrence. He hated it too; in fact, he was deeply offended, saying that Ottoline treated him like one of the poor. She had thought that he would like the colours.

Aldous guyed her later on in *Those Barren Leaves*. Not consistently: her trappings served as a point de départ and soon deviated into fiction. Nevertheless there was a grain or two of

[1] Juliette Huxley, *Mem. Vol.* and talking.
[2] The Hon. Dorothy Brett, in a letter to S. B., 1969.

truth—Lady Ottoline, like Mrs Aldwinkle, had sometimes bought the stars.

Garsington was anti-war. Philip Morrell, Liberal M.P. for Burnley, was one of the few men in public life who spoke up against it. He and Lady Ottoline made Garsington a refuge for some extremely civilized conscientious objectors. On the home farm—run by Philip with loving care—men like Bertrand Russell, Clive Bell and Gerald Shove, the Cambridge scholars, were able to do the agricultural work they had been sentenced to by the tribunals without too great a break in their mental and physical habits.

So there was "Bertie Russell with his laugh like a crazy horse and his dominating ego [this *is* what Jenny saw][1] commanding all attention"; there was Clive Bell, "kind-hearted with a noisy voice whom the farmers loved though he never did a lick of work, giving birthday cakes to the farmers' wives"; there were the Bloomsburies who "would sweep down at weekends with their superiority—Duncan Grant nearly cut his foot off dancing the sword dance"; there was Katherine Mansfield "afraid of the Bloomsburies, cautious and withdrawn"; Juliette Baillot, "very young, and beyond words charming"; Ottoline's little girl, Julian, "a beautiful child," and Philip, "always admirably dressed, trying to look like Lord Ribblesdale. . . ."

[1] The Hon. Dorothy Brett, in a letter to S. B., 1969.

Chapter Seven

Aldous at Garsington

AND there was Aldous. He lived in the house (the C.O.s. lived in cottages on the estate). He had breakfast on the lawn with Ottoline, Juliette and little Julian, and afterwards took up his axe and went off to work.

Inside the week the household was quiet, no Bloomsburies, no sword dances, no rag-time on the roof. Philip was in Parliament or at agricultural sales; Lady Ottoline spent the mornings in her tower room keeping up her diary; Julian did lessons with Juliette. At noon they bathed in the pool which was always bitter cold —Ottoline in pink jersey and Greek tunic, stately, ignoring the cold, stepping forth into the water. Aldous, diligently in the woods, did not appear.

> He had dressed himself—fastidiously—according to his new status. He wore corduroy breeches, they were jodphurs, fawn-coloured, with yellow stockings, brogues and a corduroy jacket. The jacket was dark-brown and he always had a charming coloured tie which he chose himself. Sometimes Ottoline brought him back a tie from London as a present.
>
> He looked absurdly romantic and beautiful.[1]

For a while Aldous enjoyed Bovarizing himself into a successful woodsman:

> I have been doing my usual wood-cutting [letter to his father]— useful for a house which exclusively uses logs for fuel—and have been lopping a big branch from the huge immemorial ilex in front of the house, sawing it into lengths and splitting them with wedges and beetle into suitable billets.

Yes, he cut down branches Juliette says "that was what he *could* do. He did his best." At dusk he would come in exhausted, physically exhausted.

> How very tall he was—even in that big room—with his legs wound round chairs. He just sat, saying nothing.

[1] Juliette Huxley, *Mem. Vol.* and talking.

73

He could be tangibly silent. "I think [Brett writes] he enjoyed embarrassing people with his silences. He told me so."

Exhausted, silent, draped over those armchairs: but observant, immensely observant. Brett was not the only one, hers not the only notebook. Sometimes they joined forces. "He and I [Brett] would sit over the fire in the red room and have what we called a gossip *in camera.* He was moody, always a bit ailing, always scribbling. When he did talk he was brilliant—he was ribald and cynical and brilliant. He was penniless and he was full of ambition. When Julian came down [Julian Huxley, back from America that Autumn, not Julian the little girl] he told me that Aldous was the one genius in the family."

(Julian on that visit fell in love with young Juliette; but that went unnoticed at the time. Except by Brett.)

There was much frost early that winter; Aldous was plagued by colds. He still had to do his reading through a magnifying glass. "I hope Clarke [his oculist] will give me goggles, I shall urge him to .. They w'd simplify things so much." Instead he was promoted to an eye-glass for the time being. He wore this on and off for a number of years; it amused him. "My monocle is very grandiose, but gives me a rather Greco-Roman air of rocococity."

Garsington became animated again at Christmas. "[we performed] a superb play invented by Katherine, improvizing as we went along. It was a huge success with Murry as a Dostoyevski character . . ."

The members of the party as put down by Aldous were, "Murry, Katherine Mansfield, Lytton Strachey, Brett, Carrington, Bertrand Russell and Maria Nys".

Chapter Eight

The Beginning

MARIA NYS. A name at the end of a list. Our first sight is through Juliette.

That day she first came to Garsington in the summer of 1915 and walked straight into the red drawing-room, there was Maria—

> On the top of a tall ladder with a little pot of gilt in her hand and a brush, she was outlining a panel—and there she was, very young, sixteen, with her bell hair and the large blue eyes, rather plump— she was plump in those days—quite beautiful . . . She came down, very sweet, shook hands and said hello in French.[1]

She may have been there on the December Sunday when Aldous himself came to Garsington for the first time; she was there when he came again, was there—on and off—when he came to live in the house to work on the land.

There remains now only one earlier mention of her by Aldous —a P.S. to Julian of July, 1916,

> I have at last discovered a nice Belgian: wonders will never cease.

Who was this *rara avis*, this Belgian child? Who was she and how did she come to be at Garsington?

Maria Nys, the eldest child of Norbert Nys and Marguerite Baltus, was born on 10th September 1898, at Courtrai in the province of Flanders where her parents lived in substantial bourgeois comfort in a house on the Boulevard Peereboom. The Nys's were prosperous tradespeople who with their numerous relations and connections ruled the roost of the town. Old Monsieur Nys, Maria's grandfather, owned a textile business of which her father and his brothers were partners. The Baltus's— in a rather grand way—were artists. Both families were Catholic. The marriage having been childless for some years, Marguerite Nys undertook to make three pilgrimages; Maria was born after the second. She was dedicated to the Virgin and dressed for some years in blue and white exclusively. Madame Nys in due course gave birth to three more girls.

[1] Juliette Huxley, talking to S. B.

She had been in love with another Nys brother. He married someone else; she took Norbert. Mme Nys had looks—beauty in youth, considerable distinction in old age—and a dominating personality. She was energetic, active, bright; she had interests; she was what is called cultivated, read a great deal and was in fact well-read. Courtrai (Kortrijk) is a Flemish town much given to fat good-natured jokes and jollities—"*Le Courtraisien est de nature taquinne*".[1] Mme Nys, who did not come from that part of the country, felt herself superior. Her own brother, George Baltus, painter and professor of fine arts at the University of Glasgow, was very much regarded as the crème de la crème. His wife, Vivi, who had been a playmate of the Princess Elisabeth of Wittelsbach, the future Queen of the Belgians, was the daughter of "the Rodin of Munich", Adolf von Hildebrand, sculptor, Maecenas, classicist, who had *palazzi* in Munich and Florence where he lived like a Medici giving concerts for the King of Bavaria. Mme Nys's husband, Norbert, liked to spend his time over cards and beer with his friends and brothers. Being kind-hearted and weak, he agreed to leave Courtrai, give up his cosy life and flourishing family business and move to Bellem, a village in East Flanders on the canal between Ghent and Bruges. His father gave him a million gold francs to start a business of his own, a wool business, alas, in a cotton-spinning region—"*Affaire*," his daughter Suzanne says gloomily, "*vouée à la ruine*, doomed to fail."[1]

The house by the canal was long, low, white. For the little girls there was a magic garden, barges passing by, Proustian walks . . .

It was a house of delicious smells, of confitures bubbling in copper vats, good things a-simmering, fine linen in high stacks and well-stoked stoves: a warm house where feasts were kept and Saints' days with cakes and presents, *gâteries*, ribbons, frills.

It was a feminine household—except for the odd stable boy they were not supposed to play with—their father, going up and down the country seeing about his business and his boon companions, was not much at home. It was *Mère* (they always called her that, not *maman*, even to Aldous she became *Mère*) who was the fount of so many material refinements (and how very unlike an English middle-class household of the time it was); *Mère* who created the daily life that revolved round the little girls. First there were three of them, in fairly close succession: Maria, Jeanne, Suzanne; six years later, Rose. They were cosseted, they were pampered (at Courtrai each child had a nursemaid of its own who walked it in the park), but they were also taught their

---

[1] Maria's sister, Suzanne Nicolas, the third of the Nys sisters, in a memoir of her childhood, youth, and life up to the 1960s written originally as a source for this biography.

manners and to brush their hair, and from time to time packed
off to convents for their schooling.

Maria, for her part, spent some of her earliest years in her
grandparents' house at St Trond. She was an extremely delicate
child and had to be treated for some spinal trouble. Emérence
Baltus, her grandmother—"very grand, very elegant, formidably
capable, high-handed with charm"[1]—nursed her with her own
hands, and old lady and grandchild came to love one another
very much. Aged seven, Maria was sent to the Sacré Cœur at
Liège as a boarder. At nine she returned to live with her own
family at Bellem.

The door opens. [It is Suzanne speaking] Enter my mother and
Maria. Already then she was pale, had bones as fragile as a bird's,
and those great blue eyes which dominated her face. I was impressed
—this was my sister, *ma grande sœur*, whom I had not seen for a long
time.

For a while they went on with their education at home (Maria
curious, willing, quick). They were taught by a governess and
occasionally by a Baltus cousin—*"un beau jeune homme à barbe
noire,"* who was a professor of anatomy of all things. They spoke
a profusion of languages, switching as the day went: French
basically, Flemish (when *Mère* became *Moeske*), a Flemish patois
to the villagers and servants, English to their governess. Mme Nys
read Andersen's *Tales* in German to Maria, her eldest, her
favourite. Maria was fascinated by the story of *The Little Red Shoes*
and determined to become a dancer. Her mother ended by taking
her to Brussels for lessons with the Ballet Master of the Opera.
She showed talent and was asked to take part in a Royal Command
performance. The family consulted and refused. Maria's other
childhood passion was riding. After a bad fall she was forbidden
to go out alone; she woke herself at six, saddled a horse and went
off for a long ride along the canal. Before breakfast-time she was
back in bed, glowing, telling her adventures to Suzanne who
adored her and who was discreet.

Maria as a child was high-spirited and wilful, much given to
thinking up some gay, fantastic project which she would carry
through. Once in her mother's absence, she turned the drawing-
room into a greenhouse and the greenhouse into a stage; it looked
so ravishing that she wasn't even scolded.

She read voraciously (encouraged by her mother, imitated
by Suzanne), the *Bibliothèque Rose*, Jules Verne, *Robinson Crusoe*,

[1] As described by Jeanne, the second Nys sister, the present Madame
George Neveux.

The Last of the Mohicans, Jack London, Kipling, Racine, Corneille, Molière, the *Iliad,* the *Odyssey* and *The Life of Helen Keller.*

She showed much loving tenderness for others and a great longing for wider fields. When I am married, she used to say, we shall go round the world—*nous ferons le tour du monde.* She would watch the barges being pulled up the canal, slowly, strenuously by the boatmen and their wives. One day she took her mother's hand and said: *Plus tard, je tirerai ton bateau*—Later I shall pull your boat.

Maria made her first communion (with some intensity) at the age of twelve. At fourteen she went to spend six months at Glasgow with George and Vivi Baltus. There she had more ballet lessons, was allowed to go to tea and dinner-parties meeting the learned and the famous, and to ride about the Scottish countryside—*"La grandiose et romantique campagne d'Ecosse".*

When the war broke out and the Germans invaded Belgium, she was sixteen. Refugees reached Bellem, carrying (Suzanne maintains) dead babies in their arms, telling tales of horror; the German Army was not far behind. Mme Nys packed trunks, managed to procure transport and they reached Ostend. One fine late-summer morning she and the four girls sailed for England. (Their father stayed behind to look after his affairs.)

To begin with they lived in an agreeable boarding-house run by an Irish gentlewoman—*"Une pension de famille dans le quartier chic à* Grosvenor Square"; and Mme Nys became a useful member of the Belgian refugee committee.

They had brought money to last them for two months. They were cut off from their home resources. For a woman on her own with four daughters on her hands, one a child of six and all in need of further education, the situation was a difficult one. For the girls, tearful though they had been on leaving their white house by the canal, it was all more in the nature of a lark—new friends, freedoms, travel. As money ran out, immediate solutions presented themselves: people in England were very willing to look after the Belgians; Mme Nys, moreover, had entrées through her Baltus brother. Invitations came. She and little Rose went to Kent as the guests of the vicar of Malling; Jeanne and Suzanne, after an enjoyable couple of months in a country house with a large park and masses of young people, were given places at Cheltenham College; Maria, as Suzanne puts it, went to live with a gentleman farmer.

Lady Ottoline—by way of her and George Baltus's mutual friend the painter Henry Lamb—had written to Mme Nys offering hospitality for the duration. Mme Nys, installed already in her Kentish rectory, sent Maria to Garsington in her place.

Maria was very young. If she was precocious—in her world of younger sisters, at her uncle and aunt's dinner table—she was so in the bookish, lively manner of a child. Garsington, though it drew some of the very young, was a tough place for children. Maria was bowled over by the whole thing, bowled over by Lady Ottoline. She was fascinated, she was dazzled—she adored. She was not very happy. For Aldous, with his discipline and capacity for detachment, his mental digestion, his family and academic backgrounds, Garsington was a golden windfall, an opening of horizons, intellectual, moral and aesthetic—baroque statuary, cubism and French symbolist poetry not being part of the Huxley-Arnold inheritance any more than was sensual (as opposed to educational) liberty for women. Aldous strolled about at will in the new open spaces and if at times he got a bit tipsy, there was not much danger of his losing his own way. For Maria, head-long, a little spoilt, with her intensity, her untrained mind and loving heart, it was less of an open sesame than a hard school. In later life she spoke of Garsington with affection, reticence and pain. Ottoline blew hot and cold. If the atmosphere of the house-parties was light-hearted, it was above all overwhelmingly sophisticated, always exacting, sometimes heartless. If Katherine Mansfield was scared of the Bloomsburies, it does not mean that she did not have her own pretensions. At Garsington, if you weren't very able or very amusing, you had at least to be pretty, and Maria did not think then that she was. She very much disliked being plump, and Ottoline did tease her. (That plumpness, which Aldous and some others found enchanting, was a transitory stage: as a child and again through adult life, Maria had the thinness of an El Greco adolescent.)

Lady Ottoline's maid sewed her dresses; Philip Morrell cut her hair. (The fashion was just beginning at the Slade, and Philip cut off all the Garsington girls' hair.) Lytton Strachey gave her Latin lessons; she brushed the pugs, took walks with Aldous round the pond and had her tea with little Julian and Juliette.

There was another thing, Maria had no money. No pocket money, often no money at all. Juliette, of course, had her salary; Maria was in the demoralizing situation of a refugee. She was bought presents but would have to ask for a postage stamp. For a girl so used to holding up her head in her lavish home, this was awkward and humiliating. Besides she then had that wild longing for things that can possess the young—for a necklace, a motor bicycle, a pair of gloves. Years after, when *she* had a young

79

girl in her charge, she wrote of *"Les désirs foux que j'avais à son âge"*.

It was in those early days that Maria developed her own style of dressing—fastidious elegance with a touch of fantasy. In 1916 it was yellow cotton stockings. Augustus John used to sketch her in an indigo blue pleated skirt, a wine-coloured blouse Ottoline had given her, a broad red belt and the lemon yellow stockings.

Maria had no steady occupation at Garsington; her future was vague. Mme Nys scraped up some money for ballet lessons in London. Talent was confirmed, Nijinsky briefly taught her; but she was still delicate and was told that her health would not stand a professional dancer's career. After a few weeks she had to give it all up. In the spring of 1915, before she ever met Aldous, there had been some kind of crisis. Ottoline was off somewhere without taking Maria, or Ottoline had been talking of sending her away for her own good; whatever it was, Maria in a moment of passionate grief swallowed some chloride. There was commotion, the doctor in the night, she was saved. They were very angry with her. (Later she blamed herself.) The wicked corrosive stuff burnt her insides, possibly affected her health. There exists one reference to this episode in print, a letter from D. H. Lawrence.[1]

My dear Lady Ottoline,

We were shocked about Maria: it really is rather horrible. I'm not sure whether you aren't really more wicked than I had at first thought you. I think you can't help torturing a bit.

But I think it has [shown] something—as if you, with a strong, old-developed *will* had enveloped the girl, in this will, so that she lived under the dominance of your will. . . So that when she says it was because she couldn't bear being left, that she took the poison, it is a great deal true. Also she feels quite bewildered and chaotic . . .

We English, with our old-developed public selves, and the consequent powerful will, and the accompanying rudimentary private or instinctive selves, I think we are very baffling to any other nation. We are apt to assume domination, when we are not really personally implicated. A young foreigner can't understand this—not a girl like Maria.

Why must you always use your *will* so much, why can't you let things be, without always grasping and trying to know and to dominate. I'm too much like this myself.

There, now I'm scolding you, even. But *why* will you use power instead of love, good public control instead of affection. I suppose it is breeding. Don't mind what I say.

[1] Dated 23rd April 1915 from *The Letters of D. H. Lawrence*, edited by Harry T. Moore. Heinemann, 1962. (Hereafter cited as *D.H.L. Letters*, 1962.)

Later on there was a hope of Maria getting a place at Cambridge and she went up to Newnham for a term on a trial basis. That too failed.

Maria was not quick to respond to Aldous. Ottoline still loomed very large. Aldous was gently persistent. She was aware of his damaged sight, agonizingly sympathetic. Aldous, Brett says, "needed sympathy, needed help, needed love". One day Maria went to Brett for counsel: Brett said, "Go ahead. But don't tell anyone."

Mme Nys by then—the summer of 1916—had become very tired of her position as a permanent guest. She contrived somehow to take her girls for a few weeks into the wilds of Scotland, where they walked from loch to loch, sleeping in shepherds' huts, living frugally and gaily. The younger girls had an extraordinary time; Maria, temporarily plucked from Garsington, from Aldous, mainly sulked. After Scotland, Mme Nys, listening to the siren song of a Dutch agent who was promising to make funds available to her on the Continent, decided to leave England. The trunks were packed, the girls gathered; Maria refused to go. They left without her and got stuck in Paris. They were lodged in one spacious room at the Grand Hotel Terminus where Mme Nys was known from better days; but there was hardly any cash and for two months Jeanne and Suzanne lived on tap water, French bread and jam. Only Rose got milk. Their mother, being taken out from time to time to some splendid dinner, brought home to her famished brood the only items she could bear away with any decency, cream-puffs and petit-fours. Then money trickled in and they were able to eat occasionally at some cheap restaurant in the Latin quarter. Presently Mme Nys managed to collect visas and fares and they set out by train for Italy.

Aldous proposed on a rug on the lawn at Garsington. They promised to wait for one another. He gave her a scarab ring. Maria wore it until it became too large. Suzanne has it now.

In October Maria left Garsington and went to live in a furnished room in London. Aldous went to see her as often as he could. Maria tried to earn her living—not very successfully—by giving French lessons. It must have been all very precarious and impermanent. Maria was still only just eighteen. It was unlikely that her mother would let matters be. Aldous and Maria could not meet often but when they did it was in freedom. *Carpe Noctem* —he willed them not to think beyond their dateless space of hours.

Chapter Nine

"Hélas, il Faut que l'on Vivote"

"THE worst, my dear Lewis, has not lost the opportunity of happening. It rarely does." So Aldous on New Year's Day, 1917. "Poor Maria is being hustled out remorselessly by her ghoulish mother in Florence. One achieves resignation . . incomplete and somewhat rebellious . . but not gaiety. It is altogether painful . . And then for how long? It's the indefiniteness that is so distressing. Six months, a year, three years . . ."

The thing is to get a job. "I missed one in Munitions by twelve hours. Eton won't have me. I dangle for Charterhouse . . . God preserve me!" Meanwhile there is some reviewing for the *Statesman*.

It was a cold winter at Garsington. One day as Aldous was chopping wood, a splinter hit him near his good eye. That was the end of that; they did not allow him to do any more manual work.

Aldous mooned about the place, silent and bottled up. After a long evening without a word, he would follow Ottoline to her bedroom, as if unable to bear his own loneliness, and just sit by the fire, brooding; finally sent to bed, he oozed away like a ghost.[1]

And one evening Aldous suddenly blurted out his feelings to Juliette—the awfulness of the separation from Maria, the miserable uncertainty of it all. Another night, when they were up on the roof to look at the moon—the gibbous moon of *Crome Yellow*—it all came out. ". . the death of his mother when he was fourteen years old . . . a betrayal by life . . . Two years later blindness. Believed at first to be final . . . living behind a black band, learning to be blind." He talked about his father's marrying again, his brother's suicide. Juliette, shaken but too young, could find no words.

In the spring Aldous advertised for work in the Agony Column of *The Times*; at the same time Lady Violet Bonham-Carter was trying to get him into a Government office. By Easter a clerical job at the Air Board materialized. "It is all settled and I go there next week—screw, they tell me, from £200 to £250."

[1] Juliette Huxley.

In that job, which turned out utterly time-wasting, Aldous stayed until July, living with his father and stepmother in Hampstead, at 16 Bracknell Gardens to which they had recently moved.

. . . Whether ALH can bear this Dept much longer is another question. [In May, to Julian] Porco di Madonna, the people in this place—suburban businessmen, with absolutely no interest in life but making money and gossiping about their hideous homes. They add to the soul-weariness with which this place overcomes one, as well as with physical fatigue. It is all too too bloody.

. . I have ceased to read now: it's quite impossible as I'm always too tired in the evening—and I take almost no interest in anything but my food, which is a poor subject to be interested in these days.

And to Lewis Gielgud: "There is no particular news—the misery of life proceeds." And the war too is becoming "more ghastly every day . . I think that it is folly and a crime to go on now."

In May, yet another Medical Board, again with the result of complete rejection. "But oh—the process of being rejected.

I presented myself at 10 at the Oxford recruiting office—and there I waited till 4, herded in a sort of pen with some 80 or so . . . all of whom were additionally horrible by being hospital cases of the most painful kind—halfwits, syphilitics . . goitrous cretins, men with unprecedented combinations of disease, diabetic consumptives suffering from Bright's disease, rheumatic lepers . . . There, as I say, we waited . . [in] sweltering heat . . no place to sit down: men swooned and vomited all about: when anyone tried to repose an instant on the steps of the doctors' motors, soldiers with fixed bayonets drove them away . . .

To Juliette he wrote long letters in office hours. She had sent him some of her poems.

Try using very simple words and straightforward expressions [he advised] . . use practically only the words of everyday speech . . .

Unexpected counsel rather from one who could hardly have been called the Ernest Hemingway of verse.

. . Educated speech, of course, not necessarily words of one syllable.

As he is writing they are being "pestered by German aeroplanes —a fiendish banging of bombs . . ." But Aldous goes on copying a French sonnet[1] he has written, a little obscure, he fears, as well as flippant. "But then I rarely write in French—and then only when I want to be *un peu scabreux* . . . the best language for indecency ever invented. . [only the French] can combine grossness with grace." Another day he sent Juliette his *"Hommage* to Jules Laforgue"[2] whose verbal ingenuities he found so irresistible an example in those days.

> *Que je t'aime mon cher Laforgue,—*
> *Frère qui a connu les nostalgies. . . .*

Hélas, Aldous's last stanza opened, "Hélas, il faut que l'on vivote."

Meanwhile, every day, Aldous wrote to Maria; and she to him. Those letters no longer exist.

---

[1] "Sonnet à L'Ingénue" subsequently published in *Jonah.*
[2] *Jonah.*

Chapter Ten

Interludes

AND then it is summer and Aldous is quit of the Air Board (and certain of a job at Eton in the autumn) and he has a "great new friend" and they motor about the country having curious adventures and Aldous suddenly speaks of himself as having the greatest fun. The new friend is "The inimitable Evan Morgan,[1] poet, painter, musician, aristocrat and millionaire . . . the unique fairy prince of modern life," whom Aldous met at Garsington and made to re-appear at Crome. ("Nature and fortune had vied with one another in heaping on Ivor Lombard all their choicest gifts.") In life, Morgan and Aldous encounter a young woman in a forest, "a young woman of eighteen exactly like Nell Gwyn.

. . Immense cherry trees, laden with fruit . . . Nell Gwyn . . ascends ladders and throws cherries at the young men . . . and so it begins. [It is to Carrington that Aldous narrates this story.] In the heart of Nell Gwyn the most dangerous passion is kindled . . not merely for one but for both simultaneously . . .

Scene two. In the forest at evening the mosquitoes bite; so do the young women. Rather disquietingly it begins to occur to us that the creature is perfectly innocent.

Then the strangest scene in our bedroom. We become perfectly convinced that she is completely virginal. Without any shame she caresses both of us with all the fire of her native sensuality. We explain that we cannot take her virginity; we are simply passers by . . . She is in tears about it, begs and implores that we should. We are inexorable; Evan sitting up in bed like a young Sicilian shepherd with no clothes on orders her back to her room with his most imperious manner; he is the descendant of Welsh princes; she obeys and creeps off to a cold and solitary couch. We sink to sleep. At about three I wake up, aware that someone is passionately kissing my neck and shoulders. I hasten to add that it was not Evan. Nell Gwyn has returned. I give her the hospitality of my bed for a few minutes and send her away; it was all a little nerve-racking. The next night she goes to Evan; the fate of virginity hangs in the balance, but escapes intact; this time we lock the door. On Monday we depart, and there are terrible adieus . . . However, in my case the adieu is an au revoir, for making my way from Beaconsfield to Eton on

[1] The late Viscount Tredegar.

85

Wednesday it occurs to me that it would be more amusing to spend the night with Nell Gwyn than with my tutor at Eton . . .

But the half of it can never be told; it was all so peculiar . . like something which must have happened in the Balkans, impossible in England.

Next there was Morgan's birthday party, a tremendous affair with the drink flowing and Aldous "achieving a rapprochement . . a mutual épanchement, in our cups . . sober we have always been rather alarmed of one another," with Marie Beerbohm.[1] Aldous has ceased to feel morose in the company of the gay, the charming the mercurial Evan Morgan. All in all it was not a bad summer. He stayed at Oxford with the Haldanes and the Petersens, he went to Garsington; he was writing again. His translation of Mallarmé's *L'Après-midi d'un Faune*,[2] begun at Balliol, finished at Garsington, is coming out in *Oxford Poetry* and he is contributing to "the well-known Society Anthology *Wheels*, in company with illustrious young persons like Miss Nancy Cunard, Miss Iris Tree . . . The folk who run it are a family called Sitwell . . ."

And the news from Italy is good—"will this bloody war be over in time for me to get out there before Christmas or Easter?"

When Mme Nys the year before had succeeded in leaving Northern Europe with her three younger children, they made straight for Forte dei Marmi, the village by the sea on Shelley's coast between La Spezia and Leghorn. It was still summer and the place was full of good-looking Italians *in villeggiatura*. They put up at the Pensione Tirreno where the food was delicious and plunged into Italian life. Friends of George Baltus, the Fasolas, had a house at Forte on their own beach among vineyards and pines. Signore Fasola was a disciple of Tolstoy and professor at the University of Florence, his wife was German, elderly and rich; they had a daughter, "Costanza, twenty-one years old—A dream: charming and graceful as a young goat [Suzanne speaking], full of caprices, gaiety and games".

They were introduced to other families of beautiful young women, bright adolescents—men were at the front—learned parents. It was Italian life at its most light-hearted and civilized. Mme Nys, appreciated for her charm (she had charm), her vitality, her Flemish stories, found congenial company; for Jeanne

[1] Max Beerbohm's niece. One of the sirens of the day.
[2] First republished in *The Defeat of Youth*, 1918.

and Suzanne it was the lightning friendships of the young. They swam, sailed, sketched, talked books with Costanza and some half-dozen other girls and boys, moved about the pine forests, the hills, the marble quarries of the Tuscan countryside—it was Balbec, *la petite bande*, the perennial charmed circle of youth.

In October the Fasolas went back to Florence and the Nys's went too. They found an apartment on the Lungarno Aciaioli with a view of the church of Santa Trinità across the river. (Mme Nys had resolved the problem of getting money out of Belgium, precariously; but for the remainder of the war they were never again reduced to living on jam and water, or on hospitality.)

Suzanne went to a pleasant school, Jeanne studied painting, Rose the piano; Mère took them to see all the churches, all the pictures, they drew in the Uffizi, had dancing classes and Italian lessons given by delightful persons and there was a good deal of that Florentine social life—artists, nobility and foreigners at teas, musical evenings in hillside villas and the vast, draughty, frescoed drawing-rooms of the *palazzi*. It was, Suzanne affirms, *"une existence bien agréable"*.

It was into this that Maria was translated when she arrived from England in January of 1917. She was looking thin and ravishing, and at once she carried all before her. She eclipsed her sisters. Her turn now for the lightning friendship with Costanza Fasola, with Rocca, their young dancing mistress. Once more, she was swept off her feet. By her new friends, and by what she saw —by the sheer beauty of everything about her. Overwhelmed by Italy, seduced by Italian life—for those who have lived it, the two are inseparable—she responded with what was most headlong in her nature and her life became (as Aldous put it somewhat distantly) a mere sequence of sensuous enjoyments.

Costanza called Maria *Coccola*, the Italian diminutive for dear one or my darling (and a word that in its straight sense means pip or berry); it became the name used by her sisters and later by their children. When Aldous used it, he dropped the second c.

The Russian Ballet was in Florence that winter. Maria too danced again; in the Fasola's drawing-room and with Costanza publicly for charity. Off stage she wore a sky-blue cloak, Mme Nys had made for her, cut like the cloaks carried with such swagger by Italian army officers, and on Maria it looked piercingly stylish and romantic.

In June they all returned to Forte for the summer. They took a pleasant house near the Fasolas, their young friends were there, all was as before; only that now Maria was the animator and the favourite.

Chapter Eleven

Master at Eton

THE war was *not* over and besides Aldous had to think of a financial future and support himself as well for the time being. Another office job—even if his eyes could have taken the strain of a sixty-hour week of paper work and it was clear that they could not—would have been crushing because of the dead loss of time; teaching was another matter, there being always hope of getting down to one's own work in the holidays. Aldous took up his new post at Eton. It was poorly paid; he did not think he was a born schoolmaster or would be teaching the boys anything very much.

But we get on moderately well, which is all that is needed for a quiet life.

A quiet life! That precisely, as legend has it, is what Aldous did not have at Eton.

I was, I suppose, in my second year in College [writes Sir Steven Runciman] when we were told that we were to be taught by this remarkable young writer. We Collegers were little intellectual snobs and we were much impressed. None of us had read a word that he had so far written .. but the name already had a glamour. The impression was deepened when we actually saw him.

I still have a vivid pictorial recollection of that elongated, stooping, myopic figure, with a face that was far younger than most of our masters' [he was twenty-three] and yet seemed somehow ageless, and usually hidden by an infinite variety of spectacles, eyes that were almost sightless and yet almost uncomfortably observant. He stood there looking something of a martyr but at the same time extraordinarily distinguished.[1]

The boys had been warned of the new master's defective sight and told to behave decently.

Not all of us did behave decently. At the back of the form-room there was always a certain amount of reading of magazines, passing of notes and murmured gossip. But the misbehaviour never went

[1] Sir Steven Runciman, *Mem. Vol.* and from a letter to S. B.

too far, less from the feeling that there is little fun in misbehaving
in front of a master who cannot see it than from the certainty that
misbehaviour left him completely indifferent and unmoved.

I personally think that the legend of the chaos in Aldous's Eton
class-rooms has been a bit exaggerated . . . but [possibly] the slightly
older boys were a bit rowdier than we were.[1]

And according to Eddy Sackville-West,[2] who was sixteen and in
a different division, they were.

Poor Aldous! He must have been one of the most incompetent
schoolmasters who ever faced a class . . . his solution was to read
aloud, with occasional comments the poems of Verlaine. This he
did in his scholarly, highly modulated voice . . . [it was] impossible
to hear more than an occasional word of what he read or said for
the general tumult was indescribable. Those in the back row but
one turned their backs on the rest of the form and made up a bridge
four with boys in the back row. The middle rows played noughts-
and-crosses with white chalk on the shoulders of the boys in front
of them. The majority simply conversed in loud voices. A very few,
of whom I was one, did genuinely want to listen to Aldous; but it
was useless in that pandemonium . . . From time to time, Aldous
would pause, look up, and say, in an imploring tone, "Oh! Do be
quiet!" No one took the slightest notice.[3]

Then there is Aldous's own view. Having spent the morning
correcting twenty-eight essays on the League of Nations, he wrote
to Lewis Gielgud "with such few exceptions they are all so stupid
. . ." But,

They are most of them nice fellows and treat me, all being considered, wonderfully well, though I wish I could see them more
penetratingly: I expect the secret of their quietness lies in the fact
that they are deeply engaged in something very far removed from
the sordid present, poles apart from any claptrap I may be talking
about English literature or Molière's plays.

Most of my creatures are immensely grown-up; one division consists almost entirely of members of Pop, for whom it is very difficult
not to feel awe and reverence. It is a wonderful tribute to the efficacy
of their youthful training that these superb lions refrain from rending
me as they so very well might—the most they do is occasionally to
shirk my school, taking advantage of the fact that I don't yet know

---

[1] Sir Steven Runciman idem.
[2] The late Lord Sackville, the writer and music critic.
[3] Lord Sackville, from a letter to Professor Grover Smith.

them by sight and getting their names answered by somebody else
. . . but they were regrettably caught.

Aldous was lodging in the Old Christopher, the ancient pub
in Eton High Street, where the senior Eton boys were allowed
to drink mildish beer, sharing his quarters in that strange old
house with another beak, an absurd but good-hearted clergyman
called Cobby Bevan. Aldous found him a placid though not very
bracing companion. "A very good soul ('soul' by definition does
not include mind) and we live very snugly and with no friction,
talking over our meals, which are frequent and large—for the
Reverend Bevan is something of an epicure . . . Then we retire
each to his separate room and all is well, except that sometimes
I feel almost intolerably lonely; these ushers are so nice, but so
remote, so alien."

There was not much chance for escape to London as Aldous
was seldom free before 4 p.m. and full weekends were impossible
as he had to be back for early school on Monday. If only "there
were someone jolly on the staff with whom one could walk and
talk: I say walk and talk, for as things are, all the beaks rush off
to play football or run to Maidenhead or dig potatoes when they
are not working, and the only people who take life quietly are
the antiques . ." With those Aldous took constitutionals round
the golf course, fretting and fuming at having to walk at two
miles an hour and wait minutes at each bunker. As for that
hope of writing, just as he was trying to settle down to it "in
comes another batch of essays to correct, or I have to go and
stand up in face of these sinister young men and try to keep them
amused".

All the same he managed to write a few things, and was
encouraged by hearing that Blackwells would like to publish *The
Defeat of Youth* and there was *Jonah*[1] being printed by the Holywell
Press at Oxford.

In November he has an exceptionally diverting week—luncheon
with Juliette on Wednesday in London; Gervas, on leave, on
Thursday; a tea-party at Eton on Saturday when his bright young
pupil De La Warr had invited George Lansbury to meet him.
(Aldous found Lansbury "extremely interesting, very tolerant, not
bitter like so many of these labour men . . . full of constructive
rather than destructive enthusiasms. "He is a great friend, I find,
of Lady Ottoline's brother, Lord Henry Bentinck; their view on
most things appears to be almost identical, despite the fact that
Lord H. is nominally a Tory.")

[1] *Jonah*, that bibliographical rarity, consists of twelve poems printed on a
single folded and sewn sheet of 16 pages; the issue was limited to about fifty
copies most of which Aldous sent out to his friends as a Christmas card.

Aldous now became involved in *The Eton Review* and the founding of an Eton Political Society, the moving spirit of which was his "young friend the Earl, De La Warr, who is a passionate Socialist". Aldous was asked to find out if Asquith and Haldane would come and speak to the boys. "The whole idea amused me very much and should be encouraged, I am sure."

And then there is theosophy, which appears to have excited some of the more serious-minded boys. "I point out Mrs Besant's errors in science and history, which thickly encrust her books, and try to wean them from the merely superstitious side." But except for the bunkum about astral bodies and so forth, "theosophy seems a good enough religion; the main point being that all religion contains some truth and that we ought to be tolerant."

On 1st December Aldous is summoned *again*—such is the shortage of manpower—before the military. For the rest, "the grim solitude of Eton punctuated by brief jaunts to London". He's been seeing the dashing Evan Morgan, he's been seeing Carrington, he's looked in on Katherine Mansfield "in her curious little kennel in Chelsea," and on T. S. Eliot, whom he found haggard and ill-looking as usual. On the 12th Aldous took part in a poetry reading at Sybil Colefax's,[1] a charity affair before a large and expensive audience with Gosse in the chair and Robert Nichols, Aldous, Viola Tree, the Sitwells and Eliot (in that order) reading. Aldous found the whole thing quite appalling. "Eliot and I were the only people who had any dignity: Bob Nichols raved and screamed and hooted and moaned his filthy war poems like a Lyceum villain . . . The Sitwells were respectable, but terribly nervous."

In less than a week now the Eton Half will be over. Aldous is very tired—"this teaching takes it out of one"—and looking forward to Christmas at Garsington. "What amusements we had *last* year, in spite of the somewhat wet blanket of Bloomsbury!"

Too soon this year also becomes last year and, inexorably in January, Aldous is back at the Old Christopher, wintry and bleak. His school work is now mostly tutorial, no more standing up in large forms, but some fifty elder boys coming in for half an hour each a week to have their essays commented upon, and this he found on the whole more interesting. If only there were more leisure to write, he can't even get a batch of reviews finished; all he can do is to get down a line of poetry here and there (". . a most luscious poem about Leda, the lady whom Jupiter visited in the form of a swan . . . it is the most charming story . . .")

Meanwhile the Eton Political Society was functioning and Aldous had discovered "another young aristocrat, Lord David

[1] The late Lady Colefax, the hostess, who became a friend of Aldous's.

Cecil, who is in point of sheer brains and imagination beyond De La Warr. . . . He is only sixteen, is the most brilliant conversationalist, has written one or two uncommonly good poems . . . He is one of the people who give one the sense of being enormously thorough-bred; a wonderful character in his way."

And there was Eddy Sackville-West:

> When he saw that I was really interested in French literature he thawed and we became friends. He taught me a lot about such writers as Laforgue and Mallarmé; I never lost touch with him from that time on.[1]

Still Aldous chafed at the attitudes imposed by schoolmastering: the unceasing pretence of knowing better, of being respectable and a good example; he is afraid that it will make him old. "I do my best to make my boys have no respect for me whatever." How far did he succeed?

> At first we thought his voice affected [Sir Steven Runciman], but soon some of us were trying to copy it. Above all it was his use of words that entranced us. Eric Blair—the future George Orwell— who was my exact contemporary—would in particular make us note Aldous's phraseology. "That is a word we must remember," we used to say to each other . . . The taste for words and their accurate and significant use remained. We owe him a great debt for it.[2]

And Sir Steven sums up:

> I cannot say that Aldous was a good teacher in the narrow sense of the word, I have to confess that I cannot now remember a single thing he taught us. But he was an educator in a wider sense. He showed us glimpses of the fascination to be found in an unhampered intellectual approach to things.

[1] Lord Sackville, ibid.
[2] Sir Steven Runciman, from *Mem. Vol.* and a letter to S. B.

Chapter Twelve

Strain

JULIAN HUXLEY, who had joined the Army, was being posted to Italy as a lieutenant in the Intelligence Corps and Aldous asked him to see Maria. "I hope you will go, if only to tell me what the rest of the family is like." For Aldous had not set eyes yet on Mme Nys, nor Jeanne, Suzanne or Rose.

His own existence was pretty miserable that spring. A severe attack of intercostal rheumatism; exams; icy winds—and how tired he is of being ridiculously underpaid and the war is looking gloomier every day. "Bertie Russell, did you see? has been sentenced to six months for saying the American troops were to be stationed here to put down strikes—a task to which they were so well used at home. Not a thing I'd choose to be sentenced on—it is so curiously foolish."

In April, Easter holidays and brief liberty. A week in London whizzing around "mixing one's people like discordantly flavoured drinks—Eliot for luncheon, Aunt Mary [Ward] for tea, Sitwells . . for dinner . . or else one sticks to one rich vintage all day long—Marie Beerbohm, at lunch, tea, dinner and half the night long. A very remarkable character, Marie; tremendous vitality to carry her through the arduous frivolousness of a perpetually whirling life; the marvellous niceness common to all Beerbohms, which keeps her charming and unspoiled through episodes in themselves somewhat sordid; a good mind, rather like Max's in its fantastic cleverness, which you won't discover till you know her well."

A weekend in Surrey with Aunt Sophy Huxley; more London, then retreat to Garsington where he contrived to do a little writing and reading. Then back again "to the grind and three more months of Cobby".

In May he is doing proofs of *The Defeat of Youth*, and has read "our secret treaty with Italy". (How? Could it have been by way of Maynard Keynes?)

It really makes one gasp; [he writes to Julian] one wonders which is the greatest, the stupidity or the wickedness of our rulers. I think their stupidity.

Maria and her family were now living above Florence, across the road from the Fasolas, in Castel a Montici, one of those grand

93

and spacious villas above Florence, rich in views and gardens and painted drawing-rooms, short of water and innocent of electricity. It was the spring of their second year in Italy—the fourth year of the war—times were no longer easy. The winter if anything had been more icy than the one in England; food shortages had become severe. Mme Nys, who bore the brunt, went about collecting firewood, sugar, flour, olive oil. Cooking was done on a sawdust stove. The girls were left much on their own. Sometimes Maria took a hand in keeping house. Their staple diet seems to have been figs, oranges, chestnuts and Brussels sprouts. Maria, for her own part, lived mainly on lettuce leaves and grapes.

Julian's eventual visit was brief—a man in uniform surrounded by a number of young women. Afterwards he wrote to Aldous what must have been a letter of brotherly concern. Aldous's answer reads a little chilly. "As to what you say of Maria, I think I realize her faults clearly enough." The fundamental thing about her is her very great aesthetic sensibility, and aestheticism, he thinks, is a dangerous thing. He does not believe that anyone who lives wholly on sensation is "safe". He recalls how completely Maria was bowled over when she first went to Italy. Now, judging from her letters, she has settled down a good deal.

> What I have tried to persuade Maria to do is to centre her life on thought rather than sensation, to adopt some fixed intellectual occupation, involving a certain amount of effort and mental concentration, and not merely to live on the aesthetic sensations of the moment. She is educating herself—in a rather desultory way perhaps —but the process gives her a solid foundation for her existence.

He thinks she will grow up all right. " 'Grow up!' for you mustn't forget how absurdly young she is, only nineteen . . . I only wish I was with her, for I think I could be of help to her in growing up—not to mention the fact that she would help me out of the curiosly unpleasant slough of uncertainty in which one seems to wallow so hopelessly these days." At this point Aldous may have become aware of his own dryness.

> I have spared you more lyrical effusions about her, not because I don't feel lyrically, but because it would be so tedious for you. One's aim . . should be to combine the lyrical with the critical . . Shelley and the *Edinburgh Review*. I have only given you my *Edinburgh Review* opinions about Maria—for the others see my Works passim!

Maria who never learnt to have, who never could have had, *Edinburgh Review* opinions about anything, was sustained by

Aldous's letters; and her life during those months and months of separation was, in contrast to his, delicious and indulgent. Yet from her end the uncertainty was as great. On the surface there was an improbability about the whole thing. Some thirty years later she wrote to her son.[1]

Why, why in the world did Aldous choose me out of the many prettier, wittier, richer etc young girls? Why in the world did he come back to fetch me after two long years of running around with more of those pretty and amusing ones of his own world? Knowing all the time by my letters that he could never teach me to write poetry or remember what I read in a book, or spel, [sic] or anything he did set value on.

The code at Garsington was what we now call permissive. Sexual freedom of action was a prerequisite of being civilized. Lady Ottoline had the well-known affair with, *entre autres*, Bertrand Russell; Philip Morrell pursued young women; homosexualities were accepted as a matter of course. Constancy and the loyalties of the heart were looked upon as philistine and a bit ridiculous.

And why [so Maria went on] did I who was so horrified by those Garsington men (and women) I who was so squashed by the English and terrified of them, why did I let Aldous approach me, then wait for him though I never thought he would come back to me considering the theories of the world of Ottoline's: just flit round for fun; why tie each other down. Why did I not get for a single moment entranced by the Italian men and easy life and certainly less terrifying intellectual strain of it?

[1] To Matthew Huxley in 1952.

Chapter Thirteen

Marking Time

AT Eton Aldous was dragging through another summer Half. His only bearable hours were passed in writing, talking to the three or four intellectual boys, and escapes to London. The playing fields—"those elm-shadowed expanses of soggy turf",[1] the river, the Fourth of June, colours and summer air, might not have existed; he was too miserable, and temperamentally he had no liking for routine, no feeling for ceremonial or traditional repetition. To him these were distractions from the pursuit of the significant—knowledge and art. Time well spent was spent in learning and creation. "I never really feel I am performing a wholly *moral* action, except when I am writing."

Yet there were many things that he enjoyed doing. Apart from conversation with the instructed and exceptional, he enjoyed the company of his friends, he enjoyed the company of women whom he preferred to be amusing and educatable as well as pretty.

The letters of these years are very detached from events. Julian asks about new books and Aldous answers that he is the last person to apply to "seeing that I almost never read anything under a century old, and then preferably in a foreign language". As to the state of the world, he knows nothing about it except by conversation, "and of conversation I am completely deprived here. The only modern book I have heard of at all is Lytton Strachey's *Eminent Victorians*, which I have not read—except parts in MS—but which everybody says is very good."

He gives a fastidious glance at the Pemberton Billing Trial:

> . . the after-swell of the storm in the cess-pool still heaves . . . Such as the letter sent by Robbie Ross to the public prosecutor calling him a bastard . . for not having dealt faithfully with Alfred Douglas:— poor Robbie, it is still the dismal idée fixe of the Wilde case, which everyone is getting so bored with.

(Yet when Robbie Ross died quite suddenly in his sleep a few months later, Aldous wrote, "Poor Robbie, it is very sad. He was the most charming creature.")

[1] *The Olive Tree*, 1936.

Aldous attempted to write a play. It turned out "wholly un-dramatic with a plot more suitable for a Henry Jamesian story". All the same, "I shall try and write a farce with a perfectly good machine-made plot—not an easy task, I imagine; but it will be good practice and might, if acted, make money." Here one can see the beginnings of an illusion that was going to cost Aldous a good deal in time and disappointment. He was even thinking of reforming stage convention to overcome some of the crudities of the theatre, "one must be permitted to have hundreds of scenes like Shakespeare—the cinema has already given a very good example in that respect". Anyway, "I am determined to make writing pay."

.. I have no money whatever . . . This bloody place pays me so atrociously [nothing is left after board and lodging and the haber-dasher's bill] . . . It is all very sordid and irritating.

Holidays once again, spent mainly at Garsington and at Prior's Field where all is very pleasant and the garden blooms and blazes, "and I sit with my faithful typewriter outside, surrounded by gillyflowers and peacock butterflies, and write immortal works in prose—a short story".

He is also contributing more poems to the Sitwells' magazine, *Wheels*, of which he now speaks with some approval. He rather likes "its toreador attitude towards the bloody-bloodies of this world".

He sees Gervas who is on leave and in good form on the whole confident that the war will be over in a year. But whatever happens, Aldous thinks, we may be sure it will be for the worst. "I dread the inevitable acceleration of American world domina-tion [he wrote to Julian] which will be the ultimate result of it all. It was a thing that had got to come in time, but this will hasten its arrival by a century. We shall all be colonized. Europe will no longer be Europe. . . ."

In September Aldous is at Hampstead in his father's house and in low spirits. What he longs and pines for is domesticity, domes-ticity combined with intelligence, he writes to Juliette who, too, is rather lonely in a large, isolated house in Scotland. (She had left Garsington and become governess to the children of Brett's sister, the Ranee of Sarawak.) The only thing that brightens the general darkness is the Russian Ballet "Which is pure beauty, like a glimpse into another world.

We—Ottoline, Julian, Brett, Gertler and I—had a great evening of it the other day: almost everybody in London was there, and we all went round to the back afterwards to see Lopokova the première danseuse, who is ravishing—finding there no less a person than André Gide, who looks like a baboon with the voice, manners and education of Bloomsbury in French."

Chapter Fourteen

Post Armistice

JULIAN had been in England on leave and Aldous heard that he had spent the last days of it going all the way up to Callander in Scotland to see Juliette Baillot. "I knew nothing about it from him," Aldous writes to Lady Ottoline.[1] "Is it a Romance?"

And then, at last! the war is over. Aldous's rejoicings were brief. "We have got over the jollifications of the first days of peace and are beginning to examine the facts."

The facts—well, again Aldous expects the worst. Bolshevism is a serious possibility. There is the repulsive immediate prospect of Lloyd George's triumphant return to power in the elections, and that will mean the substitution for any kind of serious parliamentary government of bureaucracy, big money interests and the press, with a consequent exacerbation of revolutionary elements. "One has to remember that two-thirds of the adult male population is highly skilled in the use of the most complicated weapons." Aldous has no desire to find himself in the middle of a revolution and rather thinks that America will be the only place where it will not break out. "Great events are both terrifying and boring, terrifying because one may be killed and boring because they interfere with the free exercise of the mind." He sent a message to Brett to vote Labour.

If the prospects of the universe were dim and dismal, they were as nothing to his personal prospects which were, Aldous said, what the Russians would call Nevsky prospects, the Nevskyest of prospects. Eton will have its normal and permanent staff back by next Half, and he will soon be out of a job. He has been sounding Oxford and has heard that there will be nothing for him at Balliol as they took on a good man during the war whom they did not want to turn out. "A future of poverty, hunger and dirt looms menacingly." Julian offered to lend some money; Aldous will accept, gratefully, if and when the time comes. At present his situation is obscure and further complicated by the uncertainties of Maria's movements. Mme Nys had gone to Naples in the autumn with the younger girls. Maria is on Capri with

[1] Who is supposed to have said, "Have I been running a marriage bureau for Huxleys?"

Costanza. Supposedly they will return to Belgium as soon as they can get passports.

Meanwhile Eton has been thrown out of gear by influenza, two hundred and fifty cases in the school. Aldous has been able to read Flaubert and Stendhal, and to do a little more work on his dual personality story. As for Julian and Juliette, "I am glad," he wrote to Brett, "you are keeping your ears pricked at your end of this strange potential romance.

> I know very little . . except that Brother J, when I wrote to him saying I thought his Scottish journey romantic, did not deny the soft impeachment, but said he had taken on Mlle as his Marraine for the war. Whether the wartime . . arrangement will blossom into any other kind of relationship in the piping days of peace remains to be seen. I know nothing.

December and still no solutions. Aldous does not even know where he will go for Christmas. To Garsington, probably. He would like to try to get to Paris as Maria might be stopping there on the way North. Money again is the problem. "It haunts me sometimes, the horror of it . . . whether it will ever be solved seems to me extremely doubtful."

Mme Nys had wished to stay on in Italy until the spring, not an unreasonable plan seeing the difficulties of travel and shortages of food in Belgium. The house at Bellem and the wool mill was damaged in the last allied offensive. The girls persuaded their mother to return at once. After days of slow travel in icy, crowded trains, delayed by strikes and breakdowns, they reached St Trond and the grand-parental house on a day of deep snow before the end of the year.

Yet there was still no question of Aldous being able to see Maria. All he could hope for was to go to Belgium in the Easter holidays. *If* he'll have the money. Only his intentions were clear. "What I want is to marry and settle down to write . . . What I want more than anything really is to get a year with nothing to do except to write."

By February he is still hoping for something at Oxford and at the same time "poking about among editors" trying to get some regular reviewing or other literary work. He is not proposing to marry on nothing at all; in fact, he sums up the position to his father, he would not like to risk it on under £500 a year. "If Maria had a little money of her own, it would be rather a comfort," but he doesn't know how far her people have been ruined by the war and whether they will be able to let her have anything at all.

As for his own people, Leonard had become chief editor of the *Cornhill* a few years before and there also was some money coming in from Prior's Field; on the other hand he now had a second family, two sons, David and Andrew, to look after and educate. Aldous's Aunt Mary, Mrs Humphry Ward, a best-selling author in her day, was facing greatly changed circumstances, her vogue and royalties having abruptly ceased during the war just when she was being faced by considerable financial liabilities in her own family. Aldous finally wrote to his father.

. . It would be a very great help if you could let me have a little—though I feel rather odious in asking you for anything: for I seem already to have claimed—and as a matter of course—so much of your work and of your life. I hope I shall do something not unworthy of all you have given me.

Julian meanwhile got demobilized with an appointment waiting at Oxford. In March he and Juliette Baillot were married. Aldous was best man. He saw them off; looking, Juliette says, lost and wistful standing on the platform.

Then, in a matter of weeks, Aldous's luck turned. He was offered a job in London. The salary was adequate and it was not teaching but a post on the editorial staff of that highly literate weekly—now long merged with the *New Statesman—The Athenaeum* under the editorship of John Middleton Murry. Aldous was to start at the end of April; his father lent him a few hundred to start life on. Aldous resigned from Eton. At the end of Easter Half of 1919 he left Cobby and the Old Christopher, dumped his books and clothes at Hampstead and set out for Belgium.

Chapter Fifteen

A Family Reunion

THEY met after a separation of two years and three months at St Trond. It was the small town in the province of Limbourg, the Longres of *Uncle Spencer*,[1] that leisurely story of gentle ironies, Longres-St Trond of the Grand'Place with the little seventeenth-century Hotel de Ville, the kermesse and the weekly pig market seething away below Grandpère Baltus's house; St Trond of the aerial music where "at the hours the bells play a minuet and trio, tinkly and formal like the first composition of an infant Boccherini".

They met. Maria was staying at her grandparents, Aldous put up by *Mère* in another house. The young English poet was accepted as a matter of course. If there was anxiety about the future it was not shown; Aldous was very well received. He fitted into "a rather oddly un-English life". At St Trond everybody, who was anybody, was everybody else's relation, and old Monsieur and Madame Baltus were the patriarchs of the town. At a family dinner they easily sat down twenty-five. At the stroke of half past one every day of the year, children, grandchildren, uncles, aunts and cousins arrived *en voisin* at the house on the Grand'Place for after-luncheon coffee in the smoking-room followed by a general armchair siesta. *En voisin* meant without a hat. All relations were rich *commerçants*, "living in large and hideous houses dotted about the town. Some make cloth, some sugar . . . A few are very cultured, the rest not at all."

It was all a very far cry from Garsington or their privacy in the London of 1916. Aldous did not see enough of Maria, but he surveyed the scene with literary detachment. He described the grandparents to his father,

. . He with the appearance of a retired colonel, deaf, very kindly and human, devoting his old age to reading which he never had time to do in his active days of cloth-manufacturing. The old lady [Maria's beloved Emérence] is a person of rather witchlike appearance, not quite so amiable as he is, I think.

Uncle George Baltus, the Glasgow professor and his wife, he found very cultured and him extremely amusing; and Mère,

[1] *Little Mexican*, 1924.

"whom I like very much," intelligent and nice, "tho' rather a creature of moods (some of the moods tiresome)". As for himself, he thought that they were fairly reassured. "They had, I fancy, rather anticipated a roaring lion: they are relieved to find a sheep."

Monsieur Nys's business had indeed been ruined (there was to be no allowance or settlement for Maria), though the grandparents' was not, thanks to Emérence Baltus who had stood up both to Germans and hard times.

The Belgian visit was brief but everything was settled. Aldous went back to England to take up his job and find a place to live. Maria with her grandmother's assistance was to see about her trousseau.

Chapter Sixteen

Adjustments

ALDOUS and Maria were married on 10th July 1919 at the Hôtel de Ville at Bellem. They were married in the simplest fashion. Aldous's father did not come over for the ceremony and nor did any other member of the Huxley family. (Nobody liked the expense and fuss of a big wedding.) Maria's father was laid up in Brussels with the gout. (Both parents, by Belgian law, had to telegraph their consent.) The only relations present were Mère and Jeanne.

Aldous had found a small flat in Hampstead[1] in a house surrounded by grass and trees, quiet as the country, fifteen minutes' walk from his father's house and only twenty-odd minutes by underground or bicycle from Charing Cross. He had furnished it practically with his own hands. He had sawed shelves, painted tables and chairs, hunted for some "nice pink wallpaper"; his step-mother had helped him to shop; his cousin Marjorie[2] had done the paper-hanging. Aldous and Brett painted the woodwork in the sitting-room dove grey; a carpet arrived from Heal's and crates from Belgium with china, silver, linen. Aldous was particularly pleased with "a marvellous instrument for heating water" which he had found and bought himself.

A little bar which you fasten to the light and dip into your water: it will boil a pint in 5 minutes—very useful . . for simple cooking, such as eggs and tea: much quicker than a spirit lamp.

Here they arrived. Maria twenty, Aldous nearly twenty-five, in the first home of his own. In her trousseau, Maria had brought silk jackets, exquisite gloves, good scent, diffusing an ambience of feminine elegance, a hint of Persian luxury, which Aldous, raw from a decade in digs and college, became quite fond of. The solitary years were over—they were going to have a Siamese cat and a pug from Garsington and live happily ever after.

When Aldous married Maria—and he had never wavered in his determination to do so from the time he spoke on the lawn at Garsington—he was very much in love with her. (In their middle-

[1] At 18 Hampstead Hill Gardens.
[2] Marjorie Huxley; Gervas's sister.

age when they had been married thirty-three years to the day and Aldous unexpectedly remembered, Maria brought it up, "What made you marry me?" she asked him. Aldous answered artlessly, "Well, you were rather pretty then." Maria roared with laughter.) For Maria in the earliest days it had been both less and more. She was less carried away by the present, what held her was a sense of doing the right thing in the long view. There was Aldous: a quality in Aldous, and this she dedicated herself to serve. If it was not explicit, it was already conscious; one may call it a sense of vocation. *Je tirerai son bateau.* Meanwhile, she was young, innocent and quite worldly, full of gaiety, love, good will; and she was very scared.

She was most frightened of the "brilliant ones", Aldous's intellectual friends and women friends, Tom Eliot, the Sitwells, the Bloomsburies, Murry, Evan Morgan, Tommy Earp; Marie Beerbohm, Mary Hutchinson, Iris Tree, Nancy Cunard. There were also the Huxleys and the Arnolds to be met. Aldous's father and stepmother were still in Scotland, and besides had written kind welcoming letters; the immediate ordeal was meeting Mrs Humphry Ward. "We go to Stocks next weekend," Aldous wrote to his father on 5th August, "—a prospect which M regards with certain qualms of terror!"

They went. Maria found "such a nice and charming old lady that all terror vanished," she wrote to Julian,[1] "except my momentary astonishment at her being so unlike Vernon Lee."

However, on Sunday by tea time "an immense family party was spreading itself as far as one could see and for one moment I really thought I would give way to terror and despair—

> a very snooty cousin and a sporty one—young ladies and old ones and an uncle and lady—very thin and stern poor woman suffering from rheumatism.[1]

How un-English Maria must have appeared to that world! And how well she knew that this precisely was original sin.

The family was very much aware that both the Huxley brothers —Leonard's boys—had married foreigners, and it took the best part of half a century to live it down. It is now conceded that they made excellent wives. Aldous's sister, Margaret, trying to explain the lack of contact between brother and sister ("the actual amounts of time during which Aldous and I merely lived in the same place were remarkably small, and we never corresponded") declares,

> When Aldous eventually got married, that didn't help as far as I

---

[1] From a letter published in *The Letters of Aldous Huxley.*

was concerned at all, because to be perfectly frank, I didn't take to Maria, not one bit! I was madly keen on games in those years, and I'm sure I didn't appeal to her at all either.[1]

Aldous, who had a marvellously useful unselfconsciousness, remained largely unaware of such undercurrents. For Maria it was, "Next week it is to your Aunt Sophy we go. She of course terrifies me to extremes though I have seen her twice—always equally energetic and wanting to rule."

To Gervas she took at once—*he* was Aldous's favourite cousin. She enjoyed the return to Ottoline, to Garsington (where they spent many of their weekends). Then there was their own flat, "delightful and comfortable," where seriously, amateurishly, they kept house. Maria was amused to see Aldous pottering about, still painting and sawing—"I never suspected him of being so handy at all." They had a daily maid who did the cleaning; no cook. There was no kitchen. What they had was "a hole with a sink", a spirit lamp and Aldous's prodigious instrument for boiling water. One might possibly manage with these if one were very experienced and very patient. Maria became the latter by sheer effort of will (temperamentally, she was extremely quick) and managed to feed Aldous. On tinned soup, bread and jam, an egg beaten into the top of the milk. She used to tell me how she would boil a potato for him over the pilot light of the geyser in their bathroom. The pilot light sprang from a movable bracket that could be turned clear of the geyser casing, and she would hold up a tiny saucepan over that single flame for as long as it took.

Aldous's Aunt Sophy, wishing to help, was much concerned. "My mother", Gervas says, "was worried about the Hampstead flat. They were very hard up . . . She thought Aldous wasn't getting enough to eat. She had them in for meals, gave them a good meal . . . But Maria did her very best. I was very very fond of her—she was awfully good to Aldous."

Aldous and Maria *were* hard up, but no more so than seems acceptable to many young couples, if anything they were rather pleased and proud of being able to manage, and at first it did not occur to anyone that Aldous might be worked above his strength. "Aldous is working very hard but is well I think and happy," Maria wrote to Julian. His work on the *Athenaeum* consisted mainly of reviewing and doing the mass of shorter notices. At once after his marriage he became "frantically busy with a host of books to review and odds and ends of all sorts to write".

[1] Margaret Huxley, from a letter to S. B., 1969.

At the same time he was doing a fair amount of work for other papers and trying "in the somewhat rare intervals" to do things of his own.

How much he was doing, and how rare the intervals must have been, becomes clear when one counts up the items listed in the bibliography.[1] In 1919, in the course of the eight months-odd he was working for the *Athenaeum*, Aldous contributed 29 signed articles and 171 anonymous notices and reviews to the paper, did 8 articles for the *London Mercury* and some reviews for the *Statesman*, published 7 poems in *Wheels* and one story in *Coterie*. His subjects included Aeschylus, Walter De la Mare, Jacob Boehme, John Galsworthy, John Donne, C. H. B. Kitchin, Lord Alfred Douglas, Flaubert, Maeterlinck, John Masefield, Rose Macaulay, Vita Sackville-West, Blaise Cendrars, Paul Claudel, Ronald Firbank, Leonardo da Vinci, Laurence Housman, Latin poems of the Renaissance, a handbook of Greek vase painting, Charles Maurras, André Gide, Mark Twain and Marcel Proust.

> It is a crowded sort of life [he wrote four weeks after his wedding to Gidley Robinson, his old headmaster who had sent a present] but I enjoy the work, and the whole atmosphere of the *Athenaeum* is so delightfully remote, in its purely literary preoccupations, from the horrors of the present that it is in a way restful work.

What Aldous needed at that stage of his life was a breathing space; time to sit back and recover, a measure of security, manageable, not crushing, responsibilities. Sadly, for him, for the child, who simply came too soon, he did not get this breathing space; in August already an ominous sentence appears in one of Maria's letters. She is speaking of their flat and how much she loves it, "I [am] already studying how one might find one more room so as to enable us to remain here all our life."

To that letter (to Julian) Aldous added the postscript: "I wish one could do without sleep, that the days were twice as long and that my strength were the strength of ten so that I could do all I want to do."

Now he had to snap up whatever might be going. He signed an agreement with Constable's to do a book on Balzac, fifty pounds on receipt of the MS and the book to be finished by the end of 1920. It will be a big task, he thought, but interesting— "I am rather appalled at the prospect of having to read *all* Balzac!"

---

[1] *Aldous Huxley, A Bibliography 1916-1959*, by Claire Eschelbach & Joyce Lee Shober, University of California Press, 1961.

Chapter Seventeen

"My Two Children—*Limbo* and *Leda*"

ALDOUS had finished his first long story, "The Farcical History of Richard Greenow", earlier in the year; by the autumn he thought that he had enough short stories—five more and a little play—to make a book, and took the MS to Chatto & Windus where Frank Swinnerton read it and approved. The book was accepted. Chatto's were the first publishers Aldous had approached; he remained with them for life.

Maria, pregnant and none too well, stayed much at home; Aldous went his round, from the *Athenaeum* offices to the London Library, to Soho luncheons with a friend, to evenings at the Eiffel Tower restaurant in Charlotte Street or Osbert Sitwell's house in Swan Walk or the Café Royal. In January he managed a week in Paris, staying with a new friend, Drieu la Rochelle, the young writer, "a charming and interesting creature," and meeting "the cubists of literature," Aragon, Tzara, Picabia, Soupault, André Breton.

Aldous's book of short stories, *Limbo*, was published on 29th January (these things were ordered more quickly in those days). The actual sales were only about 1600 copies but the book was pounced upon by the high-brows and the literate young who were carried away by the cool bugle call of that new astringent voice expressing so essentially the coming post-war mood. Anticipating a roaring lion, the Belgian family had been relieved to find a sheep; Aldous in life was one thing then, Aldous on paper another. There was nothing sheeplike in the sentiments of Richard Greenow.

Mrs Humphry Ward died on 24th March at the age of sixty-nine. Aldous was much affected. Juliette went with him to the funeral. Aldous, tears streaming down his face, wept openly.

The baby was expected any day. Aldous took on another job, a night job as it were, he became second-string dramatic critic on the weekly *Westminster Gazette*. The main critic was the late Naomi Royde Smith, the novelist (who was also poetry editor and problems editor), an influential figure in the literary world of the time (she published two first poems, Rupert Brooke's and Graham Greene's). Later she married the actor Ernest Milton. She was an extremely nice woman who became an intimate friend of Aldous and Maria.

On 19th April Matthew Huxley was born. The delivery was an extremely difficult one; Maria had a haemorrhage and nearly died. By her contrivance these facts were largely kept from Aldous. She was told—and this he knew—that it would not be wise for her to have another child.

On 20th April, the very next day, Aldous started his stint as theatre critic (to which he stuck for some eight months). Always reluctant to look too hard at disaster which might after all not occur, and which in this case had *not* occurred, he wrote to Arnold Bennett:

> My wife has just had a son and has, I am thankful to say, weathered the tempest safely and auspiciously. These works of nature really do put works of art in the shade.

Maria and the baby went to Garsington for a longish convalescence. Aldous took on a third job. Part-time work at the Chelsea Book Club, a high-brow book shop cum small art gallery in Cheyne Walk run by a painter called Arundel del Re. Aldous's role was to be knowledgeable and to sign the cheques. The enterprise soon ran into financial trouble and he was not paid. All the same he carried on, putting in a few hours a day. This meant travelling between Hampstead, Chelsea and the Strand: "I have bought a bicycle on which I now do my voyages. Very good exercise . . quite ten miles, I imagine, the double journey, which I take through two parks, so that it is very pleasant. Also from Chelsea to the *Adelphi* and the *Athenaeum* which I do by the long embankments."

What he detested most in his existence was the theatre going. Then, and later, he never ceased to complain about "the quite extraordinary badness of the ordinary play", and became more and more convinced that it ought not to be too difficult to beat the playwrights at their own game. "I shall go on producing plays", he wrote to his father, "till I can get one staged and successful.

> It is the only thing to do . . . There is nothing but a commercial success that can free one from this deadly hustle.

That May Chatto's published *Leda*, Aldous's third collection of poems. "My two children," Aldous said, "Limbo and Leda."

> *Brown and bright as an agate, mountain-cool,*
> *Eurotas singing slips from pool to pool;*
> *Down rocky gullies; through the cavernous pines*
> *And chestnut groves; down where the terraced vines*

And gardens overhang; through valleys grey
With olive trees, into a soundless bay
Of the Aegean. . . .

So opens the title poem, some five-hundred lines in rhymed couplets, on which Aldous had laboured in the darkness of the Old Christopher at Eton.

Couched on the flowery ground
Young Leda lay, and to her side did press
The swan's proud-arching opulent loveliness,
Stroking the snow-soft plumage of his breast
With fingers slowly drawn, themselves caressed
By the warm softness where they lingered, loth
To break away. . . .

Among the shorter poems were the then notorious *Philosopher's Songs*, the Fifth being possibly the most quoted of Aldous's verse:

A million million spermatozoa,
    All of them alive:
Out of their cataclysm but one poor Noah
    Dare hope to survive.

And among that billion minus one
    Might have chanced to be
Shakespeare, another Newton, a new Donne—
    But the One was Me.

The volume ends with another long poem, "*Soles Occidere Et Redire Possunt*," a poem as anguished, contemporary and fragmented as *Leda* is homophonous and serene, an illustration indeed of what Aldous called the multiplicity of man. "*Soles Occidere*" is a curious work and it is prefaced by an equally curious introduction.

John Ridley, the subject of this poem, was killed in February 1918. "If I should perish," he wrote to me only five weeks before his death, "if I should perish—and one isn't exactly a 'good life' at the moment—I wish you'd write something about me. It isn't vanity (for I know you'll do me, if anything, rather less than justice!), not vanity, I repeat; but that queer irrational desire one has for immortality of any kind, however short and precarious—for frankly,

my dear, I doubt whether your verses will be so very much more
perennial than brass. Still, they'll be something. One can't, of course,
believe in any *au-delà* for one's personal self . . . No, my only hope
is you—and a damned poor guarantee for eternity. Don't make of
me a khaki image . . . I sincerely hope, of course, that you won't
have to write the thing at all—hope not, but have very little doubt
you will. Good-bye."

The following poem is a tentative and provisional attempt to
comply with his request. Ridley was an adolescent, and suffered
from that . . . characteristic instability of mind which makes adolescence so feebly sceptical, so inefficient, so profoundly unhappy. I
have fished up a single day from Ridley's forgotten existence. It has
a bedraggled air in the sunlight, this poor wisp of Lethean weed.
Fortunately, however, it will soon be allowed to drop back into the
water, where we shall all, in due course, join it. "The greater part
must be content to be as though they had not been."

It is strange to think of Aldous fifty years ago taking up that
grudging challenge. And when did he find time to write that
elaborate poem of nearly five hundred lines? Nobody remembers
him referring to the dead friend and his weird legacy. Did Aldous
work at "*Soles Occidere*" in spare moments at Eton, in holidays at
Prior's Field or Garsington in the intervals of writing *Leda* and
"The Farcical History of Richard Greenow"? Or in London during
the first year of his marriage, in the year of the great journalistic
grind? Well, he wrote it, and there survives now of John Ridley
his own letter and Aldous's poem, in print both after some fifty
years—a far cry from immortality though, as Ridley might have
said, it's something.

Leda in a sense was the last of Aldous as a poet. Although he
went on writing and publishing verse for another ten years (in
fact never entirely ceased to), his main creative impulse after
his mid-twenties flowed no longer into poetry. His quantitative
output, the sheer fact of writing so much to earn a living had
something to do with it doubtlessly, though the demands on his
time and energy were heavier if anything during the decade of
The Burning Wheel, *The Defeat of Youth* and the Mallarmé translation; but then fatigue can be cumulative and surreptitious. The
partial silting of one channel was an unconscious, unwilled process
and not, I think, the result of any deliberate, practical or critical,
decision on his part. Aldous did not give up poetry and "confine
himself" to prose in the way described by T. S. Eliot.

. . My prestige [in 1919] was such that Aldous submitted for my
opinion his own book of Verse, *Leda and Other Poems:* I am afraid
that I was unable to show any enthusiasm for his verse. After this

attempt he wisely confined himself to the essay and that variety of fiction which he came to make his own.[1]

"Luckily," Aldous wrote in another context, "people don't leave much trace on me. They make an impression easily, like a ship on water. But the water closes up again."[2]

In June Maria and the baby returned from Garsington to the flat which had meanwhile been improved with some ingenuity. "Our little hole with the sink," Aldous wrote, "has been given gas and lined with shelves, so that it makes a really excellent little kitchen. M's room has been distempered and serves pretty comfortably as a nursery."

They had a nurse-maid for the infant, but decisions were up to Aldous and Maria. "Shall we boil the teat?" they asked Juliette. "Oh, I think so."

In August Aldous decided to give up the job with the Chelsea Book Club; he could not afford to spend his time for nothing. As it was, he felt "excessively busy and overworked" and never had a holiday. However, there was now a good job in prospect: "Sordid journalism but a screw of £400 which, at the moment and in the circs, I can't refuse. Journalism is paying in the inverse ratio of the goodness of the paper, which is rather melancholy." He added, "I should like to be rid of the whole damn thing, but there's no chance yet."

So in October Aldous left the *Athenaeum* (though he went on contributing to the paper) and went to work for Condé Nast. At first he would seem to have been caught by some enthusiasm.

> I have just helped to float [he wrote to Naomi Mitchison] a marvellous paper belonging to the *Vogue* people,—*House and Garden* (run by a "staff of experts" . . otherwise by me and a young girl). It is a huge success: more than £1000 worth of advertisements in the first number . . . I wish I reaped more of the profits than I do; but I won't do too badly . . .

Aldous and Maria were better off now and Aldous's work was less dispersed, though he had kept on the theatre job for the time being. Yet Maria was still far from well and, as might have been obvious from the first, existence with baby and nurse-maid in that flat for two was not really possible. The baby yelled when Aldous had to write or sleep. In spite of the recent alterations, they decided to give up the place. A very typical thing for them

---

[1] In *Mem. Vol.*   [2] Philip Quarles in *Point Counter Point.*

2 THE HUXLEY FAMILY

Back row (standing): Miss Churcher sec. to Mrs Humphry Ward; Dorothy Ward d. of Mrs H. Ward; Janet Ward d. of Mrs H. Ward married G. M. Trevelyan.

Centre row: Miss Ella Salkovski governess to Aldous, later to Matthew; Mrs L. Huxley; Arnold Ward son of Mrs H. Ward; Mrs H. Ward; second wife of Thomas Arnold; Thomas Arnold (1823-1900), Aldous's grandfather.

Front row: Aldous; Trevenen; Julian

3   Aldous aged about five

to do as it turned out. Again and again it was to be—convert, furnish, buy or build—Maria proclaiming that it was for the rest of their natural days—then in no time move out lock, stock and barrel. Now they suspended home life altogether. Maria and the child were to go to her family in Belgium for the winter, while Aldous was to toil on in London, put up by friends. Though gloomy enough in the short run, this was a constructive plan: Maria was to get well and Aldous to make enough money to get away from journalism for a time. Their aim was Italy by the spring with something like four or five clear months in hand.

They packed up before the New Year. Maria took Matthew to Mère at St Trond; and Aldous, after a solitary Christmas doing two or three theatres a day, was able to see Maria again in Paris, "snatching a brief and restless holiday". They stayed with Lewis Gielgud and his French wife Mimi, Aldous and Lewis trying "to write up a new play in frantic haste". (The play came to nothing.)

Aldous now spent the rest of the winter in a flat in Bloomsbury belonging to Tommy Earp. Russell Green, their mutual Oxford friend explains the amiable, haphazard set-up. Earp, Russell claims, had just inherited forty thousand pounds and proposed to take an extra flat at 36 Regent Square.

> "I like having several places, don't you know. Why not furnish it and we will live there." Tommy Earp handed me the cash to furnish the flat, and we resided there until 1924. (I must say the constant hot water was a great boon.)
> It was there that dear Aldous joined us.[1]

Russell Green of the photographic memory goes on:

> I can still see him, sitting back on the Minty basket chair [this would be after Aldous's office day at *House and Garden*] typewriter on knees, producing reports on (I fancy) orchestral concerts for the old green *Westminster Gazette*.

(Aldous had gone on to doing the infinitely more congenial concert notices; he was succeeded as dramatic critic by A. P. Herbert.)

> Before this effort Aldous would brace himself with a cup of tea, using what he termed "my silver egg", which he lowered into a cup,

---

[1] Russell Green, in letters to S. B.

poured on boiling water till infusion was complete. I noticed how pallid and strained he seemed. But it all helped to accumulate enough cash to enable him to travel, with pretty wife Maria, to write a new book.

Green was struck—as we all so often were—by the inconsistencies in Aldous's seeing.

Though I have seen him, in that basket chair, reading Braille, he was quite capable of riding his bicycle about London . . .

One day Green plucked up courage to read Aldous passages from his own first novel. "At a pause, his silvery voice emitted the damning question, 'But, my dear Russell, do you suppose that anyone will ever *read* it?' . . He was quite right—nobody ever did."

By the end of March Aldous had saved enough money. Maria was already in Italy; the Fasolas had found them a place to live. Aldous packed his books, watched by Russell Green.

I can see them now before me piled on the carpet. He took with him the new *Handy Volume* of the Encyclopaedia Britannica.

But Aldous was tired out. The London Life Association refused to insure him in his present condition. "It is absurd and rather humiliating to be a Bad Life," he wrote to his father the day before he left England, "and I am resolved [to become] definitely a Good Life . . by leading a decent existence for a few months. I shall try and get really well while I am in Italy."

PART FOUR

European Decade: 1921-1930

La bêtise n'est pas mon fort.

PAUL VALÉRY

The performance took place against
a background of relatively few, simple,
moral convictions; they were disguised
by the brilliance of the technical accomplishment, but they were there . . .
like the monotonous, insistent, continuous ground bass slowly pounding
away through the elaborate intellectual
display.

SIR ISAIAH BERLIN

Chapter One

Tuscan Summer

THEY were in Florence on their son's first birthday. "Darling," Maria wrote to him twenty-seven years later from California in another April,

> This is a little letter full of sentimental affections because we have just returned from a birthday party for little Bill.[1] And it reminds me so much of your birthday party; there is nothing again like the first one.
>
> We were in the Villa Minucci, which you cannot remember, it was cloudy and sunny as always when the lilac bloom and they were blooming all around the house and scenting through the open windows. You were as blonde and pink as little Bill and you said your first word and had your first tooth on that day. The Sitwells and Willy Walton the composer came to tea and you were as unconcerned as little Bill about the whole thing.

The Villa Minucci. It stood on the Via Santa Margherita a Montici, country then, above a valley planted with olives and vines. The Huxleys lived in a wing of it; on one side the whole of Florence lay before them in the plain below, on the other there was an exquisite Tuscan view of hills and San Miniato. They lived in two rooms, one of them large and long, a kitchen and a garden, and paid 150 lire a month, two pounds in terms of the exchange. They had divided the long room with a screen, Aldous and Maria slept in one half and sat in the other, nurse and baby had the second room and all ate in the kitchen. Maria was well again, Matthew had grown healthy and big, and there was a nanny now, Julian and Aldous's old Fräulein (Bella to Matthew) back from out of the past with "her round red face a little wrinkled, like a ripening apple".

At first Aldous did little but eat and sleep. (For much of his life he had the gift of flawless sleep, nine hours easily, ten given the time.) It was his first view of Italian Italy (he had been as far as Lake Como one Easter holiday as a boy). He kept his head about Florence. Too tre- and quattrocento for his taste—too much Gothic in the architecture and too much primitive art in

---

[1] Bill Kiskadden, godson of Aldous and Maria, a child of their friends, Dr William and Peggy Kiskadden.

the galleries. "I am an enthusiastic *post*-Raphaelite. Sixteenth and seventeenth century . . is what I enjoy . . ."

One must go to Rome for the architecture and to Venice for the painting and of course to the masses of little towns where you find "the most fabulous outflowings of baroque buildings". He had not yet been to any of these places but hoped to get to them in time. As for people. The English colony is "a queer collection; a sort of decayed provincial intelligentsia". Among the permanent inhabitants he liked Vernon Lee, and Geoffrey and Lady Sybil Scott. From "the number of awful people of one's acquaintance, or wanting to make one's acquaintance, who pass through the town, we escape by chance and cunning".

Quite soon Aldous was well enough to be thinking about work. They had an idea that the sea might suit him and Forte dei Marmi was the obvious choice: the Fasolas were going, Aldous *liked* Costanza. In May they went and took "a minute little house [Aldous to his father] with four rooms, very clean . . and well-furnished with comfortable beds and a good batterie de cuisine, with a garden . . ." Aldous hopes that now all will be perfect. It is the perennial wish expressed by those who have resolved to produce work in a new place and a given span of time. How many writers, before Aldous and after, surfacing from some lucrative, exhausting stint, have been first daunted then defeated by the daily imperative of their hard-earned and counted mornings. At Forte Aldous knuckled down point-blank to write a novel, pledging himself to finish it within two months. And writing *Crome Yellow*—such can be the reward of virtue—turned out to be not the least like reading Macaulay in Braille; it was like being in a state of grace. Happy countries, he wrote to his father, have no history.

The life of the household was even and revolved around Aldous's needs. His days fell into a pattern which he was to reproduce, *mutatis mutandis*, for much of his life. Work in the morning; a bathe in a warm sea, luncheon, walking or reading till tea; more work; a latish dinner, often with friends, and after dinner music or reading.

At Forte they ate out of doors in the shade and wore the light, free clothes of the Mediterranean summer. Aldous was thriving; born into the rain, he said, he had always had a craving for sunlight and heat.

At the hour before dinner, alone in their room Aldous and Maria talked. This became their habit. Aldous pacing perhaps, Maria sitting at her looking glass told him about the day, told him what she had seen; the early light on the hills, the first cicada, the neighbours' ménage à trois. Maria was Mercury, was the messenger, bringing the news of her world. Aldous asked, Maria told. Too *curious*, he said, too *extraordinary*; then used it, changed it, made it his own.

He *was* working well. For so many years circumstances had forced him to hold back sustained writing; in the meantime he acquired experience by the incessant practice of literary journalism. (Of a high standard of excellence. Bruce Richmond, the editor of the *Times Literary Supplement*, whose taste was a hundred per cent classical, said of Aldous's prose, using the colloquial English of the late Victorians, "He is a real swell."[1]) Now, the Peacockian novel—the form so deliberately chosen—flowed. An entertainment he called it, though not on the title page, and he was delighted by what he found was there to shape and say—the fireworks of ideas, the erudite digressions, the mild (from today's view) human ironies—and some of this joy, this freshness of a young writer's easy dip into his treasures, still comes through.

In their first Hampstead days Maria had been amused to find Aldous capable of being handy about the house. She soon decided that this would not do. Aldous's gaiety—he was a far gayer man, a more light-hearted companion, than one might deduce from the letters—his zest when stimulated, his unassuming attempts to ride bicycles and buses like everybody else, made people forget or underestimate both the extra strain imposed by his sight and the great need he had to recuperate from the events of his early years. Maria did not forget; on the immediate level she was resolved that all should be done to make his daily life peaceful, effortless and agreeable, that he should be spared concerns extraneous to his work and thoughts, should be free, above all should feel free, of any domestic and practical demands. This she carried out in sickness and in health for thirty-six years. All who knew them saw this and how she went about it, and there are revealing passages in her own letters. In the 1940s, for instance, she advised her young, and slightly rebellious niece, Claire Nicolas,

> As-tu jamais pensé qu'il fallait se préparer pour la vie intime avec un amant dans la vie intime de la famille? Une chose aussi délicate que l'amour, l'affection, l'admiration ne doit pas être dérangée par des détails dangereux, petits mais continues, de la vie journalière . . .
>
> Par le plus grands des hazards j'ai découvert, étant de ton age, que ce sont les efforts incessants, invisibles et inconnus du passant, qui nous donnent le plus de sécurité et de joie . . .
>
> . . Ton mari, ton amant, sans savoir pourquoi sera toujours heureux et calme avec toi—parceque tu fera des choses dont il ne doit pas se fatiguer à te remercier.

[1] As told by Sir George Clark.

For all this concentration on the novel, Aldous had some leisure to look at Italy. There were jaunts into Lucca, Pisa, a day or two at Siena. (". . English strangers wandering about the streets," seen by their future friend Yvonne Franchetti,[1] "tall, tall Aldous peering at the façades, beside him tiny Maria, trailing behind them a baby and a nanny . . .") English strangers—not entirely absorbed by the façades: The fascisti [Aldous to his father] ". . One cannot imagine how the Italian population suffers an entirely irresponsible private organization [which in fact it still was in 1921] to act as the fascio does—sometimes usurping powers that should belong to the state, sometimes resorting to incredible acts of violence and brutality. People look on with a sort of resignation.

"It is the same attitude as one sees over the whole world— blank fatalistic resignation to stupid and wicked governments, to anything or any person with power."

Aldous finished *Crome Yellow* in the second week of August, and the MS, re-typed by Maria, was sent off to Chatto & Windus. "Practically, I have written the whole thing, some 60,000 words, in the 2 months I have been here: which is pretty good going."

He hopes that the book will amuse, "It is pleasingly baroque." The last weeks *have* been a strain and he is looking forward to a rest, though he is already thinking of doing another Peacock, "a gigantic one in an Italian scene". Meanwhile he and Maria went to Rome; they had been lent a flat for a week. Now Aldous *was* swept off his feet. "What a place! It inspires one at once with a kind of passion to know it utterly and inside out . . . It is certainly the place where I shall come to spend my old age and if possible, large portions of my existence . . ."

He discovered that architecture, sculpture and painting gave him as much pleasure as music. When he could indulge his post-Raphaelite tastes that was—"Rome being practically invented by Bernini.

I feel sorry for people who come to Rome with the preconceived certitude of the badness of Bernini and the seventeenth century. They are left nothing but Michelangelo and Raphael, the Colisseum, the columns and arches and the insupportably dreary spectacle of the rubbish in the forums.

When Aldous's grandfather, T. H. H., visited Rome in 1885 he expressed dissimilar if equally forthright views. He railed

---

[1] The present Mrs Hamish Hamilton.

against "the ill-proportioned, worse decorated tawdry stone mountain on the vatican," and described some of the rites performed in St Peter's as "elaborate tomfooleries . . . devised, one would think, by a college of ecclesiastical man-milliners for the delectation of school-girls.

The best thing, from an aesthetic point of view, that could be done with Rome would be to destroy everything except St Paolo fuor le Mure, of later than the fourth century.[1]

Aldous left Rome inspired with an intense desire to live. "What I should like now more than anything [he wrote from Forte] is a year or two of quiet devoted simply to seeing places and things and people: to living, in fact. When one hasn't much vitality or physical energy, it is almost impossible to live and work at the same time . . . Circumstances demand that I should work almost continuously, and I can't squeeze in enough living."

Aldous had to make up his mind about the immediate future, whether to go on living in Italy or to return to England. In Italy they could live comfortably on less than 2,000 lire a month, £300 a year, and live more comfortably at that than on £800 in England. The question was could he be certain of making that £300? "I hope to have from £70 to £100 in hand in the autumn. My book, if it does as well as the last, should bring me another £100." What with getting some short stories into magazines and writing enough of them for another volume in the spring, he ought to be able to make up the rest. Then there were the drawbacks of Italy: the absence of libraries and the lack of informed and intelligent society; on the other hand the thought of plunging back into journalism appalled him. "I have been living for two years in a perpetual state of fatigue and I don't want to go back to it if I can help it . . ."

In September Aldous still does not quite know what will become of them. Condé Nast has offered £750 a year; if he accepts, they will be "pretty comfortable" in London. If only one could spend half one's time in each country—"but that, alas, seems impossible."

---

[1] T. H. Huxley to his son Leonard, Rome, Jan. 20th 1885. (From *Life and Letters of Thomas Henry Huxley*, by Leonard Huxley. Macmillan & Co., 1900.)

Chapter Two

Life in London: Westbourne Terrace

IN October they were back in London. Aldous had accepted the Condé Nast job and they were about to set up house again. They took a ground floor and basement near Paddington in one of those family houses that were being cut up into maisonettes. Hampstead Hill Gardens had been cramped, 155 Westbourne Terrace was all echoing space. The rooms were vast, and Maria's two sisters came over to help paint them. Jeanne brought her fiancé, René Moulaert, a young theatrical decorator, and he chose the colours. The ground floor consisted of a lofty front room occupied by Bella and the baby, Maria's room opening on a small inner court and, separated by a bathroom, a rather sad back room in which Aldous slept. Below was a kitchen, an immense dining-room and another sizeable back room looking out on dustbins, Aldous's study. This they painted lemon yellow to make it look more cheerful. The basement was infested with black-beetles, and there was a poor, thin local cat who chased and ate them.

Crome Yellow was published in November. For Aldous as a writer this was the end of the beginning. People were dazzled; he had made a name. Or perhaps he had only caught up with his own curiously precursory fame. Since early Oxford, with little published and less read, the literary aura had been about Aldous. Proust conjured him up on the margin of the soirée at the Princesse de Guermantes in the guise of the nephew of the "illustrious Huxley", who himself appears in the guise of an eminent physician.

L'illustre Huxley (celui dont le neveu occupe actuellement une place prépondérante dans le monde de la littérature anglaise) . . .[1]

Actuellement—yet that passage of *Sodome et Gomorrhe* must have been written before the appearance of Aldous's first novel. (Forty years later Aldous made one comment, "I never met Proust and have no idea how he came to know about me—as it was far from being true that . . I occupied a preponderant position in English literature at that time.") When his first novel did appear in 1921

[1] *A La Recherche du Temps Perdu: Sodome et Gomorrhe.*

the literary world was captivated; at the same time—such are the changes in moral fashions—a good many people were shocked as well. While the young were exhilarated, their parents and schoolmasters disapproved; so did Aldous's own family.

> When he produced *Crome Yellow* and the other novels [writes his sister Margaret] I couldn't see any of the Aldous I knew in them and was bitterly upset by their unkindness of attitude (as I saw it).

Aldous saw it too, and put his finger on it in his next book. The American heiress meets Dolphin, the poet, in the Italian moonlight. She asks, "Will you show me your books?" Dolphin replies:[1]

> "Certainly not, Miss Toomis. That would ruin our friendship. I am insufferable in my writings. In them I give vent to all the horrible thoughts and impulses which I am too timid to express or put into practice in real life. Take me as you find me here, a decent specimen of a man, shy but able to talk intelligently when the layers of ice are broken, aimless, ineffective, but on the whole quite a good sort."

Margaret called it unkindness of attitude, the general public had another word for it—the name Aldous Huxley became equated with cynicism. Aldous (again in his next book) permitted himself a retaliation.

> "Oh, you're cynical."
> Mr Hutton always had a desire to say "Bow-wow-wow" whenever that last word was spoken. It irritated him more than any other word in the language.[2]

Mr Hutton goes on to explain that he is *not* cynical.

> I'm only speaking a melancholy truth. Reality doesn't always come up to the ideal, you know. But that doesn't make me believe any the less in the ideal.

That brings us to another matter, one which also irritated Aldous, the game so dear to acquaintances and scholars of pinning down who might be who. It irritated him because he found it trivial and beside the point. He felt that this whole process of writing, this process of transposing life and fiction is far from wholly conscious and a good deal more obscure and complex

---

[1] "Permutations Among the Nightingales" *Mortal Coils*, 1922.
[2] "The Gioconda Smile", ibid.

than putting Jack Robinson or D. H. Lawrence into a book. It might be true to say that Aldous himself did not so much put "real characters" into his books as use two or three striking aspects of one as a starting point. A novelist may be propelled originally by a face, a voice, a mannerism, a psychological situation or a place, but as he goes on something else takes over, call it inspiration or the exigencies of art, he will leave out, add, develop, change. When he is done there may be little left in Mary Fortinbras's character or story resembling that of Jenny Y, the author's friend. Mrs Fortinbras has turned out quite an elaborate monster whereas Mrs Y for all her affectations is an uncomplicated soul, though both happen to scream like peacocks, dread getting old and have a house in Rome. The great public is unaware of Mrs Y's existence; for the author, his own creation has very likely blotted out her very memory; but in her circle the fat is in the fire.

Aldous often found himself accused. He had a habit of mixing up his starting points—one man's philosophy, another's sexual tastes, one trait from a member of his family, another from a character in history—and as he did not like to stop and think that any particular person might recognize fragments of himself in an otherwise outrageous context, he took little trouble to cover up his traces.

Lady Ottoline was offended by *Crome Yellow* and a breach ensued that lasted many years. Aldous and Maria were distressed, and Aldous genuinely surprised. If the setting of the novel, the country house party, was very much based on Garsington, was not this if anything a rather elegant homage to his hosts? (The actual fictional house, Crome with its privies in the turrets, did not look like Garsington but—mixed starting points indeed—like a very old house in remote Oxfordshire.[1]) And if people, a handful of people, saw Henry Wimbush as Philip Morrell, was this not again a compliment as he is made the author of that moving pastiche, the Dwarfs' Story? And if they thought they recognized a bit of Bertie Russell in Mr Scogan, a bit of Mark Gertler in the painter, and Evan Morgan (or was it Koteliansky?) in the pianist, if they said that Anne made them think of Carrington (or Maria Nys), Jenny of Brett, and Mary of Maria (or of Carrington), surely then people must also see that all these were conceived in a spirit of light-hearted comedy and that their absurdities did not belong to life and dreary *Realismus*, but to a summer's masque? Aldous was puzzled and tried to explain in letters. The Morrells remained offended.

[1] Then belonging to Clothilde Fielding, the daughter of Brewster, Henry James's dentist in Rome.

Meanwhile Max Beerbohm wrote to him about *Crome Yellow*, a very precious letter Aldous called it. Cool though he became to praise or blame, praise from that quarter then delighted him. Thanking the master, he used the identical Victorianism Bruce Richmond had used about himself: "Such a charming and all too generous letter from such a tremendous swell is an honour . . .

. . It also gave me a great deal of pleasure and encouragement, your letter. Thank you very much indeed.

Aldous was even moved to refer to his own circumstances.

Quant à moi, I am very securely wedded and possess a son of two years old, whom I shall train up to be an engineer or a capitalist—none of this literary business—with a view to being supported, during my declining years, in a state of cultured ease.

That year Aldous was elected a member of the Athenaeum Club, proposed by his father and seconded by Professor Raleigh whose lectures on Elizabethan literature he used to attend at Oxford.

Aldous very rarely discussed work in progress so that when we find him sending a draft MS to his father inviting comment, we can surely take it as an indication that their adult relationship (always affectionate) was a good deal more positive than has sometimes been said.

Dearest Father,
I enclose the story about the nun I told you about. ["Nuns at luncheon", one of the stories Aldous was writing to fill up that volume for the spring.] My impression is that the . . . sexo-religious psychology of the beginning is too long and that the story wd be better remodelled so as to give only the anecdote itself, very quickly and sharply.

Leonard Huxley, it must be remembered, was a most able—possibly underrated—literary man; and certainly in that domain was taken au sérieux by his son. "He was the perfect editor," writes John Murray who worked as his assistant on the *Cornhill Magazine* as a young man.

So firm was his basis of literary scholarship that he could afford to be gentle and humble in dealing with authors of every age or degree of experience or conceit. The gentleness caused me continual problems because, when dealing with his letters, I often did not know if the author's contribution had to be sent to the printer for proofing or returned as a rejection. So gentle and firmly helpful was he that many years later a contributor to the *Cornhill* told me that he preferred a letter of rejection from Leonard Huxley to one of acceptance from any other editor. It was L. H.'s humility and the self-effacing quality of his editorial handling of, for example, the work of Elizabeth and Robert Browning, Jane Welsh Carlyle and Captain Scott of the Antarctic that denied him the public recognition that was his due.[1]

At 50 Albemarle Street, where then as now the *Cornhill* was edited, "business and pleasure were indistinguishably blended". Aldous occasionally called. "It always seemed to me surprising that they were father and son. Perhaps it was Leonard's litheness of body and mind and Aldous's short-sightedness that were partly responsible for an apparent levelling of age, but it was the way in which they conversed, and disagreed, that strengthened the illusion. And when, on visits to the Leonard Huxleys' home in Hampstead on pleasure, or on *Cornhill* business, Julian and his step-mother were also present, the illusion of a single generation was complete."[1]

Aldous and Maria lived in the Paddington flat for a whole year, black-beetles, journalism and all, a very pleasant one. Aldous kept loose office hours at Rolls House, E.C.4 and was pretty busy writing articles on heterogeneous subjects, drumming up ideas and contributors (he solicited Norman Douglas, Lytton Strachey), even sketching covers; but he was not hounded any longer, there was some leisure and a bit of time for odds and ends of his own; his health, and Maria's, was not radiant, it seldom was—and Matthew too was often ill or believed to be ill as a child—but for London they were all fairly well. They had stimulating and attractive friends. ("We kept *table ouverte* in those early days," Maria used to say, wondering how they did it.) Theirs was still rather a hand-to-mouth existence. When Jeanne got married that April, they were unable to send their small wedding present till the week after. Then, Maria wrote, they would send three English notes, three pound notes, which Jeanne should be able to change—those were the years of the monster inflations in Europe—at a good rate. And they must come and stay, Jeanne and Moulaert, any time they please, *avec joie*, there will always be beds for them and rice *à discretion*—"*Que faut-il de plus?*"

[1] From a letter of John Murray to S. B., 1971.

They were young. Domestic life at Westbourne Terrace was gay. From Suzanne, who came to live with them for some months, we get a memory of it as fresh as paint. Suzanne, nineteen then, had a yet undirected talent (she became of course a sculptress) and Aldous and Maria wanted to assist her training. (Moreover, the poor girl needed a change of scene having lately been involved in a rather macabre incident, a piece of family lore treasured by Aldous. A rejected suitor—Suzanne was of angelic beauty—upon hearing the final No, shot himself in the Nys's drawing-room. Her father, on hearing a pistol shot, came out of his study to find a young man, smoking weapon by his side, lying on the carpet in his blood. "This is inconceivable!" Monsieur Nys exclaimed. The expiring young man opened his lips: "Monsieur it *is* conceivable.") In London, Suzanne was given a bed in Aldous's room, separated from his by a screen. Aldous produced ideas and sketches for magazine covers, she was to turn them into commercial copy. There were elliptic Boromini staircases, façades of the Acropolis adorned by *jeunes filles en fleurs,* and there was the black and white cover, over which she laboured long and hard and which was finally accepted by Naomi Royde Smith (who paid £10)—a piece of Negro sculpture set next to a white plaster statuette of Queen Victoria. As for Maria, "Coccola was adorable. She did everything to encourage me . . ." Suzanne helped with the housework, moth-balling winter clothes, getting the evening meal (breakfast and luncheon were produced by Matthew's Bella and there was a Mrs Jones to do the cleaning). Things that Suzanne would have shirked at home became a pleasure with Maria,

. . devenaient une fête et aussi m'ont rendue un peu plus pratique plus tard, dans mon ménage.

She was not allowed, however, to wash up having once been caught out not plunging soapy plates into pure water. Always wonderfully soignée, Maria had now become competent as well. She sewed beautifully—as many people do who were taught by nuns—and was making her own hats and dresses. Even the food had become sensible (for the time being): they did not live on rice alone nor on the grapes and lettuce leaves of wartime Florence; Aldous had a proper breakfast every morning, porridge with fresh cream, tea, bacon and eggs.

On Thursdays Naomi Royde Smith, Osbert, Sacheverell and Edith Sitwell came to dinner and afterwards they all went to the cinema. On other evenings they had Jack[1] and Mary Hutchinson,

---

[1] The late St John Hutchinson, K.C.

Sullivan,[1] Mark Gertler, Tommy Earp. When they were by themselves Aldous and Maria would dance to the gramophone after
dinner, foxtrots, tangoes, with Matthew following in their steps
clinging on to one of Aldous's trouser legs. (When Joan Collier
Buzzard came to see them, Matthew would meet her in the hall,
take her hand and say, "Come, I will show you Daddy.")

Aldous took a certain pleasure in his clothes, which he wore
with casual elegance. He was then and always mildly, idio-
syncratically dandified. His suits were made by a good London
tailor (Studd and Millington for a long time); they were never
blue or pin-striped or a solid colour, they were speckled, softly
patterned, snuff coloured, cinammon coloured or what Maria
called a nice brownsey grey. (Incidentally he looked very well in
dark and plain, and irresistible in tails—Aldous would have made
the most distinguished looking conductor who ever stood on
platform.) He wore a waistcoat and a watch-and-chain. His
shirts, soft collars, were usually white and his socks always white.
His ties often verged on the cubist or the floral. Sometimes he
wore a snake-skin tie, or was it a lizard tie? and I don't think
that he as much as owned an Eton one. In later years he wore
no hat—except occasionally a French beret—but then he still
sported a black hat with a very large brim indeed, to all effects
a sombrero. "Here", the St John Hutchinson's young children
would cry when they saw his long form ambling up their garden
path, "Here comes the Quangle-Wangle!"

Their poor alley cat died. (Aldous evoked her in *Those Barren
Leaves:* Mr Cardan is alone in church at Montefiascone with the
body of Grace Elver, the moron who has died of fish poisoning,
on a bier.

> Once, years ago, he had a . . . cat. She ate too many black-beetles
> in the kitchen and died vomiting shreds of her shard-torn stomach.
> He had often thought of that cat. One might die like that oneself,
> coughing up one's vitals.)

Now, Aldous acquired one of his perennial loves, a Siamese,
who did not live in the kitchen but attached itself to him. They
played together and when Aldous went back to writing the
creature would settle itself snugly on his neck.

Mark Gertler asked Suzanne to sit for him in the house on
Hampstead Heath that he shared with Dorothy Brett. (There
she saw Brett—listening to them through a great copper ear-
trumpet.) Pocket money having run out, Maria allowed Suzanne

[1] The late J. N. W. Sullivan [Mathematician, music critic and scientific
journalist].

2/6d. a week out of the house-keeping for the bus fare but had warned her of Gertler:

"Méfie toi car il embrasse les filles derrière les portes." Doubtlessly, Suzanne adds, "a memory of the time she was at Lady Ottoline's." She found Gertler charming. He did not kiss behind doors—"tout beau comme il était, pareil à un personnage de Carpaccio," and she soon met the young woman he was head over heels in love with, Carrington. Gertler did two portraits of Suzanne; between sittings they walked on the Heath, lay on the grass, he talking to her about Chekov, about life at Garsington, telling her not to go there (someone had suggested her as young Julian Morrell's companion).

Aldous was still doing concert notices for the *Westminster Gazette:* Suzanne usually went with him. On the bus he would talk to her, on his own level, about music, literature and art.

> Aldous prenait à cœur de m'éduquer, de me donner des conseils, souvent par l'intermédiaire de Coccola . . . Aldous avait la courtoisie et la politesse de son éducation d'origine victorienne, malgré l'influence de la révolution dans les mœurs à Garsington . . . Quoique Aldous était cérébralement agnostique, libertin et sceptique, de nature il était timide, donc peu entreprenant, un peu hypocrite et très critique, tout en étant plein d'égards pour les gens les plus simples telle la femme à journée, Mrs Jones.

After a concert Aldous and Suzanne would find Maria waiting up in her large divan bed, where "on s'installait tous les trois," and the sisters would take turns in reading aloud to Aldous *Les Voyages du Père Huc au Tibet,* after which Suzanne went off to sleep behind the screen in Aldous's room. Sometimes she would perceive Aldous late at night creeping about the dark, get a bottle out of a cupboard and take a swig. "Je croyais que c'était un 'night cap'. Ma mère prétendait toujours que les anglais buvaient dans leur chambre à coucher, surtout les femmes, même de l'eau-de Cologne . . ."

She was much relieved when she discovered that the bottle in the cupboard was a cough mixture. Often Aldous and Suzanne, each on their side of the screen, had nocturnal conversations. He told her stories from the Bible and one night when the flat was cold he told the story of King David and Bathsheba. "Je lui disait que c'était dommage qu'il n'était pas David et on finissait par s'endormir chacun de son côté du paravent avec regret."

Suzanne summed up those months with Aldous and Maria— "in their atmosphere of perfect lovingness"—as one of the most harmonious of her life. There was one anxiety, Maria's when Aldous was abroad in the London traffic on his own. (His bicycling terrified her, yet she never stopped him.) When friends left after dinner he liked to walk them home; one night when he was late returning, Suzanne saw Maria stand in tears by the front door.

In May, only six months after *Crome Yellow*, *Mortal Coils*, Aldous's second book of short stories, appeared. It contained what has become one of his best known stories, "The Gioconda Smile", the story he re-wrote—with such changes of emphasis and range —twenty-five years later as a play. It also contained a good deal of 1922 Aldous. To quote once more from *son semblable, son frère*, Sidney Dolphin the poet:

> His two volumes of verse, "Zoetrope" and "Trembling Ears", have been recognized by intelligent critics as remarkable. How far they are poetry nobody, least of all Dolphin himself, is certain. They may be merely the ingenious products of a very cultured and elaborate brain. Mere curiosities; who knows? His age is twenty-seven.

And here another character compliments Dolphin on his philosophical detachment, " 'Brooding on the universe as usual?'

> 'My philosophical detachment? But it's only a mask to hide the ineffectual longings I have to achieve contact with the world.'

Crome Yellow, meanwhile, had been earning its advance, and Aldous was being paid royalties. The book sold 2,500 copies in the first year and 86 the year after. (*This Side of Paradise*, Scott Fitzgerald's first novel published the year before, sold forty-five thousand.) Cash in hand, Aldous enrolled Suzanne in an art course he had seen advertised in *Vogue*.

All good things come to an end. First Matthew left with Bella to visit her family in what was now Poland. Then Maria went off, bound for Paris and Forte. For a while Suzanne kept house for Aldous and made the Siamese cat's nauseous dinner of boiled cods' heads as instructed. Then Aldous, too, went to join Maria, and Suzanne alone remained behind to finish her art course after seeing Aldous off one fine morning, cat in basket, from Victoria station.

Chapter Three

Proboque, Deteriora Sequor

THE publishing agreement with Chatto & Windus which was to have such an effect upon Aldous's literary and material life was not signed until January 1923. However, the main principle—a regular income enabling him to give up jobs and journalism and devote all his energies to his own writing—must have been under discussion, and very likely settled in rough detail, several months before. This seems to be borne out by Aldous's and Maria's moves.

Another stretch of summer at Forte, another villa, reunited with Baby "splendidly well" after his travels, preceded by a little travelling on their own: Salzburg Mozart festival, expenses footed by the *Westminster*; a day or two in Vienna where they were so appalled by what they saw of post-war misery that the memory of it still beclouded their views on European revival in the 1940s; their first sight of Venice. In the autumn they returned to London, having made up their minds to settle down in England. First, half-heartedly, it was to be the country, then became London after all. By the new year they had moved house, to Kensington this time, to 44 Princess Gardens, the first of their more conventional abodes. Aldous was able to invite Suzanne in these positive terms, ". . . When are you coming to stay with us again? We can offer you le confort moderne in this house: no horrors of the kind which abounded at Westbourne Terrace. Do come."

The "MEMORANDUM of AGREEMENT Made this Eighth Day of January Nineteen Twenty-Three between Aldous Huxley of the one part and Messrs Chatto & Windus of 97 & 99 St. Martin's Lane, London W.C.2 . . ." was clear, uncomplicated and, by today's standards, brief. The substance was contained in two clauses, numbers One and Six.

1) The Author agrees to supply the Publishers with two new works of fiction per annum (one of which two works shall be a full-length novel) written by himself during the next three years.

6) The Publishers agree to pay the Author for the period of three years . . . . the sum of Five Hundred Pounds per annum . . . such sum to be considered an advance on account of royalties upon the earnings of the Author's books.

Financially, the arrangement was almost perfect. Five hundred certain was a reasonable basic income; three years were a reasonably solid chunk of time. And this was only the foundation: Aldous was retaining his American rights—*Limbo, Crome Yellow, Mortal Coils* and *Leda* were already published in the United States[1] —and there was a reassuring and flexible option clause:

7) On the termination of the period of the three years aforesaid, the Publishers shall have the option of making another contract with the Author for a further period of three years on similar lines or as may be otherwise mutually agreed.

The arrangement was also realistic. Aldous was not paid so much that he need fear accumulating debt; no-one was doing a Mr Micawber in expecting the advance to be safely overtaken by the sales. The royalty scale was excellent: starting on works of fiction with 15%; rising to 20% after the first two thousand copies sold; and to 25% after eight thousand.[2]

So far, so good. There was the other side to the arrangement, the obligation to produce two books a year. Two books of fiction, what is more, and one of them a full-length novel; two books a year for three years running, six books in fact in a row, commonplace enough to the Victorians, but what writer of today—of similar talent and literary conscience—would, *could*, take on such an engagement? Yet that kind of contract in those post-war years was by no means rare.

Aldous did not quake. He had formed the habit of meeting date-lines under the most trying conditions; he had written a novel in two months (a daily average of a thousand words); even if he were to write the next ones at, say, half that rate he would still have more time on hand for living than he had had since he left Oxford. As for subjects—he was beginning to spread his wings and what he wanted to explore must have seemed inexhaustible at that point. Novels do not feel so difficult to write when one is young.

The books were supposed to be delivered in January and July each year "commencing July 1923". (Quarterly payments had begun that April.) During the course of the winter Aldous still had some decks to clear, finish off his journalistic commitments and wind up at Condé Nast's. "But I can see an end to it," he wrote to Suzanne in February. "After April I shall be able to write what I want."

---

[1] By Doran.
[2] Royalties on non-fiction—essays, poetry, drama—were rather lower: 10% on the first 1,000; 15% on the next 2,000 copies; 20% thereafter.

To write what I want. The wish that had been echoing through the years of lonely schoolmastering without prospects, the years of treading time. "*. . I want to marry and settle down to write . . . What I want more than anything really is to get a year with nothing to do except to write.*" And now at last Aldous might say that he had his wish (*quant à moi, I am very securely wedded . . .*) He was nearly twenty-nine; he had come a long way since the days he mooned in digs shared with a chatty old clergyman.

Yet it is doubtful that Aldous drew much solace from that reflection. The thought of our past sufferings does little more to alleviate our present ones than does the thought of earthquake in Peru. It is doubtful that Aldous during that winter and spring of 1923 gave any thought to his former condition. There is no end, it would seem, to the tricks the gods may play. Nor does the bolt from the blue come always in the form of tragedy: "There are confessable agonies," Aldous wrote five years later on, "sufferings of which one can positively be proud. Of bereavement, of parting, of the sense of sin and the fear of death the poets have eloquently spoken. They command the world's sympathy. But there are also discreditable anguishes, no less excruciating than the others, but of which the sufferer dare not, cannot speak."

It was May and of the novel to be delivered to Chatto & Windus in July not a word was down. What had happened was that Aldous had fallen in love with Nancy Cunard. Madly in love, "Against reason, against all his ideals and principles, madly, against his own wishes, even against his own feelings . . ."[1]

Nancy Cunard. It is difficult not to say either too much about her or too little. There are many—they will become more numerous—who have never heard of her; there are those who know of her as a valiant, or a strident figure on the margin of our recent history, know about her anthology *Negroe* and her early and passionate championship of that cause, of the Hours Press, the association with the French surréalist movement, the public brawl with her mother (her White Ladyship), the involvement with the Spanish Civil War; remember perhaps the great friendships with George Moore and Norman Douglas, have read her poetry and her books on those two men. There are those who knew her. To us she was the friend one loved, whose arrival one often dreaded. She always astonished: never for a second was it possible not to be aware of Nancy. Now that she is no more, she is still loved: better perhaps, more safely, than when our existences could be swept by her actual turbulent presence. Nancy, impeccably outrageously extravagantly courageous, generous, violent, self-destructive, fanatically wrong-headed, waywardly elegant,

---

[1] *Point Counter Point*, 1928.

incarnately alluring, was unique. What struck first was her appearance, and her appearance was itself a condensation of her temperament, her comportment, her ideals.

> Nancy Cunard was a fiery and furious angel, like the angel in Mathias Grunewald's triptique or the angel in Rainer Maria Rilke's *Elegies*—a terrible messenger descending with a fiery sword upon bourgeois hypocrisy and those ignorant persons who discriminate between race or colour of skin . . . If as Dante wrote, "Heaven and hell reject the lukewarm", Nancy will certainly come into her own.[1]

What did she actually look like?

> Miss Nancy Cunard is wonderful, made of alabaster and gold and scarlet, with a face like Donatello's Saint George . . . [Mary Hutchinson in a letter of 1919. And in 1924:[2]] . . Behind [her façade] one seems to see a shadow moving—an independent, romantic and melancholy shadow which one can never approach; the façade is exquisite, made of gold leaf, lacquer, verdigris and ivory.

She was often painted (not very well); there are many telling photographs; the most quintessential remains Cecil Beaton's taken when Nancy was thirty-four. There she is with her extraordinary eyes—arctic blue, tiger's eyes, triangular eyes shaped like arrow-heads, with their "*regard* (there is no English word meaning not only the eyes . . . but the way in which they confront the visible world)"[3] with her thinness—"she was dangerously thin," and her carapace of African bracelets. What the portrait cannot give are Nancy's walk and Nancy's voice.

> First and instant impression—tigress-dragonfly. No: cheetah . . . Then, seated, one *heard* her . . . Nancy's voice was a miracle. And so was the way she walked . . . she flowed swiftly forward, as I have said like a cheetah, and also like a slim and splendid fish.[4]

> The mixture of delicacy and steel in her build, hips, legs, ankles all of the slenderest, weighed with massive ivory bracelets . . . that they seemed too fragile to support . . . the head held high with its short fair hair, and one foot placed exactly in front of the other, not with mannequin languor, but spontaneously, briskly, boldly, skimming the pavement.[3]

---

1 Allanah Harper in *Nancy Cunard: Brave Poet Indomitable Rebel*, edited by Hugh Ford. Chilton Book Company, 1968.
2 Mary Hutchinson in op. cit.
3 Raymond Mortimer in op. cit.
4 Kenneth Macpherson in op. cit.

> Whatever she did, however violent she was, Nancy always looked more distinguished than other people.[1]

Nancy Cunard was born in 1896. She was thus two years younger than Aldous, whom she survived again for two years. Her father was Sir Bache Cunard (of the shipping line), though it is likely that her natural father was in fact George Moore; her mother, a legend in her own right, was Maud (later Emerald) Lady Cunard, born and raised in the American West. Nancy was brought up as a member of the ultra rich but soon managed to put an end to that. She wrote and published a foolish and insulting pamphlet about her mother, *Black Man and White Ladyship*, resulting in a life-long breach and her cutting herself off from the family money. It was generally assumed that Lady Cunard had stopped Nancy's allowance, in fact she never ceased to provide her daughter with an income: it accumulated in a bank in Nancy's name, untouched, unacknowledged, over the decades. Nancy, in her integrity or intransigence, lived in poverty, often squalid poverty. It hardly seemed to affect her. What little money came her way she gave to her friends, to artists, to refugees. She lived in rudimentary cottages in France, in cheap hotel bedrooms all over the world; her clothes often came from thriftshops and street markets; she had no possessions besides a few paintings, books and her collection of African bracelets. She hardly ate. Like Maria, she had that partly moral loathing of food; her only material wants were drink (cheap red wine) and cigarettes; her true mainstay was her own emotions and these went into causes, friends and lovers. The causes sometimes suffered. "Nancy's back: We're in trouble!" the cry would go up in Harlem. "Hold on to your hats, kids, Nancy's back."

> There was no middle way for Nancy. She was *entière*, as the French would say. She had an innocent, an almost naïve belief in the causes she so strongly upheld. She seemed incapable of abstract reflection; or of separating political reality from her own emotional conception.[2]

Nancy became *persona non grata* in the United States; the Loyalists' defeat in Spain affected her as a personal grief; during the Second World War her little house in Normandy was vandalized by occupying Germans and, more bitter to her, by local French collaborationists. As time went on, her gallant wanderings —in cargo boats, in third-class railway carriages—seemed to become more desperate; the man or two she always had in tow was still young, but her hold over men was diminishing and her

---

[1] Allanah Harper in op. cit.   [2] Ibid.

need for their company was not, and sometimes they were not very nice to her. She believed herself persecuted—by the ever-present bogies, the bourgeois and the police—and indeed she got into bad trouble, in England of all places, with the law (a breach, "how not!" of the peace). She looked emaciated; she was beginning to be very ill (emphysema, a broken hip that would not mend), and defied it all, would not keep still, it was not Nancy who would go gently into that good night. And yet in those last years there were moments when she could be ruefully mild, strangely tolerant, defeated and undefeated at the same time. Ultimately, Nancy Cunard was a tragic figure. With exquisite aptness, Allanah Harper quotes these lines from Léon Paul Fargue, a poet loved by Nancy.

> *Gare de la douleur, j'ai fait toutes tes routes.*
> *Je ne peux plus aller, je ne peux plus partir.*
> *J'ai traîné sous tes ciels, j'ai crié sous tes voûtes.*

All that was still a long way into the future in 1923 when Aldous hung about Nancy Cunard and her entourage through the London nights. She was in her gilded youth, a divorcée, independent, madly attractive to men, spoilt. ("You are late, Nancy." "But *of course*, darling.") Her energies in those days went into poetry—her own much influenced by T. S. Eliot's—not politics, her rebellion against her upbringing, against the luxury of her mother's house, against chaperones and chastity and the conventional morality of the time. Nancy and her bright friends were part of the vanguard of the post-war Twenties. Her daily existence was hectic; pleasure, the pursuit. There was already the shadow. The 1914 War had bitten very deep into the world of Nancy's generation, she was shaken early in her personal life. A charming and handsome young man called Peter Broughton-Adderley whom she had been in love with, was killed in the last months of the war; Nancy got married, briefly, disastrously, to a man of her mother's choice.

One cannot say exactly when Aldous fell for Nancy. No records of this episode have emerged. Aldous did not speak of it; on Nancy it left small mark. What remains are his own transparent generalizations scattered through the novels, wisps of the gossip of the time, and what Maria told to a few friends. Jeanne knew, and Mimi Gielgud and Costanza; Maria talked to Juliette and to Moura Budberg[1] and later on to me. Aldous then fell in love with Nancy sometime in 1922; possibly in the autumn after

---

[1] Baroness Budberg, an intimate friend.

his return from Italy. It almost certainly lasted less than a year and longer than six months. They had known each other since 1917; one recalls Aldous's rather *de haut en bas* reference when he was first contributing to the Sitwell's *Wheels* ". . in company with such illustrious young persons like Miss Nancy Cunard," and though Nancy was in Paris a good deal they must have met often enough with their mutual friends on their mutual round, the Sitwells, Eliot, Earp, the Hutchinsons, the Trees at the Café Royal, the Eiffel Tower. It was not a passion, then, at first sight; nor was it mutual. Aldous's feelings were unrequited—the unconfessable agony, the discreditable anguish he speaks about in *Point Counter Point* was the anguish of thwarted desire.

Nancy went through a good many lovers; she had the kind of bad reputation, that aura of casual lasciviousness, that can be an added bait. To Aldous it was the ultimate of the pendulum swing of his flight from puritanism, beyond the liberations of Garsington, beyond Maria's serene Latin sensuality. But if Nancy was promiscuous she was also capricious, and she was choosy. What she wanted were men who were more than a match for her, strong men, brutes. Aldous simply was not her type. He was far too gentle, too unexcessive and, with her, too hang-dog, too love-sick. Unfortunately for him she happened to like him and enjoy his company. If she did not strictly lead him on, she did not let him go.

> Tiresome as he was, his love-sickness did at least make him faithful. That, for Lucy, was important. She was afraid of loneliness and needed her cavalier servants in constant attendance. Walter attended with dog-like fidelity. But why was he so like a *whipped* dog sometimes? So abject. What a fool![1]

He was obsessed, and remained lucid. He observed as an intelligent, disapproving helpless parent might observe the aberrations of a son without being able to deflect the son's pursuits. He went on wanting Nancy, as he had said, against his principles, ideals and reason, even against his own feelings. "For he did not like Lucy, he really hated her."[1]

Aldous had little interest in Nancy, the individual. What engaged him was a distillation of her sexual power, the erotic and exquisite façade: the voice, the look, the walk.

> The strong gardenia perfume was in his nostrils; he was breathing what was for him the very essence of her being, the symbol of her power, of his own insane desires. He looked at her with a kind of terror.[1]

[1] *Point Counter Point.*

He looked at her with a kind of terror. It was thus that Aldous nightly sat at Nancy's crowded table in a public place. After dawn he walked home to Maria awake and waiting.

Life at Princess Gardens was at a standstill. Days were dominated by whether Nancy had telephoned or not. Maria not only suffered from the conventional reaction—though already then she was lightly, wisely tolerant of "infidelities"—she was disoriented: Aldous was behaving so unlike himself, and he was so unhappy. She saw little of him (he was still at Condé Nast's) and when he was at home he was dumbly miserable. Maria was sorry for him but he also infuriated her. Nancy represented all she most feared in English life, the attitudes and morals of a certain world; and to this one has to add her invincible anxiety for Aldous's safety when he was out and late. At one time she went abroad waiting for events to take shape. At another, Nancy and Aldous had a brief affair. Nancy gave in, out of affection, exasperation; after a few days discarded him. Once, for a whole night, he paced the street below her window.

There were intermissions. Nancy was out of England for some of that winter; Aldous made an attempt to follow her but she put him off. In April he joined Maria for a few weeks in Florence. But when he got back to London, there was Nancy. On top of it all he was feeling more and more ill. Nightlife was constitutionally poisonous to him; he could never stand hot crowded places, stale air and the smells of food and whisky (nor could or ever did he drink himself; anything beyond a glass or two of wine would make him queasy). Then one day there came a stop to the whole thing. Maria told the story to me some ten or twelve years after the event. She told it in a spirit of reminiscence and also with a view to educating me. I listened, I was at an impressionable age, I was learning something about Aldous, I listened with all my ears. Maria may have been telling the literal sequence of events, she may have been giving a revised memory. This is what she told me. One evening—she gave no month or date, that was not her way, but the impression was one of a long light evening in late spring—Aldous came home to Princess Gardens looking miserable and ill. Maria was seized by sudden resolution. She put an ultimatum then and there. She would leave England the next morning with him or without; for him to make up his mind, but he must make up his mind *now*. They packed all night. That is, Maria packed; Aldous hovered, sat on the lids of trunks, tried to read, scribbled in a little book; when allowed gave a hand. Maria was getting more and more exhausted and there seemed to be no end of objects to be packed. At first light she opened a window and threw out every article that was still about. Whether they fell into the street or a front garden was not clear; one does not interrupt such tales. Nor can I say what happened to the furniture or the keys, or whether the trunks went with them in the cab or were picked up later on by Thomas Cook's. All I was told is that in the morning, unslept, unbreakfasted, in the clothes they stood in, Aldous and Maria left the house, drove to Victoria and caught the first train out of England.

They went straight to Italy. There, in two months, Aldous wrote *Antic Hay*. He wrote it all down, Maria said, he wrote it all out; it was over. He never looked back. The possession—that one descent of Até—left a mark on his novels; not his marriage.

Chapter Four

The Second Novel—*Antic Hay*

ALDOUS wrote practically no letters between October 1922 and July 1923, or at least few have come to light. Only six appear in the published edition: one to Suzanne, one to E. S. P. Haynes, neither of them long, the other four mere notes. The next full-fledged letter is dated 2nd July. It is to Robert Nichols and contains this opening paragraph:

> I am ashamed at my remissness in not having written to you before ... I was leaving England in rather a hurry—Maria not having been at all well, and we deciding all of a sudden to get away out of the piercing English spring and the odious tumult of London into warmth and peace ... and ever since I have been in Italy I have been so wildly busy tapping on this machine for my living—a book to be finished by the beginning of August and hardly ten words on paper before I started.

Aldous and Maria were at Forte staying with the Fasolas and the book was going well enough to be thinking about plans, they were arranging to take a villa outside Florence on a long lease from September. "We are proposing to settle, more or less permanently—as far as any arrangement with us is ever permanent —in Italy ..."

It is a choice of sunshine, dust, grapes and scirocco—not to mention icy winters in imperfectly warmed houses—as against grey days and mud. The house itself was presented by circumstances; Castel Montici, the house Maria had lived in during the war with her mother and sisters was for rent again; the view was incomparable, disadvantages known. So "There I shall settle down to grind out two yearly books of fiction for Chatto's and any other thing I can manage. The life, I think, ought to be agreeable and one's money goes nearly twice as far as in London. I shall come back to civilization a few months each year to find out what is going on."

By August the novel was finished and the MS posted off. Once more Aldous had written the best part of a hundred thousand words in two months. He and Maria were able to go to Belgium where they were expected for her grandparents' Golden Wedding at St Trond. They found the family assembled in strength: Maria's father, Mère, the George Baltus's and the Raymond Baltus's,

Jeanne with her husband and little girl, Matthew and his cousin Ado Baltus, Suzanne and Rose. Suzanne had just become engaged and brought her fiancé, a charming looking young Dutchman, trained as a lawyer who had chosen to be a painter: Joep Nicolas. They were photographed, jubilants to baby-in-arms, in a group on the lawn, and there was of course a Gargantuan repast. There was also music. It was the unexpected produced so often by that family ("some make cloth, some make sugar . . . a few are very cultivated, the rest not at all"). George Baltus had arranged for the Pro Arte Quartet from Brussels and they played music very rarely heard yet at that time, Vivaldi, Pergolesi, Josquin des Près, Pierre de la Rue. "It was a revelation," Suzanne writes, "even for Aldous." There were long afternoon walks across country through the Flemish fields and orchards; the two future brothers-in-law took their first liking to one another, Joep discovering Aldous's conversation, Aldous Joep's painting, "Suzanne," he said, "has chosen well." But it was too hot and Aldous who was still tired developed a "sort of suppressed jaundice". Feeling pretty wretched, he travelled back to Italy with Maria, Matthew and Bella "in a heat wave of the first magnitude". In the train young Matthew kept howling for water.

> . . You used the word *wasser* [Maria recalled that journey in a letter to him twenty-five years later] . . . to our despair . . when there was none to give you. I even got so despaired that I ran out to fill the thermos to find out that it was the tap of the "eau non potable" so Bella would not give it to you. I might have to keep you quiet . . You were so loud. So I can never forget it.

At Milan, they escaped from that train, and next morning picked up the motor car they had ordered. It was their first. Aldous had deliberately saved the money to buy it, Maria had just learnt to drive. (She had passed the test, the first woman in Italy to obtain a driving licence.) The car was a 10 h.p. four-seater Citroën. They set out, the first of a thousand such journeys, in the cool of the evening, rested at Forte (Aldous still gloomy and nursing his jaundice), left child and Bella with the Fasolas, and went on to Florence and their new home on Montici.

It was still frightfully hot and there was a bad drought and trouble with the electric water pump; they had to do everything themselves and their trunks were slow in turning up. But the inside of the house was cool and certainly spacious: four rooms downstairs, one of them a *salone* twenty-five feet square, six bedrooms, several waterless baths, a study in the tower, a balcony-terrace running the breadth of the house. And the prodigious view from five hundred feet above the town—the view of Florence and the Arno valley up to the Apennines.

In a matter of weeks they are straightened out, have servants; Matthew is with them, Aldous recovered and Maria too getting reasonably well. "We are firmly settled here once more and very busy." Writing and reading; writing regularly, but at an agreeable pace (six months to go before the next book is due, and it is going to be short stories). Aldous is in fact at work on "Uncle Spencer" and "Young Archimedes".[1]

Summer "still lingers deliciously". Occasionally, they descend into Florence to see Norman Douglas or Geoffrey Scott.

> It is so pleasant up on our hill, that one rarely feels tempted to venture into the town, even for the sake of seeing pleasant people . . .

And there was the stupendous discovery of Italy. They drove to Rome.

> We went by Arezzo and Cortona—grim Etruscan town on an immense mountain with a view over Trasimene—stopping the first night at Chiusi . . . Orvieto . . Montefiascone . . . what a town! Two thousand feet up, a hill crowned by an immense Renaissance cupola looking over the perfectly circular bright blue lake of Bolsena . . to Viterbo over the volcanic hills past the incredible Lago di Vico and then on, through the Campagna, . . to Rome.

Tivoli, Frascati, Albano, Neni, Ostia . . . They went back along the Tiber valley "over a range of perfectly enormous mountains —hugely high and quite barren . . .

> apparently a way which no knowing motorist ever takes, owing to the terrible climbing . . . and the complete absence of any assistance if you break down.

Fortunately, "our little Citroën did the whole thing without turning a hair". On over the Somma pass to Spoleto, through the plains of Clitumnus, past Trevi, past Assisi ("Saw the Giottos —and my word . . .") to Perugia and by Trasimene back to Florence. It was the journey, almost exactly the Italian journey, of *Those Barren Leaves*.

These were good days; a stretch of time in mid-life when the present is satisfying and the ultimate threats still far off. There were reminders: Costanza's mother incurably ill, a question of

---

[1] *Little Mexican,* 1924.

months. And there was the world, the post-war world of unemployment, inflation, revolution, led or handled by Poincaré, Baldwin, Lenin, Mussolini, President Harding. "I try to disinterest myself from politics [Aldous to Julian] but really, when things are in the state they are, one can't help feeling a little concerned . . . Society can less and less afford to be governed by imbeciles or even by charlatans of genius . . . These monsters will end up by making such a mess that we shall all suffer."

Antic Hay was published that November. Aldous's second novel came very near the knuckle. It reflected, perhaps crystallized, attitudes of the time, and many young people began to see and judge in Huxleyan terms. Sir Isaiah Berlin,[1] speaks of Aldous as one of the great culture heroes of his youth, and the transforming power of the early Huxley, "the 'cynical', God-denying Huxley, the object of fear and disapproval . . . the wicked nihilist . . . [the delight of] those young readers who supposed themselves to be indulging in one of the most dangerous and exotic vices of those iconoclastic post-war times . . ."

Friends and strangers wrote to Aldous; the novel sold well (5,000 copies within a year of publication). Again Aldous's own family shared the disapproval. "I am sorry [he wrote to his father from Florence] you should have found my book so distasteful." He had no desire, he went on, to enter into argument as they would be starting from entirely different premises. *Antic Hay*,

. . is a book written by a member of what I may call the war-generation for others of his kind; and . . it is intended to reflect—fantastically, of course, but none the less faithfully—the life and opinions of an age which has seen the violent disruption of almost all the standards, conventions and values current in the previous epoch.

The book is, I may say without fatuity, a good book. It is also a very serious book. Artistically, too, is has a certain novelty . . all the ordinarily separated categories—tragic, comic, fantastic, realistic—are combined . . into a single entity, whose unfamiliar character makes it appear at first sight rather repulsive.

I can't say that I expected you would enjoy the book . . . I expected that my contemporaries would; and so far as I know by what people have written to me, they have.

And there, I think, I had better leave it, only pausing long enough to express my surprise that you should accuse me, when I speak of a young man's tender recollections of his dead mother, of botanizing on my mother's grave.

[1] *Mem. Vol.*

The young man is of course Theodore Gumbril Jr., he of the Patent Small-Clothes and the artificial beard, the protagonist of *Antic Hay*, not Aldous's *alter ego* to be sure, but a young man with a good infusion of Aldous all the same. There he is meditating in the School Chapel while the Reverend Pelvey, M.A., is fog-horning away at the lesson. "Could it be that he had an answer and a clue? That was hardly believable. Particularly if one knew Mr Pelvey personally. And Gumbril did." Diligently unto thy children, the reverend intones and Gumbril remembers his own childhood, his mother. Her diligence had not been dogmatic. "She had just been . . good, that was all.

> Good; good? It was a word people only used nowadays with a kind of deprecating humorousness. . . . But good in any case, there was no getting out of that, good she had been . . . good. You felt the active radiance of her goodness when you were near her. And that feeling, was that less real and valid than two plus two?
> The Reverend Pelvey had nothing to reply. He was reading with holy gusto . . .
> She had been good and she had died when he was still a boy; died—but he hadn't been told that till much later—of creeping and devouring pain. Malignant disease—oh, *caro nome*!
> 'Thou shalt fear the Lord thy God,' said Mr Pelvey.[1]

It is curious to recall here Maria's assertion about *Antic Hay* as a means of exorcism. She was referring, of course, only to one, then all too recent, episode. "He wrote it all down. He wrote it all out." *Did he?* Nancy Cunard, a member of that war-generation *par excellence*, fitted into his theme. Aldous had to put in someone like her. But *is* the fictional Myra Viveash really in the least like Nancy? Both are wilful, dangerous, alluring and have lost the one young man they cared for in the war. Mrs Viveash has been given Nancy's voice and Nancy's walk.

> He watched her as she crossed the dirty street, placing her feet with a meticulous precision one after the other in the same straight line, as though she were treading a knife edge between goodness only knew what invisible gulfs. Floating she seemed to go, with a little spring at every step . . .[2]

There is also a version of the famous *regard*:

> Mrs Viveash . . turned on him . . her pale unwavering glance. Her eyes had a formidable capacity for looking and expressing nothing;

---

[1] *Antic Hay*, Chatto & Windus, 1923.   [2] Ibid

they were like the pale blue eyes which peer out of the Siamese cat's black-velvet mask.[1]

And yet Mrs Viveash is not so much Nancy Cunard disguised, as Nancy dis-individualized, turned into a type, a type, what is more, representing but a fragment of her personality. There is no trace of Nancy's fire and crazy idealism in that poised and sophisticated figure, none of her partisanships and her violence, no hint of any passionate involvement outside a personal universe of *ennui*, disillusion, lust and a little art. It is rather remarkable that Aldous did not even attempt to explore the character of the actual Nancy, that he showed no literary interest in anything that did not lend itself to a generalization. (Perhaps this was the way Aldous preferred, or was temperamentally compelled, to handle his raw material.) As for the personal episode, he wrote about it at arm's length as it were, in one passage firmly situated in the past—exorcism by way of the wrong end of the telescope. Another character, Shearwater, is about to fall for Mrs Viveash and Gumbril suddenly feels the need to speak. " 'There was a time,' he said in a tone that was quite unreally airy, off-hand and disengaged, 'years ago, when I totally lost my head about her. Totally.'

> Those tear-wet patches on his pillow . . . and oh, the horrible pain of weeping, vainly, for something that was nothing, that was everything in the world! 'Towards the end of the war it was. I remember walking up this dismal street one night, in the pitch darkness, writhing with jealousy.' He was silent. Spectrally, like a dim, haunting ghost, he had hung about her; dumbly, dumbly imploring, appealing. 'The weak, silent man', she used to call him. And once for two or three days, out of pity, out of affection, out of a mere desire, perhaps, to lay the tiresome ghost, she had given him what his mournful silence implored—only to take it back, almost as soon as accorded. That other night, when he had walked up this street before, desire had eaten out his vitals . . . That was a long time ago.

It was Aldous's ferocious sincerities, his iconoclasm, his scepticism that struck the readers of the time; few of them when they recall the early Huxley so much as remember that there were other trends. Yet even then, Aldous wrote this passage:

> . . . Gumbril took off his hat, breathed the soft air that smelt of the greenness of the garden.
> 'There are quiet places also in the mind', he said meditatively.

---

[1] *Antic Hay.*

4a   Aldous with his aunt
     Mrs Humphry Ward

b   Aldous with his father

5*a*   The four Nys sisters *c.* 1915: Maria; Rose; Suzanne; Jeanne

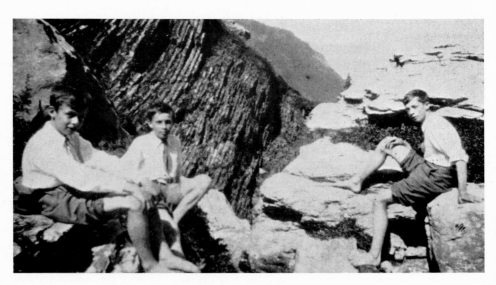

b   The Huxley Brothers *c.* 1905

'But we build bandstands and factories on them. Deliberately—to put a stop to the quietness . . . All the thoughts, all the preoccupations in my head—round and round, continually . . . What's it for? What's it all for? To put an end to the quiet, to break it up and disperse it, to pretend at any cost that it isn't there. Ah, but it is; it is there, in spite of everything, at the back of everything. Lying awake at night—not restlessly, but serenely, waiting for sleep—the quiet re-establishes itself, piece by piece; all the broken bits . . . we've been so busily dispersing all day long. It re-establishes itself, an inward quiet, like the outward quiet of grass and trees. It fills one, it grows—a crystal quiet, a growing, expanding crystal. It grows, it becomes more perfect; it is beautiful and terrifying . . . For one's alone in the crystal, and there's no support from outside, there's nothing external and important, nothing external and trivial to pull oneself up by or stand on . . . There's nothing to laugh at or feel enthusiastic about. But the quiet grows and grows. Beautifully and unbearably. And at last you are conscious of something approaching; it is almost a faint sound of footsteps. Something inexpressively lovely and wonderful advances through the crystal, nearer, nearer. And, oh, inexpressively terrifying. For if it were to touch you, if it were to seize and engulf you, you'd die; all the regular, habitual daily part of you would die . . . one would have to begin living arduously in the quiet, arduously in some strange, unheard of manner. Nearer, nearer come the steps; but one can't face the advancing thing. One daren't. . . .[1]

The passage has affinity with the opening lines of Paul Valéry's poem, *Les Pas*:

> *Tes pas, enfants de mon silence,*
> *Saintement, lentement placés,*
> *Vers le lit de ma vigilance*
> *Procèdent, muets et glacés.*

[1] *Antic Hay.*

Chapter Five
Santa Maria a Montici

THE Huxleys lived in Italy for rather more than four years. Seen as a whole those years were perhaps the most easy of their lives. They were also immensely enriching; Oxford, Garsington, London, followed by another education—in the Italian years the beloved pastime was travel, doors opened to the visual worlds of countryside and art. "C'est probablement l'Italie qui est le plus empreint dans ma visualité," Maria wrote in later life. What had so captivated her in 1917, the aesthetic sensations she had tried to present in her letters during their engagement, now came to Aldous and they were able to share a kind of impassioned sightseeing.

They always went by car. Aldous had found another interest: "If I had any strength of mind, I should stop talking about Citroëns and return to higher themes. But the temptation of talking about cars, when one has a car, is quite irresistible. Before I bought a Citroën no subject had less interest for me; none, now, has more."[1]

He read the motoring papers, technical brochures, reports of Grand Prix racing. He sat in the car, as he sat in all their subsequent ones, in the passenger seat, riveted as far back as it would go so that he might unfold his grasshopper's legs, peering through an assortment of optical glass at the landscapes whizzing by. At his side, Maria, slight as a jockey, drove. She drove very well. She brought to it the style and the control that might have gone into her dancing. She would get up at first light to wash and tend the car just as at Bellem as a girl she had got up to look after her horse. Maria became an outstanding driver, well up to professional standards, very precise, very safe, very fast. The speed was for Aldous's pleasure, the only new one, he used to say, mankind had invented since the palaeolithic age. Maria never drove in a race though this would have been tempting to a side of her; duty to Aldous and to Matthew made it inconceivable. She was always conscious that she was "driving Aldous" (and, when out alone, of her duty to come safely home); in some thirty years and what perhaps amounted to a million miles, Maria never had anything that could be called an accident.

1924 turned out a stable year. Aldous was quietly working away

---

[1] *Along the Road.* Chatto & Windus, 1925.

on their Florentine hill with a short journey now and then. There was no house move (though they were already thinking about one).

In January he had been relieved of a nagging worry. As he was finishing *Little Mexican*, his next lot of short stories, and turning up ideas for a novel, "that bloody book on Balzac, which in an insane moment years ago I pledged myself to write", came home to roost. Constable's seemed to take the contract seriously. They had written to say that the MS was three years overdue. "I don't blame them." Aldous feared that he would have to write the book. The thought filled him with horror. He was bored stiff with Balzac; the more familiar he became with him, he told his father, the less he thought of him. He found him marvellous in his energy, his power of rapidly and effectively creating, "but so astonishingly remote from life—at any rate from interior life . . I always enjoy his books; but there are very few of them I think particularly good. What an immense difference between him and a really great novelist like Dostoevsky or Tolstoy. And what a difference, in his own sphere of fantastic creation, between him and the incredibly much more fertile and juicy Dickens."

Aldous turned to Eric Pinker, then his agent, asking if there were a way of getting out of the agreement he had made "being at the time very young, very foolish and poor". Pinker persuaded Constable's to take a book on some other subject in lieu of the impossible Balzac; but now Chatto's, understandably, objected. Fortunately no money had passed, and Pinker was finally able to cancel the whole thing.

That winter in Florence was particularly icy, though there were the single miraculous days of sitting out in a morning sun. Aldous's friend J. N. W. Sullivan stayed with them. "He has a very clear, hard, acute intelligence," Aldous wrote to his father—Sullivan had contributed articles on the Einstein theory to the *Cornhill*, "and a very considerable knowledge, not merely on his own subjects—mathematics, physics and astronomy—but on literature and music. A stimulating companion." Aldous often worked the better for having a man to talk to on his walks and in the evening. The finished MS of *Little Mexican* was sent off in the last days of February. "Six short stories, the first of considerable length, about thirty thousand words . . . some quite good stuff in it, I think." Aldous and Maria went off on a trip. They got stuck in the snow trying to cross the Apennines but eventually got down to Bologna, Parma—Aldous had a *faible* for Correggio —Mantua, Padua, Venice and home again by Ferrara and Ravenna. Home meant buckling down to the next book. There were some false starts. "It is horribly difficult to find the right way of saying what one wants to say. What I am working on now . . is to be . . a discussion and fictional illustration of different views of life. *The mere business of telling a story interests me less and less*" [my italics].

How difficult to understand the mentality of a man like Bennett who could sit down and spin out an immense realistic affair about life in Clerkenwell. "When it was first done that sort of thing had a certain interest . . . But it is a purely factitious interest. The only really and permanently absorbing things are attitudes towards life and the relation of man to the world."

In April Suzanne was married to Joep Nicolas. While Aldous was getting on with his novel—*Those Barren Leaves*—Maria went to St Trond for the wedding (a proper white one with the family assembled in strength). Suzanne found her sister's presence a great comfort, and the night before they slept together in their Uncle Julien's room. Maria had sent advice already during the engagement: Suzanne must learn to spell. Spelling was Maria's own bugbear, but if her own was eccentric, Suzanne's was a family byword; neither grappled well with dates and figures. (Suzanne first chose 30th February for her wedding day.) Now Maria, five years married, gave some more advice. Suzanne listened.

I think it is thanks to her that I have not made myself unhappy in my marriage . . . [Suzanne writing].

"Un homme à femme," Maria said of Joep, "il me plairait." Suzanne took it as a compliment. In essence Maria's advice was to create an emotional and domestic atmosphere in which a man could do his work in peace: artists and writers needed experience, needed variety. How much nicer—and wiser—not to make a fuss, to consent, not hinder; not to break one's heart.

Joep and Suzanne went to Italy for their honeymoon, staying with the Huxleys well into the summer. Everybody got on beautifully; life was agreeable, so were friends and neighbours, Robert Nicolson, Sullivan (humanly a very odd fish), Costanza of course. There was an excellent cook. One of Aldous's young second cousins, Renée Haynes,[1] a girl about to go to Oxford, was also in the house.

. . It was an extraordinary kind of time [Renée Tickell talking]— because there he was—and he knew so much about everything. It was always a bit daunting, not because you felt stupid, he wouldn't

[1] The present Mrs Jerrard Tickell.

have let you feel stupid . . . he talked about Florence and painting and Italian gardens and what Italians were like. When he was talking one saw things through his lens, through his mind, they became alive. There were times though—one was much less grown up than as seventeen now—when I wished I could have gone swimming.

Matthew, four and very large and lively, ate at table. There were fearful scenes. He was difficult about his food and refused to eat meat or fish. Aldous put it down to his extreme sensitive-ness to smells and to sentimental reasons, "he realizes that meat is dead animals". Perhaps a course of mild hypnotism? And the boy was too lazy to read although he knew his letters. "We don't worry him," Aldous told his own father, "too early a passion for reading distracts from the powers of observation."

In June the Huxleys took Joep and Suzanne on a slow tour to Rome. One looks upon the 1920s as the brief golden age of motoring. Comic breakdowns were past, self-starters and balloon tyres in; cars had become reliable and there weren't too many of them—the road was for the few. But in Italy roads were narrow, winding, rough; there still obtained the dangerous habit of keeping to the right in towns and to the left in open country. Dust and pebbles flew in one's face, donkeys zigzagged, peasants dozed upon their carts. It could be broiling hot. Aldous liked to have the hood down and they had to wrap in dust-coats, veils and goggles. We looked like brigands, says Suzanne. They ploughed on, Maria at the wheel, the two men sight-seeing untiringly. They explored places little visited at the time, Etruscan tombs, abandoned Byzantine churches. There was much gaiety. One evening at a small hotel in Viterbo with the dining-room full of elderly English ladies, Joep ordered a young bubbly wine; it had been a long day, soon they were in very high spirits: Maria, Suzanne and Joep were taken by the giggles. Aldous remained impassive. He tried to hush Maria. "But why not, darling?" she said to him. "Why not?"

"Because it isn't dignified, darling."

Whereupon they only laughed the harder.[1]

For Aldous the impressions of the day were not washed off by a glass of *spumante*. He was enmeshed in the aesthetic round. Italy —"The real place. The more one goes into it, the more one is astonished by its richness." At the same time he was puzzled, not entirely satisfied, seeking. "All that these creatures poured out in

[1] Suzanne Nicolas, *Memoir* cit.

the past—and *cui bono*? What has become of all their thought and passion? It seems to have had no particular effect on anything. The fossilized remains are still here—miraculous: the tourists look at them—and that's all."

In July Aldous and Maria went again to Forte. Villa Fasola: Aldous wrote, bathed. *Those Barren Leaves* were near the end, Maria was typing fair copy. The house was full of young children, and Matthew at last was beginning to eat properly. "He now puts away beefsteak and fish like a hero," Aldous reported. In mid-August his parents set out for England in the Citroën. Aldous planned to stop somewhere on their way across the Alps to finish his last chapters, but when they got to the top of Mont Cenis the rain came down in torrents and the summer temperature dropped to near freezing point. They were driven back into the plain, the hotels were full up; after a night of sleeping in a kitchen they found rooms at "an absurd little place called Ambérieu, where we stayed ten days. When I got my work done, we drove on . . ."

Paris: a few days at the Lewis Gielguds—galleries, bookshops, the Louvre—September in London, Aldous's first return since his flight in the spring of 1923. They lodged in rooms in the King's Road, Chelsea. Aldous saw his family, attended to business with his publishers, doctors, tailor. For the moment he was feeling quite satisfied with the finished novel. "It comes off fairly well," he wrote to Bob Nichols. And a few weeks later to his American editor, Eugene Saxton,[1] ". . . It cuts more ice . . than the others and is more explicit and to the point. The characters, too, are better, I think."

After London, Holland. They stayed with Joep and Suzanne in their first home, an old farmhouse by the sea at Groet; then, inevitably, the four of them went on another trip. ". . entirely successful. Holland was a revelation, especially the country . . . But my word, how cold!" Aldous was spell-bound by the number and virtuosity of the cyclists on the road. "Il s'attendait même à ce qu'ils fassent l'amour en bicyclette" [Suzanne].

They continued into Belgium, driving down the Meuse valley in the rain. But it was "marvellously lovely," (Aldous to his father) "exactly like those strangely improbable little landscapes of Patinir . . . which I always thought mere fancies . . ."

The Huxleys returned to Italy in still, settled autumn weather by the long route south through France. Reims, Chartres, Orléans,

---

[1] Eugene Saxton, who later became a great friend of Aldous's, former editor of *The Bookman*, later editor in chief of Harper Brothers, was then on the staff of Aldous's first American publishers, George H. Doran.

Bourges—"Chartres fine, but Bourges unbelievably magnificent"
(ever after Aldous preferred Bourges to Chartres), Moulins, Lyons,
Provence; Marseilles, the Esterel, Nice, the Ligurian coast. Some
of the roads were atrocious. The car, Aldous could not forbear
to tell, "went through its ordeal in a marvellous fashion, the only
weakness being . . a leak of oil into the clutch". All the same he
envied his father for having a new Morris.

> If we get a new car, which won't be yet awhile, it will be Italian
> and more powerful than the Citroën . . Possibly the new Lancia, or
> even, if it's not too dear, the new 6 cylinder Itala which is said to
> have all the qualities of the Alfa Romeo . . .

They were back in Florence in late October. Aldous, stimulated
and refreshed, began work on a book of travel essays—breathing
space before his next go at fiction—hoping to have the MS ready
by Christmas. For the next few months they remained settled in
a quiet and pleasant existence. Aldous had put on some needed
weight, so had Matthew and Maria ("I think we should all have
been in the grave by this time if we had stayed in London").
Italy was serving them well; only Florence was beginning to pall.
"Too much fog in the valleys and too little water in the hills,
too many bores to be avoided . . ." They had a look at a house
on the coast south of Rome at Monte Circeo on the edge of the
Pontine marshes—sea air for Matthew, the advantages of Capri
without its intolerable disadvantages (an island and inhabited by
Sodomites)—they will move there probably in the spring. One
thing is sure: "I shall certainly stay in Italy . . . I shall stay here
for the next few years . . . until it is time for Matthew to be
educated. Then, I suppose, London or Oxford. Qui sa? . . But it is
still fairly remote."

Chapter Six

Those Barren Leaves

THROUGH the winter the quiet productive life continued. "The greatest luxury of this existence," Aldous wrote to Julian, "is the feeling and being well." The book of travel essays, having taken only a little longer than Aldous had bargained for, was finished in January: a few days' relaxation—catching up with letters, buying a tie—and start on a long story for the next book due.

Those Barren Leaves was published on 21st January 1925. It was well received (eight thousand copies sold in the first year). But Aldous, for his part, was no longer certain that it had come off. He was at the beginning of his dissatisfaction with his writing.

> I'm glad you liked the *Leaves* [he wrote to Naomi Mitchison that winter]. They are all right, certainly; tremendously accomplished, but in a queer way, I now feel, jejune and shallow and off the point. All I've written so far has been off the point. And I've taken such enormous pains to get off it; that's the stupidity. All this fuss in the intellectual void; and meanwhile the other things go on in a quiet domestic way, quite undisturbed.

Some of this was bound up with Maria. There was Aldous's cognizance that Maria—who did not formulate, who did not, in his sense, think—was *on the point*, by intuition, by straight experience. Aldous was becoming able to use that faculty of hers. He often called her his dragoman. It was closer than that, more organic: at times he saw in an almost physical way through her. (After her death he would speak consistently of amputation.)

That letter to Naomi ended with a new version of Aldous's old *cri de cœur*: I wish I had time to do nothing but write. Now it was: "I wish I could afford to *stop* writing for a bit." The essence of the plea remained the same: he had realized that there is a price to pay for writing two books a year.

The main theme of *Those Barren Leaves*, Aldous wrote, "the main theme is the undercutting of everything by a sort of despairing scepticism and then the undercutting of that by mysticism." Again he had deliberately mixed the unities. There is comedy (poor impossible Mrs Aldwinkle), melodrama, farce, young love, there are the Tuscan and Umbrian landscapes of the Italian journey with Irene and young Lord Hovenden driving round and round Lake Trasimene for ever. There is much about death. Death and the thought of death, the undercutting of everything by death.

Aldous happened to write this book during one of the most serene periods of his existence. "The wise man does not think of death lest it should spoil his pleasures."[1] If Aldous was a wise man, he was one marked by the experiences of his past. The pleasant life on the hill, the journeys with Maria by his side, the lively little boy, his son, the splendours of art and learning were undercut by memories of *staphylococcus aureus*, of his mother's painful senseless death. Was there a way of side-tracking lurking horror, a hope short of literal belief in a compensatory heaven? Mr Cardan, the ageing hedonist (a one-dimensional Norman Douglas figure) snorts that there is not; but Calamy, ex-guardee, big-game hunter, accomplished lover ("my greatest talent"), the man turned thirty who has come to a dead end, is willing to suspend his ways in order to find out. He goes off into the mountains to be alone to think ("to get to the bottom of the universe, eh?" says Mr Cardan).

Those Barren Leaves was a signpost in Aldous's development. It is for this reason that I am proposing to quote from it at length. All but the first passage (chosen for a visual quality) are taken from the fifty concluding pages of the novel. The house-party have arrived at Perugia; Irene and Lord Hovenden are as good as engaged and go for a stroll at dusk. "I like vis place," says Hovenden who has trouble with his th's.

.. Leaving the stately part of the town, they plunged into the labyrinth of steep alleys, of winding passageways and staircases behind the cathedral. Built confusedly on the hillside, the tall houses seemed to grow into one another, as though they were the component parts of one immense and fantastical building, in which the alleys served as corridors. The road would burrow through the houses in a long dark tunnel, to widen into a little well-like court-yard, open to the sky. Through open doors .. one saw in the bright electric light a family sitting round the soup tureen. The road turned into a flight of stairs, dipped into another tunnel, made cheerful by the lights of a subterranean wine shop opening into it. From the mouth of the bright cavern came up the smell of liquor, the sound of loud voices and reverberated laughter.

And then, suddenly emerging from the high houses, they found themselves standing on the edge of an escarped slope, looking out on to a huge expanse of pale evening sky, scalloped at its fringes by the blue shapes of mountains, with the round moon, already bright,

[1] *Those Barren Leaves*, 1925.

hanging serene and solemn in the midst. Leaning over the parapet, they looked down on the roofs of another quarter of the city, a hundred feet below. The colours of the world still struggled against the encroaching darkness; but a lavish municipality had already beaded the streets with yellow lights. A faint smell of wood-smoke and frying came up through the thin pure air. The silence of the sky was so capacious, so high and wide, that the noises of the town —like so many small, distinctly seen objects in the midst of an immense blank prairie—served to intensify the quiet, to make the listener more conscious of its immensity in comparison with the trivial clatter at its heart.

"I like vis place," Lord Hovenden repeated.

They stood for a long time, leaning their elbows on the parapet, saying nothing.

A few days later Grace Elver, the moronic girl, has died and there is Mr Cardan, who had been about to marry her to provide for his declining years, is meditating in the empty church before her funeral.

The tragedy of bodily suffering and extinction has no catharsis. Punctually it runs its dull, degrading course, act by act to the conclusion. It ennobles neither the sufferer nor the contemplator. Only the tragedy of the spirit can liberate and uplift. But the greatest tragedy of the spirit is that sooner or later it succumbs to the flesh. Sooner or later every soul is stifled by the sick body; sooner or later there are no more thoughts, but only pain and vomiting and stupor. The tragedies of the spirit are mere struttings and posturings on the margin of life, and the spirit itself is only an accidental exuberance .. like the feathers on the head of a hoopoe ... The spirit has no significance; there is only the body. When it is young, the body is beautiful and strong. It grows old, its joints creak, it becomes dry and smelly; it breaks down, the life goes out of it and it rots away. However lovely the feathers on a bird's head, they perish with it; and the spirit, which is a lovelier ornament than any, perishes too ... the body, the doomed, decaying body, is the one, appalling fact.

.. Mr Cardan wondered how he would die. Slowly or suddenly? After long pain? Intelligent, still human? Or an idiot, a moaning animal?

A few pages later comes the passage about the human hand— Calamy's discourse, in bed with Mary Thriplow. He holds up his hand. "Look .. it's just a shape that interrupts the light:

To a child who has not yet learned to interpret what he sees, that's all it would be, just a shaped blotch of colour . . . But now, suppose I try to consider the thing as a physicist . . ."

Calamy, in fact, is talking about the extraordinariness of existence.

"And the more you think, the more obscure and mysterious it becomes."

He speaks of atoms . . of units of negative electricity whirling several million times a minute round a nucleus of positive electricity. He speaks (Calamy is one of nature's guardsmen, but what we hear is Aldous's voice) of the structure of molecules, of electromagnetic radiations, of electrons moving from one orbit to another without taking any time . . covering any space . . .

Mary Thriplow (a bright lady novelist) observes that he is making her feel dizzy. Calamy remarks in passing that the behaviour of light is satisfactorily explained by one theory of electro-dynamics, while the behaviour of electrons in the atom can only be explained on a theory that is entirely inconsistent with it. He goes on:

"Well, here are two ways already in which my hand exists . . . then there is the chemical way . . . it is enough to think of it for five minutes to perceive that [my hand] exists simultaneously in a dozen parallel worlds."

Simultaneous existence in a dozen parallel worlds—this is what always exercised Aldous's mind. What most of us most of the time choose to ignore because it is too complicated, too out of stride with our daily requirements and habitual sense perceptions, too dizzy-making in fact, was for Aldous evident philosophical and literary raw material. He would think, and what had appeared comprehensible on the routine surface became utterly mysterious. This fascinated him—how he adored the *extraordinary*—it gave him a sense of adventure, of getting off the map, allowing him to believe that *anything* might be possible. It informed his writing. "This is what *interests me*," he would say. So over and over again he attempted to put across simultaneous existence, to co-ordinate disparate fields; to bring off, in literary terms, the grand composition. (Unifying, as he might have put it, the subject matters of Piero della Francesca, Blake, El Greco, Chardin, Rubens and the Elder Breughel.) He doubted whether it *could* be done in words; spoke of it having been done in music; kept on trying. It enriched his writing but at times overloaded and distorted it. Those whizzing electrons, those anatomical analyses of love-making, do we see them as lapses now or as an enhancement of reality? In *Those Barren Leaves* Calamy went on about the human hand.

"Now if, like Cranmer, I were to put my right hand in the fire . . these molecules would uncombine themselves into their constituent atoms . . . But this leads me on at once to a set of entirely different realities. For if I were to put my hand into the fire, I should feel pain . . . For I am alive, and this hand is part of a living being, the first law of whose existence is to preserve its life . . .

". . . The hand is part, not merely of a living being, but of a being that knows good and evil. This hand of mine can do good things and bad things . . . it has written all manner of words; it has helped a man who was hurt; it has touched your body." He laid his hand on her breast ". . and when it touches your body . . it also touches your mind. My hand moves like this, and it moves through your consciousness as well as here, across your skin. And it's my mind that orders it to move; it brings your body into my mind. It exists in mind; it has reality as a part of my soul and a part of yours . . .

". . these are some of the ways in which my hand exists . . . And from this one goes on to ask, inevitably, what relationship exists between these different modes of being."

What is there in common, he asks, between life and chemistry, between a collection of cells and the consciousness of a caress?

"It's there that the gulfs begin to open. For there isn't any connection—that one can see, at any rate. Universe lies on top of universe, layer after layer, distinct and separate . . ."

"Like a Neapolitan ice," says Miss Thriplow.

". . . The only hope . . is that perhaps, if you went on thinking long enough and hard enough, you might somehow get through, get out on the other side of obscurity . . . But into what precisely, into what?"

And now we are in the last chapter. Calamy has gone to live in a hut by himself in the mountains—for a week, for a year?—to think, as he had said, in freedom.
In freedom. And here Aldous returns to something that he already knew when he was writing *Antic Hay*.

"The mind must be open, unperturbed, empty of irrelevant things, quiet. There's no room for thoughts in a half-shut, cluttered mind. . . ."

Most of us pass through life without knowing that the thoughts are there at all, "If one wants to lure them out, one must clear a space for them:

156

One must open the mind wide and wait. And there must be no irrelevant preoccupations prowling around the doors. One must free oneself of those."

Calamy is interrupted by Mr Cardan and Francis Chelifer who have come to see what he is up to. The final fifteen pages consist of their argument. Again Calamy speaks of his wish of "getting through"—how many days did Gotama spend under the bo-tree?—the undercutting by mysticism is out now in the open. If you try long enough and if your mind is the right sort of mind,

"Perhaps you really do get in some queer sort of way, beyond the limitations of ordinary existence. And you may see that everything that seems real is in fact entirely illusory—*maya*, in fact, the cosmic illusion. Behind it you catch a glimpse of reality."

Mr Cardan won't have any. What bosh your mystics talk about, he says, lights and darknesses, sweet and bitters, wheels, mercury, salt and sulphur—it's a rigmarole. Chelifer concurs. Only soft-heads and sentimentalists engage in that kind of activities.

On the contrary, Calamy replies, mystics, in point of historical fact, have generally been men of the highest intelligence. Buddha, Jesus, Lao-Tze, Boehme, Swedenborg. And what about Sir Isaac Newton, who practically abandoned mathematics for mysticism after he was thirty?

"Not that he was a particularly good mystic; he wasn't. But he tried to be; and it can't be said that he was remarkable for the softness of his head. No, it's not fools who turn mystics."

And again we seem to hear the voice of Aldous:

"It takes a certain amount of intelligence and imagination to realize the extraordinary queerness and mysteriousness of the world in which we live."

Mr Cardan has to come back to the fact of death—you cannot get over that. When the flesh dies, there's an end to mysticism with all its by-products, God, justice, salvation . . .

Perhaps it is, says Calamy. Let's admit it as certain even. Does it make the slightest difference?

"Salvation is not in the next world; it's in this . . . here and now. The kingdom of God is within you—if you'll excuse the quotation . . ."

Mr Cardan shakes his head. "All this, my young friend, doesn't in any way mitigate the disagreeableness of slowly becoming *gaga*, dying and being eaten by worms . . . When my soul is at the mercy of my slowly rotting body, what will be the use of salvation then?"

"It will have profited during the fifty years of healthy life," said Calamy.

Chapter Seven

"Lève l'ancre pour une Exotique Nature!"

THE house at Monte Circeo fell through, the Florentine lease
was up at the end of June, they thought of moving to Rome
in the autumn. "After a third-rate provincial town, colonized by
English Sodomites and middle-aged Lesbians," Aldous wrote to
Julian, "a genuine metropolis will be lively. Not to mention the
fact that Rome is incomparably the most lovely place in the
world."

In March they went over to North Africa for a brief journey
into Tunisia. Aldous had been working on the title story of *Two
or Three Graces* since February; it was the sort of thing he could do
easily enough but did he want to go on doing it? "For me," he
said in a long letter to Robert Nichols, "the vital problem is not
the mental so much as the ethical and the emotional. The fundamental problem is love and humility, which are the same thing.
The enormous difficulty of love and humility—

a difficulty greater now, I feel, than ever; because men are more
solitary now than they were; all authority has gone; the tribe has
disappeared and every at all conscious man stands alone, surrounded
by other solitary individuals and fragments of the old tribe, for
which he feels no respect. Obviously, the only thing to be done is
to go right through with the process; to realize individuality to the
full, the real individuality, Lao-Tze's individuality, the Yogis'
individuality, and with it the oneness of everything. Obviously! But
the difficulty is huge.

. . And meanwhile the world is peopled with miserable beings who
are neither one thing nor the other; who are solitary and yet not
complete individuals . . .

. . What's to be done about it? That's the great question. Some
day I may find some sort of an answer. And then I may write a
good book, or at any rate a mature book, not a queer sophisticatedly
jejune book, like this last affair, like all the blooming lot, in fact.

One fine morning it was brought home to Aldous and Maria
that they were living in Fascist Italy. Four ruffians in uniform
forced their way into Castel a Montici and demanded to search
the place. Now Aldous did not like the regime. He deplored its
acts of brutality; he found it wicked. Wicked, stupid and fantastically incompetent—"curious country! [it] would be comic if

159

it weren't tragic." In fact, he was "against it" as a rational matter of course. He did not, as so many contemporary writers, feel passionate about it. Temperamentally Aldous inclined to the wide-range view; he would not be doctrinaire, would not be a labelled anti-anything. Musso and the Fascisti, he would have said if pressed, were worse, yes a good deal worse, than a democracy, say, such as France or England (with their bitter inequalities and hypocrisies); but they were part of the general inhumanity and folly, the Human Vomedy as his typewriter once slipped into naming it. As for living in Fascist Italy (as people may well ask today), there was fortunately something hit or miss about the regime, horrible though it was; it did not succeed in becoming as efficiently totalitarian as other dictatorial regimes right or left, and it did not crush out the humanity of the Italian people. It was possible for a man of conscience to live in Italy (I am speaking as one who remembers the time and was passionately and emotionally "anti"), while it would have been unthinkable for such a man to have lived in Nazi Germany.

The four ruffians on that June morning of 1925 were members of the political police and looking for an Italian professor, for Gaetano Salvemini, in fact, the historian, who had written against the regime and whom they believed to be in hiding at the Huxleys (who had never even met him as it happened). Aldous stood up to the louts and invoked his ambassador, demanding to see their warrant (they didn't have one). They searched all the same. When they found no trace of either Salvemini (who was arrested elsewhere shortly after) or incriminating documents, they ended up rather ashamed of themselves. "But it was a tiresome and unpleasant business."

It was the Huxleys' last month at Castel a Montici; they were already crating books with no very clear idea of where they'd be living next. ("Plans a bit vague," Aldous wrote to Norman Douglas, "but I prefer them so.") His glimpse of the African oases had stimulated his desire for remoter travelling. He and Maria were beginning to talk about going to India in the autumn "to take a look round". And after that, who knows? Meanwhile they made the most of family life. Maria's sister Jeanne was staying with them with her husband and child, so that there were now two small children living in the house; Sophie two years old against Matthew's five. Aldous and Maria were no longer the babes in the wood they had been in that Hampstead flat when they were barely married and did not know whether to boil the teat or how to stop Matthew from howling; they no longer had to cope with cramped quarters and overwork. The shades of having to write Balzac's life were laid. There was space now for young children. Aldous read to Matthew, took a mild interest in

Sophie, playing tricks on her dolls; Maria loved her. "Je me suis attachée d'une manière toute nouvelle et si profonde," she wrote to Suzanne . . . D'ailleurs elle m'aime aussi . . . car elle sent que je l'adore; une petite créature déjà si vivante et alerte et surtout si bonne . . ."

Suzanne herself had just had her first child, also a girl, Claire. (The Huxleys sent her Matthew's old pram, a vast and splendid English affair.) Aldous became greatly attached to his nieces (there were to be five in all) but it was Sophie who lived with the Huxleys during most of her childhood and adolescence, and became almost their second child.

The Huxleys left Castel a Montici for good at the end of June. They went by car to England, leaving Matthew with his grandmother at St Trond. It was not an easy parting for Maria—the Indian idea was expanding into one of a much longer journey. In London the thing took on concrete shape as Aldous was able to arrange for a series of travel articles to cover the worst of the expense. "Seeing that one practises a profession that does not tie one down, I feel that one ought to see as much of this planet as one can."

It was *le tour du monde*, the journey round the world Maria had talked of as a girl. She still longed to go; Aldous needed no urging; they were leaving the small boy in responsible and loving hands, but the separation in terms of distance and time—with no return except by sea—was a serious one. As usual, Maria made her choice; as often, she was divided. She and Aldous spent the rest of the summer in London, seeing to passages and equipment. Invitations accumulated; the last story for *Two or Three Graces* was all but finished. On 15th September they sailed from Genoa bound for Suez.

Chapter Eight

The Journey Round the World—India

THEY landed at Bombay "hot, muggy and expensive" on 2nd October; met "the local intelligentsia, journalists, politicians, etc., frail little men, very gentle and underfed-looking . . . no wonder the British rule"; went on to Lahore by train—two nights and a day, tolerable in spite of heat and dust—stayed with a young Indian barrister Aldous knew at Oxford, looked at some Mogul monuments "in a style of architecture I really don't like at all"; then up to Kashmir by way of Rawalpindi, "a desolate beastly sort of place", reaching Srinagar by October twelfth. During their first ten days in India, Aldous wrote home, they had lived strenuously, seen many people and things and travelled sixteen hundred miles.

People called at their hotel, bore them off to look at sights. They met Provincial Governors, English Residents, Chief Justices, heads of customs, medical officers, missionaries, Maharajas. "Once one has a little start in this part of the world, one goes automatically a long way."

At Srinagar they were lent a bungalow and stayed for a month. Their windows looked out across a valley to blue foothills and snowy peaks, the days were brilliantly clear, the air bracing, the nights deeply cold. They continued to live strenuously. They saw temples and gardens, were taken on day-long drives, visited the gaol and lunatic asylum. They saw the Tartar traders from Yarkhand come down the mountainside and bought two fur coats for a few pounds, a sheep-skin for Aldous and a beautiful Russian arctic hare. From Srinagar they set out for nearly three months of continuous land travel. Taxila, Peshawar, down again to Lahore, Amritsar; a tour through Rajputana: Agra, Ajmer, Chitor, Bikaner, Jodpur, Udaipur; Indore, Bhopal, Cawnpore for the All India Congress in December, Lucknow, Delhi, Benares, Calcutta . . .

Aldous went down well with Indians and more improbably with all types of English. (Once he dined as a guest in the mess of a rather stolid infantry regiment; one of the officers later told Gervas that Aldous asked innumerable questions, taking an intense interest in what daily military life was like.)

Maria did their packing and unpacking; Aldous went to Thomas Cook's to collect post and tickets, and wrote letters; together they counted their money which seemed to be slipping rapidly between their fingers. "Great wads of it have to be handed out every time one gets into the train; for fares are high and distances enormous."[1]

Once or twice they became extremely worried. (Neither of them was ever good at working out sums in perspective, a workable budget was beyond Maria's arithmetic and Aldous's patience; what they did was fall into a money panic now and then. Now they decided to travel second-class. The compartment filled to overflowing by a holy man in yellow robes and his followers; at stations more followers crowded in to kiss his feet. The holy man hoicked and spat all over the compartment, he and his admirers exhaled the sour stink of garments long unwashed. The day was very hot. Aldous sat reflecting on the fact of cleanliness dividing man from man. After seven hours of it, they paid out twenty-two rupees and had their luggage transferred into a first-class carriage.

They carried phials of disinfectant to drop into their drinking water; Maria shrank from the insects and small squashy animals and was often disgusted by the food that politeness bade them swallow. At a political party they were offered a meal of ice cream, hot dumplings stuffed with curried mice, chocolates and spice-flavoured mineral water. Aldous, stoical by principle and schooling (few things in adult life could equal the breakfast porridge at Hillside), described it as "altogether most curious and amusing," Maria on such occasions would look imploringly at her husband. Aldous avoided catching her eye or returned a glance of disapproval.

What were Aldous's impressions at this first meeting with the East, with India? Most of them can be found in *Jesting Pilate*, the diary of the journey which he began at sea and wrote as he went along, and in half a dozen letters home. Later he often talked about it with or without second thoughts. At the time his main emotion was one of horror. At Srinagar there had been the blue foothills and white mountains in the distance, in the streets, on the doorsteps wretchedness and dirt . . . "Srinagar fairly festers. The people are dressed in ancient rags and suffer agonies from cold . . ."

After a century and a half of Western domination, peace and settled government, the country was still as poor as in the days of anarchy. "Millions are still without enough to eat, all their lives . . . Custom and ancient superstitions still as strong . . .

. . Nine Indians out of ten cannot read or write, and the tenth, who can, detests the Europeans who taught him. The educated . .

---

[1] *Jesting Pilate*. Chatto & Windus, 1926. All quotations in this chapter unless otherwise indicated are from *Jesting Pilate*.

profess democratic principles; but their instincts are profoundly and almost ineradically aristocratic . . . Meanwhile the mountains of evitable hardship and superfluous suffering are piled up. . . .

At Jaipur one of the great landowners lent his elephant to the Huxleys, "a superb and particularly lofty specimen". One morning emerging from the palace precincts,

> Our monster halted and, with its usual deliberation, relieved nature, portentously. Hardly . . had it resumed its march when an old woman . . darted forward and fairly threw herself on the mound of steaming excrement. There was fuel . . I suppose, for a week's cooking . . . Our passage had been to her like a sudden and unexpected fall of manna. She thanked us, she blessed the great and charitable Jumbo for its Gargantuan bounty.

The elephant lurched on. Aldous's thoughts were moved to mournful eloquence:

> Why are we here, men and women, eighteen hundred millions of us, on this remarkable and perhaps unique planet? . . immortal souls, first cousins to the angels, own brothers of Buddha, Mozart and Sir Isaac Newton . . . is it to go about looking for dung?

Hard enough to find a reason anywhere, West or East, but in India Aldous saw no conceivable answer. "India is depressing as no other country I have ever known. One breathes in it, not air, but dust and hopelessness."

Aldous's secondary reaction to the East was exasperation.

> *There was an old man of Thermopylae,*
> *Who never did anything properly.*

"To the Westerner all Indians seem old men of Thermopylae. In the ordinary affairs of life I am a bit of a Thermopylean myself. But even I am puzzled, disquieted and rather exasperated by the Indians." He was struck by the extraordinary sloppiness of the ceremonies, the casual mixture of the magnificent with the cheap in the abodes of the potentates—ante-rooms filthy with pigeon droppings, marble halls furnished with bamboo chairs, the brass bedstead standing in the throne room . . . And those cows!

> To the eye of pure reason there is something singularly illogical about the way in which the Hindus shrink from killing cows . . but have no scruples about making the life of the sacred beasts . . a hell on earth. So strict is the orthodoxy of Kashmir, that Bovril is con-

fiscated at the frontier . . . And yet nothing is done to protect these god-like animals from any cruelty that does not actually result in death . . . To the eye of reason, I repeat, it certainly seems strange. But then the majority of human actions are not meant to be looked at by the eye of reason.

And as for Hindu spirituality, it is interesting to recall some of Aldous's remarks then.

To my mind "spirituality" (ultimately, I suppose, the product of the climate) is the primal curse of India and the cause of all her misfortunes. It is the preoccupation with "spiritual" realities, different from the actual historical realities of common life, that has kept millions upon millions of men and women content, through centuries, with a lot unworthy of human beings. A little less spirituality, and the Indians would now be free—free from foreign dominion and from the tyranny of their own prejudices and traditions. There would be less dirt and more food. There would be fewer Maharajas with Rolls Royces and more schools . . .

It is for its "materialism" that our Western world is usually blamed. Wrongly, Aldous thought. For materialism—"if [it] means a preoccupation with the actual world in which we live —is something wholly admirable". If Western civilization is unsatisfactory, that is not because we are interested in the actual world, but "because most of us are interested in such an absurdly small part of it".

And what about English rule in India? On the whole Aldous seems to have been in no doubt about this issue, though at times he wrote himself into his long-range view. He is quite unequivocal, for instance, in a letter to Lewis Gielgud from Lahore.

The sort of Englishman one meets here in trains, stations, restaurants and Dak bungalows is beyond words repulsive. Stupid, uncultured, underbred, the complete and perfect cad. In their company, one understands the Indian nationalistic aspirations. As a matter of fact, I understand them even when I am in the presence of the nice Englishmen. We really have no business here. And there is no doubt whatever that we are steadily making the country poorer and poorer . . .

In the published diary he qualifies. Are the Indians in a position to govern themselves at once? Would they do the job as well as the English, or better or worse? Nobody is able to say. Politics are not a science. His own prejudices "happen to be in favour of democracy and self-determination, and all the rest of it. Yet if

I had been brought up a little differently ..." Nor does he see that the mere fact of his liberal prejudices on the one hand, and his being an Englishman on the other, "makes me . . responsible for either the integrity of the British Empire or the liberation of the Indian people.

When I am honest with myself, I have to admit that I don't care two pins about political principles. Provided that it guaranteed my safety and left me in peace to do my work, I should live just as happily under an alien despotism as under the British constitution.

Yet on the very page before (the diary entry of another day?) he sounds a different note. Easy enough, he says, to suspend judgement on the Indians' ability to govern themselves, but "if I were an educated Indian, I should almost certainly have gone to gaol for acting on my belief—"the belief that even if it could somehow be proved that [self-government] would bring, as its immediate consequences, communal discord, religious and political wars . . inefficiency and corruption—even if this could be proved, I think I should still go on trying to obtain Swaraj. There are certain things about which it is not possible, it is not right to take the reasonable, the utilitarian view."

The high point of the journey was probably the visit to the Bose Institute at Calcutta. Their guide was Sir J. C. Bose himself, the famous researcher who had worked earlier on the effects of stimuli on metal and then on vegetable organisms, the man who had proved the "sensitivity" of plants. Aldous and Maria were shown round for three hours and saw the experiments in full blast. Here indeed was grist to Aldous's mind: Bose had devised instruments that made visible things that had so far been impossible to see even with the aid of the most powerful microscope. They watched the " 'heart beat' of a plant . . recording itself point by point on a moving plate", they watched a plant feed in the sun and stop feeding when the sun was shaded, watched it exhale minute quantities of oxygen; they saw "its sudden shuddering reaction" to an electric shock, and saw its 'heart' becoming more rapid when a grain of caffeine was added to its water.

Aldous had been sceptical—"But when you *see* the plants making records of their own sensations—well, you've got to believe."

Through the afternoon, they followed Bose "from marvel to marvel". He showed them the full-grown tree that had been brought from a great distance under an anaesthetic, and transplanted; the tree had taken root immediately in its new place and flourished. They saw a plant die. "We administered poison. A mortal dose of chloroform was dropped into the water. The graph became the record of a death agony.

> .. The poisoned flower manifestly writhed before us . . . As the poison paralysed the "heart", the ups and downs of the graph flattened out into a horizontal line . . . But so long as any life remained in the plant, this medial line did not run level, but was jagged with sharp irregular ups and downs that represented in a visible symbol the spasms of the murdered creature desperately struggling for life. After a little while, there were no more ups and downs. The line of dots was quite straight. The plant was dead.

Its last moments were so distressingly like those of a man, that Aldous was shocked into feeling a new sympathy. Fascinating, that afternoon in Calcutta; also immensely disturbing in its implications. The aliveness of matter "may seem absurd and impossible . . But a little thought is enough to show that it is . . . *a priori* probable.

> Life exists. Even the most strict and puritanical physicists are compelled, albeit grudgingly, to admit the horribly disquieting fact.

> I am always a little uncomfortable when I find myself unable to admire something which all the rest of the world admires—or at least is reputed to admire. Am I, or is the world the fool?

Some of Aldous's readers were disappointed by his attitude to India as expressed in *Jesting Pilate*; nothing in the book, however, has given so much offence, has rankled so long in East and West as Aldous's lack of reverence for the Taj Mahal. He failed to admire it. "The Taj Mahal is one of the seven wonders. My guide assures me that it is 'perhaps the most beautiful building in the world.' " Aldous and Maria drove out for their first sight by the light of the setting sun.

> Nature did its best for the Taj. The west was duly red, and orange and yellow, and, finally, emerald green, grading into pale and flawless blue towards the zenith . . The sacred Jumna was like a sheet of glass between its banks . . The gardens were rich with turf, with cypresses, palms, and peepul trees, with long shadows and rosy lights . . . Nature, I repeat, did its best. But though it adorned, it could not improve the works of man. The Taj, even at sunset, even reverberated upside down from banks and river, even in conjunction with melancholy cypresses—the Taj was a disappointment.

Worse. "Milk-white amongst its dark cypresses, flawlessly mirrored, it is positively the *Toteninsel* of Arnold Boecklin come true." Aldous goes on with evident relish about the interest (which he does not share) in the expensive and the picturesque as such. It is the "inordinate costliness" that most people seem to like about the Taj. "The average tourist is moved to greater raptures by St Peter's than by his own St Paul's. The interior of the Roman basilica is all of marble . . and marble covers a multitude of sins. St Paul's is only Portland stone." Back to the Taj. The minarets, "these four thin tapering towers . . . are among the ugliest structures ever erected by human hands". And the classicism is the product not of intellectual restraint imposed on exuberant fancy, but on an actual deficiency of fancy. The Temples at Chitor, by contrast, "are specimens of true classicism. They are the products of prodigious, an almost excessive, fancy, held in check and directed by the most judicious intelligence . . . And when you compare the Taj with more or less contemporary European buildings in the neo-classical style . . . take Palladio's Rotonda at Vicenza for example . . . [how] much richer, more subtle and various than the poor, dry, negative elegance of the Indian building."

Chapter Nine

The Range, the Confluence of Associations . . .

TAKE Palladio's Rotonda at Vicenza . . . Aldous's measure was still Italy. At Taxila, the ancient city in North India where Alexander rested, the landscape merged into the Roman Campagna.

> The outworks of the Himalayas play the part of the Alban and Sabina mountains. Ranges of woodless Frascatis and desiccated Tivolis subside into a grey and rolling plain. On sudden and unexpected eminences . . stand the Indian equivalents of Neni and Civita Castellana . . .[1]

In the week Aldous had sailed, his latest book came out in England. *Along the Road*, his second collection of essays. His first, *On the Margin*, published two years earlier, had been recognized for the particular combination of lightness and learning. (And point: what he had to say in the early 1920s on re-reading *Candide*, for instance, is only too acutely relevant today.) Most of the essays of the first volume, though, had been originally written for the *Athenaeum* and other journals; they were the products of Aldous's most hard-worked years and much of what he wrote was what he had been asked to, rather than what he might have wished to write. A Wordsworth centenary comes along, there is a Flemish exhibition, someone has written another damn thick book about someone else—the subject has got to be mugged up and, as every literary journalist well knows, he has also got to rev up ideas and emotions; this, useful training though it may be, in the long run tends to exploit rather than develop what original talent he may have. When Aldous came to write *Along The Road*, his working conditions had changed: he was free to choose his subject and his length; he was able to let himself rip in a form that suited him—a form which he refreshed and of which he became a master. Tracts of his novels read like essays; conversely he often attacked an essay with a novelist's latitude. *Along the Road* was written *con amore*, with exuberance. The book is about travel, works of art and places, and most of the art and places are in Italy. Yet Italy is but the home-base, the playground of what Kenneth Clark has so well called "the range, the confluence of

[1] *Jesting Pilate.*

169

associations, the power of speedy cross-classification,"[1] that was so characteristic of Aldous's mind, works and conversation. He is snowed up in his Citroën among the Apennines in a howling wind, and he is off to the sands of Yarmouth in a Beerbohm Tree production of David Copperfield, in another flash it is Hilaire Belloc's rhyme on the Polar bear and the Great Wall of China, in the next the second volume of the *Encyclopaedia Britannica*. Obliged in the flesh to spend the night at the inn at Pietramala, his mind moves to 1813 when men could travel in spite of the Napoleonic wars and make experiments on iodine at Mount Vesuvius, and English scientists were presented with medals by the Emperor. And now he is getting down to Sir Humphry Davy, young Michael Faraday and James Clerk Maxwell. "A Night at Pietramala" is a serene essay, postulating a serene view of the continuity of science. How satisfactory, Aldous exclaims, "these lives of born men of science always are!

> There is an integrity about these men, a unity of purpose that to the rest of us distracted mortals seems wonderfully enviable and wonderfully beautiful.[2]

If *he* could choose his next existence he would like to be a man of science—"by nature, inevitably . . . The only thing that might make me hesitate would be an offer by fate of artistic genius. But even if I could be Shakespeare, I think I should still choose to be Faraday."[2]

Men of science ought to be happier than other men. "And when one reads their lives one finds that in point of fact they generally were happy. [Whereas the artist] must fatally pass much of his life in the emotional world of human contacts . . . these form the subject matter of his art . . . I personally would rather be subdued to intellectual contemplation than to emotion, would rather use my soul professionally for knowing than for feeling."[2]

Along the Road contains the essays on Leon Battista Alberti, on Breughel and on Piero della Francesca which much influenced contemporary taste. Aldous's physical sight, as we know, was defective; when he looked at a picture he would put a squat little telescopic instrument to his good eye and peer at the canvas from a distance of a few inches. Yet the fact remains—I am quoting once more Kenneth Clark, and who should know better?—that what Aldous "wrote about painting proves him to have been one of the most discerning lookers of our time.

> . . Aldous had an astonishing faculty for seeing what an artist really meant. This allowed him to follow what I believe is one of

[1] *Mem. Vol.*   [2] *Along the Road.* Chatto & Windus, 1925.

the most enlightening of all forms of criticism—the description of the subject of a picture in the artist's own terms . . .

Should we say that Aldous's gift of perception was not so much a matter of eye, as a part of a general sensibility to all forms of orderly or impassioned communication . . . It is true that Aldous responded with equal intensity to all the arts . . .[1]

And with so much pleasure. One of the most endearing experiences was to follow Aldous round a gallery or a museum: he was so pleased, so eager, so oblivious of his own exertions.

The river [Patinir's] flows in a narrow valley between hills. A broad, a brimming and a shining river. The hills are steep and all of a height . . The sky is pale above this strip of fantastically carved and scalloped earth. A pale sky from which it must sometimes rain in Chinese white . . . and the green of the grass and the trees is tinged with white till it has taken on the colour of the "Emerald Green" of children's paint-boxes.

. . Peering into the little pictures, each painted with a million tiny strokes of a four-haired sable brush, I laughed with pleasure at the beauty of the charming invention. This Joachim Patinir, I thought, imagines delicately . . .[2]

It is in the essay on Piero della Francesca that Aldous declares his values. The essay is called "The Best Picture". "You smile . . . the expression is ludicrous . . ." There are a great many kinds of merit and classifications are futile. "But there does exist, none the less, an absolute standard of artistic merit. And it is a standard which is in the last resort a moral one."[2]

Whether a work of art is good or bad depends on the quality of the character which expresses itself in the work. Not that all artists are conventionally virtuous. "Longfellow was a bad poet, while Beethoven's dealings with his publishers were frankly dishonourable." The virtue that is necessary to a good artist is "the virtue of integrity, of honesty towards oneself". Bad art can be negatively bad, that is merely incompetent or dull; it can be positively bad, that is "a lie and a sham". When the lie is well told one is taken in—for a time. In the end the lie is always found out. "Sometimes the charlatan is also a first-rate man of genius and then you have such strange artists as Wagner and Bernini, who can turn what is false and theatrical into something almost sublime."[2]

The best picture is Piero della Francesca's "stupendous"

[1] Lord Clark of Saltwood, op. cit. *Mem. Vol.*
[2] *Along the Road.*

Resurrection at Borgo San Sepolcro. Christ is standing, "a banner in his right hand, his left foot already raised and planted on the rim of the sepulchre, preparing to set out into the world.

. . But the being who rises before our eyes from the tomb is more like a Plutarchian hero than the Christ of conventional religion. The body is . . like that of a Greek athlete; formidably strong . . . The face is stern and pensive, the eyes cold. The whole figure is expressive of physical and intellectual power. It is the resurrection of the classical ideal, incredibly much grander and more beautiful than the classical reality. . . .

The picture is great, "absolutely great, because the man who painted it was genuinely noble as well as talented.

And to me personally the most moving of pictures, because its author possessed . . those qualities of character which I most admire . . A natural, spontaneous, and unpretentious grandeur—this is the leading quality of all Piero's work. He is majestic without being at all strained, theatrical or hysterical—as Handel is majestic, not as Wagner . . . Piero seems to have been inspired by what I may call the religion of Plutarch's *Lives*—which is not Christianity, but a worship of what is admirable in man.[1]

---

[1] *Along the Road.*

Chapter Ten

The Journey Round the World—Malaya, The Pacific, Japan, The United States

THE Huxleys left India—"rather glad to escape"—early in February, sailing from Calcutta for Burma. There were still another four full months of travelling before them; much of it by sea and more leisurely; they had reached a saturation point and were taking their impressions with detachment. They spent some weeks looking at Burma and Malaya, ending up at Government House in Singapore. From there they went to Java, cruised among the islands, changed to a ship that went along the coast of Borneo to Zamboanga in the Southern Philippines, where "(with luck) we shall get another ship to take us to Manila in time to catch the liner leaving for Frisco on April 7th. It ought to be very pleasant."

It was. The ships were Dutch and comfortable; Aldous read what he could find and wrote up his travel diary. He would not allow Maria to help herself more than very sparingly to the caviare that was profusely offered (one of the few things she liked to eat); taking advantage, he explained to her, was vulgar. Off North Borneo they were faced with violence. A member of the crew entrenched with a dagger threatening to run amok. Only a week before another determined sailor had stabbed to death the captain in his own ship and twelve others within five miles of Singapore. While the ship's officers conferred and the passengers stood huddled, Aldous reflected on "the precarious artificiality of all that seemed most solid and fundamental in our civilization, of all that we take for granted.

> An individual has only to refuse to play the game of existence according to the current rules to throw the rule-observing players into bewildered consternation . . .
> They are appalled, they are at a loss, they are helpless.

The sailor, fortunately, lost his nerve.

In Japan they only spent a few days, landing at Kobe, going on to Kyoto by rail, joining ship again at Yokohama. It rained incessantly, the streets were deep in mud and the light as grey as a Scotch November. From the train they saw dim country bristling with factory chimneys. Kyoto looked like a mining camp. Yokohama like a camp that had not yet been finished. In Kyoto they walked through the city and it was like walking through an enormous Woolworth bazaar. "Such a collection of the cheap and shoddy, of the quasi-genuine and the imitation solid, of the vulgar and the tawdry . . ."

The news from home had not been reassuring. Matthew was not well and the doctors advised sending him to Switzerland to improve his lungs. Madame Nys was against this, and Aldous and Maria had to accept her judgement. Although they heard soon after that the little boy was better and Switzerland no longer urgent, they realized that they would have to give up their plan of moving to Rome on their return; instead, it would have to be some suitable mountain place. From Udaipur they had cabled Mme Nys, "Belgium for the moment—the mountains with us when we come back."

In April they were crossing the North Pacific and what Aldous called the somewhat Extreme Orient was behind them. The shock of re-entry into the West was near. One morning Aldous was handed the ship's bulletin of daily news. "Mrs X of Los Angeles," he read, "girl-wife of Dr X, aged 79, has been arrested for driving her automobile along the railroad track, whistling like a locomotive."

This piece of information had been transmitted through the ethereal holes between the molecules of air. From a broadcasting station more than five thousand miles away it had come to our ship . . . The labours of half a dozen men of genius, of hundreds of patient and talented investigators, had gone to creating and perfecting the means for achieving this miracle . . The ether reverberated with the name of Mrs X . . . The wave that bore it broke against the moon and the planets, and rippled on towards the stars and the ultimate void . . . Ah, the fire of Prometheus is put to the strangest uses . . .[1]

Meanwhile Aldous and Maria admitted interest in the exploits of Mrs X. She was bailed out, they presently heard, by her ancient husband, went home and began to smash the furniture . . . "What ultimately happened we never learned. The anonymous powers

[1] *Jesting Pilate.*

174

which purvey wireless news are strangely capricious. [One morning] the name of Mrs X no longer rippled out towards Aldebaran and the spiral nebulae. The bulletin announced that Bébé Daniels had fallen off her horse."

The last weeks of the voyage were spent in the United States. They landed at San Francisco and took the Daylight Limited to Los Angeles. It was the America of the boom years, the jazz age, prohibition America; the Huxleys were at the end of a long and wearing journey. Aldous's comments on bootlegged cocktails and *Yes, Sir, that's My Baby* were predictable. California fascinated him there and then, though he found Hollywood "altogether too Antipodean to be lived in".

They crossed the continent by train, spent a few days in Chicago, went on to New York. If there was one person Aldous wanted to meet, it was Miss Anita Loos. He adored *Gentlemen Prefer Blondes*. He wrote her a fan letter.

.. I was enraptured by the book, have just hugely enjoyed the play, and am to be in America so short a time that I have no leisure to do things in the polite and tortuous way . . .

They met. Anita Loos was in her twenties; Aldous found her ravishing. "One would like to keep her as a pet," he wrote to brother Julian.

Of course the Huxleys were rushed and fêted. Aldous became interested in the phenomenon of American vitality, a psychological by-product of prosperity, he concluded. "In less fortunate countries the precariousness of existence keeps large classes of the population in a state of chronic fear. Unemployment is a haunting apprehension . . . so little is needed in Europe to precipitate a man . . . Fear is the enemy of life." In the America of 1926 that fear did not exist.

.. Americans live with confidence, and therefore with enhanced vitality. A generous extravagance, undreamed of in other parts of the world, is the American rule.[1]

But this vitality is externalized "in places of public amusement, in dancing and motoring . . . What is known as 'night life' flourishes . . . And nowhere, perhaps is there so little conversation .. Hence there appears to be even more vitality in the Americans than there really is.

[1] *Jesting Pilate.*

. . It is all movement and noise, like the water gurgling out of a bath—down the waste. Yes, down the waste.[1]

Presently the voyage was over. In *Jesting Pilate* Aldous summed up on a note of human unity. All values everywhere are broadly the same, "Goodness, beauty, wisdom and knowledge. . . ." In a letter a little later on he almost reversed it,

The more I see of human beings, the more I am convinced of the specific, almost generic, differences between them. One species can hardly communicate with the other. It is, perhaps, unfortunate that they can breed together. No, on second thoughts, it is probably a good thing.

At the end of May, willingly, they sailed for England.

[1] *Jesting Pilate.*

Chapter Eleven

Taking Up—New Starting Points

AFTER their return Aldous spent an agreeable June and July in London. Maria went to St Trond. He saw his family, dined with friends, strolled about the summer streets; he was staying with his Collier aunt, Aunt Ethel, in Hampstead, using the Athenaeum during the day. There was time to sit at last for his Uncle Jack. The Hon. John Collier had done a portrait of Maria in 1919, a large canvas, three-quarter length, Maria sitting, hands folded, in a décolleté dress. It was shown in the Royal Academy of 1920. Curiously, the portrait John Collier painted now, seven years later, turned out a companion piece—Aldous, rising thirty-two, looks as absurdly young as did Maria. It is a charming portrait, to my mind, academic or not, even a rather moving one. There he sits, young Aldous, in his nice brownsy suit and his floppy sofa-cushion tie drawn through a ring in the fashion of today, contriving to look at the same time romantic, casual and noble. John Collier's granddaughter, Jill,[1] aged sixteen, watched the painting's progress in the studio.

. . It was one of him sitting, sort of gazing into the distance . . . It was the first time I ever knew anything about Aldous—and I thought how fascinating he was. I fell in love with him, literally, as a portrait before I had actually met him.

The portrait was exhibited in the Academy of 1927.[2]

The three-years' contract with Chatto's had run out in January. Aldous had fulfilled it in so far as he had written and delivered two books per annum thrice running, though only two of them, instead of the agreed three, were novels, *Antic Hay* and *Those Barren Leaves*. Two volumes of short stories, *Little Mexican* and *Two or Three Graces* (just out), two of non-fiction, *Along the Road* and *Jesting Pilate* (about to be delivered), and *The Discovery*, an adaptation of the play by Sheridan thrown in, made up the bag. (Chattos were preparing also a collection titled *Essays New and*

---

[1] The present Mrs Anthony Greenwood, née Gillian Crawshay Williams.
[2] Both portraits are in the possession of Rina (Madame Marcel) Eustration, who lives at present in Marseilles.

Old, containing exactly that.) There was a small over-all deficit in royalties against the annual advances, amounting to £76.9.5d. Chattos now proposed a new agreement on the same lines and Aldous signed it on 7th June. It was again for three years and two books per annum "one of which at least a full-length novel", and "possibly three other books during the said three years". Royalties on fiction were increased to an initial 20% up to 8,000 copies, and remained at 25% thereafter. The advance, Aldous's main fixed income, was increased from £500 a year to £650.

In August Aldous went to join his family at St Trond. He found Matthew "very well and in uproarious spirits", eating copiously; yet a longish stay in a high, dry climate was still indicated. They decided to try Cortina d'Ampezzo in the Dolomites, a resort at seven thousand feet with a reputation for winter sun. By September the Huxleys were installed in a nice warm house with long balconies and the right exposures, a small house simply and comfortably furnished (the rent, Aldous noted with satisfaction, was under £9 per month). Maria loathed the mountains and the cold however dry and sunny, and the lack of friends. Aldous chiefly looked at it as a good place to work in, and Matthew, the object of the exercise, was getting more robust. Old Bella had been replaced by a highly trained young governess, Mademoiselle La Porte, whom Aldous and Maria found a charming person, intelligent and a treasure. Fortunately, Matthew also liked her and was learning quickly.

They "existed in tolerable contentment". Julian and Juliette briefly appeared on their way from a journey in the Balkans (Aldous regretting not having had the time to go with them); *Jesting Pilate* came out in England (". . an elegant chaos"); Aldous was immersed in "the first bits and pieces of an ambitious novel".

In October, brief escape to Florence. Aldous got a tiresome tooth infection and had to see his dentist. It was there that Aldous and D. H. Lawrence met again, eleven years after their first, single meeting during the war in Hampstead.[1]

Lawrence and Frieda had returned to Europe the autumn before from their years of wandering, from Ceylon, Australia, Mexico and the ranch at Taos, from his long experience of search and flight. He was already a very ill man, struggling to keep alive. "Last year I nearly fell into the Styx," he had written to

[1] In point of fact, they had met once again very briefly in the intervening years, at a London party probably in the winter of 1923-24.

Middleton Murry, ". . all I want is to live and be well alive, not constrainedly half dead."[1] *The Plumed Serpent* had come out nine months before, Lawrence was writing *Lady Chatterley's Lover*; he and Frieda were wintering at the Villa Mirenda at Scandici. The Florentine encounter was the starting point of the friendship between Lawrence, Aldous and Maria; it flowered almost at once. (It had only three and a half years to run.)

What got Aldous was Lawrence's *extraordinariness*, his difference in kind; a quality he looked for and accepted with humility and joy. ("I like him so much.") Lawrence confronted with Aldous on his own might have bristled. At Aldous's reticences, his good manners, his incisiveness of word—though that was undercut by gentleness of being—by Aldous's intellect and all that it entailed. As it turned out, the Huxleys were among the very few people with whom Lawrence did not at one time or another have a quarrel. Between him and Maria there was a straight intuitive affinity: they got on right away. Maria loved him; Lawrence, in Aldous's words, "was very fond of her". As well they had much fun. The four of them; as there was of course Frieda. She could irritate Aldous (" . . . being with her makes me believe that Buddha was right when he numbered stupidity among the deadly sins.") Much later, when Frieda was all that was left, they became very fond of her. This and much else was in the future: in point of time the meeting in Florence was short; a couple of walks, a picnic (at Vernon Lee's whose conversation Aldous admired), a meal or two at a trattoria. Traces are in letters.

. . Aldous Huxley just telegraphed, asking us to lunch Friday . . . Aldous Huxley, a writer and his wife came for the day, in their fine new car . . . Maria driving.[2]

. . Aldous Huxley was here on Friday; how he loathed India! I think it frightened him with a sense of squalor.[3]

. . I have started painting, quite seriously, on my own. Maria Huxley . . . brought me some canvases that her brother [*sic*] had daubed on . . . Maria looks like a *very* small edition of Ottoline: like Ottoline's Cinderella daughter—same peculiar long cheeks, and rather nice eyes. I liked her, too. . . .

The Huxleys seemed very bored. They are living pro-tem up in Cortina, North of Venice, in the higher mountains, because their child is supposed to have a lung. And they are very lonely—nobody

[1] D. H. L's Letters, 1932 edition.

[2] D. H. L. to Dorothy Brett, 18th October 1926, from *The Letters of D. H. Lawrence*, 1962 edition.

[3] D. H. L. to Earl and Achsah Brewster, 25th October 1926, from *D. H. Lawrence Reminiscences and Correspondence*, by Earl and Achsah Brewster. Martin Secker, 1934.

there . . . I wish they lived a bit nearer so that I could walk over and see them . . .[1]

Some snapshots were taken; the Huxleys returned to their mountains.

[1] D. H. L. to Dorothy Brett, 24th November 1926, from *The Letters of D. H. Lawrence*, 1962 edition.

Chapter Twelve

One Year

MOUNTAINS and November rains and the "inordinately large and complicated novel". Aldous was attempting to give plot and action to the hand theme in *Those Barren Leaves*. "I want to make a picture of life in its different aspects, the synchronous portrait of the different things an individual simultaneously is . . . Very difficult, and I doubt if I shall succeed . . but . . interesting."

He had been reading Gide's latest novel, *Les Faux Monnayeurs*. He usually found him disappointing—too elegant, too literary. Now he was interested, "The only good book he has written . . . in its way very good.

> It is good, I think, because it is the first book in which Gide has ventured to talk about the one thing in the world that really interests him—sentimental sodomy.

It was also, it might be said in passing, one of the things that *least* interested Aldous, he was rather hoity-toity about sodomites sentimental or otherwise; whereas Maria got on extremely well with what she loudly and to their faces called our bugger friends, Aldous was made rather uncomfortable by evident male homosexuality. About Lesbians he was tolerant, even had a *faible*— after all he shared their taste—as long as they were feminine and not too orthodox.

Aldous and Maria persevered for another long three months. "We sit perched on an icy solitude," Aldous wrote on Christmas Day, "which would be intolerable if it didn't do us all so much good." They had young visitors, Maria's sister Rose—now old enough to enter the picture—came out with another girl and a little Belgian boy as company for Matthew. On New Year's Eve Aldous and Maria took the girls to a dance, their first, "at the smart hotel.

> It was very funny to be and feel a chaperon looking after those two ravishing creatures . . straight from the convent . . in white frills . . who missed not a single dance and got very gay on almost no champagne. Aldous and I looked pompous and spent most of our time playing at games and though winning many silly prizes losing much money . . .

"Perhaps it'll bring us luck in the New Year . . . It's already started: We shall go away soon . . . to London . . . Aldous's work be praised for that necessity . . . London for a long time . . . Cortina I have hated for so long so intensely that now I quite like it."[1]

The event of the winter was a new car. "A really rather tremendous car," Aldous called it. He had sold two articles in America "for a thousand dollars apiece! Crazy—and it probably won't be repeated." So they parted from their faithful Citroën that had cost so little and behaved so well and whose "habits had been as regular as those of Emanuel Kant", and bought the new Itala six cylinder two litre, the car with all the qualities of the Alfa Romeo. "What a machine . . ."

In February Arnold Bennett spent some weeks at Cortina, "in excellent form . . . My word,

> what sums these literary nabobs can command . . . [Bennett] revealed a few of the secrets. He himself never writes for less than two shillings per word, like an Atlantic cable!

Aldous ran into trouble with his novel—"The thing is simply getting too formidable for me." (The thing became *Point Counter Point*.) *Antic Hay* had taken under three months, *Those Barren Leaves* six; Aldous was used to going on with a book till it was finished. Now, with some fifty thousand words down, he felt that he needed time for "further thinking and ruminative living", and decided to stop altogether. Meanwhile there was nothing to send to Chattos for spring publication. From the money point of view this was not so worrying; *Jesting Pilate* had sold 3,000 copies, *Two or Three Graces* 2,000 in the regular and another 3,500 in the cheap edition, and an extra £200 had been made by the limited edition of reprinted essays. These were not large sales but good enough to wipe out the deficit and put Aldous a couple of hundred pounds ahead. He began to write some essays for autumn publication, something he could count on doing with reasonable certainty and speed.

All the same he was worried about the novel. A standstill in work is often outside the writer's conscious control and accompanied by a sense of having somehow made *fausse route. What* if the thing will never move again? There is nothing to do but wait (and meanwhile try to handle the waiting time in some constructive fashion). Perhaps it was a good thing to go on writing hard at something else; perhaps it would have served Aldous

[1] Maria Huxley in a letter to Eugene Saxton, published in *The Letters of Aldous Huxley.*

better to be idle. There was no choice, he had to earn his living; he could not afford to follow his own instincts as Lawrence, who could afford it even less, would certainly have done; but then Lawrence, as Aldous said, obeyed his daemon, was possessed in a real sense by his creative genius,[1] whereas Aldous, in humility and honest doubt, did not believe in his. (And how he often longed to be possessed, longed for the overriding impulse, whether it would have driven him into being Faraday or a great musician or a mystic or into seizing for himself a richer slice of life.) When the book stopped he went about the house morose and silent.

They left Cortina in late February (Matthew glowing with health), meaning to stop in Florence for a little motoring in the Tuscan spring. Instead Aldous went down with influenza. They saw Lawrence,

> Aldous still absolutely gone in the grouches—is writing a political novel [*sic*], heaven save him. [D. H. L. to Brett] I feel myself in another world altogether. They seem to me like people from a dead planet ... It's no good, for me the human world becomes more and more unreal, more and more wearisome.

The Huxleys drove on to England, and remained in London until May when they were suddenly called to Belgium. Maria's grandfather was dying, Monsieur Baltus, the old gentleman, now really old, who looked like a retired colonel and had spent his active days manufacturing cloth and his declining ones in reading, who had given Aldous his first welcome at St Trond. It was a formal death-bed.

> We were all there—kneeling around his bed. [Suzanne in her memoir] . . The Monk, Père Auguste, a family friend, an intellectual from the neighbouring Capuchin monastery, read the prayers. My grandmother was kneeling with us. Grandfather's last words were, "Emérence," his wife's name; she rose and gave him her hand—*et tranquillement il a poussé son dernier soupir.*

The recollection of that first death-bed remained potent with Maria. When in California, decades later, a dying woman asked for her help, she wrote to her great friend Rosalind Rajagopal, trying to clarify her feelings. ". . We all knelt around my grandfather's bed and prayed with the monks and the nuns and the older servants . . . But I could not tell—brought up as Catholics, heaven and hell clutter up all one's reactions and that personal God too . . . Perhaps I was too young. I think I mean not

_____
[1] Introduction to *The Letters of D. H. L.*, 1932.

interested, only impressed."[1] Her active pity went to her grand-mother who, very frail, took a dose of valerian in the night and nearly died herself.

I can still see Coccola [we are back with Suzanne] a very tender nurse by her side, holding her hand, renewing the ether compresses although the smell of ether made her ill . . .

Aldous tried to keep aloof. "It will be impossible [he wrote to Lewis Gielgud] to get out of staying several days [after the funeral] as M's grandmother finds her presence particularly com-forting. In the circumstances we cannot refuse to stay.

All this is . . at once lugubrious and farcical—the real Balzacian comedy of a funeral in a little town; friends and relations in crêpe; lettres de faire part; prodigal sons turning up to be reconciled and pinching the cigars and a thousand francs for a black overcoat; the poor old man's body in full evening dress; monks and sisters of charity padding about; preparations for a colossal funeral banquet —all very fantastic and everything happening to the strains of the steam organs and electric pianos of the inevitable Flemish kermesse just round the corner. . . .

That year they had another long summer by the Mediterranean. They had missed Forte two years running; now they came back with relief. Forte was the hub of their Italian life, here Aldous felt in health, had a sense of basking however hard he worked; there were sea, olive trees, cicada sounds in soft nights; they had attractive, gay, affectionate friends at hand. For Maria the mechanics of living were easy. They were in a new house, the Majetta; basically all were much the same, smallish, clean, quiet and equipped with the necessities of outdoor life—a garden and a vine-wreathed pergola. Aldous was working away at his essays (despatched in July). The Léner string quartet was staying prac-tically next door, there was live music at night: Beethoven trios. Rose was expected again, George and Vivi Baltus were in their castello above Carrara; the Gielguds, Lewis and Mimi, were coming to stay in August; as usual their closest, their permanent Italian friends were more or less in residence. Yvonne Franchetti —adorably pretty, a joy to Aldous and already to young Matthew —and her husband Luigino, the pianist. And of course Costanza. She would come swinging into the house early of a morning, sit down on Aldous's bed and tell him—all ears—about everybody's

<hr/>

[1] Letter dated Llano, 27th February 1943.

love affairs including her own. The name of her first and brief
lover was, to Aldous's utter joy, Dottore Cherubini. Costanza was
now married, after some experiments and romantic attachments,
and beginning to have daughters. She had finally accepted one
of the boys of the *petite bande* of their youth, his name was Ecki
Petterich and he was a German intellectual, very German, in a
sugary artistic way, with Greek ideals. (The marriage fizzled out
after some years.) The Huxleys did not like him much. In a
certain way—says Jeanne, who knew it all so well—Costanza
belonged to them.

Aldous and Maria had a way of drawing people into their life.
Costanza was the first; she set the pattern. There were variations,
it could be a woman on her own, a single man, or a man and
wife, but wherever they were they gathered an eclectic family
about them. It was a matter of sharing daily things, hearing con-
fidences (entirely one-sided on Aldous's part), sharing the friends'
troubles. These relationships might wane with time and geo-
graphical separation; they never ended in a quarrel.

It was the summer Rina came to them, Rina Rontini. She was
the child of Italian peasants, one of nine; at the age of eight—
after one and a half year's schooling in all—she was sent away
from home into the mountains to mind sheep. Not for wages—
for her daily food. "My mother didn't have to feed me any more."[1]
In that manner she lived till she was fifteen, then, through an
elder sister in service with the Fasolas, she was sent to Forte to
the Huxleys. "I knew nothing—the *patience* Signora Maria had
with me. She taught me. When I think of it, the things I couldn't
do ... Luckily there was a cook ... The *patience* ..." Rina loved
Baby (as Matthew was called well into boyhood), Maria she
worshipped, for Aldous at first there was awe. "I was shy as a
girl, I was shy being in the house with him. But he was kind—
era sempre gentile—oh yes, he talked, he talked to everyone, but
not *like* everyone." (And Rina is laughing—she is dark-eyed with
the bone structure showing now in the fine Tuscan face—makes
a gesture that includes the street, the city she now lives in.) "You
see, he didn't talk like a *Marseillais*."

Her own trouble was sweets. "I hadn't ever had even sugar to
eat, so I had this craving ... I took cakes, I stole chocolates. I
couldn't help myself. Signora Maria would hide the chocolates,
lock them up; I could always get at them. I knew it was wrong—
it made her sad. But it was *plus fort que moi*. And you know what
she did the first thing after the war, in 1945, Signora Maria?
She sent me a parcel with chocolates from America."[1]

Rina remembers her youth and ignorance; what Aldous and

---

[1] Rina Rontini, the present Madame Marcel Eustration, talking to S. B.

Maria spoke of was her goodness and intelligence. And she was observant. Aldous liked to hear about what was going on, to hear, she says, about the funny things. She told him to come out to see the Contessa della Gherardesca next door give sugar to her horse from a gloved hand, the groom standing by with napkin and the lump of sugar on a silver salver. Aldous was enchanted and Rina had to call him every morning for the Contessa's *zucchero*.

Into that Forte life Lawrence arrived: in June, by himself, for a couple of weeks, not in an easy mood. "Stimulating," Aldous wrote, "but difficult to get on with, passionate, queer, violent." Rina found him gentle and expansive—"*He* really talked to everyone."

Gentle to Rina; less so about the Huxley's friends. Wretchedly unwell, he was apt to lash out. ". . He is a Jew, Barone Luigi [Franchetti]—and as rich as Croesus. He plays the piano very well, and is quite nice . . . but I have absolutely no basic sympathy with people of assured incomes. All words become a lie, in their mouths, in their ears also. I loathe rich people."[1] Nor did he share the Huxley's love for Forte, ". . beastly as a place: flat, dead sea, jellyfish and millions of villas." And the sun and bathing were bad for him; within days of his return to Florence he went down with a bronchial haemorrhage. Aldous and Maria rushed to him. They found him in bed, "touchingly gentle now and very ill.

> . . And the poor wretch is not strong enough . . to move into the cool of the mountains . . . I hope profoundly he'll get over this business. The doctor seemed to think he'd be all right; but with these haemorrhages . . the end can be quite sudden and unexpected.

As we know, Lawrence pulled through. He managed to get away to Austria. "It is such a mercy to be able to breathe and move. I take little walks in the country," he wrote to the Huxleys, and in the autumn they had a letter full of new plans which ends with this spirited passage:

> I'm glad Maria has met Mrs Beeton . . . Right-o! Maria! You wait a bit, and I'll be eating your puddings for you. God gives us a good meeting, as the Methodists 'd say.—Though I'm sorry Rose has gone. The boy must miss her terribly, lessons or not!—Maria, have you greased the car?—I feel I don't want to do a thing, except curse *almost* everybody. Never mind! *Hasta la Vista!*
>
> D. H. L.[2]

[1] *The Letters of D. H. L.*, 1962. (To Koteliansky, 13.6.27.)
[2] Ibid., 1932.

Aldous had gone back to the novel. It grew but he was "getting more and more involved in its difficulties". He wished that he could afford, he wrote to Julian, to spend four or five years over a book like Flaubert. "There might be a chance then of making it rather good." Instead he was still aiming at spring publication, and they stayed put in the "balmy warmth" of autumnal Forte, "I sit working on the beach with nothing but a pair of bathing drawers." Yet Italy *per se* was getting more irritating daily—petty regulations, police persecutions. At the moment the Italian press was fulminating against birth control. "I see that Musso wants twenty million Italians in twenty-five years. Presumably to fight France with . . ." As for the rest of the world, he'd been reading *The Mind and Face of Bolshevism*

> It's really humiliating that human beings can be so stupid as the Russians seem to be. They really are the devil. Europeans must join together to resist all the enemies of our civilization—Russians, Americans, orientals—each in their own way a hideous menace . . .

Proper Studies, the new book of essays, was published in November. The book can be read as an exposition of Aldous's current views on the social fabric—democracy, education, equality, eugenics . . . Much of the inspiration came from the Italian sociologist Vilfredo Pareto.[1] "He really does take the lid off and shows you the works [Aldous to Robert Nichols] at some length unfortunately . . . three thick volumes in Italian [and the writing] slow, subfusc and grim . . ." Aldous's regard for Pareto (who has three faintly dismissive lines in the *Britannica*[2]) was lasting. In 1934 he wrote,

> About old Pareto—I . . . feel he is one of the very few people who have approached sociology in a genuinely scientific spirit, without any metaphysical axe to grind, without violent political prejudices (beyond that conservatism and disbelief in progress which seems always to come to people who spend a lot of time studying the facts of human activity) and without, above all, any propagandist zeal for any *one*, or all explanatory hypotheses. This last is what makes most sociologies such rubbish. The mania to explain everything in terms of one set of causes—economic, climatic, psychological, religious and so forth. Pareto is prepared to admit that there are a great many causal factors always at work . . .[3]

[1] Vilfredo Pareto (1848-1923) Author of the monumental *Trattato di Sociologia Generale*, 1916. English Translation *Mind and Society*, 1935. Reviewed by A. H. in *N.Y. Herald Tribune Books*, 9th June 1935.
[2] Expanded to full article in recent editions.
[3] In a letter to Marjorie Seabrook.

In *Proper Studies* Aldous, too, attempted to approach sociology in a scientific spirit. The result is a very intelligent and arid book, perhaps his most arid. It has the aloofness of *Jesting Pilate* without the lightness, and in spite of many nails hit on the head, I cannot find it a sympathetic book. But let D. H. Lawrence have the word.

Dear Aldous,—

Many thanks for *Proper Studies*. I have read 70 pages, with a little astonishment that you are so serious and professorial. You are not your grandfather's *Enkel* for nothing—that funny dry-mindedness and underneath social morality. But you'll say I'm an introvert, and no fit judge. Though I think to make people introverts and extraverts is bunk . . . You are an extravert by inheritance far more than in *esse*. You'd have made a much better introvert, had you been allowed. "Did she fall or was she pushed" . . . But, my dear, don't be dry and formal and exposition all that—What's the odds! I just read Darwin's *Beagle* again—he dried himself—and *tant de bruit pour des insectes!*—But I like the book.

There is a P.S. to this letter:

I don't mean I didn't find the 70 pages good—they're very sane and sound and good—only I myself am in a state of despair about the Word either written or spoken seriously. That's why, I suppose, I wrote this, when I wasn't asked . . .[1]

The Huxleys had been without anything like a permanent home since they left Florence over two years ago. Soon Matthew would have to go to school. Once more they thought of settling in England. It was to be the country—in easy reach of London, and Aldous is looking forward to it rather, looking forward, he wrote to Julian, to being more in England. "If only the sun shone!"

Their immediate plans were for another Alpine winter, joined this year by Julian and his family. (Julian was working at his share of the encyclopaedic work on biology, *Science of Life*, in collaboration with H. G. Wells, and was geographically his own master.) One gloomy day Aldous nearly called it off.

I have realized [he wrote to his brother] with increasing certainty that my novel can't be finished, as I hoped, by the beginning of January and that I shall need at least an extra month's work to get it done . . I shall have to go on working at it all through January

---

[1] *Letters of D. H. L.*, 1932.

—seven or eight hours a day, which would make rather nonsense of a joint holiday. So that I think . . it would be wisest if I . . . dug myself in somewhere with Maria . . . I really must get this bloody book off my hands and I know that I should find the task almost impossibly difficult in the midst of a friendly party . . .

Matthew and Mademoiselle could go if Juliette was able to take them on, and Aldous would lend Julian his own skis . . . By next morning Aldous had changed his mind. He sent a note,

My Dear J,
    Thinking it over again—after all I could get my work done all right, particularly if we were in a house; and it would be very nice to be together.

And so Juliette took a house for all of them, the Chalet des Aroles, at Les Diablerets in Switzerland.

Presently, late in the year, Aldous and Maria left Forte. They spent Christmas in Florence. On Christmas Day they drove out to Scandici and picked up Frieda and Lawrence who had written that he wanted to go where they could "eat turkey and be silly—not sit solitary . . ."

Chapter Thirteen

A Family Holiday—Involvements with D. H. Lawrence

THEY were a large party, in their capacious chalet at Les Diablerets, the two brothers, Juliette and Maria, their three children, Anthony, Francis and Matthew; Mademoiselle, visiting relations. The men wrote in the morning, then came outdoor exercise, picnics, teatime talk, reading aloud in the evenings— Julian and Aldous had regained the family holidays of their youth; taking turns, they got through the whole of *The Pickwick Papers*. Everybody felt well. In his memories,[1] Julian speaks of it as a cheerful, a happy time. As a mountain resort, a ghastly species, Aldous complained, Les Diablerets was a poor specimen. But the sun was marvellous. He very much wanted Lawrence to join them ("I'm waiting to hear . . what it's really like and how dear it is,"[2] Lawrence wrote). Presently he and Frieda arrived and settled "two minutes away across the snow in another wooden hut".

The men laboured. To Aldous it soon became clear that he could not get the novel done in time. Even in those days of quick production a book for spring publication had to be in by February. For the second year Aldous was about to fail his contract. Maria restored his peace of mind by firm advice. "Darling—tell them." On 23rd January Aldous sat down and wrote to C. H. C. Prentice of Chattos, a letter typical of his attitude to his publishers and his money dealings.

> I feel very apologetic; but this wretched book refuses, in spite of incessant labours, to get finished. I might perhaps contrive to scramble through the final additions and alterations in the course of another month; but I'd much prefer to take more time and produce for the autumn something which I hope would be better. I hope this won't be a great inconvenience; but I do want to get this thing thoroughly ship-shape.
>
> Meanwhile I am bothered by the thought that this delay of mine may involve you in financial loss; and since I haven't fulfilled my side of the contract, I think it would be only fair if the next two quarters' instalments were at least reduced. . . .

[1] Sir Julian Huxley, *Memories*, Vol. I. Allen & Unwin, 1970.
[2] This and all subsequent quotations from Lawrence are from *The Letters of D. H. L.*, 1932, unless otherwise stated.

Prentice's answer arrived a few days later.

Dear Huxley,

It is a pity about the novel, but to push it through, simply in order that it should come out quickly, would be a great mistake. Please do take your own time over it. Autumn will be quite all right . . . *Point Counter Point* is rather a critical book; so it would be madness to prevent you from doing all to it that you wanted . . . Do you think the MS will be ready for us by April? . . . [Harold] Raymond and I are both in the highest fizzle of curiosity.

It is charming of you to suggest that the next two quarterly instalments should be reduced. There may not be a necessity for this, but it does just look possible that the current year will show a deficit. *Proper Studies*, being not quite the kind of book that many people expected, has not started off so briskly . . . There is, however, the possibility that the royalties from the other books . . will have completed the annual sum . . . Perhaps it would be the easiest thing to go on paying your quarterly cheques as usual, and to carry on any deficit from this year to the next . . . It is really awfully good of you making the suggestion, but we do not wish to incommode you in any way.

There had been hope that sun and altitude might do something for Lawrence. At first all he could say was, "I'm no worse". Later he wrote to Orioli,

I think the place is really doing me good, I do feel stronger. I don't love snow, exactly—it's so beastly white, and makes one's feet so cold. But sometimes it's beautiful. Yesterday we drove in a sledge to the top of the pass and picnicked there, with Aldous and Maria and Rose, and Julian Huxley, Aldous's brother, and his wife Juliette. I really liked it. It does put life into one.[1]

He had brought the MS of *Lady Chatterley's Lover* and Maria was typing it for him. Maria, Aldous and Juliette were the first people to read it. "Aldous and Maria liked it very much—so they said." Juliette, apparently, was "*very* cross, morally so . . ." Nor did Lawrence and Julian see always eye to eye. When the Huxley brothers talked science to one another, Lawrence "exploded with a snort of impotent rage".[2] What infuriated him particularly were evolutionary and physiological ideas; he believed of course, writes Julian, that

[1] *The Letters of D. H. L.*, 1962.   [2] Sir Julian Huxley, op. cit.

More power exercised by the "dark loins of man", greater freedom for our instincts and our intuitions, would solve the world's troubles. His anger was particularly directed against myself, as a professional scientist. I learnt to disregard his outbursts of fury, but we had many stormy passages.[1]

And "Well, of course," said Aldous, "I never understood his anti-intellectualism . . . His dislike of science was passionate and expressed itself in the most fantastically unreasonable terms. 'All scientists are liars,' he would say, when I brought up some experimentally established fact, which he happened to dislike. 'Liars, liars!' It was a most convenient theory.

> I remember in particular one long and violent argument on evolution, in the reality of which Lawrence always passionately disbelieved. "But look at the evidence, Lawrence," I insisted, "look at all the evidence." His answer was characteristic. "But I don't care about evidence. Evidence doesn't mean anything to me. I don't feel it *here*." And he pressed his two hands on his solar plexus.[2]

But then Lawrence could give so much, and what he gave was so valuable (as Aldous said in the London interview) that it was absurd and profitless to spend one's time with him disputing about a matter in which he absolutely refused to take a rational interest. This anti-intellectualism was all the more curious,

> as he was an intellectual . . . I mean as a young man he was a great passer of examinations. [Chuckle in Aldous's voice] I mean he had a large store of knowledge, he didn't like to say so, but *he did*. He was very well read. . . .

By mid-February Julian had had to return to England, Frieda had gone to Germany, Maria was in Florence. *Gli autori* and the children stayed on, Juliette and Mademoiselle looking after them "like angels". Aldous was still glued to his "bloody novel . . . Such are the difficulties of fiction," he wrote to Lewis Gielgud, "especially to one who, like myself, isn't really a born novelist but has large aspirations."

Plans were vague again; he was tempted to fall in with Lawrence's idea and go out to live for six months on his ranch in New Mexico. In the meantime he and Maria went to London (in the Itala) to look at schools. Leaving Matthew in Belgium, they took a furnished flat in Onslow Mews for three months.

---

[1] Sir Julian Huxley, op. cit.
[2] Intro. to *Letters of D. H. L.*, 1932.

Your letter and Maria's today—[Lawrence wrote from Florence]
and first sound you've made since leaving Diablerets—those 2 postcards were ghosts . . . The printer is printing my novel. [The
miserable trouble over Lady Chatterley had just begun. Lawrence
had decided to print the unexpurgated version in Florence—a
thousand copies to be sold by mail order one by one.] Secker won't
do it—*meno male*—but what about the copyright . . . you must help
me. I'll send you a little batch of order forms, and I'm sure you
and Maria will make a few folks buy. That novel must be put down
their throats. Mind you stand up for it, when the pigs begin to
grunt. . . .

The letter ends with a litany:

Let's go to New Mexico in autumn. Let's be amused.
I've said May fifteenth for my novel.
Damn everybody!
What is Julian's address?
We *must* put salt on the hypocritical and snaily tails, the good
public.
Dear Maria, don't be downhearted.

And a few days later,

My dear Maria,
Your letter yesterday. Glad you are happy in London. You
wouldn't be happy in Italy—it only rains . . .
. . Secker wrote that he didn't see how the novel could possibly be
expurgated for public sale—so I'll just go on with my private one . . .
Did you get some of the little order-forms? . . And I've made my
design of a phoenix rising from the nest in flames for the cover . . .
Shall send you a specimen.

It is a long letter and in it Lawrence touches on what he and
Maria seem to have understood so well about one another.

I think myself it's rather nice to be busy and practical on the outside—and day-dreams, as you call it, inside. The things one cares
about are all inside, like seeds in the ground in winter. But one has
to attend to the things one only half cares about. And so life passes
away . . . Luckily the inside thing corresponds with the inside thing
in just a few people. I think it is so with us. We don't fit in very
well outside—but the inside corresponds, which is most important.

The sale of *Lady Chatterley's Lover* is already forbidden in Italy.
Now Lawrence decides that no more English publishers are to

be shown the novel. Aldous went to Curtis Brown's on his behalf. "They are furious in that office," Lawrence writes him, "that I publish my novel: daren't say much . . . I shall ask [them] to send the MS to you—do you mind? Perhaps Maria will deposit it somewhere for me. . . ." And in the p.s.: "Dear Maria—if you're passing Curtis Brown's office with the car, will you call and demand the MS of *John Thomas*, and carry it away from them. I don't want them to have it any more. And you can do what you like with it."

Lawrence had been correcting Orioli's page-proofs, "and it was *almost* Maria's typing over again. Dear Maria, all those little mistakes you made, and I followed like Wenceslas's page so patiently in your footsteps: now it's a Florentine printer. He writes dind't, did'nt, dnid't, dind't, din'dt, didn't like a Bach fugue. . . ."

Aldous and Maria and other friends were getting orders for *Lady C.* Maynard Keynes, the St John Hutchinsons, Lady Colefax subscribed; cheques were coming in. The price was £2 and $10 respectively. Lawrence was already thinking of a sea voyage with Frieda. "Believe me," he advised Aldous, "that's the thing to do: publish for oneself at £2. It's the solution for us small-selling authors."

Matthew's first school had been chosen, Frensham Heights, near Godalming, near Prior's Field, in Huxley country. He arrived from Belgium to be fitted out. "There are moments," Aldous groaned, "when parenthood really is a whole time job." What with shopping, zoo-visiting, calling on relations. . . . Presently the boy went off to school and Aldous did his last revisions. In the second week of May the T/S was sent in. *Point Counter Point* was off his hands. He was a free man once more. He and Maria left London for a stay in Paris before going on to Forte.

Chapter Fourteen

Cottage on the Seine

IT was not going to be Rome after all; nor as yet New Mexico,
nor the house in the Home Counties. Aldous and Maria saw
a house just outside Paris and took it then and there on a long
lease: 3 rue du Bac, Suresnes, beyond the Porte Maillot. It was a
compromise solution, and for such one usually finds a number of
good reasons. None of them were climate. The sun was not likely
to shine much more on that part of the Seine valley than it would
on Surrey. If Aldous shied again from settling down in England
it was perhaps because of an instinct that he functioned better
where he was not actually belonging; the freedom of the outsider
in perpetuum did suit him; like so many idiosyncratic and distinguished Englishmen and women before him he chose to live in
foreign parts without losing an essential Englishness. Italian plans
had to be shelved because the political nonsense had become too
intrusively obnoxious. Suresnes was near a civilized metropolis
and at the same time quiet; it was a handy distance for Matthew's
holidays (Aldous and Maria's bright idea of the best way for an
unaccompanied boy of eight to travel was to fly and many of
Matthew's childhood journeys began by his being put on one of
those small aeroplanes at Croydon); Lewis Gielgud lived in nearby
Passy; the literary world of Paris might prove pleasant it was
hoped; and Maria would be with her sister. Indeed it was planned
that the Moulaerts, René, Jeanne, Sophie, should have a permanent
apartment in the house. Moulaert, who had mixed the colours
for the flat in Paddington, was to do a professional decorating
job.

The landlord agreed to put in central heating; Maria found
materials designed by Dufy for sofas and cushions; armchairs
made to Aldous's measure were ordered from Maple's in London.
(Most of this furniture has endured.) Aldous, for his part, was
pleased.

> I look forward to getting into the "Cottage" at Suresnes . . . The
> surroundings are really delightful—a tiny provincial town enlivened
> by Sunday boating, with the river at the door and the Bois—where
> one can walk on weekdays for an hour and hardly see a soul—3
> minutes away; and the whole a quarter of an hour from the Rue de
> la Paix.
>
> (Though I wonder if we shall ever be there. We have already

planned to visit Germany, Spain and Khartoum in the course of the next year! But then, what are plans for unless to be unmade?)

They left Paris for their summer at Forte, seeing Lawrence in Switzerland on the way (three days at Chexbres above the Lake of Geneva—Lawrence surprisingly well, all things considered). Thence over the Simplon into Italy, Aldous's first experience of a modern motorway—"40 miles . . where you . . are guaranteed a perfect surface, no crossroads, no towns and no traffic except fast moving cars". Rina and yet another Forte house were waiting for them, Il Canneto, minute, in the pinewoods, very green, neither noisy nor dusty.

The weather—it always seems to have been—was perfect. Aldous had acquired an electric fan and so could work in the hottest hours after luncheon; "the difference between still and moving air," he remarked to his father, "is really incredible." What he was working on were "beastly proofs" and notes for some biographical essays on Pascal, Burns, Baudelaire . . .

Point Counter Point was to be published in the autumn, meanwhile Aldous learnt that it had been selected in advance "by a thing called the Literary Guild of the USA as their book of the month, which means a considerable sale over and above the ordinary figures and a corresponding quantity of filthy lucre. Which is very agreeable."

They returned to Paris in October, staying with the Gielguds as their house was still full of workmen. Suddenly, once again, Maria was called to St Trond. Emérence Baltus was dying. Maria was in time. Aldous and Jeanne followed for the funeral.

In late October they moved into the new house which was hideous. A narrow red-brick and stone frontage with gabled windows, a strip of back garden, the whole too small and not very convenient. A living-dining-room took up the main floor, the first held two bedrooms (Aldous worked in his), a bath and a tiny sitting-room for Maria. A crooked little staircase led to an attic floor with two rooms for the Moulaerts and a minute one for Matthew. As it turned out, Moulaert never came to live there; he had met another young woman in the summer and gone off with her. (He finished the decorations.) The house was well run, with "Rina adorable and perfect," Jeanne describes their new life; Maria had her dresses made at Nicole Groult (*haute couture* thought more individualistic and approachable than the classic establishments) and looked ravishing in the evening. They were very social, with people for luncheon nearly every day (after nightfall, they found out, Suresnes became inaccessible by public

transport), Drieu la Rochelle, Gabriel Marcel, James Joyce—"*he*
was a very strange man*," Aldous would say. Their dining-table,
by Moulaert, had a looking-glass surface that allowed a weird
view of faces chewing, disconcerting to new guests.

The houses were very close, the Huxley's next-door neighbour
happened to be a middle-aged French writer, "not a great writer".
Rina whose story this is explains, "comme Monsieur, mais un
écrivain de livres de poche à frs. 1.50". *Contrepoint* was being
written up in *Les Nouvelles Littéraires* and the poor man was
jealous. When Aldous stepped into his garden the *homme de lettres*,
lying in wait, would turn the garden hose on him. Aldous got wet
and Maria very angry. After the third time, she went to the
police who came to remonstrate with this unamiable character.
He told them, "Cet Anglais n'a qu'à rentrer chez lui."

When Aldous took a day off, they would all set out in the car
to Fontainebleau or Chartres . . . Yvonne Franchetti came to
stay, and Mary Hutchinson's young daughter Barbara.[1] There
were money panics. One evening as Aldous was talking about
the bills and the need for cutting down, Maria, after a moment's
reflection, called in Rina, "*Domani niente uovo bollito*—no boiled
egg tomorrow". Thereafter Aldous asked Jeanne's advice on
money matters. "Il trouvait que j'avais du bon sens. Il est évident
que je connaissais mieux la valeur de l'argent que Coccola."

Suzanne, living with her sister and brother-in-law in London
six years earlier, had been a young girl, a learner of the adult
world. Jeanne, at Suresnes, was a married woman with a child
of her own whose life had just gone to pieces. She was unhappy,
and not particularly sociable. She was setting out to earn her
own and Sophie's living. France, the year before the Wall Street
crash, was already in a state of financial instability; it was a hard
time for an untrained young woman who had wanted to be an
artist. She turned to hand-painting scarves and dress materials
which for a while sold well. Aldous was affectionate and did much
to make a cheerful home for her and the little girl; Maria was
terribly concerned and beset by guilt about her own happy and
so much easier existence. Their life *à trois*, in Jeanne's words,
was both cozy—with long late-night and morning chats across
the landing—and difficult. There was a profound—a very profound—attachment between these two sisters; yet they were, and
remained, so different in many ways. Jeanne very straight, blunt
at times; Maria, "toute souplesse, charme et savoir faire (avec un
côté bourgeois si on veut). Je n'aimais pas les formes extérieures,"
Jeanne says of herself. "J'ai dû leur rendre la vie peu agréable."

Maria also tried to look after Rina's future and sent her to

---

[1] Barbara Hutchinson, the present Mrs Nico Ghika.

evening classes to improve her R's. Rina admits to going to the cinema instead.

Everything was going wrong for Lawrence. Now the pirating of *Lady Chatterley* had begun. In December he wrote from Bandol:

> Would you or Aldous do a little thing for me when you are in Paris? There have come out *two* pirated editions of *Lady C.* in America; they are being sold in London at £3 . . . I believe they are being sold in Paris too, in Galignani's and other shops . . . I do wish when you are in town you would ask these shops if they have copies of the book, and how much, and ask to see one . . and tell me if it's the pirated edition—and tell them, the brutes. The pirated editions were *photographed* from my edition, so they may look superficially the same. . . .

They were indeed selling the stolen edition, asking 5,000 frs a copy, more than £60 or $250! Aldous advised offering the legitimate Florence edition to the Paris book-sellers "at some reasonable rate between the original 2 guineas and the 5,000 frs asked by the pirates . . . [to] undersell the devils and at the same time turn an honest penny". In the same letter Aldous reported about himself: the house, the weather, reading. The house is beginning to look like one . . . The weather is a damp cold hell . . . His reading, "a tiresome book by Virginia Woolf—*Orlando*—which is terribly literary and *fantaisiste* that nothing is left in it at all . . ."

Unfortunately Lawrence did not have sufficient stock in hand to undersell the pirates (so many copies had been confiscated by the US customs). "If only I had 2,000 I could kill the pirates," he wrote. Aldous went to Sylvia Beach to see if she could be interested in re-publishing *Lady C.* We know that she was not. So Aldous went into the possibility of photographing the Florence edition, and wrote at length to Chattos to get the facts about this new process. Did it cost less than ordinary setting? How many copies from the plate? Do most printers undertake the job? "I'm sorry to bother you . . . but I am anxious to get all the information I can to help Lawrence in his campaign against the pirates . . ."

At this time Aldous's own novel was being bought at a great rate. Before the year was out the sales of *Counterpane*, as Lawrence called it, had passed the 10,000 mark. Aldous had ceased to be a small-selling author.

Chapter Fifteen

Point Counter Point

ALDOUS had a correspondent whom apparently he never met. Mrs Flora Strousse who lived in Philadelphia and published under the pseudonym of Floyd Starkey. She wrote first and he occasionally answered with a frankness both unusual and detached. The situation has been irresistible to other writers. Aldous began with Dear Mr or Miss Floyd Starkey, soon went on to My dear Starkey, and this is the kind of thing he wrote, "I have almost no ideas about myself and don't like having them—avoid having them—on principle even—and only improvise them, when somebody like you asks to know them . . . 'know thyself' was probably one of the stupidest pieces of advice ever given . . . introspection which distracts one from the outside world is a kind of suicide. . . ." When *Point Counter Point* came out, he wrote to her, "I have at last written a rather good, but also a rather frightful, novel."

Meanwhile D. H. Lawrence wrote to Aldous. "I have read *Point Counter Point* with a heart sinking through my boot-soles and a rising admiration.

> I do think you've shown the truth, perhaps the last truth, about you and your generation, with really fine courage. It seems to me it would take ten times the courage to write *P. Counter P.* than it took to write *Lady C.*: and if the public knew *what* it was reading, it would throw a hundred stones at you, to one at me.

Lawrence admired, he did not like the book. "I do think that art has to reveal the palpitating moment or the state of man as it is. And I think you do that, terribly. But what a moment! and what a state!" And Lawrence went into a rave about Aldous's thrilling only to "murder, suicide and rape.

> All I want to do to your Lucy is to smack her across the mouth, your Rampion is the most boring character in the book—a gas-bag. Your attempt at intellectual sympathy! It's all rather disgusting, and I feel like a badger that has his hole on Wimbledon Common and trying not to be caught. Well, *caro*, I feel like saying good-bye to you—but one will have to go on saying good-bye for years.
>
> D. H. L.

199

Point Counter Point was published in October 1928 and became a best-seller on both sides of the Atlantic. It was translated into every conceivable language, European and Asiatic, enjoyed a huge vogue in France and Germany, broadened Aldous's English public and became one of the cornerstones of his international reputation, not to say his fame.

Since then—the best part of a half century—a good deal of printer's ink has flowed. Aldous's ambitious novel has been weathering eclipses as well as heights of fashion. It has been acclaimed as a great novel, debunked, disserted upon, fitted to many a Procrustean bed; it has been regarded as a work of stark realism, cynical despair, universal range, excessive intellectualism, eroticism, defeatism, a rogue's gallery of satanic creations, and a major portrait of English society of the time. Cyril Connolly has pointed out that the opening reads like a story in a woman's magazine—" 'You won't be late?' There was anxiety in Marjorie Carling's voice, there was something like entreaty." The book has been called vulgar and it has been called sublime; and of all the scoldings, Lawrence's is perhaps the oddest. "*Murder [etc.] is what you thrill to* . . ." The murder in *Point Counter Point* appears to be dragged in, much like the death of Leonard Bast in *Howard's End*, with a visible effort on the author's part.

It is Lawrence's famous subjectivity that comes out in his splenetic complaint. The narrowness of scope he was capable of indulging in is pointed up by a passage of Sir Isaiah Berlin's.[1] Sir Isaiah places Aldous with Ezra Pound and J. B. S. Haldane among the major intellectual emancipators of his generation:

> As men of letters—led by Voltaire, the head of the profession—rescued many oppressed human beings in the eighteenth century; as Byron or George Sand, Ibsen, Baudelaire, Nietzsche, Wilde and Gide and perhaps even Wells or Russell have done since, so members of my generation were assisted to find themselves by novelists, poets and critics concerned with the central problems of their day. Social and moral courage can, on occasion, exercise a more decisive influence than sensibility or original gifts. One of my own contemporaries, a man of exceptional honesty, intellectual power and moral responsiveness, inhibited and twisted by an uncertain social position and bitter puritanism on the part of his father, was morally freed (as others have been by psycho-analysis, or Anatole France, or living among Arabs) by reading Aldous Huxley: in particular *Point Counter Point* and one or two short stories. Light had been thrown for him on dark places, the forbidden was articulated,

1 Sir Isaiah Berlin, *Mem. Vol.*

intimate physical experience, the faintest reference to which used to upset him profoundly and affect him with a feeling of violent guilt, had been minutely and fully described. From that moment my friend advanced intellectually, and has become one of the most admired and productive men of learning of our day. It is not this therapeutic effect, however, that appealed to the young men of my generation so much as the fact that Huxley was among the few writers who, with all his constantly commented upon inability to create character, played with ideas so freely, so gaily, with such virtuosity. . . .

And now follows what is, to my mind, the most acute analysis of a constant element in Aldous's writing:

The performance took place against a background of relatively few, simple, *moral convictions; they were disguised by the brilliance of the technical accomplishment, but they were there, they were easily intelligible, and like a monotonous, insistent, continuous ground bass slowly pounding away through the elaborate intellectual display,* [my italics] they imposed themselves on the minds of boys of seventeen and eighteen—still, for the most part, eager and morally impressionable, no matter how complex or decadent they may in their naiveté have conceived themselves to be.

Aldous's intentions in *Point Counter Point* are largely expressed by the stanza from Fulke Greville on the title page.

> *Oh, wearisome condition of humanity,*
> *Born under one law to another bound,*
> *Vainly begot and yet forbidden vanity,*
> *Created sick, commanded to be sound.*
>   *What meaneth nature by these diverse laws,*
>   *Passion and reason, self-division's cause?*

Diverse Laws—"Just what I want." This was what he tried to put across (contemporary English society being but the raw material to hand), this, and again the queerness of reality, the *extraordinariness* of everything. "That's what I want to get into this book—the astonishingness of the most obvious things," says Philip Quarles, the novelist inside the novel. And for that any plot or situation would do. "The whole book could be written about a walk from Piccadilly Circus to Charing Cross." But it was not. Aldous was aware of the limitations of the discursive novel, the novel of ideas. Not only must you write about people who have ideas to express—·01 per cent of the human race. Hence the real, the congenital novelists don't write such books. But then I never pretended to be a congenital novelist."[1]

In *Point Counter Point* Aldous tried to balance talk with action; ideas are translated into the lives of men and women, into case histories if you like. The characters act as well as talk; things happen to them. Was Aldous really as reluctant or defective a novelist as he made himself out to be? When it comes to his major characters, one can see what he (and his critics) meant—his talent for generalizing is allowed to get the better of his talent for exploring the particular. And he over-insists. To what extent are Rampion, Spandrell, Illidge, Burlap credible in the round? The question raises questions within questions and one of them is that of genesis —like *Crome Yellow, Antic Hay*, like in fact the lot, *Point Counter Point* has been regarded as a roman à clef. Let's take Mark Rampion now. We know what Lawrence himself thought about him—a gasbag and a bore. Floyd Starkey, Aldous's unseen correspondent, asked him straight. Aldous answered, "Have I 'done' Lawrence? No. Kingham [another Lawrentian character, in *Two or Three Graces*] was concocted before I knew him—at least I'd only seen him once . . . Rampion is just some of Lawrence's notions on legs. The actual character of the man was incomparably queerer and more complex than that."

Aldous "did" Baudelaire in so far as Spandrell's disastrous adolescent history was Baudelaire's; he did John Middleton Murry in *some* aspects of the revolting Burlap; he did Maria in Elinor, Philip's wife; Matthew in their child; he put something of himself into Walter Bidlake and a good deal into Philip Quarles. And there again are the shades of Nancy Cunard whom this time he did not attempt to do at all, Lucy Tantamount is any stylized siren of the 1920s; what he did was the tale (recollected in tranquility) of a young man's unrequited physical passion for a woman he dislikes.

The actual character was incomparably more complex—Mark Rampion *v.* D. H. Lawrence; Philip Quarles *v.* Aldous Huxley. All the same, there is very much of Aldous in *Point Counter Point*—Aldous on himself, though selective and with little regard for fairness, is biography at first hand and as such must have its place here.

Was Aldous ever really influenced by D. H. L.? If so, did it last? How serious, later on, was the influence of his friend Gerald Heard?

. . In point of fact [Philip Quarles says of himself] . . he had never deeply and whole-heartedly admired anyone. Theoretically, yes; but never in practice, *never to the point of wanting to make himself a disciple,*

---

[1] From Philip Quarles' notebook in *Point Counter Point*. Chatto & Windus, 1928. All quotations in this chapter, unless otherwise stated, are from this book.

a follower. [My italics.] He had adopted other people's opinions, even their modes of life—but always with the underlying conviction that they weren't really his, that he could and certainly would abandon them as easily as he had taken them up . . .

. . At different times in his life . . he had filled the most various moulds. He had been a cynic and also a mystic, a humanitarian and also a contemptuous misanthrope; he had tried to live the life of detached and stoical reason and another time had aspired to the unreasonableness of natural and uncivilized existence. The choice of moulds depended at any given moment on the books he was reading, the people he was associating with. Burlap, for example, had redirected the flow of his mind into those mystical channels which it had not filled since he discovered Boehme in his under-graduate days. Then he had seen through Burlap and flowed out again . . . After a few hours in Mark Rampion's company he really believed in noble savagery; he felt convinced that the proudly conscious intellect ought to humble itself a little and admit the claims of the heart, aye and the bowels, the loins . . . The moulds were emptied as easily as they had been filled . . . But the essential liquidness that flowed where it would, *the cool indifferent flux of intellectual curiosity* [my italics]—that persisted and to that his loyalty was due.

If there was any single way of life he could everlastingly believe in, it was that mixture of pyrrhonism and stoicism which had struck him, an enquiring schoolboy among the philosophers, as the height of human wisdom and into whose moulds of sceptical indifference he had poured his unimpassioned adolescence. . . .

And here is Aldous speaking of his indifference to possessions. He calls it his under-acquisitiveness and regards it as hereditary as well as developed. "The instinct of acquisitiveness has more perverts, I believe, than the instincts of sex. At any rate, people seem to me odder about money than about even their amours . . ."

In any case I find myself uninterested in possessions and rather unsympathetic with, and without understanding of, those who are. No predominantly acquisitive character has appeared in any of my stories . . .[1]

And here on his dislike of human contacts,

. . From those who served him Philip demanded little, for the good reason that he wanted to have as little as possible to do with them. Their presence disturbed him. He did not like to have his privacy

[1] From Philip Quarles's notebook, op. cit.

intruded upon by alien personalities. To be compelled to speak with them, to have to establish a direct contact—not of intelligences, but of wills, feelings, intuitions—was always disagreeable to him. He avoided it as much as he could; and when contact was necessary, he did his best to dehumanize the relation.

The exception was of course Maria. Elinor Quarles, if no portrait, is a tender evocation.

"What I want to do is to look with all those eyes at once. [Philip is off on the different levels of reality.] With religious eyes, scientific eyes, economic eyes . . ."
"Loving eyes too."
He smiled at her and stroked her hand.

And now they are in India, in a garden under a full moon. To Elinor the night evokes "Gattenden" and their first summer. "Do you remember those evenings, Phil?" she asks. "Which evenings?" he answers. She begins to cry, but after a while is laughing at him and herself. "You do your best to be nice to me," she says. "You make such efforts. It's sweet of you." He protests,

"You know I love you."
"Yes, I know you do." She smiled and stroked his cheek. "When you have time and then by wireless across the Atlantic."

Presently the Quarles are back in England. A month ago, says Elinor, as their taxi drives out of Liverpool Street station, "we were in Udaipur". Philip agrees, it certainly seems improbable. These ten months of travel have been like an hour in the cinema, she says. She begins to doubt whether she's ever been away. "It's rather a dreadful feeling." "Is it?" says Philip. "I suppose I'm used to it. I never do feel that anything has really happened before this morning." They pass St Paul's, he brings up the Taj Mahal, then goes on, "I often doubt whether I ever had a childhood".
"That's because you never think of it. Lots of my childhood is more real to me than Ludgate Hill here. But then I constantly think of it." (Now this was entirely Maria—St Trond, Bellem *were* her present.) Philip says, "I don't often try to remember. Hardly ever in fact. I always seem to have too much to do and think about."
"You have no natural piety," says Elinor. "I wish you had."
At one point Elinor is stung into asking Philip where he would be if she left him. "Where would you be?"

. . Where *would* he be? . . . in the ordinary daily world of human contacts he was curiously like a foreigner . . finding it difficult or impossible to enter into communication with any but those who could speak his native intellectual language of ideas. Emotionally, he was a foreigner. Elinor was his interpreter, his dragoman . . Elinor had been born with a gift of intuitive understanding and social ease. She was quickly at home with anybody. She knew, instinctively . . just what to say to every type of person.

He tries to see their marriage from her side, make her reflect on his emotional poverty.

. . After an outburst, she would settle down and try to love him as reasonably as she could, making the best of his kindness, his rather detached and separate passion, his occasional and laborious essays at emotional intimacy, and finally his intelligence . . that could understand everything, including the emotions it could not feel and the instincts it took care not to be moved by.
. . All that the intelligence could seize upon he seized. She reported her intercourse with the natives of the realm of emotion, and he understood at once, he generalized her experience for her . . he classified it, found analogies and parallels. From single and individual it became in his hands part of a system. She was astonished to find that she and her friends had been, all unconsciously, substantiating a theory, or exemplifying some interesting generalization. Her functions . . were not confined to mere scouting and reporting. She acted also directly as personal interpreter between Philip and any third party he might wish to get in touch with, creating the atmosphere in which alone the interchange of personalities is possible . . .
Left to himself Philip would never have been able to establish personal contact.
. . Elinor . . acted as go-between . . . not only for her own sake, but for the sake of the novelist he might be . . . Heroically, she had even encouraged him in his velleities of passion for other women. It might do him good to have a few affairs. So anxious was she to do him good as a novelist, that on more than one occasion seeing him look admiringly at some young woman or other, she had gone out of her way to establish for him the personal contact . . . Elinor took the risk, partly because she thought that his writing ought to come before anything else, even her own happiness, and partly because she was secretly convinced that there was in reality no risk at all . . . The cure by affairs, if it worked at all, would be gentle in its action . . . Philip's infidelities amounted to very little and had had no appreciable effect on him. . . .

Elinor discusses him with her mother-in-law who says, "Even as a little boy he always shut doors." "And now," says Elinor, "he has his work, which makes it worse . . It's like a castle on the top of a mountain, his work. He shuts himself up and he's impregnable."

Old Mrs Quarles smiles sadly. "Impregnable . . . Perhaps in the end he'll surrender of his own accord."

And now a domestic scene: Philip as a father. The little boy is trying to read from a magazine. The big word begins with a D, it is a dentifrice advertisement but the picture shows a fox-trotting young couple. Little Phil unhesitatingly reads, "Dancing". "You old humbug," says his father. "I thought you said you could read." "But they *are* dancing," says the child. He is told to try again. He takes a long look at the picture. "Dynamo." Now his father starts to tease him, "Or why not dinosaurus, while you're about it? . . Or dolicocephalous? Or dicotyledon?" Little Phil is deeply offended.

"Try again. Try to *read* it this time. Don't guess."

The boy turns his head away. "It bores me . . . But would you like me to make you a drawing?" He turns back with a captivating smile.

"I'd like you to read," says Philip.

"But it bores me."

"Never mind. You must try."

"But I don't want to try."

"But *I* want you to. Try."

Little Phil bursts into tears. Elinor intervenes. Philip says, "If you imagine that's the way to educate a child . . . seeing that he has the misfortune to be an only child, one really ought to make an effort not to spoil him". Elinor presses her cheek against the boy's hair. "Seeing that he is an only child, I don't see why he shouldn't be treated as one." Philip retorts that it's high time for them to settle down so that the boy can have a chance of being brought up rationally.

"And who is going to do the rational upbringing?" asks Elinor. "You? . . At the end of a week you'd be so bored that you'd either commit suicide or take the first aeroplane to Paris."

"Naughty father!" says the child.

Aldous and Maria were here [Lawrence wrote to Lady Ottoline from Bandol in the winter after the novel]

> . . . neither of them very well, run down . . . and Maria going very thin and not eating enough. I think the *Counter Point* book sort of got between them—she found it hard to forgive the death of the child—which one can well understand.

And at the same time to the Brewsters,

> . . The Huxleys left a week ago . . . I'm a bit worried, as they are neither of them well. He was run down and livery, and if she doesn't

watch out, her lungs are going to give her trouble again. People live the wrong way of their nerves, and of course it destroys them. She minded *Point Counter Point*—his killing the child—it was all too lifelike and horrible—and the love affair with Lucy was A's affair with N C.[1] I think Maria hardly forgives it. And perhaps now he's sorry he did it. But it has made them money. And Maria wants money—says so. Yes, she wants to buy a new car in Paris. But I say there are many men in a man, and the Aldous that wrote the *Point Counter Point* and killed the child is only one of the Aldouses, and perhaps by no means the best or most important. I think he's really nicer—realizing the things one mustn't do, if one is to live.[2]

The child in the book has Matthew's ways as a small boy. Like Matthew, he muddles up his longer words to his governess's distress and everybody's else's joy. The gardener pulls the mow-lawner, there are hop-grassers and crack-nutters. In life, Matthew once came back to their Swiss hotel saying he'd been playing a nice game with some Seraphic Jews. *Like* Matthew; not *Matthew*. So have painters used their wives and mistresses to stand in for Salome or Joan of Arc, used the models that came handy. The child in the novel dies of meningitis (a death probably suggested by that of the Mitchison's eldest boy the year before). For a writer with the bit between his teeth such an end is the inevitable conclusion to a theme (pointless horror, the irony of fate); Thomas Mann in much this way "killed" his favourite grandson in *Dr Faustus*; little Phil in Aldous's novel—whatever the resemblances and starting points— is a character in fiction, on paper, a creation with its own compulsive reality and no reality in life. And like Philip Quarles, Aldous had no natural piety; superstitious dread was among the emotions he was unable to feel. For him there was no reasonable connection. (And indeed Matthew, the heavens be praised, continued to flourish.) For others, as inevitably, the connection was there. Women on the whole are more superstitious, or more sensitive. Lawrence, more feminine in his perceptions, guessed or knew Maria's feelings.

Point Counter Point as a whole is not easy to pin down. I should like to end by condensing some evocative lines. There is the passage of Everard Webley's slow drive through Hyde Park on a summer evening, in love with Elinor, on his way to Elinor, seeing the world transfigured—a psychedelic passage before the word. Unfortunately it does not lend itself to quotation without context. Instead

---

[1] Both names were replaced by asterisks in the 1938 edition of the letter.
[2] *D. H. Lawrence Reminiscences and Correspondence,* op. cit.

here is an extract from the opening set-piece, the evening at Tantamount House in Pall Mall. The concert has begun. In *Barren Leaves* Calamy held up his hand against the light and talked; now Aldous tried to give the sense of synchronous existence in action.

Meanwhile the music played on—Bach's Suite in B minor, for flute and strings. Young Tolley conducted with his usual inimitable grace . . . as though he were dancing to the music. A dozen anonymous fiddlers and 'cellists scraped at his bidding. And the great Pongileoni glueily kissed his flute. He blew across the mouth hole and a cylindrical air column vibrated; Bach's meditations filled the Roman quadrangle. In the opening *largo* John Sebastian had, with the help of Pongileoni's snout and the air column, made a statement: there are grand things in the world, noble things; there are men born kingly . . . But of an earth that is, oh! complex and multitudinous, he has gone on to reflect in the fugal allegro. You seem to have found the truth; clear, definite, unmistakable, it is announced by the violins; but it slips out of your grasp to present itself in a new aspect among the 'cellos . . . The parts live their separate lives; they touch, their paths cross, they combine for a moment to create a seemingly final and perfected harmony, only to break apart again. "I am I," asserts the violin, "the world revolves around me." "Round me," calls the 'cello. "Round me," the flute insists. And all are equally right and wrong; and none of them will listen to the other.

In the human fugue there are eighteen hundred million parts. The resultant noise means something perhaps to the statistician, nothing to the artist. It is only by considering one or two parts at a time that the artist can understand anything. Here . . is one particular part; and John Sebastian puts the case. The Rondeau begins, exquisitely and simply melodious . . It is a young girl singing to herself of love . . singing among the hills, with the clouds drifting overhead . . solitary as one of the floating clouds, a poet has been listening to her song. The thoughts that it provoked in him are the Sarabande that follows the Rondeau. His is a slow and lovely meditation on the beauty (in spite of squalor), the oneness (in spite of such bewildering diversity) of the world. It is a beauty, a goodness, a unity that no intellectual research can discover, that analysis dispels, but of whose reality the spirit is from time to time suddenly and overwhelmingly convinced. A girl singing to herself under the clouds suffices to create the certitude. Even a fine morning is enough. Is it illusion or the revelation of profoundest truth? Who knows? Pongileoni blew, the fiddlers drew their rosined horse-hair across the stretched intestines of lambs; through the long Sarabande the poet slowly meditated his lovely and consoling certitude.

Chapter Sixteen

And Another Year

ALDOUS was in London briefly in January 1929. There he signed his third agreement with Chatto & Windus. Three years go quickly. He had delivered three books instead of six to nine, one novel instead of three. The new agreement was more realistic; two novels in three years, three further books "if possible". The annual advance was raised to a thousand pounds. Beaverbrook made a handsome offer for a weekly book review which Aldous ruminated and presently declined. The most enduring consequence of that London visit flowed from Aldous's first meeting with Gerald Heard. Raymond Mortimer introduced them, Gerald being one of his greatest friends.

On a typical London January evening thirty-five years ago [Gerald Heard's description of the first encounter[1]] Aldous Huxley sailed into my view . . . his approach, his "port", had about it something of a galleon's. He came in, as it were, under full sail, a long coat billowing around him. The voice, however, was as neat as a seamstress's stitching. And, indeed, the long fingers made the precise movements of a needlewoman handling thread and seam . . .
. . the discourse . . was not only ironic and entertaining, but fantastically informed.

Now Gerald Heard himself was a tremendous talker who would shoot off ideas and information from the split second he entered a room. He was as extraordinary to listen to as Aldous if a good deal less lucid.

Our host . . [Raymond] had asked no other guest. We stayed talking till past 1 a.m., when all buses had finished their routes, all taxis ceased their cruising. Consequently each of us had before him a more than three-mile walk. To my surprise, for our directions were divergent, Huxley accompanied me all the way to my block of flats and then, changing tack, sailed off for another couple of miles of solitary striding to his own rooms. But not before he had invited me to another session the following week. . . .

Hardly returned to Suresnes, Aldous, with Maria, left again. For the South of France to see Lawrence who was wintering in Bandol

---

[1] Gerald Heard, *The Poignant Prophet*, *The Kenyon Review*, 1965.

at the Hotel Beaurivage. "I would like to see you both," he had written. "But these little *en passant* glimpses like Lavandou and Chexbres don't amount to much, do they?"

Or did they? Florence, Forte, Les Diablerets—"We saw a great deal of him," Aldous said thirty years after, in the London interview. John Chandos led him off: "You said something very strong, you said—in your preface to *The Letters*—'He is one of the very few people I feel real respect and admiration for. He is something superior and different in kind.' "

"Of course, you are quite right," said Aldous. "He was perfectly extraordinary as a human being. He was extremely fascinating, and he was always stimulating. A little alarming to be with . . ."

Chandos put in: "Why did he quarrel with people?" Aldous [chuckling] "He somehow did it on principle, I believe. Or perhaps that's wrong—it was a very strange thing, he would burst out in that *curious* way against people. But it was always a pleasure to be with him, and hear his comments on things; his reactions to nature were always very very fascinating. I mean it was a great pleasure to go for a walk with Lawrence. The way he perceived the world— so intense, and exciting."

Chandos says, "But he was always hectoring people—he must have had atrocious manners?" "Well, no," says Aldous mildly, "he was very charming generally. Sometimes he would get sort of cross. But he could be very amusing. Entertaining. I mean he was happy; Happiness is the greatest virtue, he would say. And he *was* happy. He was happy sort of sitting on a grey stone—very like Words- worth's Expostulations and Reply . . . and of course a lot of his life was spent in this way. And then he would get the urge to write: and then write for eighteen hours a day. It was very extraordinary to see him work, it was a sort of *possession*; he would rush on with it, his hand moving at a tremendous rate. And he never corrected anything; because if he was dissatisfied with anything he would start again at the beginning.

". . of course one of the things I often speculate about is what would have happened to him if he had lived on to a reasonable age. It is absolutely extraordinary to think that this man who died at the age of forty-four produced this *immense* volume of stuff which he did—some of it is very fine. I do think the short stories and some of the very long novelettes are most remarkable. And some of the longer novels. I don't think all of them are successful, by any means. And some of the later poems, I think, are very beautiful. But it's amazing to think that all this was produced by a man who died at forty-four and who was *sick* for a great deal of the time . . .

"But *where* would he have gone from the point he was at when he died? This is a very interesting speculation. I don't think he could have *remained* where he was, because I mean there was a

certain ambivalence even in a book like the *Plumed Serpent* where
he is inviting us to go back to the dark gods and the dark blood
and so on; but in the next breath he's saying how awful the
Mexicans are because they are so slow and unintelligent and so on.
It's a *very* odd book. You get these tirades against the Mexicans,
almost in the terms of an English colonel talking about the natives;
in the next breath you get these tremendous invitations to sink
yourself in the dark blood. So there was even then a kind of ambivalence. I think he would even then have come round to what
seems to me a more balanced view—I mean this *whole* thing that
we have to make the *best* of both worlds . . .

"The point is that you *must have both*. The blood and the flesh
are there—and in certain respects they are wiser than the intellect.
I mean if we interfere with the blood and the flesh with our
conscious minds we get psychosomatic trouble. But on the other
hand, we have to do a lot of things with the conscious mind. I mean
why *can't* we do *both*—we *have* to do both. This is the whole art of
life: making the best of all the worlds. Here again is one of those
fatal examples of trying to make everything conform to the
standard of only *one* world. Seeing that we are amphibians—it's *no
good*."

Aldous and Lawrence's meeting in the winter of 1929 lasted for
some ten days. It was the meeting referred to in Lawrence's letters
to Ottoline and the Brewsters. "Neither of them well . . . the *Counter
Point* book . . ." The Huxleys had arrived in late January; the time
has some significance because of the ensuing weather. In the night
of the 28th there was a sudden severe frost in Southern Europe,
followed the next morning by an icy wind that lasted through
several days, one of the worst cold spells in memory. Palm trees
froze on the promenades, thousands of cars were stranded. At that
time houses and hotels had little heating and people were huddling
in the doorways of department stores and in the cinemas of Toulon
and Marseilles. It had begun before the weekend on the French
coast and gradually spread into Italy, but at Bandol it was all over
on the Monday morning—the sun shone on a wind-still day and
a limp and blackened vegetation, "one sat out again," as Lawrence
wrote, "and felt the brightness." But the intense cold had given
Aldous one of his liver attacks, a bad one verging on jaundice.
Unwisely he and Maria had left by car for Italy on that bitter
Sunday. (Their car, Italian registered, had to be repatriated unless
they paid a huge duty to the French and went through a morass
of paperwork, the bureaucratic pettifoggery being even worse than
it is today.) They had a frightful journey. The cold wave followed
them; Aldous was getting worse. On the Italian Riviera their

magneto gave out which meant spending forty-eight hours in an inn at Albenga where "the only mode of heating was by hot bricks". Later at Chiavari they found the road wiped out by a landslide and had to wait some hours in a cutting *tramontana* for a train to put the car on. They reached Florence with the roads deep in snow and the Arno frozen solid. At last their hotel was warm; a modest hotel, Il Moderno, to which they returned in gratitude for years.

. . The miserable population, quite without proper clothes or houses for such a season, [is] dying in thousands. Out of 250,000 inhabitants 65,000 were ill. And Florence was balmy compared with Trieste and the Adriatic ports, where the sea froze and the trains were blown off the rails by the wind.

They left their car in a garage waiting for a buyer (it was not the best moment for selling the Alfa Romeo-like machine) and crept back by train to Paris.

There Aldous went back to work on the essays, "I'm busy, but not exuberantly well," he wrote to his father, "this quasi-jaundice has left me a little dubious physically." And the journey had taken it out of Maria. Lawrence wrote to her

. . I'm a bit worried about your health, so please be a good child and *really* take care for a while—don't bother about *anything* else. Now do as you're bidden, and don't go squiffing about any more, but keep still and warm and well fed: and don't buy a car just yet. Just be without one for six weeks, really. You need a rest from driving.

. . . Well, let us know you are safely arrived, and safely in bed, and warm and well fed. I shall fidget till I know.

D. H. L.

Could you get me Nancy Cunard's address? I'll ask her if *she* will do *Lady C.*

But they had every intention of getting a new car. "After much trying and testing and on the recommendation of the A.A. engineers in London we have fixed on the new touring model of the Bugatti which has a most extraordinary performance and is a very sound piece of engineering and building." It was ordered from the works at Turin and the body was to be custom-made.

In March Lawrence arrived to see about a new edition of *Lady Chatterley*. He stayed at the Hotel de Versailles on the Boulevard Montparnasse, felt ill and was borne off to Suresnes for a few days and put to bed in one of Jeanne's attics.

I arrived here [he wrote to Rhys Davies] with a bit of 'flu or something—felt very cheap—but they are really very nice and kind to
me, and look after me so nicely.

Joep Nicolas was in the house and it was here that Lawrence sat
to him for his portrait. Looking after Lawrence was not simple.

. . We actually got him to agree to undertake a treatment [Aldous
to Julian], alone, minus Frieda, and we also actually got him to go
to a doctor in Paris. He was to go back to the Dr. to be X-rayed.
(Meanwhile, however, the Dr. told M that . . he could hear that
one lung was practically gone and the other affected . . .) Then
Frieda, who had been in London, returned. L. felt himself reinforced. He refused to go back to the Dr., refused to think of the treatment and set off with Frieda (of whom he had bitterly complained
when he was alone with us) to Majorca. So that's that. It's no good.
He doesn't *want* to know how ill he is: that, I believe, is the fundamental reason why he won't go to Doctors and homes. He only
went in Paris because he was feeling iller than usual and was even
more frightened of dying at once than of hearing how ill he was . . .
and meanwhile he just wanders about, very tired and at bottom
wretched, from one place to another, imagining that the next
place will make him feel better and, when he gets [to] the next
place, regretting the one before and looking back on it as a
paradise. . . .

The coach-builders were late and the Bugatti only ready by
Easter. Maria and Rina went to Turin to fetch it, and drove it
back across Mont Cenis. The Bugatti was Aldous and Maria's high
point in cars, and their one great personal extravagance (paid for
by *Point Counter Point*). It was a slim, powerful two-seater, scarlet,
with the upholstery in dove-grey leather. Maria sat close under the
large sports car wheel; Aldous's seat had been built to measure for
his outstretched legs. (There was a kind of third perch in the back,
a sort of side-saddle on which one balanced with one's knees up to
one's chin. The boot held their two or three Revelation suitcases
and a portable typewriter.) Ettore Bugatti, the constructor, was
amazed to hear that a woman was going to drive one of his
monsters, and asked to meet her.
The engine needed serious driving in, and Aldous and Maria
did this on a forced journey through France into Spain as far as
Madrid and back again (after one first look at the Prado). Afterwards they went to London.
During the time he nominally lived in Paris, much of Aldous's
work was done in hotel bedrooms elsewhere. (He could set up his
workshop with a minimum of paraphernalia.) In London, Jill, the

cousin who fell in love with his portrait in 1926, now actually met him. He was thirty-five.

I was invited to dinner at my grandmother's house—the Dragon [Aldous's Aunt Ethel]. I must just describe the Dragon to you— she was known as Grand-Dragon to the grandchildren, and I think she originally got the name because she was the chaperone on the trips to Switzerland when there were a whole lot of relations there and she was always put to make sure that everybody behaved themselves. She wasn't really a dragon, only in some ways: the kindest dragon you've ever known. And a lovely person. She had these Sunday night supper parties, which were always cold chicken and then some sort of a mousse—always the same—and she had these two cats who would sit on each side on the chairs waiting . . . And there I met Aldous. And he was sitting, not quite opposite, but nearly opposite me to the right, and I couldn't take my eyes off him. And I wasn't sure whether he was looking at me or not, because he wore these tremendous pebble glasses . . . But afterwards, Maria told me that *he* couldn't take his eyes off *me*. But I didn't know this until many years later.

At the time it was my brother's twenty-first birthday. And when we were all waiting in the drawing room for ten o'clock which was the exact hour at which we all had to leave the Dragon—this was an understood thing—we still felt keen to carry on the evening: I turned to Aldous and said, "Aldous, will you come to the Gargoyle night club where my brother is having a twenty-first birthday, because he would love to meet you?" And Aldous said, "*Yes*". And Maria grasped my arm and said, "*Jill—but how did you do it?* We have never *been* to a *night club* before. We never go to a *night club*."

Anyway he came with us, and we went to the Gargoyle. As we came down the steps, past the huge Matisse painting, my brother was sitting at the bottom of the stair with a whole group of friends and he leapt up: "How-did-you-do-it!? HOW-DID-YOU-DO-IT!?" He was so excited that I brought him. And he sat down at the table with us. And instead of everybody dancing and the music playing, the band stopped, people stopped dancing, they all came and sat round Aldous to listen to him. He didn't *hold forth*—he *conversed*. I can't tell you at all what he talked about; but he was just fascinating, and even the waiters came and listened, and the place was silent except for Aldous talking.[1]

They did not live much in the house by the Seine. Barely returned from London, they left for their Italian summer. They had turned

[1] Gillian (Mrs Anthony) Greenwood, talking to S. B. in 1968.

against Suresnes—hating it mortally, Lawrence put it—and Aldous
realized how little suited he was to life in the north.

> I have reached a point [to Starkey] where I value sunshine more
> than people, culture, arts, conversation. So I'm off to Italy . . .
> (Incidentally, it's full of people, culture, etc. as well as sunlight.)
> I believe and rather hope that the days of the Nordics and their
> beastly northern countries is nearly over. Civilization will return to
> the warm and luminous places where it was born.

They spent ten days in Rome, made a tour of the Etruscan
towns, then settled down in their little house. It was their last
summer at Forte, the last of their living in Italy. There were wind
and clouds and Aldous felt melancholy; then once more the weather
became "incredibly serene". Their newest acquisition was an
inflatable rubber boat. Aldous had begun some short stories.
Matthew presently arrived with Rose; he had learnt to swim quite
well; "we are also improving his French reading . . by means of
the excellent Jules Verne . . ." Lawrence had appeared for a few
days in June, even worse in health than he had been in Paris in
the spring.

> . . no energy . . . [Aldous to Julian] It's pathetic to see the way
> he just sits and does nothing. He hasn't written a line or painted a
> stroke for the last 3 months. Just lack of vital strength. He still talks
> a good deal and can get amused and excited into a semblance of
> health for an hour or two at the time. But it is only a semblance . . .
> He has gone to Germany now—or is just going: for he has been in
> Florence these last days—of all places in this weather! We have
> given up trying to persuade him to be reasonable. He doesn't want
> to be and nobody can persuade him to be—except possibly Frieda.
> But Frieda is worse than he is. We've told her that she's a fool and
> a criminal; but it has no more effect than telling an elephant.

Aldous appears to have been convinced then that Lawrence's
illness was "unnecessary, the result simply of the man's strange
obstinacy against professional medicine". Yet some thirty years
later he made a curious remark to Sidney Nolan and his wife; he
said that Lawrence had died of chagrin, that T.B. was a disease
of chagrin. Was it a new conclusion, was it an echo? In that mellow
letter Lawrence wrote to Ottoline in 1928, there is this passage:

> You ask me, do I feel things very much?—and I do. And that's
> why I too am ill. The hurts, and the bitterness sink in, however
> much one may reject them with one's spirit. They sink in, and there
> they lie, inside one, wasting one. What is the matter with us is
> primarily chagrin. Then the microbes pounce. . . .

In July Aldous took the cure at Montecatini for a week to get over the after effects of his liver attack. A curious experience . . the Carlsbad of Italy. "Have you ever been to a spa?" he wrote to Robert Nichols. "If not, go. It's the most grotesque vision imaginable . . ." Soon after he made good use of it in *After the Fireworks*. The Huxleys returned to Suresnes in late September and stayed put for a few weeks. But Paris seemed really rather frightful and the traffic must have doubled in the last year—on the whole Aldous had not found much of what he wanted; "French literary society is really a bit too literary . . ." He bore away some anecdotes which he told in later years with anthropological benevolence. Here is one about James Joyce that survives in his own voice.[1]

Well, *Ulysses* is obviously a very extraordinary book. I don't know exactly why he wrote it. Because a great deal of *Ulysses* seems to me to be taken up with showing a large number of methods in which novels *cannot* be written. I suppose it's a great book—to me it remains a little bit too static. The character of Bloom—But I think there are splendid passages. I don't think it's a success as a whole.

He was a *very* strange man. I used to see him sometimes in Paris. His—what one might call—magic view of words—I shall never forget sitting next to him once at dinner and mentioning to him, which I thought would give him pleasure—and it *did*—that I'd just been re-reading the *Odyssey*. And his immediate response was—he said to me, "Now do you realize what the derivation of Odysseus, the name Odysseus is?" I said [sotto voce] "No, I don't." And he said, "Well, it really comes from the words Udyce, meaning nobody, and Zeus, meaning God, the Odysseus is really a symbol of creation of God out of nothing." Well, I mean this is exactly the sort of etymology which would have been made by Albertus Magnus in the 13th century—with no relation of course to anything we would regard as realistic. But this completely *satisfied* Joyce's mind.

Chandos: But he was enormously a man of words.

Aldous: Absolutely a man of words.

Chandos: This was the lovable thing about him—I love words in my own way . . .

Aldous [with much determination] Yes, but I mean, surely one has to realize the limitations of words. Joyce—seemed to think that words were omnipotent. They are *not* omnipotent.

Where to go next? Now there was money for a house of their own. Maria's idea was a cool stone house in the depth of a garden. They did not feel that they could return to live in Italy; political

---

[1] London interview of 1961 cit,

facts apart, it seemed time to move on. The South of France? They had rather liked the coast round Bandol . . . Meanwhile they went off in the Bugatti on a tour of Spain. Jeanne stayed behind and put up jam. Suresnes was isolated at night, Sophie was away at boarding school, sometimes she felt afraid. Like Maria, Lawrence was concerned about her situation. "Yes, I have often thought of you," he said to her in the course of a long letter of advice,

> and of our talks. I like you because you seem to me quite honest, you say what you mean, and nearly all people equivocate when a subject really touches them, so I think that in the end you will come out all right, after this horrible period of frustration. . . .

The second Spanish journey (described as usual by Aldous to his father) began with a week in Barcelona, then Tarragona, Valencia (Lawrence had a post card from Maria saying they were happy; he was fretting about them, "Spain is *hard*"), Alicante, Murcia, Almeria; across the Sierra Nevada to Granada losing their way and wandering for some time in the mountain byways of Andalusia. Then Ronda in its staggering position, Jerez, Cadiz on its strange promontory, Seville, Cordoba (a letter *from* Lawrence, "I'm so anxious when I think of that *enormous* way from S. of Spain by Biarritz to Paris. Too much, too much . . . When we've motored for one morning, I'm so thankful to have done"). To Madrid through the desert plateau of La Mancha and Castile, "one isn't surprised at Don Quixote going mad in a country like that". To Burgos "with such a wind that the mud was lifted in sheets from the road and hurled against our windscreen . . . It was a comfort to get down to Atlantic softness at S. Sebastian . . ." To Starkey Aldous summed it up,

> Really, the strangest country in Europe . . . one of the oddest in the world even. Half very sympathetic, half very repulsive. But always very odd and full of the most extraordinary things, natural and artificial. The El Grecos, for example, which I admire much more (tho' hating them in a way) than when I saw them last . . .

They got back to Suresnes in late November. "So you are safely back," Lawrence wrote, "that's one mercy, anyhow, and we needn't think of you on rainy, windy days and imagine the little red car ploughing on, ploughing on."

With the death of Maria's grandparents, St Trond as a home base was no more. For that one Christmas the house at Suresnes served for a family gathering: the three Huxleys, Jeanne and Sophie, Madame Nys and Rose.

Chapter Seventeen

Do What You Will

IN the course of a letter to another impersonal correspondent (Scudder Klyce, who had sent him his recent book, *Dewey's Suppressed Psychology*) Aldous discussed his own viewpoint in *Do What You Will*. He began by saying that he had never managed to make his statements logically watertight, "a feat.. which the literary quality of what I write (such as it is—that quality!) renders less vitally necessary. For after all the most perfect statements and human solutions of the great metaphysical problems are all artistic, especially, it seems to me, musical. Beethoven's "Missa Solemnis" for example, and his posthumous quartets, Bach's "Art of the Fugue" have always struck me as the subtlest, profoundest and completest metaphysical works ever composed . . . Such pieces of music, and certain passages in Dante and Shakespeare, certain paintings, certain architectural monuments get closer to the essential fact than any professional philosopher's discourse . . . I do not delude myself with the belief that I am a great artist; but at least I possess a certain literary talent, the use of which serves in some measure to take the place of a sadly deficient logic!

. . . Being an unmetaphysically-minded person preoccupied with phenomenal appearances, not ultimate reality, I think mostly of the diverse Many and not much of the final One. My essay . . ["One and Many"] in . . *Do What You Will* is a statement of the observable facts of diversity so stupidly overlooked by contemporary science and contemporary religion. Any tentative solutions of the problems raised are never . . . metaphysical solutions, only practical, ethical, sociological and psychological solutions.

Do What You Will (finished in May 1929, published in October) consists of twelve essays. The essays on Baudelaire, Swift, Spinoza's Worm, Wordsworth in the Tropics, the brief and savage account —"Silence is Golden"—of the first talking film. The main argument is developed in the opening essay, "One and Many", and in the equally long one on Pascal, and could be summed up as, "The final mystery is unknowable.

Men's confused perceptions of it are diverse and contradictory. The truth—the inward truth, I mean, since that is the only truth we can know—is that God is different for different men, and for the same man on different occasions. The testimony of the mystics cannot be made to prove more than this.

. . A rational absolute is a contradiction in terms. The only absolute which a man of intelligence can believe in is an irrational one.[1]

God is different . . . So are men. A sense of planetary unity? "To me it seems in the highest degree unlikely that mankind will ever feel itself intimately and lovingly one. The differences of race and place are too enormous.

A Northerner can never feel as a man of the tropic feels; America imposes a mode of being that is radically unlike the modes of being possible in the Old World. There is such a thing as absolute alienness. An absolute alienness which no amount of . . movies and thousand-mile-an-hour aeroplanes . . will ever, it seems to me, completely abolish.[1]

And as for government. There can never be an absolutely right kind of government. "For the simple reason that societies change and that the forms of government must change with them." Aldous's tentative solutions for our various dilemmas were psychological solutions chiefly, and addressed to the fairly exceptional individual, to *l'âme bien née*, in fact. "If one is well-born and well-bred one does not behave like a pig; one behaves like a human being."

To those, *Do What You Will* offered, in distinction to Pascal's worship of death, a creed of "life-worship" the fundamental assumption of which is that "life on this planet is valuable in itself, without any reference to hypothetical higher worlds, eternities, future existences". (Aldous quoted Blake, "It is not better, then, to be alone and love Earth only for its earthly sake?") The end of life "is more life . . the purpose of living is to live . . . The life-worshipper's philosophy is comprehensive. As a manifold and discontinuous being . . he is at one moment a positivist and at another a mystic: now haunted by the thought of death . . and now a Dionysian child of nature . . . His aim is the full realization of all his potentialities—to balance excess of intelligence by an excess of intuition, of instinctive and visceral living . . ." (Much of *Do What You Will* was a continuation of ideas turned up in *Point Counter Point*. Mark Rampion is talking on. The impression of the Lawrentian ship was still upon the water.) "The life-worshipper will be in turn . . excessively passionate and excessively chaste." However, the most

[1] *Do What You Will*. Chatto & Windus, 1929. As all quotations in this chapter.

suitable postulants for this creed, Aldous branched out, "are probably those who have been strictly educated in Christian or bourgeois morality, in the philosophy of commonsense tempered by religion, and have afterwards revolted against their upbringing". Yet the ideal of completeness was mostly realized "by such men as Burns . . as Mozart, as Blake, as Rubens, as Shakespeare, as Tolstoy before he deliberately perverted himself to death-worshipping consistency, as the adorable Chaucer, as Rabelais, as Montaigne . . ." By artists, in fact, And one thing all life-worshippers have in common is a hatred of the empty fooleries and sordidness of average human existence.

Incidentally the progress of science and industry has enormously increased the element of foolery and sordidness in human life.

The great new menace. How clearly Aldous saw the trends in 1929! The machine—dangerous because it also is a creation-saver.

Creative work, of however humble a kind, is the source of man's most solid, least transitory happiness. Leisure has now been almost as completely mechanized as labour. Men . . . sit and are passively amused by mechanical devices. Machinery condemns one of the most vital needs of humanity to frustration which the progress of invention can only render more and more complete.

Already then there was no workable answer. Machinery had increased production, and production had doubled population in one hundred years. Scrap the machinery . . and you will kill about half the population . . . The machinery must stay; it is obvious. It must stay, even though, used as it is now . . it inflicts on humanity an enormous psychological injury that must, if uncared for, prove mortal. . . .

The real trouble with the present social and industrial system is not that it makes some people much richer than others, but that it makes life fundamentally unlivable for all.

In that same year Aldous published *Arabia Infelix*, a limited edition of poems written at intervals during the last decade. It contained what is perhaps his finest poem, an acceptance of life as it is given, the serene and luminous *Cicadas*.

Chapter Eighteen

Endings

> I am suffering agonies at the moment over the rehearsals of a stage version of *Point Counter Point* which has been concocted by an ingenious young man and which is to be produced the day after tomorrow—God help us!

THE young man was Campbell Dixon, the producer Leon M. Lion, and the play, *This Way to Paradise*, opened in London on 30th January at Daly's, a very large theatre far from full. On the first night the actors were so nervous that they forgot their lines. It was Aldous's first personal experience with the theatre and though repelled he was attracted as well. ". . Rather awful, very instructive." He described it all in letters to Lawrence and Robert Nichols. The play was a kind of patchwork made up from scenes of the novel; Aldous had had no hand in it. "Lots of things in it made me rather shudder." At the dress rehearsal though, "the whole performance miraculously [came] to life"; and again, after the horrors of the first night, everything got much better. "Some of the scenes turned out finally very well indeed, particularly the last where they play the Beethoven A minor quartet while the audience waits in a long-drawn anticipation for the man to be killed. The effect was exceedingly good, theatrically, and the music created an extraordinary atmosphere . . The scene absolutely held the audience. It showed me what very astonishing things can be done on the stage with a little imagination and the necessary minimum of technique."

Through February the play did quite well. Aldous returned to Suresnes after the first week and then and there began to write a play of his own. "The only thing that deters one from experimenting much with the theatre is the theatrical world . . . God! what a horror to have to depend on other people for your creation—not to be personally responsible for the whole, but be compelled to use instruments . . . Have you ever had anything to do with actors and producers?" Nevertheless Aldous was bitten. When he was young and poor he had flirted with the idea of the successful commercial play; now he was after something else. "There are a few good producers in the world and . . if one could see one's own dramatic ideas well realized by one of them the thrill would be enormous."

This Way to Paradise closed on 30th March.

Aldous has made great literary use of the sense of horror which in his life, however, was mitigated by an uncommon equability of temperament. Sufficient unto the day—he was not a man to torment himself (nor others) neurotically without present cause. When he was reasonably in health, when work was going and the immediate sky was clear, he was—one can say this—happy. In a letter to Starkey of that winter he tried to clarify the contradiction. He writes about solitude, about the hopelessness of communication:

> Still, one can be very happy all the same. And in spite of the appalling possibilities of unhappiness and the appalling frequency with which the possibilities are realized, I think on the whole it's most decidedly worthwhile—not for any good reason, of course; but for some mysterious good unreason . . .

He ended this letter with, "I wish you very well, dear Starkey."

Aldous was never much of a reader of modern fiction, and when he did read he remained aloof to much that was moving or exciting to his contemporaries. He was apt to be impatient, for instance, with Virginia Woolf (of whom he *was* fond); she did not provide what he was looking for. "Have you read a novel called *The Man Within* by Graham Greene?" he asked Robert Nichols.

> I think it's most remarkable . . . Much better (between ourselves, for it's a frightful heresy!) than Virginia's *To the Lighthouse* which I'm now rather belatedly reading. It's the difference between something full and something empty; between a writer who has a close physical contact with reality and one who is a thousand miles away and only has a telescope to look, remotely, at the world.

Aldous and Maria were now at Suresnes for their last weeks. They had done with the place. Jeanne had already moved out. (Into a flat of her own and a job on the editorial staff of *Le Jardin des Modes*, Aldous had got for her by writing, on Maria's initiative, to his old boss Condé Nast.) The last action of Aldous's Paris life was concerned with Lawrence. "The latest is that *Lady C* is being proceeded against by the French police! [he wrote to Julian] Don't mention it to L. if you're writing . . . If the affair can be arranged —I've been ringing up all the influential literary men I know—he need never know."

In such matters it was Maria who suggested ways and names. They would talk it over, make the decisions together; then Aldous acted. He did not like using the telephone; asking favours he liked

even less. He got on to Paul Valéry whom he knew quite well; to
Gabriel Marcel; to his friend Drieu la Rochelle who though young
was well-known in the *monde*. Possibly he also spoke to André
Maurois who had written the preface for the French edition of
Counter Point. He did not ask Gide. Literary men *have* influence in
France and the nasty business was allowed to peter out.

Lawrence was sinking. On 7th February he had written a postcard from Vence to Maria.

> I have submitted and come here to a sanatorium—sort of sana-
> torium—and Frieda is in the hotel—I came yesterday. It doesn't
> seem very different from an ordinary hotel—but the doctors are
> there to look after one—I'll tell you the results . . .

Five days later he wrote to her again.

> . . Here I came at last, as I was getting so feeble and so thin. It
> isn't a sanatorium, really—an hotel where a nurse takes your
> temperature and two doctors look after you once a week—for the
> rest, just an hotel. They examined me with X-rays and all that. It
> is as I say—the lung has moved very little since Mexico, in five
> years. But the broncs are awful, and they have inflamed my lower
> man, the *ventre* and the liver. I suppose that's why I've gone so thin
> —I daren't tell you my weight . . . I've got a good balcony and
> lovely view—and the air is much better than Bandol . . . It's dull
> here—only French people convalescing and nothing in my line. But
> I'm feeling more chirpy, and shall try to get *on my legs*. It would
> be fun to see you, end of this month. When I hope I can walk a
> bit. I wish we could have been somewhere to have a good time like
> Diablerets. Or I wish I could sail away to somewhere really thrilling
> —perhaps we shall go to the ranch . . .
>
> Perhaps we might have a few jolly days, if you came down—just
> jolly, like Diableret.

But on 21st February:

> Dear Maria,—
> . . I am rather worse here—such bad nights, and cough, and
> heart, and pain decidedly worse here—and miserable. Seems to me
> like *grippe*, but they say not. It's not a good place—shan't stay long
> —I'm better in a house—I'm miserable.
>
> Frieda has Barbey with her—and Ida Rauh. When do you think
> of coming?
>
> D. H. L.

This was the last letter but one Lawrence wrote. The postscript
said, "This place no good."

Aldous and Maria arrived in Vence on 24th or 25th February. They found Lawrence even worse than they had feared. "Terribly changed," Aldous wrote. "He gave one the impression that he was living by sheer force of will and by nothing else. But the dissolution of the body was breaking down the will."

Rina was with them and allowed to see Lawrence once or twice, bringing him flowers. On the afternoon of the 27th, a Thursday, the Huxleys drove over to Villefranche to see the Robert Nicholses.

Aldous and Maria are as sweet as ever [Robert Nichols wrote the next day to Dr Henry Head[1]] . . . Little Maria is much upset over Lawrence. She loves him very much. I am very sorry for her. Her face is worn and peaked over D. H. L. I'm going to see if I can be any use to her. She drives an awful pace in her Bugatti, but I think we rag her too much about it.

The place was no good—once more Lawrence insisted on change. So Frieda rented a villa[2] and on that Saturday, the 1st of March, took him over in a shaking taxi. Lawrence lay down on the new bed, exhausted. Frieda slept on a couch where he could see her.[3] Aldous and Maria had gone to Villefranche again for the day and night. When they came back the next afternoon, on the Sunday, they found Lawrence very weak and suffering much pain "and strangely égaré, feeling that he wasn't there—that he was two people at once".[4] He kept saying to Maria, "Look at *him* there in the bed!" It was as though Lawrence were up in a corner of the ceiling looking down on the body in the bed."[5]

Frieda went out for a few minutes.

"Lawrence grasped my two wrists with his hands and said, 'Maria, Maria, don't let me die.' But he was more peaceful a little later; he was interested in the material phenomenon, I think. He told me he saw himself, his head, just there, next to me, and that he knew he would die."[6] Maria held him in her arms. Frieda, and her daughter Barbara, came back. At 9 p.m. Aldous went to find the doctor, who came and gave some morphine. Lawrence became less distressed. He said, "I am better now." Frieda was holding his ankle. "It felt so full of life, all my days I shall hold his ankle in my hand."[7]

[1] The late neurologist.
[2] The Villa Robermond, now Villa Aurella, at Vence.
[3] From Frieda Lawrence's own account as given in *The Intelligent Heart: The Story of D. H. Lawrence*, by Harry T. Moore. Heinemann, 1955.
[4] Aldous in a letter to Julian of 3rd March 1930 from Vence.
[5] Told to Christopher Isherwood by Maria.
[6] Maria in a letter to Rosalind Rajagopal of 27th February 1943; a letter part quoted on page 183.
[7] Frieda Lawrence, cit.

" . . and he settled off to sleep—to die quietly at 10.15 . . . He went so quietly at the last."[1]

There is a close account of the next day but one in a letter by Robert Nichols written on 8th March 1930 to Dr Henry Head and his wife. Nichols drove over to Vence on the Tuesday morning and knocked at the door of the Villa Robermond.

[I] was greeted by a tall young woman—Barbara—Frieda's daughter by her first husband. Aldous was seated in a smallish tiled room with Thys, the Paris publisher of *Lady Chatterley's Lover*. Almost immediately Frieda came in and grasped me by both hands. She said: "I'm so glad you've come. He would have been so pleased." And then as I found myself unable to speak, "Don't make me cry again." We sat down. She appeared somewhat exalted. "He was so brave, such a fighter; such a MAN."
We sat down and chatted, smoking innumerable cigarettes. For some time I did not gather that Lawrence was in the next room. Mrs Lawrence opened letters and telegrams. A huge wreath of dark crimson carnations arrived from two or three American painters who did not know Lawrence personally but much admired his work. F. was much touched (she was by turns voluble and silent and when she was silent she stared in an odd manner, the pupils of her all but hazel eyes like pin-points.) Barbara opened the door to take the flowers in and I saw Lawrence's nose "sharp as a pen" and his little Greek satyr's beard sticking up (his feet covered by a sheet were towards me). Any time Barbara went in . . she came out crying . . .
. . Little Maria appeared. She looked ghastly—her face was greyish and one could see the blue veins at her temples. From time to time she shivered and enormous tears gathered in her blue eyes. They are a peculiar colour—clear as sapphires, one sees through the lens to the iris and their blue is not the blue of the sky but the blue of water in a white-tiled swimming bath—absolutely translucent and to me very beautiful. They seemed the bluer because the lids were rather red. I must admit that almost my first thought was "This woman is a lot worthier of Lawrence than Frieda" but I doubt whether Lawrence ever really appreciated her. Indeed Barbara told me later that when Aldous and Maria left to come down to me, Lawrence said: "I like them but don't love them anymore." "Because they are intellectuals?" I asked. "I suppose so. I suppose at the last, he felt they weren't his sort." "He felt they were lacking in human warmth?" "Yes." I can understand that. I take it he went back to his miner's world. Probably his pronounced mother-complex worked. But of course A. and M. have plenty of human warmth only it is

[1] Aldous in a letter to Julian of 3rd March 1930 from Vence.

very civilized warmth. I dare say poor little Lawrence wanted somebody to take him in their arms and probably would have recoiled
from it at the same time. [How contradictory this is to what had
actually happened; and yet in another sense perhaps not . . .] Aldous
and Maria will I hope never find out that he said this. Frieda is so
stupid (not malicious) that she might let it out.

A. and M. were magnificent throughout. Frieda would have been
lost without them.

Lawrence went very quickly. He refused oxygen saying it made
the pain worse. I fear he suffered frightfully. Just before they gave
him morphia ("I think I'll have a little morphia now!"—he had
refused it for a long while) he ordered Frieda's bed to be moved to
across the foot of his own. Barbara said he smiled as he watched
the long-armed Aldous working it. But I like Aldous working it
better than that smile.

Though they had not been at the villa long (a day?) Frieda had
contrived to get the kitchen into a hell of an unwholesome mess.
Little Maria, though nearly a wreck, spent the morning scrubbing
it out. Aldous and she had the greatest difficulty in persuading Frieda
to take the most ordinary precautions such as burning clothes etc.
When D. H. L. was very ill they were hard put to make her keep
a special cup for him. She is one of life's natural "squatters", a gypsy
and totally unpractical.

Aldous has been at great pains over money affairs etc. If she
follows his advice all should be well, but she is so stupid and such
a fool that she is quite likely to do the wrong thing.

All the while that we talked in the front room I could feel the
presence of Lawrence next door. What I principally felt was the
fighter. And I stuck to this with Frieda.

Aldous took Barbara and Frieda and myself down to lunch at the
hotel . . . We went back to the villa and Maria and Thys went
down to lunch. It seemed hours till four o'clock. We sat in the
kitchen, which smelled of ether, and I talked my head off. Maria
said it was the only thing to do as I was the least hit of those
present . . .

At length I went out for a stroll and saw the hearse approaching.
It was a rickety old thing drawn by one horse and accompanied
by a sort of chorus of grave-diggers—old characters in workaday
darkish clothes with waistcoats half-buttoned up . . but I liked
them. They were respectful. A dreadful silence fell on the house
and they could be heard knocking their boots on the steps to take
the mud off.

Lawrence had been coffined while we were at lunch. The doors
to the bedroom were thrown open and the old Jobbernols set about
lifting the oak coffin. It appeared—though Lawrence was frail and
smallish—perfectly enormous, and I feared they'd drop it. While

this was going on the silence seemed to stretch itself tight from
horizon to horizon . . . Aldous was standing absolutely impassive,
rather straighter than usual and very pale. His face was beautiful
—and there was so to speak a marvellous pianissimo in it. Maria
seemed in a dream and the big tears rolled two at a time down
towards her nostrils.

We got hold of all the flowers and followed. Aldous had something
to arrange and Maria was alone. She looked terribly forlorn and
greyer in the face than ever. Aldous came back and took charge of
her and I took charge of Frieda. She was quite wonderful. "It's how
he would like it," she said, "just friends. And see, the sun's come
out!" And so it had and the landscape was beautiful—it's lovely up
at Vence and the birds were singing and the huge mass of rocks
above the villa towered in a perfect sky . . .

Frieda didn't want the car to follow the hearse but it had to. The
crawl to the cemetery was rather a nightmare. But then I suppose
it always is! There is something of going to execution in it. But it
had redeeming features. Every man took off his hat on the way—
though one (Englishman of course) only did it at the last minute
after I had stared him out of countenance and even then he kept
his pipe in his mouth. I stared at him because a moment before
Frieda made her only remark on the ride (Aldous and Maria, Frieda
and I stuffed in one tiny taxi, my car was ahead carrying other
people), "See how they take off their hats to Lawrence—isn't it
nice!" Yes, they took off their hats. More people took off their hats
to him on that ride than had ever done in his life. These Southerners
respect death. And they are right: death should be respected. There's
mystery in it, and when one is convoying a fighter like Lawrence
one feels it more than ever. Women crossed themselves. The sky
became more and more beautiful for it was just after four and the
drama of nature was just beginning to move again after the stillness
of a day made more still by descent of rain in short spells from a
moveless [sic] grey sky. I led the way with Frieda. She said: "It's
like being all old soldiers together." And so it was.

We came out on the lowest terrace of the cemetery: a beautiful
position. Below the rampart of the cemetery the ground falls away
through an orange orchard. A wonderful valley opens out and far
away the sea glitters among haze. We all paused. "How beautiful
it is," said Frieda. The coffin had gone on to under a further wall,
beyond a solitary cypress. Here we sort of broke up into separate
units. Not a word was said. The coffin was lowered into the grave.
There was a little pause. The Jobbernols looked at us. Perhaps they
expected a speech. Mrs Lawrence advanced and dropped some
flowers on the coffin. Two or three of us did that and I said "Goodbye,
dear Lawrence," because I couldn't bear to let him go absolutely
without a word. At that I heard Maria begin to cry softly behind

me. Then the Jobbernols began to fill the grave, pitching the stones in the earth to one side before they pushed in a shovel—curious long shovels they used, the oval shape perhaps as that used by the Romans. By God, my dears, it was grand. Why make speeches in the face of death? We don't know enough to say anything. The work was soon done . . .

. . One of the Jobbernols made to put the flowers on the grave. But Frieda said, "Let us put the flowers on ourselves." So I went over to the pile of flowers and handed them over. But Maria wouldn't put any on. She stood like one about whom the heavens had fallen. I stayed a little after most had moved away and put up a prayer to whosoever rules the remains that I might be—that we all might be . . . Then I went back to Frieda and she was quite calm . . . as we went up the path she suddenly stopped. The hearse was there. "It's empty now," she said in all but a whisper.

On their way back from the funeral, Aldous, Maria and Robert Nichols stopped exhausted in a wayside café and drank tea. They talked about the fortuitous nature of Lawrence's illness, how little care he had taken of himself; and Nichols, in the course of that very long letter, also says this: "I am bound to add as a statement of mere fact that I am afraid Frieda Lawrence was worse than useless as regards D. H. L.'s health.

On the Friday (I think, but it may have been the Thursday) before he died, D. H. L. said to her, "Frieda, you have killed me." Aldous told me this . . Aldous would not repeat such a terrible saying unless he felt it to be true. And he said, "I like Frieda in many ways but she is incurably and incredibly stupid—the most maddening woman I think I ever came across. Nevertheless she was the only sort of woman with whom D. H. L. could live." Poor Maria felt the whole thing frightfully. She was devoted to D. H. L. I think perhaps she loved him better than she loved anybody except Aldous among the few people she knew well. I felt more sorry for her than for anybody. The only good that has come out of the episode is that I am now nearer these two, Aldous and Maria . . . I feel profound affection for her. She agrees with Aldous about Frieda but she spoke without an atom of resentment and with great compassion. . . .

A day or two later, Aldous, Maria and Rina drove away to look for their next house up the coast. Mme Douillet, the owner of the Hotel Beaurivage who had befriended Lawrence, gave them advice and help and before the week was out they had found one on a bay at Sanary near Toulon.

PART FIVE

The Apparent Stability: 1930-1935

"Meanwhile, one must be content to
go on piping up for reason and realism
and a certain decency."
ALDOUS HUXLEY, *Texts and Pretexts*

Chapter One

Villa Huley

VILLA HULEY—the mason had painted on the gateposts in huge, bright, green letters meaning to give them a surprise. Aldous and Maria thought it unkind to wipe out or correct this blaring advertisement of their presence and let it stand for the time being. Soon they ceased to see it. The letters remained, scarcely faded by the sun, in the long years after when the house stood empty.

Then the country round Bandol and Sanary was unspoilt, a classical landscape of hills, olives, vine. The new house though was on a slightly scruffy promontory between the two villages, called La Gorguette, where the dominant vegetation was thin pines and the land already destined to advancing development. (Aldous and Maria were apt to acquire their houses as quickly as they got rid of them.) There were advantages: the sea and a small beach at less than three hundred yards, main water and electricity and a short if bumpy drive to the good road. The original Villa Huley was a cramped little house built by a retired French *fonctionnaire* around 1910. By knocking down walls, cutting windows and enlarging here and there, the Huxleys changed it beyond recognition. The house was re-made, hand-made to their needs by the local builder. This turned out expensive; Aldous worried, but the new play was like a lottery ticket in his pocket ("I hope and pray that someone will take it . . .")

The outside became white-washed and green-shuttered. There was no entrance hall—one walked in, sandy feet, rain or shine, right into the living room. This was a large, well-proportioned L-shaped room, the walls terracotta wash, the floor red-tiled. At once one became aware of a fresh light scent of rosemary, geranium, lime and rose: Maria's pot-pourri in a deep urn by the door. To the right, shut off by long pale greenish oil-cloth curtains, another legacy of René Moulaert's, was the looking-glass dinner-table and a row of squat green oil-cloth covered chairs; to the left the living-room proper—Mexican rugs, the vast Dufy sofa and chairs from Suresnes before a fireplace; beyond in the sleeve of the L, Maria's desk and sewing box and a settee for two. Here she typed Aldous's books; and here they came, one by one, Matthew, Sophie, Raymond Mortimer and Eddy Sackville-West, Gerald Heard, Rina, myself, offering gossip, pouring out our troubles, our stories, answering anything she might ask (and my goodness, she did ask, out of her own

quick interest *and* to pass on to Aldous), to be scolded, comforted
and teased.

The living-room led into a hall—coat-stand, piles of straw hats—
and to the stair-well in the centre of the house: one broad flight up,
one narrow down to the kitchen which was on a lower level. Off
this hall was a pantry with a food lift and the telephone, a solid
wooden instrument with a crank. One was able to make and receive
calls from, I think, 7.30 in the morning until 9 o'clock at night.
Across the hall was Aldous's room, the room he worked in, his
library. It was a good-sized room, almost square, with tiled floor
and bookcases to the ceiling. There was a roll-top desk, a swivel
chair, his very long chaise-longue and the armchair made to
measure. French windows, well-shuttered, gave on to the large
East terrace they had built but did not use as nobody except Maria
and the Siamese cats went into that room unasked. Messages and
crises were not relayed to Aldous during working hours. Sometimes,
when he was not actually writing, the door might be open and one
could see him standing up with his nose inside a book. When the
heat of the day was waning, the shutters were flung open to a
pleasant enough view of the garden. There was as yet no other
roof in sight. (Quite soon, though, a monstrosity began to rise brick
by brick across the fence; shoddy, gabled and pretentious it attained
a spindly height. It housed at first a summer-school and when that
failed a *pension de famille*, the Huxley household referred to it as
Nuremberg.)

There were five bedrooms and one bath upstairs (the spare rooms
had modest *cabinets de toilette*). Maria's room was large and light,
an East room with a balcony to step out on, light modern furniture
in pearly and coral tints. The looking-glass on her dressing-table
was framed by sea-shells. The key-note—the key-note of the house
—was order and quietness, and the luxury of this. Aldous's bedroom
narrow as a passage, led out of Maria's and contained little beside
a row of wall-cupboards, a chest of drawers and his extra-long bed
(with extra-long sheets from England and an extra-long red quilt).
The other bedrooms faced West. Matthew's, the largest and nicest
with toy- and book-shelves; the other two for guests. Rina lived in
a cottage in the garden.

Aldous had insisted on adequate central heating, and they installed a water filter for their tea (always Jackson's Earl Grey) and
an electric refrigerator, a rare luxury at the time. The kitchen
range was coal; bathwater was heated by a stove that had to be
hand-fed with small sticks. The Siamese (the protagonists of
"Sermons in Cats") were three, Matou, Pussy and their off-spring
Matelot.

It was a very pleasant house, the house at Sanary, and it had
dignity. It was not beautiful; none of their houses ever was,

nor really intended to be, and some of their friends sniffed and shuddered. There were few objects, no good pieces; such bric-à-brac as they collected on their journeys was not fashionable. Maria had one of D. H. Lawrence's paintings in her bedroom and a Marie Laurencin print; downstairs there were a very fine landscape by Joep Nicolas and his portrait of Maria, the rest of their pictures were by Aldous.

I have described the house as it was in its heyday. At first there were neither telephone nor Nuremberg; Mexican rugs, Joep's and Aldous's paintings, all came later. At first, the spring of 1930, there was chiefly brick-dust, hammering, gaping holes and crates. It was in this setting that I, in turn, had my first glimpse of Aldous. It was in the early afternoon of a warm day in spring; I was living at my mother's[1] and step-father's, and the Roy Campbells were staying with us for a few days. After luncheon Roy demanded to be taken to say hello to Aldous who, he had been told, was building in the neighbourhood and whom he had not seen since the days of Tommy Earp and Russell Green's Bloomsbury flat which he had sometimes shared. To me this was a shock. I had read *Antic Hay* (I was an adolescent with passionate intellectual longings), I had read the stories, I had read and re-read *Point Counter Point*. Aldous Huxley's writings were the overwhelming revelation. I was not prepared, I did not think of, an encounter with the writer in the flesh. (Oh perhaps in some dim adult future, when I should have proved myself, become a visible writer . . .) I thought about the books—constantly—of the man who wrote them I knew next to nothing (except rumours about his sight). Publishing being rather more impersonal then, I had not even seen a photograph. Had I been asked to place him—say, in one of those pen-and-paper games my family too indulged in—I might have visualized a disembodied existence in a tower at Balliol. An actual house in this fishing port, on our doorstep practically, if one were to believe Roy, was not credible. At any rate it came too sudden and too soon. My mother, also, was not enthusiastic. She admired Aldous's essays, taking a cooler view about the novels (we used to argue about this); writers, she told Roy, should be read not seen; and besides she did not hold with a pack of strangers dropping in on the poor man. Roy became aggressive. One needn't stand on ceremony with old Aldous, he declared, many was the night at Oxford when he'd carried him home and into his bed dead-drunk. This I refused to believe. (It was indeed a complete fabrication, made up, not in malice—Roy in many ways was a very sweet character—but in one of his spurts of obstinate mythomania.) Roy in those days drank red wine almost continuously, continuously from breakfast. He insisted; somebody

---

[1] The late Lisa Marchesani.

had to drive him. Nori Marchesani, my young step-father, volunteered. We set off on what had the hallmark of a wild-goose chase, Roy having no idea of the direction we were to take. Mary Campbell sat in front, Roy and I in the back. He was holding on to a shopping net with two full bottles. We stopped whomever we saw to make enquiries (it was the siesta hour) and quite soon struck lucky. Yes, an *homme de lettres anglais* was building on La Gorguette, about a mile from our house! We drew up in front of the Green Letters. These were the gateposts, there was no gate as yet. We stepped across some planks and approached a hole in the façade. Inside, sitting on the floor beside a large revolving book-cage, sorting books, was Aldous.

He was dressed in khaki shorts, sandals without socks and a light shirt; he looked up and one saw the large round spectacles. Roy spoke, "Aldous—this is Roy." "Roy," Aldous said in a high silvery tone. He got to his feet, uncoiling length. "Dear Roy—how are you?" He shook hands with a little smile, very friendly. Roy introduced his wife.

He struck me—he was looking absurdly young that moment on the floor—as he must have struck Juliette the first day at Garsington, and L. P. Hartley from across the stairs and that young woman who saw him at Oxford lectures standing by a pillar. It is more than forty years ago; the snapshot in the mind is static, clear. I can look at it at will, interpret now, feel; use the words of today, note his absorption—we came upon him when he thought himself alone— the apartness, the vulnerability, the curious young bird's unprotectedness that has caught so many women. Can it be transmitted that snapshot? Of Aldous by the book-cage, head bent gracefully, thick dark hair dishevelled, long tapering hands moving about books . . .

The next one—Aldous standing head forward, stooping from the shoulders, swaying to one side—is blurred by the overlay of so many later ones. He began to talk—now it was the voice that drew attention—almost the first thing he said was that someone ought to paint a horror picture of The First Day in the New Home. Not that it was the first day, he had been camping in the house since April and had just come back from a brief escape to England on poor Lawrence's business. My step-father, who was on alien territory but had his own perceptiveness, caught my eye: "I must get her," and was gone. At that stage Maria appeared (much intrigued, she told us later, to see the back of a car shooting out of the drive and wondering who was fleeing from their premises and why). Maria, as I said, appeared. This was another turn, as I had no idea that Aldous might be married. Roy—they hadn't met—had probably forgotten. She moved forward swiftly, an ephesian figure in full white sailor trousers and a linen shirt, the face all eyes and profile, auburn hair held by a ribbon and a flower, falling to the shoulders. An Angel of the Annunciation by El Greco with a touch of Degas (in my mother's words). *She*, meanwhile had arrived. The car had come back, there were two more of us, Maria took it in her stride. My mother, though still young, was already very ill then and often rather wayward and eccentric; there were still some traces of a beauty that had been considerable. She was a great talker, as well as a good listener, when there was something worth listening to, and a most amusing story-teller; she also had much charm. Aldous responded. Maria asked us to stay for tea. We settled round a table in an arbour; the ensuing talk was a dialogue between Aldous and my mother. They talked about life in Paris, they talked about local history. Aldous declared himself to be fascinated by a character called General Rose, after whom the main street of Sanary was named, who had built a folly for his mistresses at the age of ninety. The rest of us listened. Roy was meek and mild. (I longed for answers to so many questions but knew that it was not the time.) They talked about French novelists, made jokes about the Goncourts, Maupassant. *Une Vie*, Aldous said, was a much longer and much less effective version of what Wilhelm Busch had so admirably done in his life of *Die Fromme Helene*. While they were talking, there went on a mimed obligato to which most of us paid little attention but which mesmerized Maria. (She told the story later.) Rina came in with a large full tea-pot and placed it in front of Maria. My mother, going on with what she had been saying and without taking her eyes off Aldous, reached across the table, seized the pot and drew it to herself. She was notoriously absent-minded and had no doubt forgotten that she was not in her own house. However, she did not pour out. For some time nothing happened. My mother, hand on tea-pot, went on talking. Maria now made a discreet move to regain possession. My mother grasped the pot more firmly, drew it closer to herself and, still without losing the thread of her conversation, opened the lid, peered inside and quickly dropped the lid again.

Maria was filled with admiration. She had recognized a peer in savoir faire. What presence of mind, what tact! For she was convinced that what my mother had seen and somehow *known* to be inside that tea-pot must be a dead dormouse at the very least. The party took its course. Our cups stayed empty (according to Maria; I have a notion that Rina was signalled for a fresh supply). Roy, by the way, had not dared to bring in his provisions. My mother went on sitting with the tea-pot practically in her arms, only relinquishing her grasp to help herself to the excellent thin brown bread-and-butter. Brown bread was rare in France, and she finished off the platter.

We had been back at our house for an hour that evening when

we heard the snort of a powerful car outside. The red Bugatti stopped, tore off again: Maria had left some tuberoses and a small brown loaf for my mama.

Aldous was not D. H. Lawrence's literary executor. Lawrence died intestate. Frieda and his brother George, who became joint administrators of the estate, asked Aldous and some others to advise on literary decisions. There was, for instance, the question of a biography. Frieda and Aldous felt that it was still too early for a truthful life of D. H. L. Aldous suggested a memorial volume instead, reminiscences by various people interspersed with Lawrence's own letters.

> e.g. an account of his childhood by his sister; early manhood by a schoolmaster friend, and, for a later period, by Ezra Pound; shortly after his marriage an account by David Garnett . . . war-time by Middleton Murry (perhaps) and also Lady Cynthia Asquith and Lady Ottoline Morrell; perhaps a page by Bertrand Russell . . . also Richard Aldington; and Norman Douglas; for the Australian time his collaborator in *The Boy in the Bush*, Miss Skinner; for the American period, Mabel Dodge; for the last 2 or 3 years in Italy and France, perhaps myself.

The recollections to be printed as nearly as possible in chronological order, adding when necessary a bald statement of dates and doings. Aldous offered ("this goes without saying") to do whatever work for nothing. That rather good idea petered out.

During the three months following Lawrence's death, Aldous kept moving between Bandol, Sanary, London and Paris. "I'm hunting up Lawrence letters," he wrote to Robert Nichols,

> What a queer devil he was! The queerer, the more I think and know about him. So many charming and beautiful things in him, such a lot that wasn't sympathetic. I gather . . that you got Frieda a bit on the nerves. Well, I'm not surprised . . .

The idea was to get hold of and copy as many of D. H. L.'s letters as possible at once so that they should not be dispersed or lost. As to what to publish, Aldous's own view was clear. ". . The selection should be as far as possible impersonal. I don't like the body-snatching business."[1] "The rather indecent display of personalities which has become so unpleasantly common now is

---

[1] To Richard Aldington, 1st June 1930.

something which, if I have any say, shall be avoided."[1] "What may happen many years hence is the affair of posterity."[2]

"Here all is exquisitely lovely," Aldous wrote to Juliette from Sanary in May. "Sun, roses, fruit, warmth. We bathe and bask. Best love to all."

Aldous and Maria's first Sanary summer lasted well into September. The house got into shape, daily life reassumed its even pattern. It was still very much as it had been in Italy. Maria got up early. She loved the light and solitude of dawn. Unhurried, day-dreaming, she would garden. Asked what she was doing in those morning hours, she would say, "I paint my artichokes." (To keep off insects.) Family breakfast was at about ten. Aldous would look sleepy and be comfortably silent. There was no post as yet or newspapers. Quite soon he would get up, still silent, and go into his room. The door shut behind him.

He was working during that summer on essays and on the play he started at Suresnes, *The World of Light*, and he was also trying his hand again at poetry. By one o'clock he would emerge—a little sun-bathing on the roof, then everybody in their bathing dress walked down to the sea. Aldous carried the inflated rubber boat. He and Maria wore large hats against the sun which they kept on in the water. Out they swam, the two of them, rather slowly, farther and farther, talking all the while—"swimming together conscientiously," as little Sophie saw it, "with straw hats on, discussing important subjects." On land again, Maria inveterately took photographs—the French had gone to eat, the pebbly beach was theirs—Matthew, looking pensive, holding up a toy ship; Eddy Sackville-West, as thin as a fakir, emerging from the waves; Raymond Mortimer laughing in the spray; Rina, also laughing, in a bathing cap; and of course Aldous. "Aldous was usually cheerful, anchored still, one felt, in his morning's work, but ready for the break, willing to join the talk," I wrote, I find, in the *Memorial Volume*; now, having thought about it so much more, I still believe that this was so. He *was* cheerful and present on one level; he often teased the children. Back in the house, one washed off sand and put on clothes. Few clothes, shorts, espadrilles, and those magically cool Egyptian cotton shirts Aldous and Maria wore interchangeably. Rina banged a gong. Luncheon was indoors. The dining cubicle with the green shiny curtain, the glassy surface and the filtered light coming through the shutters, had an under-water quality. Rina handed round the dishes. (The house ran simply but with smoothness—

[1] To Helen Corke, 7th May 1930.
[2] To Brett, 23rd June 1930.

one did not interrupt conversation proffering things.) Food was risotto or pasta, a green vegetable, some mild cheese, always fruit. Plates and bowls, Italian mostly, were pretty, the Tuscan glass green-tinged. There were carafes of cooled white and red wine and plain water on the table, local wine at noon; at dinner it was claret. Everybody talked. Maria exchanged words with Rina in Italian. Maria's Italian was delightful to listen to; it was the one language, and like Aldous she did know a good many, she spoke without a foreign accent. Her French passed as French, not Belgian, but had alien undertones to acute French ears; her English had a cadence of its own. Luncheon was not long, though unhurried (time was not allowed to be talked away, there was an invisible bar of dis-cipline). Not that Aldous went back to work at once; now he often painted during the dog hours, setting up his easel to do a view from Maria's window or Maria or a child on a chaise-longue.

The post would have arrived while everyone was bathing and been left on a sofa. Book parcels, unsolicited manuscripts and all. Nobody ever seemed to wish to look at it at once. For a writer in working spate this matter of answering letters—keeping on indoors, solitary and cramped, after the day's work—can be a cruel business. For Aldous the problem was perennial. No wonder so many of his letters begin with "Time has been sliding away . . ." Somehow bills got paid and letters opened. Maria did what she could, which had its limitations. Accounts, forms, bank statements, made little sense to her; she typed fast but with all the mistakes Lawrence had found in her script of *Lady C*; she did not often date her letters and the hand-written ones were hard to read. Yet to her friends and sisters she wrote those long, descriptive letters, typed late at night when Aldous was asleep.

The Huxleys did not subscribe to an English newspaper. (No *Times*, no *New Statesman*.) They took in a French daily which generally remained folded in its wrapper, as did the polyglot reviews that were sent from all over the world. Aldous subscribed to *Nature*.

After painting, tea. China tea and a plate of ginger nuts, in Aldous's room, in the garden, anywhere. Then another stint of work.

Before dinner there might be a quick dip in the sea or, if it was cool enough, a stroll. Then Aldous and Maria went upstairs to have their baths and change—the hour of their private talk. Presently they came down (dinner in summer was round nine o'clock): Aldous in a gleaming shirt and endless white cotton trousers (beautifully laundered by the Italian maids); Maria in a cloud of scent, a fresh flower in her hair, often also in white ducks (hers were made at the cost of about fifteen shillings at the naval bazaar on the quai of Toulon). There was a sense of release about these evenings, something of what Aldous had spoken of as the "profoundly satisfying consciousness of being 'in order'."[1] Dinner was lightly *en fête*. And afterwards they went out into the summer night, the garden where hammocks used to swing under the eucalyptus and the lime. Aldous brought his black box, the hand-wound gramophone. There was music. There was silence.

Such was the tip of the iceberg, the manifest part of their daily round. People who were brought up at Prior's Field speak of the atmosphere of goodness and kindness in the home life of another generation of Huxleys. Time and place had changed and Aldous and Maria's home life was in some ways eccentric, yet again the atmosphere was a compound of seriousness and gaiety, of gentle-ness, niceness, grace. Like his mother Aldous possessed invisible moral authority. There were things one did not do, did not wish to do, in his house, his presence. (There was also of course that dread he had, and communicated, of coming close to uncovered emotion.) Aldous's entourage adopted a certain standard; even strangers did, such as porters and waiters in the more excitable countries. Perhaps Aldous never realized what a good influence he was. (I once said rather naively to a mutual friend, "But *you* don't do such things?"—it was something fairly harmless—and he answered, "My dear, you mustn't think of me only as you see me at the Huxleys.") Much of it was a matter of tone. There never was a harsh word between Aldous and Maria. Nor between them and others. Which does not mean that Maria did not speak up or criticize; she was *very* outspoken, she was *very* critical; in fact she could be quite didactic, particularly with her sisters and the children. One was not allowed to get away with things. And that went for Aldous too. He wasn't let off doing what Maria thought he ought to do; she kept down his sins of omission. And how she could puncture pretension. By teasing or laughing. How often one heard her say, "Matthew, don't be pompous." and to Aldous, the least pompous of men, "Darling, don't be pompous!" (What she was up against was the irreducible masculine pomposity about accurate facts and not making oneself conspicuous in public.) When Maria had to scold in earnest, it was done in sorrow and concern. Once when Rina had again succumbed to the lure of sweets, I came upon them crying in each others' arms. Whereas if Aldous girded himself to rebuke or educate, he generally did it by letter; which of course was so much worse for the recipient.

[1] In "On Grace", *Music at Night*. Chatto & Windus, 1931.

We have left them in the Mediterranean darkness, under leaves and sky.

Moonless, this June night is all the more alive with stars. Its darkness is perfumed with faint gusts from the blossoming lime trees, with the smell of wetted earth and the invisible greenness of the vines. There is silence; but a silence that breathes with the soft breathing of the sea and, in the thin shrill noise of a cricket . . . Far away, the passage of a train. . . .

Music, you say; it would be a good night for music. But I have music here in a box, shut up, like one of those bottled djinns in the *Arabian Nights*, and ready at a touch to break out of its prison. I make the necessary mechanical magic, and suddenly, by some miraculously appropriate coincidence (for I had selected the record in the dark . .), suddenly the introduction to the *Benedictus* in Beethoven's *Missa Solemnis* begins to trace its pattern on the moonless sky.

The *Benedictus*. Blessed and blessing, this music is in some sort the equivalent of the night, of the deep and living darkness . . .

There is, at least there sometimes seems to be, a certain blessedness lying at the heart of things, a mysterious blessedness, of whose existence occasional accidents or providences (for me, this night is one of them) make us obscurely, or it may be intensely, but always fleetingly, alas, always only for a few brief moments aware.[1]

1 *Music at Night*, written in 1930.

Chapter Two

The Bad Utopia

IN the three years after *Point Counter Point* Aldous did not attempt any major work. *Do What You Will* was followed by *Brief Candles*, a collection of stories; the longest, *After the Fireworks*, was perhaps his last go at story-telling *per se*. It is an accomplished tale, very literary, with a characteristically hybrid genesis—"an elaboration and emendation of an incident recorded in the letters of Chateaubriand. When he was sixty, a very young girl at a watering place came and threw herself at his head. He wrote her a most exquisite letter, which is extant. And there", Aldous explained to Starkey, "the matter ended, even though she did invade his house one evening . . . I thought it would be amusing to give it the cruel ending [the man giving in: the girl getting tired of him in a matter of months]. As one couldn't use Chateaubriand himself—that monstrous pride and loneliness and, underneath the burning imagination, that emotional aridity would have been impracticable to handle—I made the hero one of those people . . [whose identity would be guesswork] who know how to shirk natural consequences and get something for nothing . . ." Aldous's third working year—from the death of Lawrence to May 1931—was ragged. "Time, like an Indian thief [once more to Starkey] has got away with weeks and months of booty, leaving how little, so far as I'm concerned, in return—some essays, a few poems, some on the whole rather melancholy reflections."

Actually Aldous had got through a fair amount of work. He had been tinkering with the idea of a new novel: "a kind of picaresque novel of the intellect and the emotions, [to Robert Nichols] a mixture between *Gil Blas*, *Bouvard et Pécuchet* and *Le Rouge et le Noir* . . quite impossible to do—but will be fun to try". Nothing apparently came of this, but he had finished his play; he had written some of his best or his best-remembered shorter essays, "Tragedy and the Whole Truth", "Meditation on El Greco", "Sermons in Cats", "Music at Night"; he had written a dozen or so new poems. In publishing terms, this meant four titles in ten months. In November 1930 *Vulgarity in Literature*, a somewhat drawn-out essay in a limited edition; in April 1931 the play, *The World of Light*; in May, *The Cicadas*, plumped out with some earlier poems; and in September, *Music at Night*. Meanwhile Aldous had also been painting, and coping with a flow of D. H. Lawrence letters as it had been decided to publish a substantial collection of these presently.

6   The Huxley Children *c.* 1903
From top: Julian, Trevenen, Aldous, Margaret

7   Maria in the twenties

As for travel, the Huxleys had been staying relatively put. They had left Sanary in September for England from where Aldous had gone on to Berlin and Paris, accompanying his friend Sullivan on "a tour of great men [Sullivan was interviewing eminent scientists] . . a most entertaining piece of sightseeing". (Later he gave Robert Nichols an account of a night he and Sullivan spent at a homosexual dance-hall in Berlin which Nichols related in one of his letters to the Henry Heads.

> . . Incidentally he [Aldous] danced with one of the male prostitutes rather than hurt the fellow's feelings. This last slipped out. He didn't mean to tell it. But I asked him how [they] . . dealt with the men who came to their table. He added, 'I was just a little tipsy when I did it. But I can assure you, my dear Bob, a couple of times round that hall and I was sobriety itself. Horror is a wonderful disintoxicant.')

In October Aldous came back to England and, with Maria, went to Nottingham to see D. H. L.'s relations and then up into the Northern Midlands for some articles he had been asked to do on conditions in the mining villages. It was a bleak time; Aldous was appalled. "What a world we live in. I was staying in the Durham coalfield this autumn, in the heart of English unemployment, and it was awful.

> If only one cd believe that the remedies . . (Communism etc.) proposed for the awfulness weren't even worse than the disease . . . The sad and humiliating conclusion is forced on one that the only thing to do is to flee and hide . . .

They went back to Sanary and did not move again until well into the new year when they went to London for the last two winter months. They stayed in rooms in Dalmeny Court, Duke Street, St James's, rooms which never saw daylight but were well heated and comfortable enough and provided with a pantry where they could boil their own kettles and need not go out for every bite. The situation was perfect for Aldous's routine—two steps from the London Library and the Athenaeum.

Some of Aldous's recent verse, we just noted, was to be published in late spring. He asked Robert Nichols for an opinion. "If you have time," he wrote to him, "will you glance at these and tell me what you think of them when we meet. Some, I think, are all right. But I don't really know and rely on your judgement."

Now Robert Nichols was devoted to Aldous; he was also a very emotional young man, a man of feeling, as another age might have called him, and he showed his feelings. (He had an extraordinary harrowing way, a marrow-piercing way, of reading poetry.) One can imagine how he affected Aldous; Nichols, for his part, gave an analysis of their relation (in that letter to the Henry Heads of 1930).

. . . Aldous and Maria were as sweet as ever. I adore them. I fear Aldous finds me rather a bore—I'm so naïve beside him, so much the "life is real, life is earnest" young man and also so disconcertingly emotional—for when I see him my india-rubber face will give away how I wear him in my heart of hearts. But he's really fond of me and that's one of the reasons he feels shy. I think he's scared that I shall close his ship and set about boarding him emotionally. Nature has erected on the edge of his emotional garden a board "trespassers —against the will of the owner—are apt to be prosecuted". Sometimes I note him rein himself in from emptying a cold douche on my head. He really is a saint. He would like me to steal aboard and somehow arrive without his notice. That I try to do though I feel terribly inclined to rush on board with a loud "O Aldous!" and when I get there I keep one eye on the clock. He is a great man, a great human being and not at all cold really. He also has tremendous pluck.

And now, in his house at Winchelsea, Nichols was expecting the Huxleys once more.

My beloved Aldous and Maria are coming this weekend . . . [to the Heads, 30th January 1931] He desires me to advise him on some poems to be added to those in *Arabia Infelix* . . which contains the superb *Cicadas*—and published in an ordinary edition. It is very difficult. There is not one of those poems without a good idea, but Aldous hasn't always the power of melting the thought with music —for poetry must have music; if possible various music or it isn't poetry. There is one largish splendid poem called *ORION* among those he sent me. A. H. hasn't the technical resources of T. S. E.— but he's *game* which T. S. E. isn't. He wrestles with his despair. The following comparison is absurd as far as class goes, but as to character one might say that at the present moment, in the prevailing atmosphere of profound discouragement, Aldous is a sort of Beethoven trying to fight his way through, and T. S. E. is a sort of Chopin (recollect I am not speaking of class: I am speaking of character, of spirit). The spirit—and the will to pay—in Aldous is making a desperate battle . . . He has terrific courage and formidable mental integrity—he is a hero: one of the few heroes among the writers of our time . . . In fact, now Romer [Wilson]'s dead—and D. H. L.— I hardly see another.

The World of Light, Aldous's first play, had been accepted, by Leon M. Lion, and was being produced at the Royalty in March.

Aldous watched the rehearsals. "He sat there in the darkness of the stalls," wrote Denys Blakelock[1] who played Hugo, the principal part, "silent and as I thought disapproving." And yet after the opening Aldous wrote him a most complimentary letter.

> I wish he could have said a few of [the things he wrote] during the rehearsal period . . . But he was a shy remote man and I think he would have found it impossible to make contact with a company of actors.[1]

Mr Blakelock speaks of the play as "one of the most distinguished and provocative pieces of writing for the theatre of that decade". . . . Yet it was far from a success. It made less money, Aldous said, than any play since the Agamemnon of Aeschylus. *The World of Light* is the world of spirits. In Act Two the stage is plunged in darkness and the audience stares at a realistic seance—floating objects, musical box, luminous trumpet. This seance is smashed— seconds before curtain— by the arrival of the spirit in persona and alive. The medium (one thinks) has been unmasked. And yet the messages he transmitted—the thoughts of the living man—turn out to have been minutely accurate. The extra-sensory communication was genuine, only the seeker's premises were at fault. But this is not quite cut and dried; Aldous did not commit himself. It is even difficult to make out whether he was using the spiritualist theme as a trimming and a dramatic bait, or whether he regarded it as parallel or as subordinate to the play's other theme, escape. (Escape from emotional aridity, an undesired marriage, conventional duties, escape into gratuitous action.) Aldous rather side-tracked a critic's demand (Desmond MacCarthy's) for a more definite solution.

> [It seems] justified . . even tho' there would not in fact have been such a solution in life, it is perhaps one of the functions of art to provide definite solutions—to consummate wish-fulfilments . . . The difficulty was (a) finding any plausible solution at all and (b) finding one that could be got into the terribly limited space at a playwright's disposal. A difficulty so great that, after many attempts, I stuck to the mere verisimilitude and left the situation hanging in the void.

In Sanary, in April, Aldous began to write his Bad Utopia. He wrote it in four months. It all began light-heartedly enough. It was time to produce some full-length fiction—he still felt like holding back from another straight novel—juggling in fiction form with the

---

[1] Denys Blakelock, *Round the Next Corner*. Victor Gollancz, 1967.

scientific possibilities of the future might be a new line. Twenty-five years after, an American acquaintance asked Aldous whether he had any idea that *Brave New World* would be considered prophetic, that it would be regarded as an influential philosophical work. "He replied with a kind of tender but self-deprecating affection for his own past that he had been having a little fun pulling the leg of H. G. Wells. At least it had started out that way until he got caught up in the excitement of his own ideas."[1]

Wells' views on the effects of applied science were rosy; Aldous had his doubts. Take eugenics for instance—the increase, by deliberate breeding, of some of the inheritable qualities such as intelligence and ability. An intrinsically desirable change, you might say, but would it have desirable results? What would happen to a society compelled by law to breed exclusively from its most gifted and successful members? Four years earlier already, Aldous had had this to say on the subject.

. . It is obvious that all the superior individuals of the eugenic states will not be permitted to make full use of their powers, for the good reason that no society provides openings for more than a limited number of superior people. No more than a few can govern, do scientific research, practise the arts . . or lead their fellows. But if . . every individual is capable of playing the superior part, who will consent to do the dirty work and obey? The inhabitants of one of Mr Wells's numerous Utopias solve the problem by ruling and being ruled, doing high-brow and low-brow work in turns. While Jones plays the piano, Smith spreads the manure. At the end of the shift, they change places; Jones trudges out to the dung-heap and Smith practises the A minor Etude of Chopin. An admirable state of affairs if it could be arranged . . .[2]

"Personally," Aldous went on, "I find my faith too weak . . . The intellectually gifted are notorious for the ruthless way in which they cultivate their gifts."

In Aldous's counter Utopia, then, human beings are deliberately bred inferior as well as superior; Gammas and Identical Epsilon Semi-Morons as well as Alpha-Pluses. The principle of mass production, as one of the World Managers explains, is at last applied to biology. The theme, the well-known theme of *Brave New World*, is the effect of science applied to human beings by their rulers at some approaching future point. (The theme was not the progress of science as *such*; Aldous's intention was not scientific prophecy, no foretelling of any probable specific technological development,

[1] Mrs Arthur Goldschmidt of New York, in a letter to S. B. 1968.
[2] "A Note on Eugenics", *Proper Studies*. Chatto & Windus, 1927.

such as if and when we might split the atom—bottled babies were just a serviceable extravagance—it was psychological prophecy.) The theme was that you could dominate people by social, educational and pharmaceutical arrangements:

> iron them into a kind of uniformity, if you were able to manipulate their genetic background . . . if you had a government sufficiently unscrupulous you could do these things without any doubt . . .

And this, Aldous said in the London interview in 1961, "This *was* the whole idea of *Brave New World.*"

These things—projected forty years ago for the year 600 After Ford—were Pavlovian conditioning of children before and after birth, hypnopaedia, mind-changing drugs and pleasure-giving drugs, planned sexual promiscuity (". . as political and economic freedom diminishes, sexual freedom tends compensatingly to increase"), compulsory contraceptives, the prolongation of youth, euthanasia, total centralization of power, total government control and above all a foolproof system to standardize the human product. Today, we are still a longish cry from globally controlled production of human beings. Yet (as Aldous pointed out in 1961) "We are getting more and more into a position where these things *can* be achieved.

> And it's extremely important to realize this, and to take every possible precaution to see that they shall *not* be achieved. This, I take it was the message of the book—*This is possible: for heaven's sake be careful about it.*[1]

One can see how Aldous became caught up in his idea in that summer of 1931, writing away in his cool room by the Mediterranean. An artist, starting on a piece of work does not know what it will be until he has made it. Nor where it may lead him. The new line led Aldous into some extremely fruitful fields; it was the line which ultimately led him to his last novel, the Good Utopia, *Island.* Meanwhile, if repelled, he was fascinated also by what he conjured up and let himself rip over Malthusian belts, *The Delta Mirror* and synthetic music.

> The scent organ was playing a delightfully refreshing Herbal Cappriccio . . . "Going to the Feelies, this evening, Henry?" inquired the Assistant Predestinator. "I hear the new one at the Alhambra is first-rate. There's a love scene on a bearskin rug; they say it's

[1] London interview, 1961.

marvellous. Every hair of the bear reproduced. The most amazing tactile effects."[1]

Much in the book is crass or funny; much is horrible. Throughout there obtains the yardstick of the Aldous who admired Piero della Francesca for proclaiming all that is most admirable in man. The inhabitants of the World State of 600 After Ford have little left to be admirable about. Material security is complete; environment stabilised and safe (and superlatively hygienic); war is unthinkable, death not thought of; abilities and wants are bred to measure for one's station in life. There is no sickness, no old age, no solitude, no questions; no sleepless nights. Anxiety and depression are muffled by drugs that have no after or side effects and no one ever has to wait for the fulfilment of a desire. It is an existence without frustration, maladjustment, fear, rebellion, poverty or crime—there is no past, no art, no God.

A life-span without war, violence and the dread of cruel disease—is it not worth the silly slogans, the scent organ, the Feelies and the lack of an unknown freedom? But then the price—in our terms—is also the freedom to reject servitude, the freedom to choose, to grow, to change. The price is deep and graduated human relationships, is virtue, is courage, endurance, faith exchanged for uniformity and spiritual squalor. There is no doubt on which side Aldous comes down on.

"You all remember," [says the Resident Controller for Western Europe] "you all remember, I suppose that beautiful and inspired saying of Our Ford's: History is bunk. History," he repeated slowly, "is bunk."

He waved his hand; and it was as though, with an invisible feather whisk, he had brushed away a little dust, and the dust was Harappa, was Ur of the Chaldees; some spider-webs, and they were Thebes and Babylon and Cnossos and Mycenae. Whisk, whisk—and where was Odysseus, where was Job, where were Jupiter and Gotama and Jesus? Whisk—and those specks of antique dirt called Athens and Rome, Jerusalem and the Middle Kingdom—all were gone. Whisk—the place where Italy had been was empty. Whisk, the cathedrals; whisk, whisk, King Lear and the Thoughts of Pascal. Whisk, Passion; whisk, Requiem; whisk, Symphony; whisk . . .[2]

---

[1] *Brave New World*. Chatto & Windus, 1932.
[2] Ibid.

Chapter Three

Living

BRAVE NEW WORLD was finished by late August. "I have at last, thank heaven, got rid of it." Aldous wrote off his arrears of letters and threw himself into painting. "I'm taking a holiday from writing in painting in oils ... a most exhausting process, I find, but extraordinarily pleasure-giving." So were the subjects he chose to paint, a swing in the garden, trees, a sea-shell and fan, portraits of his family and friends. No symbolism, no horrors, no abstractions: but joy and interest in the visible world and the problems of getting it on to canvas. What were they like, Aldous's pictures? Well, given his limitations (a Sunday painter with unpredictable sight) they were rather remarkable. Without any great claim to originality, they were not obtrusively derivative—though Aldous knew how to pick up a trick or two—and they had a certain personal quality. The colours are often subtle, the drawing a bit lop-sided; he took much trouble over composition. His paintings do what they did to him: they give pleasure. There is perhaps more than that in a few of the portraits. Three, the very charming one of Maria in a lamb's fur jacket and the heads of Eddy West and Gerald Heard—Gerald very Grand-Inquisitorial in sharp profile (all in Rina's possession), which I recently saw again, show a degree of physiognomic perception.

On the periphery, the life of the house went on. Friends had come and stayed, J. W. N. Sullivan, the second Mrs Arnold Bennett (now a widow), the children for their holidays. "Matthew exceedingly flourishing, I am glad to say; we are reading Monte Cristo aloud." Aldous attempted to help him with his Latin and to teach him the piano. These lessons were not a success. Aldous exhibited controlled conspicuous patience. He was easier with Sophie, a girl and a niece—responsibility at one remove. "To me," she says in a memoir[1] "Maria and Aldous were a couple out of a fairy tale.

Maria so exquisite, always delicately scented, wearing lovely silks and furs, gardenias and coral ear-rings, and doing the craziest exercises on her bedroom floor ... (They always had a passion for exercises, crazy diets, bizarre doctors etc.) Aldous was to me immensely long, wearing snake-skin ties in London ... He was, at

[1] Written for this biography by Sophie Moulaert, the present Mrs Willem Welling.

247

times, quite conscious of me and very attentive and polite, always listening and answering my questions although he sometimes referred to me as a "female" which hurt my feelings very much. He used to come to my room and enjoy standing all my beloved dolls upside down. I would .. fly into a rage which left him baffled, and he would then at great pains explain to me that there was no good reason why dolls should *not* stand on their heads. I would think he was heartless.

.. Aldous and Maria were constantly present during my whole childhood. My parents being divorced, my mother always turned to Aldous for advice concerning my education and my future.

But Sophie too says that Aldous was "quite a bad teacher.

Although he enjoyed it . . . We worked together on Macbeth [that was some years later when Aldous was tutoring Sophie in Eng. Lit.]. After having me read a few lines, he would try to explain them to me but never went very far as he would digress on Shakespeare himself, and philosophy and politics and the fact that Macbeth was 'utterly un-understandable!'

Maria was often far from well (a delicate constitution: anaemia, fragile lungs, a queasy metabolism, not helped by not infrequent pregnancies—always interrupted—and severe attacks of migraine). When she felt ill, though, one knew it only afterwards—"I'm so much better." That summer Aldous tried to do something new about the anaemia which so far had resisted, he said, everything prescribed. He made Maria take dried animal stomach tissue. "I decided on the strength of the accounts I read in a medical paper .. the results have been excellent." For the time being.

They had not stirred from Sanary since April. Aldous had hoped to accompany Julian on his first journey to the Soviet Union, the book prevented it. He and Maria now proposed to go to New York in the autumn, but when the pound went off the gold standard in September, their plans changed. "Partly for reasons of expense and partly because I want very much to be on the spot when the crisis is being solved—or not solved! .. One develops a strong sense of patriotism when the moment comes . . ."

Thus Aldous went to England to stand by, followed some weeks later by Maria. They first put up in Dalmeny Court again, then moved round the corner into Rosa Lewis's Cavendish Hotel.

The [gods??] treated me very well this week for Aldous turned up for a night. [Robert Nichols wrote to the Heads on 3rd October] .. He's only gone about an hour ago . . . Aldous was in fine form though pale. He is more himself than ever; he really does now seem in possession of his whole self. He is far and away the most intelligent and humane man I have ever known save Henry [Head].

He goes on to comment on Aldous's range.

Here are some of the things we touched on—unemployment (effect on character of workmen)—Crébillon—steam-cars—the nature of music (pattern as opposed to content)—drug-taking in Siberia (consumption of a fungus and its effects)—the book of Job . . . the new process for procuring petrol from coal by electrolysis . . . Siamese cats—validity of different forms of experience . . . D. H. Lawrence—Provençal poetry . . "Mistral must have been a silly old bird . ."—Bolshevism—Noel Coward at Monte Carlo—alarming spectacle of the scientists at the British Association—the popular Don Juan played every November in Spain—modern free verse and T. S. Eliot—the appalling fashionableness of drunkenness in the U.S.—the difficulty of dealing with manuscripts sent for him to look over . . . Homer, how sensible Homer is, how sane, what an enormous gap there is till you come to another broad and wholesome writer—he intoned Chaucer—Oh, and something else. We went for a walk and looked at the sheep—I pointed out one like Wordsworth—he capped it with 'in vagrant and in pensive mood'—and indeed that's exactly how the old ram looked lying under a chestnut tree with his head on one side, gently puffing—his slant eyes fixed on us. We lingered quite a long time by the sheep—picking up conkers from the chestnut trees—baubles he loves as I do for their beautiful rich brown glossiness and their veining—but he is firmer-minded than I am—I know they will fade in an hour and their lustre be gone, but I carry them home, while he has the good sense to feast his eye and finger-tips on them and then throw them away. He loves beauty even more than I do. It's lovely to see him holding a split chestnut-fruit in his fingers, close up to his face, admiring the dappled treasure lodged in the pith as white as the flesh of a magnolia. By the way his eyes are better. He's been seeing what he calls 'my two dear quacks' in Westminster—Hitchcock and Duppock—or some such names. They have soothed his blind eye by exercising it with green light and he can now just see a little with it. They have also given him very different glasses of immense power and a queer pair which he calls 'my white-eyed poppies' which look like this that is, they have a sort of pebbly lens in the centre surrounded by a sort of silver shield. 'But,' he says, 'I daren't put them on in public—they make everybody laugh. I don't mind them laughing but there are tender-hearted people who might be hurt at the notion that I was hurt . . .'
. . To return to the sheep. After we'd looked at them for some time he said, 'You know the early Christians either had no luck or they

were very dense. Fancy choosing a sheep as a symbol. Gentle—yes
—but oh how stupid!!' He talked about the poet Beddoes too—how
good his letters were, how interesting, what a queer fellow he was.
I forgot how we got on to that. O yes, poets taking over scientific
discoveries, trying to incorporate the findings of their poems—what
a hash they usually made. I didn't bring up Goethe as an example
of the opposite because I don't think he really admires Goethe—
though he admired him more than he used to, finding him a bit
bookish I daresay—and he has been very nice about Goethe to me,
so much respecting my almost incessant admiration of Goethe. . . .

His taking to painting—for relaxation. 'But, my dear Bob, the
strain, the strain! It's so devilish exciting. And the discoveries one
makes! Quite ordinary, of course—any painter who knows his job
can put you up to the wheeze. But the thing is to discover them
for oneself. You can't imagine the lusciousness of putting on paint
. . . Well, one day I discovered that if you waited till your paint
was half-dry and then brushed it over—caressed it—with a dry
brush, you got the most marvellous effects—a bloom! My dear Bob,
I wouldn't have sold the excitement and the pleasure I had in
making that discovery for a million pounds. Incredible!' I really
think Aldous was more animated over this than I ever heard him
on any subject and, contrary to what people who don't know him
may well think, he can be very animated in conversation.

. . . Darling Aldous—the more I think of him the more perfect
he appears to me and the more I love him. And to think that I
once fancied I was and could be a greater writer than he. Benighted
and besotted idiot!

A good deal of Aldous's time in London then was taken up with
the business of Lawrence's letters, the rest he spent in libraries: he
had begun to ruminate an anthology of poetry with comments.
After the New Year they went back to Sanary for a quiet and
pleasantly industrious winter putting the idea on to paper—*Texts
and Pretexts*, the most serene perhaps of all his books. "A mixture
between an Oxford Book (tho' not very Oxonian in choice of
selections) and a book of essays. It's a pleasant thing to do and
should be quite agreeable, I think, to read . . . There's a great deal
of queer, good, interesting stuff in English poetry that never gets
into most anthologies . . ."

And what an appalling amount of bad stuff by even the best of
authors. "It's unbelievable what 80% of even Shelley is like. As for
Wordsworth, Browning, Spenser . . ."

Raymond Mortimer came to stay in February—"a charming
guest"—for the rest of the winter and early spring, Aldous and
Maria were by themselves, Aldous in good spirits, painting, working
hard. Aside from the anthology, he was thinking about his intro-

duction to D. H. Lawrence's letters—"a big job"—and re-reading his grandfather's life and works in preparation for the Huxley Memorial Lecture he had been asked to deliver. "He was really a very impressive figure . . . unquestionably the genuine article . . .

> Do you know the *Life and Letters* by my father? [Aldous wrote to Starkey] it's a good book. And the essays are first class and really astonishingly up-to-date. People try to make out that he was a dogmatical-materialistic old ass, who couldn't understand the finer shades. But it's not in the least true. He was quite as much aware of things as any of the Jeans-Eddington people. And how well he wrote! and what a heroic figure of a man! This century doesn't seem to breed them as the last did. But enough ancestor-worship!

Aldous could not really remember his grandfather who died ten months after his birth. T. H. Huxley's aura may have loomed more formidably over his childhood than it did over his brothers' who had known the private face of "the adorable 'Pater' ".[1]

Brave New World (published 2nd February) was extremely well received in England, selling 13,000 copies in the year and 10,000 the year after. It was not much liked in the United States, at first, pessimism and the guying of material bliss being still unacceptable at the time, and the sales were relatively minute. (Well under 3,000. The large, continuing, sales came later.)

Aldous's first American publisher was Doran. In 1927 the firm had amalgamated with Doubledays. Aldous had weighed the pros and cons, well, "are one's interests better looked after by an individual or a Ford factory?" and taken the line of least resistance. Now his Doubleday Doran contract was running out, nudged by Pinker, he was considering a change. This was talked about in London. Wheels turned within wheels. James Hamish Hamilton wrote by air mail to Eugene Saxton (then head of Harper & Brothers),

> Naomi [Royde-Smith, not Mitchison] the arch gossip says that Huxley is dissatisfied with Doubleday . . .

Harpers responded, so did other American publishers (Farrar & Rinehart are supposed to have been the main rival suitor). Cabled bids flew across the Atlantic, dealt with by Pinker in London while Aldous made up his mind in Sanary. Harpers' terms were substantial. A three-year contract with a $21,000 guarantee to be paid

---

[1] Sir Julian Huxley, *Memories*, op. cit.

at the rate of $7,000 a year. But they were demanding six to seven books. These were presently reduced to five. Aldous's choice was influenced by his fondness for Eugene Saxton, who had been at Doran's in the early days. (The friendship began when they met —Aldous and Maria, Eugene and Martha Saxton—in New York in 1926 at the end of the Huxleys' journey round the world.) Pinker obtained some refinements in the Harper contract and it was signed on 9th February. (Seven years later Harpers were also able to take over the copyrights of all of Aldous's earlier books from Doubleday.)

By contrast the renewal of Chatto's agreement, due again that March, was by now a matter of course. (Incidentally, Aldous had fulfilled the last Three Year Plan almost *à la lettre*—one novel; one long story, novel-length by today's standard; plus three short ones; two volumes of essays and three miscellaneous slim volumes.) In commercial terms his books were doing well in England at the moment, better even than in the *Point Counter Point* year. It might be of interest to look at one complete account. Here are Aldous's gross earnings from books sold in the United Kingdom and the British Empire in the year ending 31st March 1932. (Ten per cent of these earnings went to Pinker, a good deal more to the Inland Revenue.)

	£	s.	d.
MUSIC AT NIGHT	481	17	6
THE WORLD OF LIGHT	77	15	–
THE CICADAS	113	5	–
BRAVE NEW WORLD	881	14	–
10,000 in 7/6 Ed.			
VULGARITY IN LITERATURE	6	–	–
BRIEF CANDLES	8	6	3
POINT COUNTER POINT	86	5	–
Phoenix Library Repr's	360	18	6
	£2,016	1	3

Chatto's present agreement, unchanged in terms of books (two novels plus three miscellany), raised the advance from £1,000 to £1,250 a year, and the initial royalty rate from 15% to 20%, and to 25% thereafter.

When Aldous had been long close to a piece of work, he liked to make a break by a few days' recreative motoring. This had all been very well in Italy, now he complained about the comparative

paucity of art in Southern France. (Nîmes, Arles, Orange, he maintained, one should have seen before Italy, not after.) They decided
on Cannes for the nonce. They drove off—it was mid-March—
Aldous, Maria, a mutual friend a very pretty blonde, and myself.
Maria got us there, *porte à porte*, in two hours and fifteen minutes,
or was it two hours and twenty-five? At any rate it was pretty good
going. (How we all four fitted into the Bugatti, I can no longer say,
except that our blonde friend was literally a light-weight.) During
the drive Aldous appeared to be in a kind of speed-induced trance;
only when we were coming down from the Esterel he began to
point out landmarks and speak about the colours; when Maria
hesitated about a turning, it was he who told her which way to
take. This was most startling. One had learnt that when approaching Aldous one had to do what Roy Campbell had remembered
and so exactly done, one had to make oneself known by voice.
Maria had a quick way of identifying for him the person coming
in, "Oh Eddy, there you are," "Oh Lewis, you're back already,"
—for Aldous was generally not able to distinguish a face on the
other side of the room.

We put up at a comfortable and not fashionable hotel, very
pleased by the Niagaras of bath-water (at Sanary one was always
minding the level of one's cistern). In the evening Aldous and
Maria went off to have dinner with H. G. Wells at his house near
Grasse. It was to be their first meeting since the publication of the
leg-pull, and Wells was supposed to have been very annoyed about
the nature of Aldous's Utopia. (According to Gerald Heard, he
wrote him a letter accusing him of "treason to science and defeatist
pessimism"[1]; and Wells's old friend, Moura Budberg, used the
identical word—in her deep, slow Russian voice—"H. G. was very
cross, he said it was *defeatist*".) Aldous and Maria though went off
cheerfully enough that evening and came back with nothing worse,
as far as I remember, than a rather gossipy account of Wells's
ménage. But to Harold Raymond[2] Aldous wrote a few days later,

. . I'm glad the book still does so well. In Cannes we saw H. G. Wells
who, I fear, wasn't best pleased with it.

Aldous enjoyed strolling along the Croisette, on the shop-side,
peering into the windows, discoursing about women's clothes, economics, sex and fashions. One morning he spent at the aquarium
at Monaco. We mainly ate Chez Oscar on the port of Cannes, a
place that is no more, where the food was delicious. This was inconsistent. Aldous and Maria had a thing against good restaurants,

[1] Gerald Heard, *The Poignant Prophet*, *The Kenyon Review*, 1965.
[2] Then head of Chatto & Windus.

grand restaurants they called them. Grand or granders was a word of theirs, granders might mean a first night or a white tie, "Is it going to be granders?" It had overtones of tolerant persiflage—grand friends were all right, even a grand party; grand restaurants were not. The expense, the disgustingly rich food . . . A liking for such indulgence really shocked the Huxleys. "He's the kind of man who likes grand restaurants," was near dismissal.

Later that spring Aldous and Maria went on a real journey. First to Brussels as they had been asked to dine with the King and Queen of the Belgians. Albert I, a man of diverse interests, had wished to meet Aldous and this was arranged through Maria's Uncle, George Baltus. Aldous bought himself a pair of white kid gloves and they went off to the palace.

> We dined en intimité [Aldous wrote to his father]; only Maria's Uncle . . ourselves, Willie de Grunne (who was at Balliol with Julian and Trev and is now the Queen's chamberlain) and a lady in waiting and A.D.C.

It went off "very pleasantly.

> She [the Queen] is a really charming woman—a typical cultured idealistic Bavarian of the late 19th century generation, reminding me very much of Maria's aunts-by-marriage, the daughters of the sculptor Hildebrand. He is also sympathetic—a very thorough, rather ponderous mind, grinding exceedingly small and rather slowly. Curiously enough, speaking French with that typically royal German accent which distinguished royal English up to the times of Edward VII!

What really fascinated Aldous was that the palace "like all palaces,

> was a bit mouldy in its splendour: actually moths flew out of the sofas when one sat down! A great difficulty was talking in the third person, which etiquette demands and which is directly cramping to conversation when one isn't used to it.

Etiquette equally demanded that one must never turn one's back upon the royal persons, leaving guests were required to vanish by walking backwards gracefully and straight to and through the doors. The King decided that Aldous should not be called upon to perform this feat and a compromise solution was arrived at. Their Majesties themselves got up at the appointed time and left their guests.

Raymond Mortimer joined Aldous and Maria in Belgium, and they went on to Germany together. They did some sightseeing at

Bamberg, Würzburg and Cassel, then to Berlin. I had gone there
earlier and for about a week we coincided. Aldous was still full of
the royal visit, the royal accent, the third person singular and the
moths in the upholstery—he would beat the air thumping an
imaginary sofa cushion. And the food had not been hot—the
general way of palaces because of the great distance to the kitchens.
On Germany he looked with a kind of aloof voyeurism: the grossness of the provincial crowds, the bulgy consumers of whipped
cream in the cafés on the Kurfürstendam, the ubiquitous sign of
the depression in the streets. It was, one must realize, less than a
year before Hitler came to power. There *was* an ominous feeling
about the country (I am sure this is not mere hindsight); in Berlin
people appeared to be both restless and resigned, waiting for *anything* to happen, revolution from the extreme left or right, and in
either case a cataclysmic breakdown of the social order. (Surely
one of the reasons why Nazi rule became acceptable to the mass
of the German people—impervious anyhow to the wickedness of
what the Nazis said and did, and self-protectively ignorant—was
because there was at first no apparent breakdown of the social
order, which instead even seemed to have been saved.) Aldous and
Maria met no educated Germans on that journey, they were
tourists. For once they had come by train; I by car, and on the
principle that any car was better than none, they submitted to be
driven about in mine, a very old open Ford roadster. The radiator
leaked so badly that it had to be topped up hourly from a tin.
Worse: I was still on pocket money and could not afford to travel
as I did; I had started from Sanary with a large drum of petrol (on
tick—to be paid for on my coming of age) and this drum which
had to be returned was now empty and rattled about in the dickey
with unsuppressible din. This amused Aldous who chose to give
me a hand with the water tin in front of the uniformed minions
of the Eden Hotel. We drove to Potsdam, where Aldous did a minor
verbal Taj Mahal on Sans Souci. Maria had bought a new Rolleiflex,
I had a box Kodak, between us we took Aldous in front of the Old
Residence, Aldous peering at a newspaper kiosk, Aldous skimming
along the street in flapping overcoat and wide-brimmed hat, looking
for all the world like Professor Picard. With Raymond we went to
the Kaiser Friedrich Museum, to the Zoo, the opera (*Ballo in
Maschera*); one evening we went to have a look at a large and
glittering night club whose speciality was table telephones: middle-
aged couples and a sprinkling of commercial blondes ringing each
other up across the floor. The whole thing was of deadly vulgarity,
a repulsive combination of facetiousness and lust—a Germanic
Lyon's Corner House with the lid taken off and invaded by an
infernal din of human shrieks and jazz. Aldous duly remarked how
extraordinary it was and how depressing. (He did not venture

again, this time, into the less orthodox regions of Berlin nightlife.)

In June we were all back in Sanary (Aldous and Maria for a
solid spell of time until December). Raymond had returned with
them; Eddy West arrived from Knole; I, our house being shut
down (my mother in a clinic, my step-father evaporated) was put
up too. We made a quiet and, I think, extraordinarily happy house-
party. Raymond, as Aldous has said, was a very charming guest,
so was Eddy. Nothing much was happening. If we went out, it was
for walks en famille and picnics. Eddy, who was working on a book,
was given Matthew's room. (He was writing that remarkable, that
very strange novel of his, *Simpson*, the story of an English nanny,
which incidentally he finished eighteen months later, again in
Sanary, in a house in the back country that belonged to D. H.
Lawrence's friends the di Chiara's and was then inhabited by Eva
Herrmann, the American artist, and myself.) Raymond and I fell
into the routine of our industrious betters, he working on the
material for a book on suicide he thought of writing, I hopefully
filling notebooks. Maria loved Raymond and Eddy, and this made
a circuit of affection; Aldous was very much at ease with them.
He and Eddy talked music ("Eddy is a pianist nearly up to concert
standards," Aldous would say with admiration); there was constant
general talk about books and art. Aldous had the habit of airing
subjects he was writing about in conversation. One remembers
Ernest Hemingway's expressed dread of talking it out; Aldous did
this with unconcern. Perhaps the passage *was* already on paper.
Perhaps it was his way of working himself in. Aldous rarely talked
about his work as such and so one often did not realize that he was
quoting himself until months later when one saw in print an almost
literal repetition of a passage heard. Now he would talk about
Swinburne's peyotl trances and Shelley's dreamy vagueness in the
words of the future *Texts & Pretexts*, and prequote with glee the
lines of Coleridge that he regarded as the prime example of unsifted
poetical rubbish.

> *Why need I say, Louisa dear,*
> *How glad I am to see you here,*
> *A lovely convalescent;*
> *Risen from the bed of pain and fear*
> *And feverish heat incessant.*

(Aldous still quoted Louisa Dear twenty-five years later in Hollywood to Edith Sitwell.)
We were looked after breakfast, lunch and dinner. The delicious

fried rabbit and zucchini flowers we took on picnics appeared and vanished without any of us lifting a finger. Beside Rina, there was Giulia, the cook, an Italian with an austere face and a fierce devotion to her masters (guests and friends were judged); and Camilla, a girl from a Tuscan village, more shy than sullen and of great good nature. Nothing, as I said, much happened. Suzanne's last word on her stay with Aldous and Maria in the 'Twenties was harmonious. *Harmonious*—looking back on it, I think of it as one of the happiest times of my life.

There was one event. A Sunday morning Raymond and I went on some errand into Bandol. We were strolling along the port in the sun. A bright little sports-car flashed past us with dotty speed, missed the turning and leapt into the sea. There it sat, stock-still and silenced in a flash, in twenty inches of water with the young man in his gay clothes at the wheel and the girl beside him in her dress laughing their heads off, waving at Raymond and me. It made his day, Raymond said. We told Aldous and Maria, they laughed with us and Maria said, "things like that *will* happen to Raymond".

Too soon we dispersed. The young men to England, I with the foolish or the enviable adventuresomeness of youth, to Istanbul.

Aldous sent off *Texts and Pretexts*, caught up with his reading, began and finished another play; painted. They built a small studio above the garage, white cube upon white cube, a structure of Moorish simplicity. Other guests stayed and went. They saw friends and new friends up and down the coast. Julian and Juliette, returning from an American tour, arrived on their first visit. The subject of the new play, *Now More Than Ever*, was high finance, with a Kreuger figure as the central character. This play was never produced, or published, and the typescript appears lost. (I read it at the time and retain an impression of it being rather exciting and without the ambiguities of *The World of Light*.) Aldous re-read *War and Peace*, "a great consolation and a tonic," and discovered Hermann Broch. He had already been impressed by Broch's earlier novel *The Unknown Quantity* (in the English translation); now *The Sleepwalkers* bowled him over. His face lit up when he spoke about it: *there* was a novel that had brought off complexity ... I recall an image Aldous used—a skater seeing through the ice beneath him. To Martin Secker, who published Broch, he wrote,

. . I read the trilogy with steadily increasing admiration. It is the work of a mind of extraordinary power and depth, and at the same time of extraordinary subtlety and sensibility—of a philosopher who is also an artist of exceptional refinement and purity. It is a difficult book that makes great demands on the reader—nothing less than his whole mind at the highest pitch of attention . . .

The studio was finished. Flat-roofed it turned out to be stifling. Aldous painted nudes—one member of the household posing, another reading aloud. He was using gouache (I had brought Eva Herrmann from my travels, who became a great friend of the Huxleys and was experimenting with the medium then); Julian too was roped into the painting circle, Aldous persuaded him to try his hand at a still life he himself arranged. He so enjoyed doing things with Julian—the bond of affection, and shared interests between the brothers was visibly very great. In the Sanary summers a good many people came to lunch and dinner; once or twice a week Aldous and Maria dined out. Edith Wharton, Charles and Marie-Laure de Noailles, and Madame de Béhague of the Paris salon, had houses at Hyères, where Paul Valéry and his wife and son spent the summer holidays. At St-Cyr were Meier-Graefe and his wife in their shaded *mas*; nearer home the Kislings at Bandol. Meier-Graefe was in his sixties, a man of vast presence (tall; a fine head; heavy beautiful hands), a life enhancer if ever there was one, a *viveur*, at the same time oddly delicate, moody, sharp, very difficult. Aldous had no more than heard of his main body of work (*Impressionism, Van Gogh*), but had read with some enthusiasm *The Spanish Journey* written in 1911 when Meier-Graefe had set out to praise Velasquez and stayed to discover El Greco. Meier-Graefe was a relentless worker; *his* hours were from dawn till about 4 p.m., sustained by fruit and pots of China tea, his output half a page a day. In winter he travelled, in summer he wrote. Unlike Aldous, to whom this would have been a shocking waste, his evening recreation was a game of bridge. One went to see the Meier-Graefes for tea or dinner out of doors on their terrace above a cypress alley. Bush, Meier-Graefe's wife, his third—she had eloped with him, running away from boarding-school—was very young, practically a girl, and already as competent as she had to be: driving the car, running the house hospitably, typing the books, managing at the same time to get on with her own painting and to be gay and giggly. Other eminent and elder men of letters were courting Bush and she always had a following as well of young and handsome men without literary pretensions. Meier-Graefe called her *Püppchen*, Poopers to Aldous. As the fates turned out, she eventually married one of the few contemporary writers, and the only one in the German language besides Kafka, whom Aldous admired, Hermann Broch. With the Kislings, Kiki and that force of nature Renée, there was not much contact. Aldous was not attracted by the robust sensuality of their style—those great feasts of garlic, fish and wine, the nights at *bals musettes*, the *couchages* that were not analysed in literary terms but blurted out—Aldous was bored, felt inadequate and withdrew behind polite French words. The Kislings shrugged off the Huxleys as bloodless intellectuals. Then one day Renée and Maria discovered their shared feeling for plants and cats, and Maria discovered Renée's Colette side, her exquisite perceptiveness of living things and the delicacy and humanity she was capable of. There sprang up between these two women an incongruous friendship (Renée Kisling looked like a splendid monster, a piece of archaic sculpture bedaubed in gaudy colours), a friendship all talk of gardens, offerings of fruit, sea-shells and scented herbs. But the bridge to Aldous was not flung.

It was at about that time that the Handleys too came into the Huxleys' lives. Len, Major Leonard Handley ex-Indian Army, and his wife Sally. The Handleys had been everywhere, tried their hand at anything. They had lived in Army stations, sailed with Chinese pirates, shot and filmed in the jungles of three continents, lectured to ladies' clubs in the U.S.A., got stranded in Panama. Wherever they went disaster overtook them. Lecture agencies failed, natives ran amok, elephants charged their cameras. They survived; just. They were always broke. Now they had taken a bungalow in Bandol with a view to mending their fortunes by writing. Len had already published one novel, *The Gay Sarong* (how that title entranced Aldous), Sally was working on scripts and lectures. She was in her twenties, blonde, willowy, very very pretty, chronically ailing and utterly intrepid. She was as disillusioned as the young women in the novels of Evelyn Waugh but without their vocabulary and sophistication and with a natural adherence to the morals and manners of the middle-class; hers was flat, non-cynical hopelessness camouflaged by a sense of humour that thrived in catastrophe, and she was one of the world's born story-tellers. Len looked kindly, loyal and conventional, and the first two he was. He adored Sally. They both wanted a child but their wanderings and strange luck were not conducive to completed pregnancies. (Happy to say, they eventually had a daughter.) Now the Handleys had taken a fancy to Aldous's work. They would walk over to La Gorguette, hang about the Villa Huley, babes in the wood that they essentially were, and stare at the gate. One day they were pulled in by Maria. Scheherezade began her tales, the looks did the rest, they were asked again. Soon they were friends. But there was something else—Sally was a Jonah. The well-serviced car that gave her a lift shed a wheel, the ships she sailed in sank, houses caught fire; it was no joke (I, too, came as near disaster as I'd ever care to on a little outing with Sally). The first time the Handleys asked Aldous and Maria to dinner, they had hardly sat down when a woman burst upon them meat-chopper in hand. She meant business. Maria and Sally protected Aldous while Len managed to disarm the woman which was not easy as her strength proved great—she was the femme de ménage who had turned murderous lunatic without warning. After gendarmes and ambulance had borne her away, they all went into the kitchen, very hungry now, and Sally set to retrieving a little supper over a spirit lamp. The spirit lamp upset. Oh yes, they managed to put it out, it was not really a big fire. Maria went home thoughtful.

It was one of the points about Sanary that so many people of wildly different ways of life were there at the same time. Painters had come since the turn of the century; later it was painters and writers, then more writers, some eminent, some beginners. Their language varied and their incomes and tastes. Some wrote more than others. Thomas Mann had lived in Sanary, and Brian Howard. They came by way of friends, through chains of circumstances. Katherine Mansfield's 1914-war winters led to Lawrence, led to the Huxleys, led to the Huxleys' friends. Sooner or later everybody met, *this* was the point: Sanary was no city—one newspaper kiosk, one post office, one paint-shop, two chemists, three cafés.

In these early 1930s there were two new literary ménages, one Anglo-American, one all American, the Connollys and the Seabrooks. Young Cyril, not yet thirty, before *Enemies of Promise*, before *The Rock Pool*, reviewing books (not every week) for the *New Statesman*, "with a book unfinished, beginning a second,"[1] and Jean, younger still—eighteen? nineteen?—with that slow erotic charm, talented, witty in her own right, but wilful, lazy, prone to discontents, self-destructive. There they were in that wind-battered house on the sea road east of Sanary in that time that is gone forever with their ferrets, "the English Rose . . . who saw three continents from a warm sleeve,"[1] and the lemurs, "living for beauty—

> October on the Mediterranean, blue skies scoured by the mistral, red and golden vine branches, wind-fretted waves chopping round the empty yachts; plane-trees peeling; palms rearing up their dingy underlinen; mud in the streets, and from doorways at night the smell of burning oil. On dark evenings I used to bicycle in to fetch our dinner, past the harbour with its bobbing launches and the bright cafés with their signs banging; at the local restaurant there would be one or two "plats à emporter", to which I would add some wine, sausage and Gruyère cheese . . . then I would bowl back heavy-laden with the mistral behind me, a lemur buttoned up inside my jacket with his head sticking out. Up the steep drive it was easy to be blown off into the rosemary, then dinner would be spoilt. We ate with our fingers beside the fire,—true beauty lovers. . . .[2]

[1] *The Unquiet Grave*, Cyril Connolly, 1945.
[2] Ibid.

The Seabrooks, Willie and his wife, Marjorie Worthington the novelist—a stiff, gentle woman with a soft voice and an unhappy face, were in their early middle-age; he on the affluent wave of international best-sellers, *Jungleways, Magic Island,* travellers' tales of his ventures into primitive societies, a man in the clutches of self-doubt and success. They were camping—with chauffeur, gardener, cook—in a barrack of a house on La Gorguette, high rooms dark with heavy furniture, the oppressive gloom of which they had reinforced with knives, masks and pieces of barbaric sculpture. Seabrook was a very strange man indeed (the rough diamond with the soft centre on the more obvious level) beset with inner problems. Like Jean Connolly, he bore the marks of American Prohibition. His great thing at the time was his exploits among the savage islanders. He would boast of having boasted to Parisian hostesses: "Reprenez donc un peu de rôti de veau, Monsieur Seabrook?" "Ah Madame, si vous aviez goûté la chaire humaine . . ." Yet he could feel very sorry for himself. He would lament his lack of intellectual and literary refinement, he was a craftsman, he would say, a cobbler, and he wanted to write like Tolstoy and like Aldous Huxley. Here his admiration was unrancorous and uncritical. "Mon illustre voisin," he would say to local tradesmen for the fun of it, "mon illustre voisin," in his very American French, "Aldóuss Usseley."

The neighbours became friends. Marjorie Worthington was an endearing creature once one got through her cloud of shyness, and there was something touching also about Seabrook, or a side of Seabrook. A number of disagreeable and sensational stories were going round about his sexual savageries, yet he never hinted at these practices to the Huxleys, and when dispensing hospitality to Aldous and other writers he could be meek with an *empressement* that was positively genteel. (Only once he made a very rum remark indeed to Maria in front of the gorilla cage he kept in the studio he had on the port of Toulon.) One consequence of the Seabrook-Huxley friendship was that Rina became engaged to the Seabrooks' young chauffeur, Emilio, a glib Italian.

The Seabrooks, the Handleys; not the Connollys. Between Aldous and Cyril nothing flowered then (their rapport came; but that was many years later). Why? Who else was there in Sanary at the time who could be called to anything like the same extent Aldous's peer? Cyril when he first came loved Aldous (these are his own words); had indeed come to live in Sanary to be near him; yet the response fell short even of the Huxleys' usual curiosity and kindness. Fan for fan, was Aldous not sensitive to the qualitative difference of Cyril's admiration? Not struck by his erudition, conversation, talent? Struck, yes. Not greatly interested, perhaps. What attracted Aldous then was the unfamiliar and bizarre—Willie Seabrook, Len and Sally were *terra incognita*; Cyril had gone through his own mill, College at Eton, Balliol. Cyril may have reminded him of the attitudes of his younger self which he was beginning to wish to slough off, aestheticism, pure art, the love of words; at thirty-eight Aldous at heart was no longer the literary dandy who had captivated Cyril's generation. Yet this cannot have been the whole story. Aldous still enjoyed, for instance, Raymond Mortimer's company. I rather think that the crux here was Maria and that it goes to show how much Aldous let himself be directed by her. When she did not choose to build his bridges, he was quite content to remain cut off. Now, Jean Connolly disliked Maria who made her feel that she could never put a foot right. When she and Cyril dropped in they would be intercepted: *"Aldous is working."* Years after Jean still spoke of the watchdog with bitterness. In fact Maria *was* on her guard; Sally might threaten Aldous's life and limb, the Connollys were out for his time. Maria was also prejudiced. Neither she nor Aldous approved of their style of life; they did not see it as romantic or delicious. Eating your dinner with your fingers reading before the fire meant leaving grape skins and the skeletons of sardines between the pages. The ferrets stank; the lemur hopped upon the table and curled his exquisite little black hand around your brandy glass. Your *brandy glass*—exactly: liqueurs after luncheon. The Connollys did like grand restaurants. *And* they would not descend to any disguising of their tastes. People, as I have said, tempered their behaviour to the Huxleys' standards; the Connollys were more irrepressible and to Jean it would not have occurred to make friends on anything but her own terms. Maria would forgive you anything as long as you deferred implicitly to Aldous.

What matters, rather sadly, is that this casual coolness of the Huxleys amounted then for Cyril as rejection. It affected his own work. (He has written about his feeling of paralysis at Sanary by the thought of Aldous drumming away on his typewriter across the bay. He felt—again his printed words—a kind of mental poor relation.) And yet it was a fortuitous shutting out, a lapse in awareness—those elders, Aldous and Maria, too, were young still—it might not have been impossible to have broken through by some intuition or right word.

Autumn by the Mediterranean—reflections on the state of the world. To Naomi Mitchison, politically active (on the left) who sometimes challenged him, Aldous wrote à propos of the Scotboro case, "It's terrifying what can be done by people who have the monopoly of means of propaganda—private money grubbers in the U.S.A., Musso and Co in Italy, Communist party in U.S.S.R...

Yes, I perfectly believe that a lot of people are happy in Russia—
because happiness . . is a by-product of something else and they've
got a Cause . . . the working for which gives them happiness . .
but it is always as history demonstrates, in the nature of a temporary intoxication . . . In Russia where propaganda is more efficient, it may last a bit longer . . . The next remedy is love, for
an individual or for one's neighbours in general. This is the most
powerful antidote against the misery of individual existence . . .

Well, well—it is all very obscure and distressing. [These are fragments from a very long letter] I wish I could even see clear into the
economic problem. This system is bad, and on a large scale, seems
not to work. But at the same time without some private property,
what is to become of individual liberty? Private property is the only
guarantee possessed by individuals against the tyranny of the State
[and let us remember that the State is not an abstraction, but just
Jones and Brown invested with power]. Proudhon insisted on a
limited amount of private property—and I think he was quite right.
The difficulty arises in determining where the limits are to be placed.
What a world!

In September the first edition of the letters of D. H. Lawrence,
with Aldous's long preface, was published by Heinemann. The
letters were a tremendous lot, as Aldous had written to Brett the
year before:

The early ones are particularly interesting and delightful—such
high spirit: which he lost as he grew older and iller. The horror of
that creeping disease! I am cutting out feeling—hurting passages,
uninteresting bits and things which are repeated in several letters
to different people. . . tho' it's often worth keeping repetitions because
of the subtle variations . . .

For the rest, Aldous had kept editorial notes and comments to the
minimum. The book did well. "Which I'm glad of for Frieda's . .
sake:

tho' the stupid woman is embarking on enormously expensive legal
proceedings against L's brother now—quite unnecessarily in my
opinion . . Her diplomatic methods consist in calling everyone a liar,
a swine and a lousy swindler, and then in the next letter being
charming . . Since L is no longer there to keep her in order, she
plunges about in the most hopeless way. I like her very much; but
she's in many ways quite impossible. She was only possible for someone who happened to be in love with her and married to her—and
not only in love and married but, as Lawrence was, in some strange

way dependent, on her presence, physically dependent, as one is dependent on the liver in one's belly . . . I have seen him on two occasions rise from what I thought was his death-bed, when Frieda, who had been away, came back after a short absence. The mysteries of human relationships are impenetrable.

Matthew, aged twelve and a half, was moved to a new school, the Elmhirsts' Dartington in Devonshire, "an experiment which may, I think, turn out to be something very remarkable". As for the boy,

> Mentally he is the image of M's family—quick, with a remarkable intuitive power for grasping the essentials of a situation, a natural gift for living; but with a quite unusual incapacity to grasp and apply general principles . . . He is just the opposite of me; for he knows how to deal with people, but not with abstract ideas.

Joep and Suzanne came to stay for October. The weather was sparkling, they enjoyed a month of long walks and hard work. Joep did landscapes and portraits of Aldous and Maria (since destroyed by fire); Suzanne did the fine bust of Aldous, later cast in bronze; Aldous was inspired to paint a good many gouaches. He had begun to meditate his next novel. There were misgivings even then. He found it difficult to get under way, but hoped that one day the thing might flow.

> If it does start flowing [to Eugene Saxton in November] it might well be finished by the end of next summer.
> But this is all very uncertain and I shan't be able to say anything definite for another few months. If it didn't come satisfactorily, I shd ask Harper's to suspend all payments until such time as I was able to cope with the thing—abandoning myself to journalism while the novel ripened: for I know by bitter experience that I can't force myself to write anything that isn't ripe. I hope this won't happen: but if it should, well, then I'll ask Pinkers to make the necessary business arrangements to suit the situation. Meanwhile, I am just accumulating notes and writing experimental pages.

In December Aldous and Maria briefly went to London planning to be back for Christmas. But Matthew went down with influenza and they had to hang about. They were able to leave in time to reach Sanary for a small New Year's Eve celebration, dinner at the house with Charles and Marie-Laure de Noailles, my mother (temporarily restored to health) and me. We wore versions of evening dress and the character of the party—the Huxleys having announced their plan of leaving again almost at once on a long

voyage, their second *tour du monde*, Rina called it—was festive and
valedictory. Matthew had improvised decorations, a toy railway
circuit on the dinner-table: you flicked a switch and a carriage
laden with salted almonds, fruit or sweets came to a halt before
your plate; it worked precisely and was a great success. After midnight Maria went into the kitchen and made some hard-boiled
eggs which we ate then and there. This struck Madame de Noailles
as an exotic lark. She would never dare, she told Maria, to put a
foot into her own kitchen.

Chapter Four

Beyond the Mexique Bay

THE novel would not flow, Aldous abandoned himself to travel. He and Maria sailed from Liverpool in January on the cruise ship Britannic for the West Indies. They called at Barbados, Trinidad, Caracas, changed ship at Jamaica and continued to British Honduras and Guatemala. They went up to Quirigua, flew to Copan, in the second plane ever to land there, and saw the Maya ruins (their course is pretty well covered in Aldous's published travel journal). In March they were in Guatemala City; there, at dinner with the Finnish Consul who happened to be an English poet, they met Roy Fenton, the Consul's younger brother. The meeting transformed their journey. Roy Fenton talked about his coffee plantation on the slopes of the Pacific; Aldous, nostalgically, platonically, talked of the unattainable, of primitive Mexico, wild Mexico, the country of *The Plumed Serpent*. On an impulse Fenton said to him: Come with me and I will take you there. It was both a friendly offer and a dare. What Fenton was proposing was the overland journey to Oaxaca, the extremely tough ride over the Sierra Juarez. Aldous said yes.

I found Aldous—charming. I found him—well—very open-minded. [This is Roy Fenton speaking. Now; after these forty years]. In fact, quite different from what I had expected from reading his books. His attitude seemed to me quite humble at times. There was no side. Yet one felt—from little things that peaked out from his mind, that came out in conversation—that all the time he was exploring—it was as if he were looking for something. How shall I put it? He seemed to be looking for an experience.

It was Fenton who got cold feet. After another good look at Aldous and Maria. He warned them. He made his conditions. (Mexico was a rough place, a rough place struggling through rough times. A man looking after his estate was very much a rule unto himself, leading his men, going about armed, relying on his skills.) Aldous and Maria would have to go into training. Fenton asked them to come up to his *finca*, Progreso, for a couple of weeks of riding and general toughening up. The three of them set out from Guatemala City. Six or seven sweltering hours in the train to Retalhuleu, transfer to a small Ford bus for the last twenty miles to the coast. At last "we were in a street of decrepit shanties; there

266

were children in the dust and wandering pigs. Then, suddenly, vast and blank under the glaring white sky, the Pacific . . . Far out, a steamer lay at anchor . . . The air was as hot as fly-paper. A sentry in khaki, with bare feet and a two-foot bayonet at the end of his rifle, ushered us into a room, where a young *mestizo*, extenuated with heat and malaria and the unspeakable boredom of life at Champerico, very slowly did what was necessary to our papers . . .

"We walked out to the end of the jetty. There, twenty feet below us, a boat was wallowing among the rollers. One at a time, in an apparatus like a ducking stool, we were swung out into space and lowered towards the waves. When the boat heaved up within jumping distance, one jumped. A quarter of an hour later we were safely on board the steamer that was to take us up the Mexican coast."[1]

They landed in a rocky bay without a jetty. A whale boat took them from the ship to fifty yards off shore, at which point they and luggage transferred into a hollowed tree trunk, a kind of flat-bottomed canoe, like a coffin. Aldous described the process without turning a hair.

> You squat, cautiously balancing your weight; the coffin shoots forward on a wave and runs aground; then you wait till the retiring Pacific has left the sand relatively dry, and make a dash for it.[1]

In point of fact, according to Roy Fenton, Aldous had trouble landing. Presently a car took them as far as it could go. They reached Pochutla, one of those heart-breaking Mexican villages—the huge blazing plaza, the two or three Indian women squatting in the dust with half a dozen scrofulous tomatoes arranged before them in a pattern or some gory bits of meat in a cloud of flies, the bandstand and the painted church with the crumbling façade . . . They moved on. Another half-hour brought them to the end of the carriage road. Mules were waiting. At the house of the local bandit they got into gaiters and buckled on those enormous Mexican spurs. A bridle-path led them into the uplands. At first they travelled through a zone of *tierra blanca*, intolerably glaring slopes of white earth under a ferocious sun. Roy and Maria rode in front, talking; Aldous trailed behind. With his long legs, he was having difficulty in keeping on the mule. His feet were only a few inches from the ground and his spurs quite useless. Gaining altitude they came to a wood of low oak trees. "We were passing under very small stunted gnarled little trees [Roy talking[2]] in a white incandescent landscape that made Aldous screw up his eyes, and he looked

[1] *Beyond the Mexique Bay*, A Traveller's Journal. Chatto & Windus, 1934.
[2] Roy Fenton, talking to S. B. in 1968, '69, '71 and '72.

through a little telescope thing in his hand, a tiny telescope, which brought distance close up at the risk of not seeing the branches that were hanging in front of him."

He was still forty yards behind the others; Maria was still talking.

"I found her an oddly contradictory character. At times I thought she was extremely solicitous for his comfort, and his welfare —*and yet!* At times a little bit inclined to be haphazard."[1]

Suddenly there was a great yell behind them and an OUCH! They turned to find the mule walking on and Aldous sitting on the ground.

He remounted. They climbed on. And then, almost suddenly they "were in perpetual summer. The mountain side was dark green with coffee bushes, and above the bushes rose tall trees, the larger of them survivors from the original forest . . . We were already on Roy's territory . . but the coffee *fincas* in these mountains are like small kingdoms . . ."[2] they were still more than an hour's ride from the metropolis of the estate, Progreso.

They found a comfortable house on a terrace at the head of a valley. The view was the stupendous one of those latitudes. The mornings were bright summer, the nights cool, the evenings perfect. Here Aldous and Maria rested for some weeks.

It was a place of seclusion and domestic bustle, of great natural beauty and of peace. Peace, in spite of the bandits and the revolutionaries roaming without, in spite of the flaring knife fights among the Indian hands. "The memory of Progreso has the romance and the peace almost of an hermitage; till I suddenly remember how we laughed and then I laugh again in memory of it. The parrot, the animals around the beds, and the dogs and the donkey . . ." So Maria later wrote to Roy. At once there had been a *rapport* between the three. Roy was still under thirty, strong, very handsome, very male; there was a man of action, who could cope with practical living, with danger, who was also kindly, thoughtful, who had read, who could talk; a complex man, one would guess —and a very unusual combination among Aldous's friends. No wonder that he was drawn to their generous host.

During the day Aldous and Maria pottered about on their own, watching the wheels of the estate go round, the *mozos* pruning the coffee trees with flashing blades, the women slapping their washing against the stones. In the afternoon Roy took them riding—"mule rides in the paradise of shade trees", in Maria's memory. And in Aldous's:

Towards evening, when the day had cooled off . . we would walk or ride among the *cafetales*. Our favourite path followed a level con-

[1] Roy Fenton talking.   [2] Aldous, op. cit.

268

tour line round the flank of the extinct volcano that dominated the estate, winding out on to projecting bastions and round again into the valleys indented in the mountainside. One walked through an undergrowth of dark and glittering coffee bushes, and out of the undergrowth sprang great trees, each tree a column standing isolated from all the other columns and visible, in this uncrowded forest, from its base among the coffee to its high green ceiling of spreading branches and leaves. It was the jungle, but domesticated; a vast essay in tropical landscape gardening, richly, romantically beautiful. I thought all the time of that passage in the Fourth Book of *Paradise Lost* . .

> *So on he fares, and to the border comes*
> *Of Eden, where delicious Paradise,*
> *Now nearer, crowns with her enclosure green,*
> *As with a rural mound, the champaign head*
> *Of a steep wilderness . . .*

At night the men talked. "Aldous had very strong views about certain things. [Roy speaking] But he didn't try to force them on you. He would simply give them as a factual thing that he felt very strongly. And at that time, it was in 1933, I felt, I knew, there was a deep worry behind his thinking . . . Of the future, of what the world was going to come to . . . The advent of Hitler and the Nazis. And that was *there behind a lot of his thinking*. He came back and back to it. In the most extraordinary contexts. We were discussing Mexican mythology, and the Spanish Conquest—Aldous was trying to look at some analogy with the present time. While I felt you couldn't equate the two civilizations at all. There was a barbaric element in the Aztec thing which fascinated Aldous. This queer cruel cult . . . He was all the time trying to find a way of seeing WHY they had evolved this philosophy of having to appease the sun by slaughtering so many people; not out of vengeance, not in anger, but because they felt they *must* appease the sun . . ."

Roy knew what they would have to face on their coming journey. "I was rather worried. Though I had been very surprised on occasions to find how tough both of them could be when it came down to physical discomfort. But we were going to pass through country in which there was absolutely *nothing*. Nothing between us and the place we were going to." Meaning no water? "We would be travelling for the best part of fourteen, fifteen, sixteen hours a day over country with NO water, NO shade, NO people."

In *Texts and Pretexts* the year before Aldous had written (having evoked Rimbaud)

. . There are hours and days, there are even whole epochs in the life of every human being . . when rest is the last thing of which soul and body feel a need; when all desire tends quiveringly towards a strenuous and exciting heaven.

The great morning came. They left in darkness. At 3 a.m. Roy, Aldous and Maria with two *Indios* on baggage mules.

. . Dark with a double night; for our road lay under trees, [Aldous distilled it in *Beyond the Mexique Bay*, in *Eyeless in Gaza*] and the black vault of foliage shut out the stars . . but the mules picked their way securely up and down the headlong windings of the track . . .

The air was deliciously fresh against the face and sometimes, in the darkness, one would ride through the perfumed aura of an invisible lemon tree . . . the scent . . was like the brief and inenarrable revelation of something more than earthly—a moment's ecstasy, and then, as the mules advanced, hoof after hoof, up the stony path, the fading of the supernatural presence, the return to a common life symbolically represented by the smell of leather and sweat.

The path climbed. When two hours later the sun rose they found themselves on an upland of bare rocks. Roy addressed them: "Now, we've got to 6,000 feet, and we have to descend into the valley of the Copalita river, which will bring us down again to about 1,800." They descended, slowly, very slowly, the most sheer steep slope of the Copalita range. Again, Aldous might be knocked off his mule at any moment by overhanging branches which he failed to see. They reached the valley by 8 a.m.—having covered only ten miles in five hours—and forded the river in the blistering sunshine. They dismounted and ate. Then the real business of the day began. Their goal, the goal they *had* to make before nightfall was San Pedro el Alto, the first inhabited place on their route. "I said to Maria, 'I'm afraid now comes the really tough part, we are now going to climb over the most vast bald empty mountain range, the wildest emptiest country on earth. And we shall have to be up to 12,000 feet before six o'clock this afternoon.' And this was about half-past eight in the morning."

The heat was tremendous.

. . The main range of the sierra was now before us; ridge above ridge . . . There was no shade, and the vast bald hills were the colour of dust and burnt grass . . . For five more hours we climbed uninterruptedly up one of the steepest paths I have ever seen. It was one of those vast chaotic landscapes that look as though they might go on for ever—a great desert of nonenity, endlessly not there, and empty, quite lifeless . . .[1]

1 From *Beyond the Mexique Bay*, 1934, and *Eyeless in Gaza*, 1936.

Up and up they went.

> .. The sweat .. poured like water off [one's] face and soaked through
> shirt and cotton breeches . . . [one] could scarcely think or even see.
> The landscape seemed to advance and retreat before [one's] eyes,
> turned black and sometimes faded away altogether . . .[1]

"They kept on. [Roy speaking] They kept on; they never complained, they just kept on.

"And then we had a sudden relief—little donkeys appeared with
the striped mail bags of the Mexican Federal Administration,
carrying the mail from Oaxaca to the coast." [Roy speaking; now
Aldous:]

> We drew aside respectfully . . Their long ears flapping at every
> stride, their slender feet twinkling in small precise movements among
> the stones, the little asses stepped delicately by, one by one, each
> under an enormous burden of red, white and green mail bags.

"And the two chaps [Roy again] who were shepherding them
shouted Burr-rro! with that rumbling roll that keeps donkeys
moving along the Mexican roads and ranges; and Aldous watched
this and he took it up and got the greatest joy out of trying to roll
his rr's as magnificently as the Mexicans. He shouted Burr-rro! The
tremendous enjoyment he got out of that."

After fourteen hours in the saddle they reached San Pedro el
Alto, a tiny village at the very top of the sierra, built on a knife's
edge between two gulfs. The light was starting to go. It was still
hot but the heat was a kind of veneer over an essential core of
mountain cold. "And we got off our mules, extremely stiff so that
you could hardly walk, extremely thirsty. Maria, poor girl, having
a fearful battle with migraine. A terrible attack. We got the only
shelter we could get, a store-room belonging to the village shopkeeper. It was extraordinarily clean, for what it could have been.
We put down our blankets and things as best we could, and
wrapped ourselves in every bit of wool we had brought. We asked
the shopkeeper to let us have some supper. It took a bit of time
coming. Meanwhile Maria lay down; Aldous and I went out for a
stroll."

> .. The tiny plaza was like the deck of a ship, a flat space, thirty
> or forty yards from gunwale to gunwale, and on each side a drop;
> in the distance the mountains rolled away, crest after crest, like waves.
> Towards sunset, the boys of the village came out to play a kind

[1] From *Beyond the Mexique Bay*, 1934, and *Eyeless in Gaza*, 1936.

of football in the plaza—deck football; if you kicked too hard the ball flew over the edge and you had to scramble down a couple of hundred feet to find it. In the last, almost level light, the scene was curiously moving—had an intensity, somehow, the more-than-reality of a work of art. It was partly, I suppose, because there was no background. We were on a little platform at the top of everything, with only the sky all around us. Every figure stood out clear and rather flat in strangely significant isolation, against the pale bright vacancy. A donkey, tethered to a post and compact, self-contained, like Sancho Panza's ass in one of the Daumier paintings of *Don Quixote*; men passing, their heads stuck through the slits of their exiguous blankets, hunched and hugging themselves against the increasing cold; and in the centre of the narrow space the boys playing, brilliant in their white trousers and gaily coloured shirts, shining as though transfigured by the supernatural light of evening.[1]

All at once it was piercingly cold. They went back to their quarters. Supper was hot and remarkably good. The shopkeeper lingered to talk. Had they come far? Very far; from Europe. Yes, he knew about Europe . . . What chiefly interested him was the cost of the journey. "I gave him the figures—somewhat diminished, I confess . . partly from a certain sense of shame. Our host was doubtless one of the richest men in the village; but his whole annual income would probably not have bought a single first-class ticket across the Atlantic. He listened carefully: then, after a pause, 'I can't understand,' he said at last, 'why you should want to *gastar su capital* on coming to San Pedro'."[1]

Their beds were three wooden planks in the large freezing room. On these they slept quite soundly.

Next morning they washed in turns in a little basin outside on the stone parapet. They set off for another day's descending, climbing, descending, but the extreme desolation lay behind them. There were pinewoods, once or twice a stray dog slunk past. Aldous promptly ripped out, Perr-rro! That night they stopped at Ejutla, in relative civilization. They put up at the inn, found beds and bed-bugs. Before dinner Roy and Aldous went down to the bar. This was a crypt-like room with a sagging vaulted ceiling propped by thick wooden pillars. They sat down at a small table and ordered some beer. Leaning against the bar stood a smartly dressed young Mexican in riding-breeches drinking mezcal and boasting in a tipsy voice about the alligators he had been shooting in the swamps. Presently he turned, took in the foreign gentlemen and, with the slow formality of the drunk, asked them what they would have. Roy ignored him; the young man insisted. Aldous

[1] *Beyond the Mexique Bay.*

8*a*   Aldous with a goose

b   Aldous with young Matthew *c.* 1926

9a Aldous, Sybille Bedford, Eva
    Herrmann, Sanary 1930s

b Raymond Mortimer,
   Sanary 1930s

c Eddy Sackville-West,
   Sanary 1930

d Aldous, climbing in the Sanary
   Back Country 1930s

attempted some polite refusal in Spanish. The young man chose to take offence. He staggered forward, "*Ustedes me desprecian*". He crashed into their table and sent the drinks flying. His hand went to his belt. "Look out!" Roy yelled at Aldous, "get out of this, for God's sake!" Aldous, who was nearest to the man, jumped up and got himself behind one of the pillars. The young man fumbled out his revolver and waved it wildly. The proprietress screamed. The young man began to stalk Aldous. Aldous darted from behind his pillar and ducked behind the next one. It was a long moment. A shot went off as someone crashed a chair on the drunk man's arm —the bullet did not hit anyone and the man was quickly over-powered.

Next day there was a half day's ride to Ocotlàn from where they were able to take a train to Oaxaca. The adventure was over.

In *Beyond the Mexique Bay*, a few months later, Aldous wrote a fairly extensive account of those days. Curiously, the incident at Ejutla was entirely omitted. "It had been a damned unpleasant experience," Roy said; "and I wrote him twice after the book was published to ask him why." Aldous did not answer.

At Oaxaca they saw the archaeological ruins of Mitla and Monte Alban, then went north to Puebla and Mexico City. They looked at pyramids and ruins, met politicos and diplomatists and "a lot of literary gents—some charming and most intelligent," who gave Aldous a banquet. A Mexican gentleman sent in his card one morning, a Señor Eduardo Huxley, who wanted to know if he were a relation. Aldous decided that he was. "His grandfather, whose photo he showed me (taken in Ealing .. a man with .. a nose which seemed to me rather of the family type) was called Dr Edward Huxley .. born .. in 1825. His son, George Spooner Huxley, came to Mexico, married a Mexican, produced a family .. One brother, whose name I saw in the birthday book, was called Jesus Huxley! (Grand Pater wd have liked that, I think.)"

As usual, Aldous was describing it all in one of his travelogues to his father. He had been remiss on this journey, had not written for more than a month, not since they had left with Roy from Guatemala. Now, 29th April, he was making up for it, writing on board ship—"glad to be on the homeward road"—on their way to New York. His father never saw that letter. Leonard Huxley died of a heart attack on 3rd May 1933. The news awaited Aldous in New York. He and Maria returned by ship to England.

Chapter Five

1933

"THIS is our permanent address and en plus—I hope it will be our address for a long time," Maria wrote from Sanary to Roy Fenton. "It is such a joy to be home. But Europe *is* in a mess." They had found Sanary, on their return in June, full of German writers at their first stage of exile. ".. so we cannot escape from that Barbarous German news. And France's great wall is terminated and she can now only be attacked through Switzerland . . . The dollar goes down the price of life goes up.

> I am not sure that on the whole the wilds of Mexico and Mexican coffee plantations are not the best to live in at the moment where other problems are more vital than politics. . . . I . . think of the dark bushes the shade trees and the ravines—how lovely it all was —but very much a dream!

Aldous, still anxious to stave off his novel, was going on with the Central American book, "the travel book we both long for" (but his publishers, shaken by the slump, felt gloomy about the prospects of a subject book).

> I am writing about our travels—that is, about everything from politics .. to art [Aldous to Naomi Mitchison] Tell Dick[1] to study the history of the five Central American republics. They illustrate very clearly the modern fallacy of supposing economics to be at the bottom of everything. In C A there were no economics, only evil passions . . . I was re-reading Wordsworth's account of his visit to France during the Revolution . . .
>
> > *The land all swarmed with passion, like a plain*
> > *Devoured by locusts. . .*
>
> Which is exactly Europe in '33—the awful sense of invisible vermin of hate, envy, anger crawling about . . .
> Yes, you may say by all means that I am not becoming a carthlick . . . I have never more passionately felt the need of using reason jusqu'au bout . . .
> Do you think I am kind and unpossessive? Quien sabe? Perhaps I am only a person of rather delicate constitution who likes a quiet

---

1 Lord Mitchison.

life. How senseless psychological judgements really are apart from physiological judgements! And of course I am also to a considerable extent a function of defective eyesight. Keratitis punctata shaped and shapes me . . .

Aldous snatched time for painting. "Like mad. Really it is an ideal art . . . (when one thinks of the horror of using a pen or a typewriter!)

I long, when I have reached a certain level of competence, to launch out on something more ambitious. It is deplorable that only bad painters shd now undertake important and intrinsically significant subjects and that good ones should live in terror of all that is obviously beautiful, or dramatic, or sublime.

It was a hot summer with a large crop of grapes and figs. The children had arrived, and strings of visitors. Maria watered her jacaranda trees, 5 inches high, grown from seed she had brought from Mexico. The house was full of their Central American trophies; Roy sent them sacks of coffee beans and a crocodile skin which Matthew unpacked on the station platform. The rubber boat leaked, Gene Saxton from New York—endlessly kind—arranged repair. The newest import from the U.S.A. was the Hay Diet, starch *or* protein at any one meal, faithfully imposed by Maria. So it was toast and rolls for breakfast one morning, two plain boiled eggs and no bread at all the next; a mound of spaghetti for dinner or bare roast beef. Rina married her Emilio, a rash young marriage; the Huxleys gave her the two John Collier portraits as a wedding present.

What with the economic slump and Rina's living out, Maria decided to manage the house with part-time help, and cook dinner herself. As their dining-room was upstairs and the kitchen in the basement, this entailed some not inexpensive alterations, turning the present kitchen into a dining-room and an adjacent verandah into a kitchen. They also switched from coal to the new bottled gas, and put a geyser in the bathroom. The new cooking verandah was long and narrow like a passage, as well as exposed to sun and cold.

. . I hope that the net result of all the changes [Aldous to Julian] will be that we can run the house more cheaply. At the present rate of exchange it costs a lot; but I hope that the French will find themselves forced off their perch of gold . . .

The Huxleys did not take much to the German refugees. "Rather a dismal crew," Aldous wrote to Julian, "already showing the disastrous effects of exile. Let us hope we shall not have to scuttle when Tom Mosley gets into power."

One may find this callous; perhaps it was only candid. Those literary refugees were indeed the victims of barbarous events, fore-runners of catastrophe; they were also our neighbours. They were men and women in a very unhappy situation, coping with the sudden and entire disruption of their lives: they had lost their homes, their language, their possessions (which in many cases meant their libraries); they had left friends and relatives in Germany who might be in danger and in concentration camps. Some of them, Jews and men of the political left, had escaped because they had to; others had *chosen* to go, or not to return, to Germany for moral reasons. (Thomas Mann, for one, and Meier-Graefe.) At the same time this particular wave of refugees was in an exceptionally privileged position—unlike the thousands, the millions, of fugitives to come, they were not hounded (for the time being) and they were not destitute. They had been unable to bring any money but they went on earning an adequate if diminished living from their translation rights, being well-known enough to have a sizeable English reading public. And, again by reason of their eminence, they were safe from the refugee's acutest anguish—papers. To be sure, they *were* beset by the recurrent problems of passport, visa, residence permit; but the problem got solved or shelved, often at the last minute, by Mrs Roosevelt or a Hollywood studio or (later on) by the popular front government in France.

The roll-call was impressive. The Thomas Manns, Lion Feucht-wanger, Franz Werfel with his wife Alma Mahler Werfel, Bruno Frank and René Schickele had taken villas in Sanary; Heinrich Mann was at the hotel in Bandol, Arnold Zweig at a pension; Golo, the Mann's second son, lodged with the Seabrooks; Brecht, Emil Ludwig, Stephan Zweig came on visits. In their wake were wives, secretaries, translators, agents, fans. (The locals pocketed their rents and tips, and called them Boches, Jews, war-mongers and spies.) One might ask how they came to congregate at that one place. Well, they hadn't had much time to make a choice. They got into France because it had a land-border with Germany, and stayed because it had a democratic government; they went South because it was cheaper than Paris and because of the climate, and to this particular part of the coast because the Meier-Graefe's were already there and because the eldest Mann children, Klaus and Erika, who had often been to see Jean Cocteau at Toulon, recommended it.

Aldous and Maria soon met about all of them at a monster garden party given by the Seabrooks. I remember it as an incongruous occasion. It was a broiling afternoon; tea and drinks flowed. Petit fours melted in the sun. Willie Seabrook, in the grip of a failure of nerve, had whipped off his shirt and confronted his guests in khaki shorts and hairy chest. Heinrich Mann, even more stiff and formal than his brother, arrived in a high collar and black coat, extending, like Monsieur de Charlus, two fingers to anyone offering to shake hands. Maria came with Guatemalan belt and Mexican satchel bag; Aldous, in white cotton from neck to heel, kept to her side; and so did the confrères, each holding court within a cluster of his wife and entourage. Only Feuchtwanger circulated, making the round of the younger and more attractive women telling them about his latest sales figures. Like Arnold Bennett and the transatlantic cable, his word-rate ran high.

What struck the Huxleys was the regard some of them had for themselves. They threw their weight about; they *were* pompous. Their womenfolk referred to them as *Dichterfürsten*, princes of poetry. And though united in their horror of the Nazis, they were far from being one big happy family; only Willie Seabrook would have dreamt of gathering them all in one front yard. They were roughly divided into two main clans. One, the *haute culture*, revolved round Thomas Mann—the Magician as his children called him—and his friends and peers; the other clan was dominated by Lion Feuchtwanger, and the bond between him and his satellites oddly enough was communistic leanings and/or financial success; each clan patronised the other. Both, with an *hauteur* worthy of de Gaulle, looked down upon the Anglo-Saxons—Aldous Huxley and his friends.

The *Haute Culture* formed a reading circle. Once a week Mann, Frank, Meier-Graefe and Schickele, in turn, read from work in progress to their families and an invited audience. I must give a glimpse of one such evening. It was at the master's house (a villa belonging, ironically enough, to the mother-in-law of the German Ambassador to Egypt). Thomas Mann sat at the centre of a high table on the terrace, his three colleagues beside him. Behind them were chairs for their wives and Erika Mann. In the grounds below this platform, on steps, cushions, garden bench spread the hoi-polloi—a Swiss woman poet, the younger Mann children, the Schickele's schoolboy son, a well-known English critic, Aldous and Maria, my mama, Eddy Sackville-West, Heinrich Mann's Juno-esque mistress and myself. Erika approached the platform bearing her father's manuscript. For some fifty minutes he read a chapter from *Joseph and his Brethren* in a not very carrying voice. Afterwards the high-table was served with Riesling and chicken salad. Some suitably graded refreshments—I seem to remember fruit cup and biscuits—were distributed among the groundlings. Only Meier-Graefe, impervious, pulled up a chair and made his young wife sit beside him, feeding her with white of chicken off his plate. It made Aldous's evening.

In the autumn Gerald Heard came to stay for some ten days. "very nice and more encyclopaedic than ever—also more pessimistic than ever, advising us all to clear out to some safe spot in South America or the Pacific Islands before it is too late. He enjoys his glooms: but the fact does not necessarily mean that the glooms are unfounded. The German spectacle is really too frightening." Aldous tried to do his bit by taking part in a Congress of intellectuals in Paris presided over by Paul Valéry. He came back from it shrugging it off, depressed.

Poor Seabrook had been in a bad way for some time, drinking too much, unable to finish a book. In October he decided to leave everything and go to America for treatment. "The Huxleys drove us to the Toulon railroad station in Maria's red Bugatti," Marjorie Worthington wrote in her memoirs.[1]

> Because she drove so fast, we reached the *gare* ahead of time and had to wait what seemed like ages on the dark platform for the Blue Train which would come roaring in from Ventimiglia at nine o'clock. I remember Aldous walking up and down the platform, talking a blue streak. Maria sat on a bench with Willie, consoling him, listening to him, mothering him. He often poured out his heart to lovely ladies, and this night there was a heavy load to unburden . . .
> . . I failed to gather what [Aldous] was talking about . . . he remained serenely on his own intellectual plane . . . that's where he was this night at the railroad station, seeing two friends off on a train, feeling very sorry for them but not able to cope with the emotions . . .

In November Eva Herrmann and I went to Madrid and the night before we left my mother had a small dinner-party with the Huxleys and the Meier-Graefes. Meier-Graefe tried to prepare us, talking of El Greco, of Velasquez, of Goya, his own first sight of them twenty years ago. He talked all evening—with such freshness and such fire that Aldous too was caught. Maria saw it and when we said goodbye lightly made a promise. A few days later a telegram from Sanary reached us in Madrid. The thin blue slip, survived by chance among my papers, recalls the pang of pleasure on first reading the unsigned message.

llegaremos jueves besos

Arriving Thursday. They came by air; we met them. The hotel was opposite the Prado, the weather autumnal, wind-swept, clear. Every morning we stepped across into those overwhelming halls. Aldous tried to see everything, even the vast collection of drawings

---

1 *The Strange World of Willie Seabrook*, Harcourt Brace & World, 1966.

in the attics. El Greco had always fascinated him, now he was carried away by the astonishing variety of Goya—the garlanded girls, the portraits, the *Desastros de la Guerra*. Here was a man who had painted in turn the rulers, the *voluptés*, the horrors of the eighteenth century and who had lived long enough into the nineteenth to outlive Jane Austen by eleven years and Beethoven by one. We would leave the Prado full of talk, wild with eye-strain at about three o'clock and eat a good long Spanish luncheon at the hotel. Later in the afternoon we would gather in the Huxleys' room to read aloud the Spanish chapter of Buckle's *History of Civilization*. At sunset, at the hour of urban animation, we strolled the evening-streets; and night after night it would seem, we went to the theatre. This was Aldous's choice. And it was not that we were seeing Calderón or Lope de Vega—those plays were contemporary, if old-fashioned, drawing-room stuff, incredibly long-winded, with plots even Maria, who had startled us with a sudden fluency in Spanish, did not follow. The acting, so Aldous maintained, was superb. Dinner again at our hotel; Spain, in the second year of the Republic, was still a masculine civilization and we were the only *respectable* women dining in a public place. The others were mostly high-class German tarts in fox-furs (these were Aldous's observations). In this manner we spent the best part of two weeks. We went to the Escorial—it shook and depressed us, but how fascinated Aldous was by that monument to power and to death, how eloquent. Once we ate a freezing picnic in the clear light up in the Guadarrama; but what possessed our minds dreams were our mornings, was the Prado, were those canvasses of kings and dwarfs and saints.

We also laughed a good deal. Maria dug up the louche advertisements in the evening papers for Aldous—"Masseuse *gran reacción*..." We laughed at nothing and at ourselves, at the contre-temps that are the travellers' lot, at my putting away so much of the Spanish food, at Eva's concern with comfort, at the Huxleys' economies that boomeranged. In a very hard slow train we went to Toledo for a few cold days; we went to Segovia and thence to Avila in a commodious hired car, having *proved* to Aldous and Maria that this actually cost less. They accepted the logic of the figures but this transport was so much more *agreeable* that their consciences still quailed. At Avila we were in the heartland of Castile—a November evening in grey walled streets that overwhelmed one with a sense of being outside our time. But there is another memory of the town of Saint Theresa. Beds. We stopped at the first inn. We walked into the lighted hall.

> *¿Tienen habitaciones? Quieremos dos cuartos*
> *con dos camas cada.*

There were rooms. Upstairs Maria and Eva discovered that the
sheets had been slept in. Horror. They pulled bells. No one came.
In Spain at the crunch, they would pay no attention to a woman.
Maria told Aldous that *he* must go. "You must be firm, darling.
The porter understands English." We trotted after him. Arriving
at the desk, Aldous turned and said in his bell-like voice, "Darling,
how shall I put it?"

We had tickets to fly back from Madrid to Marseilles by Air
France. When we got out to the aerodrome, the waiting plane
was marked with the swastika. Lufthansa. (The German line alter-
nated with the French.) Eva Herrman and I refused to travel on a
Nazi plane. Aldous thought it was a pretty futile protest, but gave
in to our emotional indulgence and eventually we were put on a
Spanish plane. It was a small one and I cannot remember other
passengers. The air was calm, the earth below looked tremendous;
Aldous got out his notebook. I imitated him. Then something went
very wrong indeed. The plane lurched sideways and dropped to
about 25 feet. Lop-sided it proceeded to hug the coast line of the
Costa Brava just clearing bathing-huts and cliffs. The engine noise
was shattering. I looked at Maria for some reassurance, but her
face had an inward look and her lips were moving; she was, she
said matter-of-factly afterwards, composing herself for death. I
looked at Aldous— he was being sick into a paper bag. The plane
limped on for a full thirty minutes; it made Barcelona and we
landed. Smiling German airmen in Lufthansa caps met us by the
gangway.

That night, our last night in Spain, we had dinner in the Plaza
de Cataluña. A bomb had just been thrown. A tram lay over-
turned, people had been hurt, there was a lot of police. Aldous did
not fail to remark on the waste and folly. "Everyone knows that
home-made bombs have never been the *slightest* bit of use." What
was? What was any use? We talked about the new Spanish Republic.
Eva, rather warmly, expressed hopes—schools, the vote for women
... Aldous let it pass. We talked of re-armament, of Germany—
What was one to do? At what cost? At *whose* cost? It came back,
our talk, as it still does, to the dilemma of the liberal. What Aldous
said was abstract, far-seeing, aloof. In a way it was maddening. At
last one of us said, "Well, if that's no good either, what would *you*
do?" and Maria came in, "Yes, darling, do tell us."

Aldous's answer, his mood, his exploratory talk, I can no longer
pin down. At the time it was startling. Up to a minute ago he
appeared to be the man who said, "I have never more passionately
felt the need for using reason *jusqu'au bout*." Now it was as if his points
of reference had vanished. I wrote about that evening once before,

in a travel book, twenty years ago (and twenty years nearer the event). I would be tempted to put it differently today, but find that first account, midway between the past and present, standing in the way. It will have to serve.

> . . That night there was a new note. Benevolent rationalism seemed a little worn: there was a hint . . . that man was helpless indeed and therefore could be helped and help himself. It was not in anything that was definitely said, and I cannot remember words; only [that Aldous's] answer was disturbing by an undercurrent of thoughts yet unformed, a sense of tendrils on the move towards the unseen end of the stick, by something we were too shocked to recognize as hope.

Instead, one felt a sense of grievance at the shift from a trusted intellectual position (the first reaction of readers in the coming years).

> . . Then the *paella* we had ordered arrived; we ate into the saffron rice, drank Manzanilla and talked of this and that, but again and again that night the conversation led to, hovered, and not quite stopped short, of some disquietening threshold. Once or twice, always in that graceful, courteous voice, a word was dropped from the upsetting vocabulary of the tract. The Self, the All, the One . . .

At one point the Hay Diet, of all things, set it off again. Maria noticed that rice *with* prawns and chicken was not at all the thing; Aldous said it didn't matter. Not matter? Don't you believe in it? Of course he didn't believe in it, Aldous said. Maria was shocked —But why on earth then have we—? "Well, because of the discipline, darling." And when I exclaimed at that, Aldous loud and clear said something about mortification. Rebelliously I stuck to the *paella*, and there came the intimation that this would shut one off from that which was not mentioned as surely as political passion. Next day we flew back to Marseilles by Air France.

Beyond the Mexique Bay had been finished a few days before Aldous left for Spain. (Too late for autumn publication—it came out the following spring; 1933 was the first year since 1920 Aldous did not have a book out.) Now he was digging himself in for a winter at Sanary with the novel.

Chapter Six

A Store of Gaiety . . .

FOR a time all went well. Aldous was writing apace; the stack of typescript waxed.

> The theme, fundamentally, is liberty. What happens to someone who becomes really very free—materially first . . and then mentally and emotionally. The rather awful vacuum that such freedom turns out to be. But I haven't yet worked out the whole of the fable— only the first part.

At present this was no obstacle, the particular time sequence of the future *Eyeless in Gaza* led Aldous on into going ahead. The theme is presented in the opening chapter—we find Anthony Beavis, the central character (an unmarried man), in his house in the South of France in 1933, looking at old photographs, about to become aware of *the awful vacuum*. From this base in time the novel moved into various phases of Anthony's past. All action is precisely dated—November 6th 1902, June 17th 1912, December 8th 1926 and so on—but each period or episode is broken up into several chapters, and the order of these chapters is deliberately shuffled. Events begun in chapter five may be continued in Chapter X or Y. The conclusion of the fable—Anthony's future—was to be inserted in like fashion in due course of inspiration. As yet it was not revealed; Aldous did not see into post-1933 in fiction any more than he did in actual time. (Incidentally, I am convinced that it was this business of juggling with the dates which was Aldous's earliest *donnée* for this novel and that the opening of chapter one—"The snapshots had become almost as dim as memories"—was indeed his first line.)

Life in Sanary was quiet that winter and became more so when in February Maria went to London for medical treatment. I came to stay to look after Aldous under Maria's instructions. No man could have been more undemanding and more even-tempered, and during the day there were Giulia and Camilla to look after *us*. We ate breakfast, lunch and tea together, sometimes in complete silence. While Aldous wrote, I wrote (at Maria's desk, an essay on *Beyond the Mexique Bay*, then still in page proof). While he painted, I read aloud. We went for walks; at night I cooked our dinner which we ate in the new basement dining-room, facing each other across a wide table covered with green linoleum. I had been told to stir an egg yolk into Aldous's soup and smuggle cream into his vegetables, and this worked unless one got carried away. (Cream was hand-made by working butter and water through a gadget.) With dinner we drank a nice claret—a youngish Ste-Estèphe, home-bottled, that came by barrel from a négociant at Bordeaux my mother had discovered—and it was now that I might trot out some general question I'd been saving. Aldous's reactions were unpredictable. He could be quite marvellously set off by some congenial query about tadpoles or the doctrine of the Shakers; one fared less well when one really wished to keep him to the point. He was discursive, never argumentative; but he might stray anywhere, though he could be impatient himself with wide vague questions. Sometimes there was no response. Aldous would emit a kind of low-pitched *hmm* . . . It was not only as if he'd pulled the shutters down, whatever was behind the shutter had been withdrawn as well and was very far away; for the person in the room with him, there was nothing there. (Other people have talked of the prohibitive quality of that silence. He had other, peaceful silences.) Did he know what he was doing as he had said to Dorothy Brett when he was a very young man?

The only outings during those weeks—apart from picnics in the winter sun—were driving Aldous to the dentist and a charity matinée at the British Vice-Consul's at Toulon where, without any preliminary fuss, he sat down and read the Dwarfs' story from *Crome Yellow* to a mainly female audience. Once Mrs Wharton, Edith Wharton, came over with her entourage. We were sitting round a tray of Cinzano in the sitting-room when Camilla announced luncheon. Aldous opened the door for Mrs Wharton and impelled her down the steepish stairs with gentle taps with his cupped hand on her behind. The entourage froze; Mrs Wharton turned her head, not abruptly, identified and gave him a sweet smile.

To me it seemed a good life, a writer's life. Aldous admitted to doing 500, 600, 700 words a day; yet he must have missed Maria, and if he was working too intensely to be very bored, he was certainly under-stimulated. Sure enough, Maria had hardly returned when they decided that he must have a break. Italy. Rome for Easter—showing it to Matthew "before Mussolini . . destroys it all in order to dig up more rubbish heaps of imperial glory". It should have been a radiant journey. It rained a great deal; the Fascist thing had become more open and unbearable; one saw too many places in too short a time. There were many good moments. Maria had gone ahead to have the Bugatti seen to at Nice. Aldous, Camilla who was to visit her family, and I followed in my car. (Camilla had consulted Maria in distress: what was she to do if she had to obey a call of nature? Aldous was briefed and every fifty kilometres or so suggested a stop to have a look at the view.) We spent the night at Nice; Raymond Mortimer was there and it was an animated dinner. Next day Aldous and Maria, Camilla and I, in separate cars, went into Italy. We managed a rendez-vous beyond Genoa and the four of us sat down to luncheon on a Ligurian waterfront (I mention it because of the way Maria turned an ordeal into a treat for that shy girl, Camilla). It was one of those trumpery election days and we were depressed by the strutting and the blown-up features of the Duce glowering from every hoarding, house and wall.

. . an organized attempt at apotheosis [Aldous to T. S. Eliot]—as for Caesar or Augustus. I happened to be reading Edwyn Bevan's *Later Greek Religion*, and his chapter on the deification of kings from Alexandrian times onwards was fantastically topical. One understands, in Italy and, I suppose, in Germany too, why the Jews and early Christians were so much concerned about idolatry.

We slept at La Spezia, strolling—Aldous in a mellow mood—late into the night (the rain had not caught up with us yet) and temporarily parted on the Campo Santo at Pisa the next morning, Aldous and Maria going on by way of the Etruscan cities to Rome to meet Matthew whose school holidays had begun; I to Lucca, depositing Camilla, thence to Florence to pick up Eva Herrmann. When we got to Rome the Huxleys, tempted by the new autostrada, had left for Naples. They had hardly returned—Bernini churches, a picnic at Tivoli, a visit to the truly idolatrous *Mostra del Fascismo* —when we all went off again on respective itineraries, the Huxleys to San Sepolcro and to Ferrara for the special exhibition of Cossa, Costa and Cosimo Tura. We converged in Florence and in no time at all, it seemed, we were back in the same small hotel in Nice—rather tired, rain-sodden and grumpy about having spent too much money.

Money. The house was not running itself noticeably cheaper with a succession of dailies. *Beyond the Mexique Bay*, out since April, was selling rather well considering the times. Aldous now could have enjoyed a small private income from his share since his father's death in Prior's Field school. After talking it over with Maria, he had written to his step-mother who was one of the governors of the school.

My dear Rosalind,
Thank you for your letter and the cheque. So long as the boys [Aldous's half-brothers, David and Andrew, aged 18 and 16] are

still being educated, I had rather not draw any money that may come in from Prior's Field, which I regard as a family thing rather than a personal one. I am therefore returning you the cheque and the receipt . . . Dear Rosalind, I hope that, if . . . the problem of the boys' education becomes more difficult, you will not hesitate to let me know; for I should like to be able to do anything within my power for David and Andrew . . .

Love from us both.

Ever your affectionate
Aldous

(I have said nothing about Aldous's feelings and reflections after his father's death the year before. I do not know what they were. Nothing has come to light in his extant letters; letters to him were destroyed, and I doubt if many of his friends wrote to him in the accepted manner; it seemed to be an understood thing that one did not. Certainly one did not *say* anything. (I met them at the station a few weeks after, on their return from Mexico by way of London. Silence was expected. Very little came through even from Maria.) They had not reached England in time for the funeral. Leonard Huxley was buried in Surrey, in Compton churchyard beside Julia Huxley's grave.

In June of 1934 Aldous went to London on his own for a few days, then came back into the Mediterranean summer—the sequence of hot blue days and exquisite nights. The book still moved. The children were there, friends came: Robert Nichols, the Drieu la Rochelles, Victoria Ocampo, Clive Bell, Jeanne. The interests of the year were photographing insects through an enlarging lens, and human hands. Stimulated by Dr Charlotte Wolff,[1] whom they had just met, and her researches in that field, Maria collected prints of their friends' hands—a not unmessy process with a roller and thick ink. No-one escaped, not even the Hyères contingent arriving spic and span; Paul Valéry and Edith Wharton submitted. Afterwards the prints would be passed on to Dr Wolff and she and Maria would sit for hours poring over them. There were a number of young people in Sanary that year, some pretty girls, friends of Matthew's on one foot as it were, friends of his parents' on the other. How many picnics we had in those summer nights, in the woods under a moon, on beaches by a warm and phosphorescent sea. We drank planter's punch made from Aldous's

---

[1] Charlotte Wolff, M.D., F.R.Ps.S., author of *The Human Hand, A Psychology of Gesture*, etc. etc.

recipe, played games, the levitation game and Aldous and Maria's version of blind man's buff; Aldous sang:

I'll sing you Twelve O
Green grow the Rushes O.
What is your Twelve O?

At midnight we bathed.

"I wonder whether you could come," Maria wrote to Eddy Sackville-West, "and fetch a store of lazy gaiety to face the coming winter—it is more than gaiety in fact—it is serenity and detachment . . . The warm starry skies . . the scents and the peace . . with all my grapes ripening and the last tuberoses . . .

> You have never been here when the cumulative madness of five months of sun and country and stars make the world unreal in its pleasures and beauties—and when the northern sobriety is very northern and unreal indeed. I shall be so sensible this winter *but I am so happy now.*

They broke up early. Aldous needed a change of scene, wanted to do some articles, make some ready money. By 20th September they were in London. Four months, they planned. They found a flat, "a comic flat, 150 yards from Piccadilly Circus," Maria wrote to Roy, miraculously cheap: £5 a week. It was a studio under a raftered roof at 18 St Albans Place behind Lower Regent Street, with two large bedrooms: "a great deal of light . . much cupboard space. Of course we have to pay for this old-fashioned roominess by old-fashioned discomforts of heating by gas, no porter and no hot continual water. But it is very quiet, essential to peasants as we have become."

There was room for Rina (back with them for the time being); Aldous was able to do a bit of painting. "London is cheerful on the whole." He fell into his round—the novel, a little journalism, friends, walks in the park; Maria was suffering from her usual revulsion.

> My first reaction [still to Roy] are violent horror at the mechanization of the whole thing, the bad air and the, mostly, unfresh food. Also the amount of food appals me. The amount of unnecessary horrors invented to tempt humanity to spend its so bitterly earned money. The vulgarity of the crowds, its vacant look and its hustle in solid continuity in all the streets . . . How I hate it all. Passionately. But I will settle down to it . . .
>
> I wonder if you can imagine us here. I can imagine you so well

on your dare-devil tours which you combine with good business . . .
God preserve you of drought and storms. And above all from
drunken mozos. And from all the crocodiles and the chain of
horrors laying in wait for one in those countries . . .

To Aldous London seemed prosperous as well as cheerful: "The
English have convinced themselves that they're well off at the
moment and are acting accordingly—which appears to have the
same result as *being* well off." Julian had been made director of
the Zoo. "What good news . . ! I don't know what the disadvantages of the job are—but it seems to me to have a lot of advantages
from financial security to a house that . . compares not too un-
favourably with that of the gorillas!"

At this time, J. W. N. Sullivan, Aldous's old friend, was faced
with disabling illness as well as financial trouble being unable now
to meet a publishing debt. "I shall ask you to let me guarantee
the debt," Aldous wrote to Ralph Pinker, "or rather to pay it
provisionally out of any monies which may come into my account
with you.

. . I shouldn't want you to mention this arrangement to Sullivan,
of course. Merely tell him that the debt can be repaid in instalments
as he earns it. In this way he won't be worried . . .

In November Aldous and Maria came to one of their quick
decisions. They signed a seven-year lease for a flat, or set, in Albany.
This meant a permanent base in London. *If only one could spend half
one's time in each country*—libraries and intelligent, informed society
in England; warmth and country-life in Mediterranean France—
that old wish of Aldous's was being realized. Rent and rates came
to about £400 a year. They could always sublet the thing in summer
they told themselves; a set of rooms sounded less of a burden than
a flat or house. Again it was only a minute's walk from Piccadilly
Circus, again they were to enjoy unique urban quiet—no wheel
ever entered Albany that private back-alley of Georgian houses in
the heart of London, the past abode of Byron, Bulwer Lytton and
the gentleman burglar Raffles. "Do you know Albany from literature?" Maria wrote to Matthew.

They furnished it cheaply. Second-hand tables and chairs, new
beds. They managed to get rid of their comic flat but this meant
moving out by mid-December. Suddenly they were under pressure.
Maria had to go into a nursing home for a few days; when she came
out she was not strong enough for all there was to do. Aldous was
beginning to sleep badly, a new experience and it upset him. Maria
thought that it came from his worrying over money, the cost of
setting up house on top of Christmas. They disapproved of the

whole business—the rich giving to the rich, spending money on things hardly wanted. But to their younger or less well-to-do relations and their poorer friends they would send cheques, most generous cheques. They never added up the total on a piece of paper. Aldous took mild sleeping pills, sipped Sedobrol; Gerald Heard advised breathing exercises:

.. of the Yoga sort with accompanying mental concentration and
.. attempted elimination of irrelevant thoughts and feelings [letter to Robert Nichols] .. frightfully difficult and takes so long.

Presently Aldous was sleeping better again, but now Matthew arrived from school nervous and tired. After days of chaotic efforts they were in E2, their ground-floor flat in Albany.

They were at home on the afternoon of 31st December—tea at a round table that filled the darkish hall, sherry afterwards. People came and went, Aldous's step-mother, Gerald Heard, Evan Morgan (I think), Tommy Earp, Eddy West, Naomi Royde Smith, Lady Ottoline Morrell, Ivan Moffat, Matthew's contemporary; Raymond Mortimer, Eva Herrmann, Marion Dorn, Ted McKnight Kauffer . . . There were presents. Someone (Victor Rothschild?) had sent a handsome Strassbourg pie. Aldous and Maria did not approve of *foie gras*; for some moments its fate hung in the balance, then Maria said it would make a supper for Matthew, Raymond and Sybille. At one stage Lady Ottoline broke her string of pearls: large and beautiful pearls, if not well-strung, bounced and rolled over the floor like so many peas disappearing under carpets and the second-hand sideboard. We were on our hands and knees. Pearls collected in a saucer in front of Ottoline. But how many?— How many more had to be retrieved? Ottoline, quite unruffled, refused to count. Presently she took leave (pearls in a paper bag); we stood up, she made the round—the appropriate wish, the right remark. To me it was—in the great hooting voice—"You *will* enjoy the Strassbourg pie."

Afterwards Maria changed into a dressing-gown and we had supper in the bowels of the earth (in Albany, kitchens were either underground or on the attic floor). We drank champagne. Leaving in the small hours, Aldous came out with us for the night air. My car, parked in the front-yard beside the residents' Daimlers, would not start. Aldous and Raymond heaved to and pushed it into Piccadilly, broke into a run: they pushed and ran for a hundred yards till the engine caught. The car leapt forward and they fell behind; I waved, they waved, *Auguri*, we shouted, *Auguri!* Rather a nice beginning for the New Year, I thought.

PART SIX

Watershed?: 1935-1937

"Faith .. is the choice of the nobler
hypothesis. It is the resolve to place the
highest meaning on the facts which we
observe."

GERALD HEARD

".. the product, I suppose, of a
rationalist upbringing, I remain an
agnostic who aspired to be a gnostic—
but a gnostic only on the mystical level,
a gnostic without symbols, cosmologies
or a pantheon ...

ALDOUS HUXLEY, from a letter of 1962

"Ultimate reality cannot be understood except intuitively, through an act
of will and the affections. *Plus diligitur
quam intelligitur.*

ALDOUS HUXLEY, *Grey Eminence*

Chapter One

E2 Albany, Piccadilly

SOON in the new year Aldous went over to Paris having rashly engaged himself to do some articles for *Paris-Soir* on the subject of *La France au seuil de l'année 1935*. He scurried about for a week interviewing schoolmasters and cabinet ministers, then returned to London exhausted and disgruntled for a breather. He started to sleep badly again. He worked, but the novel wasn't going and the flat, still far from finished, was a restless place. So he went off again to *La France au seuil* while Maria pulled things into shape. Albany was both rather wonderful and a bit preposterous. Their two front rooms were well-proportioned with high ceilings and tall windows, giving on, uncurtained, to the covered walk which, except that it was flanked by flower boxes, was like a promenade deck aboard ship. These rooms they made quite civilized; a handsome desk and deep chairs in one, Maria's usual wide bed and coral dressing-table in the other. The rest of the flat consisted of the entrance-and-dining hall already described, below a murky sky-light; a strip of a back-room where Aldous slept and a strip of a bath. The basement kitchen, down some twisty little stairs, was a mess of pipes with a coal-fed boiler in the middle which supplied hot water and erratic heating. Each Albany tenant was allotted a couple of servants' rooms three flights up under the eaves, connected to the master flat by a system of bells. There was also a system of rules, implicit and explicit, a statute in fact. You were expected to be waited on hand and foot.

Albany was founded in 1803. To obtain a lease you had to be a gentleman, a bachelor and have no connection with trade. The vestibule off the main portal is still adorned by the busts of the more illustrious past inhabitants, Lord Byron, William Lamb, Frederick, Duke of York. You might not keep a dog, cat or parrot. The same goes for musical instruments (in the 1930s this rule was held to include wireless sets). The amendment allowing wives was passed in the early 1920s not long after the vote for women. Children were still out. Albany was always run by a gentleman trustee living on the premises. In Aldous's time it was a Captain Adams. The famous covered walk runs parallel to the Burlington Arcade from the main entrance in Piccadilly to a discreet gate into Vigo Street, fifty yards from Bond Street. Both ends were guarded by porters in uniform and top hats, the Piccadilly one day and night whereas the gate into Mayfair was left (shades of Caroline

Lamb) locked and private after 10 p.m. Tenants had a key. The porters were formal and friendly; if you were carrying a parcel, which wasn't very Albany in any case (though Maria appeared with vegetables in basket), you were relieved of it at the gate. Permit me, ma'am—whereupon the porter disappeared from sight into some subterranean passage like Alice's White Rabbit, and materialized again by your front door. They were three, one round and short and red, one built like a grenadier and a slight young man called Simpkins whom Maria took to in particular. Simpkins had a sister, Bessie, and soon it was arranged that she would come and do for the Huxleys for a few hours daily (Rina having returned to France and her Emilio). The rest of the housework and all the cooking Maria did herself (again not quite Albany). As for those servants' rooms, one they used for a box-room, the other Aldous and Maria in their kindness decided to lend to me (I had been living in digs and they wanted to save me money). The bells served. One for breakfast, two for a telephone call, three when the bathroom downstairs was empty (my attic room had only a cold-water basin and was lit—in 1935—by gas).

After Aldous returned from Paris for the second time, having finally got out of the French articles, the insomnia came back in force—he lay awake most nights, and next morning was hardly up to wrestling with the novel. Next night he could not sleep because of work undone—what *was* to become of them if he was unable to write? So the spiral went; every day he failed to get on better, the outlook seemed a little worse. On 25th February he wrote to Harold Raymond.

My dear Harold,
     I ought to have thanked you before for a very kind and generous letter—but this sleeplessness leaves one in a sorry state of incapacity to do anything. If, as I hope, I get over the state fairly soon, I trust to have the book finished by next autumn. Otherwise—God knows. Meanwhile, I don't want to let my indebtedness to Chatto's pile up; and, seeing that I can live on my own resources for a time, I think it will be best if you suspend payment till I get properly under weigh again.

Aldous tried country weekends, massage, vitamins, a hypnotist (who did some good but not at the right hours), went on with Sedobrol that old French standby, a sort of Oxo cube with something soothing added (he would not let himself slide into sleeping pills, it was to be "the minimum of dope"). He persisted with Yoga exercises. Gerald Heard was very good to them, popping in and out almost daily, reassuring Maria. To him Aldous was able to talk. In letters too he touched on aspects of his trouble. Writing had its advantages, he told Bob Nichols, but offered no support "but what one can supply from within.

> when one's ill or unhappy, one needs something outside oneself to hold one up. It is a good thing, I think, when one has been knocked out of one's balance . . to have some external job or duty to hang on to.

What Aldous was looking for, I think, was some way of breaking through, some way of getting out of himself. Harold Raymond's wife, Vera, who was running the library at Bart's Hospital, suggested that Aldous should take on distributing books in a man's ward. He set off quite eagerly (by underground to the City) but the job turned out to offer small opportunity for practising the human touch. It was too rushed. What was required was quickness of feet and some memory for faces, though an easy manner and a ready word would not have come amiss. You were supposed to load up a trolley with books to suit all tastes, as well as books requested by individual patients on your last visit. With these you entered the ward at the stroke of 2 p.m. You went from bed to bed proffering and suggesting while fishing in the lockers for books to be returned. You approached the alert and tried not to disturb those who appeared asleep or sunk in lethargy. On the other hand you must not leave out someone because he had dozed off for just a minute. Some were vague, a few were very definite about wanting a work on wild flowers or the Amazon river or mathematics. Most were slow. There was some demand for "serious" books and more for romances than thrillers. You had to memorize requests, there was no chance to write them down as you had to be out of the ward by tea-time. So after your first round you galloped your trolley back to the library, which was quite a distance, through the corridors and up a baggage lift, filled up with the requests and galloped back again to leave the right book on the right bed just before the nurses came in with the trays.

Aldous tried his best. Vera Raymond and Maria tried *their* best to extricate him without making him feel useless. At last Gerald told him that it was all right to give it up. Maria and I took over the job and to Bart's we went (we were given a ward each) every Monday afternoon for the remainder of that winter and a part of the next.

It was Gerald, also, who persuaded Aldous to give one of the Sunday evening lectures at Dartington Hall as the Elmhirsts had asked him to do. He went down one weekend with Gerald and Maria. It was during term and they partly went to see Matthew. Now, on principle the school allowed a boy to work when and at what he chose. Matthew for the moment chose to concentrate on carpentry and the like (he did become an inspired *bricoleur*); Aldous was displeased and worried, probably thinking far too much ahead, coming out heavily on the side of family tradition. He spoke to Matthew, a rather delicate schoolboy as Aldous once had been, and Matthew who thought he had been doing all right (his headmaster thought he had) was upset. Aldous's visit, and the lecture which the school attended, was all a bit of an ordeal for him.

Aldous's subject broadly was the new idolatries. Science, he said, had produced a mental climate antipathetic to the religions of the old tradition. Meanwhile the impulses which make men religious still persist.

> . . Men still desire to be ascetic, still feel the urge to give to something greater than themselves . . they still hunger for certainty . . . the emotional substitutes for religion still persist but the intellectual premise in which the emotions could express themselves has been taken away. Those who in the past have worshipped supernatural beings now find it impossible to believe in their existence . . . and set up natural beings who are worshipped instead . . .
>
> . . They sing Te Deums at Mussolini's birthplace so that the living dictator is in competition with the old saints . . .
>
> Our problem therefore is to find a new religion that is better than the old in that it accepts science, and better than the new substitute. We want to live in a world that makes some sort of sense, we want to find some intellectual basis for our efforts, we want to know where we stand in relation to the universe at large.

Daily life was by no means all sackcloth and ashes. As usual in London, Aldous and Maria were surrounded by friends. Their most intimate at that period besides Gerald were the Hutchinsons, St John and Mary, and the McKnight Kauffers, Ted and his American wife Marion Dorn. They also saw a great deal of Naomi Royde Smith who lived in what Maria called the *quartier*, and of course of Raymond and Eddy. There was usually someone for luncheon or tea, Moura Budberg quite often, Clive Bell, Bertie Russell, Tom Eliot, Naomi Mitchison, Vera Raymond, Madge Garland, May Voss. Hugh Mills, the playwright, then a very young man in advertising, called with his wife Christina, leaving a typescript, asking advice. The Huxleys went out less because of Aldous's health, though they dined at the Hutchinsons and the Kauffers, went to some of Sibyl Colefax's luncheons and to Ottoline's tea in Gower Street, saw Helen Anrep and the Kenneth Clarks; now and then Aldous would take one of his man friends to lunch at the Athenaeum. In Albany all meals but tea were eaten in the kitchen, Maria serving from stove to table which was quite a new thing then. (Some people, Aldous's cousin Jill told me, said that it was "beneath their dignity".) Once the Bernard Shaws came to luncheon and Mrs Shaw was put out by G. B. S. having to negotiate those stairs.

Maria was in one of her anti-food phases, anti-eating, anti-cooking, anti-cooking smells. She was very worried about Aldous without letting on and lived mainly on black coffee (still sent by faithful Roy, and unimaginably good even though Maria brewed it in a milk jug). What she produced for Aldous and her guests was simple and delicious—eggs poached in cream in those small china dishes, fresh vegetables, the good kinds of tinned soup, once in a while a chicken done in a cocotte (no roasting smell), smoked salmon, avocado pears. Good bread, good butter. Nor was it as extravagant as it may sound. There was a shop in Soho where you could get decent smoked salmon for four shillings a quarter of a pound (I used to be sent out for it when people stayed for supper). Maria *did* say, as she is quoted, "Such a saving to live in Albany—so convenient for Fortnum's." It's a bit misleading. She did use Fortnum & Mason's, but only for their wine (sherry, a little champagne, non-vintage, and some very modest claret; the wine department happened to be one of the most reasonable in London so was in fact a saving) and for the soups, the butter and the avocados, still exotic then, which the Huxleys had taken to in Guatemala. Her serious shopping Maria did in Soho street markets, wrapped in the blue Italian officer's cloak, made in Florence so many years ago, which she had not ceased to wear.

Although Maria never really got to like London she had the knack of making the best of things. When we remarked upon her stepping out into Piccadilly in slippers and dressing-gown to put a letter in the pillar box, she'd say, "but I'm in my *quartier*—c'est mon quartier".

One thing, I am sure, that was not right for Aldous was the room he worked in. That front sitting-room was a goldfish bowl. Not only was there the mildly distracting spectacle of the Albanites strolling up and down the covered walk, carnation in buttonhole, raising their bowler hats, but Aldous too, at his typewriter, was a sight revealed. (The typewriter by the way was tolerated; just. It was not so much the noise as the association with trade—might you not be writing business letters? The line was drawn at mine; Maria personally went to see Captain Adams. What did you tell him? we asked when she returned successful. "I gave him my word that you would only use it to write poetry.")

Yet, I repeat, all was not sack-cloth and ashes. Man, as Aldous never ceased to point out, is a multiple amphibian. Concerned about his relation to the universe at one moment, with other occupations and desires at the next. The Handleys were in England, on some disastrous lecture tour, turning up at the wrong hall on the wrong night, leaving their slides in taxi-cabs. As well as being amused by Sally, Aldous had mild designs "You'd better take her out to dinner, darling" said Maria. Their life in this respect was much as Aldous described it in *Point Counter Point*. The cure by affairs . . . Maria thought that he enjoyed such distractions, needed the change and his mind taken off his work. They amounted to very little, the distractions, and were either short or intermittent over the years. Aldous was never in the least involved. The women concerned were always very attractive in one way or another, some were beauties. Aldous had no fixations as to type or age. It might be a fluffy blonde just as soon as someone middle-aged and amusing. What Aldous offered, apart from the essential thing that he *liked* making love *and* made no bones about it, was friendliness, good humour, a measure of affection. What he did not offer was courtship. He would have grudged the *time*. Aldous seriously pursued only two women in his life—Maria and Nancy. So it was dinner and bed, or nothing. (It was rarely nothing: Aldous was seldom rebuffed; in that respect also the Nancy experience stood apart.) The logistics were largely Maria's. "You can't leave it to Aldous," she would say, "he'd make a muddle." She did it with tact, unbreachable good manners and a smile (ironic). She sent the flowers. Not actual flowers, that wouldn't have been Aldous's style, she saw to it that he sent a book. This he might inscribe with an elegantly turned allusive stanza of his own composition (in French: he still enjoyed *d'être un peu scabreux*). Maria did up the parcel. She did more than that. In a very subtle way she prepared the ground, created opportunities, an atmosphere, stood in, as it were, for the courtship.

Why did she do it? Well first of all, as she has said, for Aldous. For his work. It was also part of her generosity, and her sense of realism. "Surely, he'd get tired of only *me*?" Besides what did it matter? She really did not mind, Maria took what I should call the aristocratic view of sex. And she knew that she was wise—it never got out of hand. She did see to *that*. Not that it was necessary. And Aldous? Men have asked me: "Allowing one's wife to help one getting a girl—isn't that terribly undermining for a man?" They were shocked. Well Aldous did not feel in the least diminished, he never seemed to feel the need to assert his manhood. The situation would be unthinkable in many marriages; to understand it one has to look at it in the light of Aldous's and Maria's. It was a measure of how certain they were, and how free, and of the great niceness that there was between them. There was some brother and sister element in their relation: they could share each other's escapades. And this kept things in light perspective, protected Aldous from involvement. One might call it eating one's cake and having it. And why not? Maria would have said; it wasn't as much as all that, why grudge it to Aldous? And no one was ever hurt.

The women? One or two of them would have been glad enough to grab Aldous for good, but everyone understood soon enough that there was nothing doing. There was some resentment; on the whole the atmosphere of good humour and urbanity became contagious. Most of them were friends, devoted also to Maria. There was never any seduction of the innocent, anyone concerned was far too seductive to have remained single.

To return to Sally Handley. Here there must have been some initial misjudgement. Hers was not the aristocratic view. For once Aldous *was* rebuffed. She was deeply shocked. He took it with the best of grace, and so did she (remaining disconcerted). Aldous had stepped off a pedestal. What puzzled her most, she told me, was the delicacy of his approach—she could have dealt more easily with a straight pass. "You would have thought," she said, "he was a *Chinaman!*" I repeated this to Aldous (irresistible). The wretch went off to the British Museum to get a picture post card of some grinning mandarin which he sent to Sally, signed, "From your devoted Chinaman, A. H."

I should like to give a different glimpse of Aldous at that time. The Hutchinson's daughter Barbara had recently got married to Victor [Lord] Rothschild and Aldous often went to stay with them at Cambridge. Here Sir Isaiah Berlin first met him.

I expected to be overawed and perhaps sharply snubbed. But he was courteous and very kind to everyone present. The company played intellectual games . . Huxley plainly adored such exercises, but remained uncompetitive, benevolent, and remote. When the games were over at last, he talked, without altering his low, monotonous tone, about persons and ideas, describing them as if viewed from a great distance . . . He spoke with serenity and disarming sincerity, very simply. There was no malice and very little conscious irony . . only the mildest and gentlest mockery of the most innocent kind. He enjoyed describing prophets and mystagogues—but even such figures as Count Kayserling, Ouspensky and Gourdjief, whom he did not much like, were given their due and indeed more than their due; even Middleton Murry was treated more mercifully and seriously than in the portrait in *Point Counter Point*. Huxley talked very well: he needed an attentive audience and silence, but he was not self-absorbed or domineering, and presently everyone in the room would fall under his peaceful spell; brightness and glitter went out of the air, everyone became calm, serious, interested and contented.[1]

[1] *Mem. Vol.*

In March Chatto's and Aldous made their fifth agreement. The terms were the same as in the last, £1,250 a year etc., with one significant revision—three books in three years (one remembers the original six), works of fiction *or* non-fiction. For the first time since 1923 Aldous had no contractual obligation to produce a novel. The Raymonds' kindness and affectionate concern were a great help to Aldous and Maria (it went well beyond, and was different in kind, from a publisher's looking after an—in the long run—extremely profitable author). And it was never Chatto's who suggested suspending payments, it was Aldous who refused money during difficult times. This was necessary for his peace of mind; there were two unshakeable Huxley tenets: one educated one's children and one did not get into debt.

By the spring, without any attributable cause or treatment, Aldous was sleeping better; sleeping normally, Maria thought. He felt ready for getting back into the novel with a will. An acceptable sub-tenant was found for Albany, and in April full of hope they left for Sanary.

Chapter Two

"L'Année Horrible"

MARIA wrote to Roy from France on 4th May, ". . you don't seem to have received . . my gloomy account of that winter, as grey as it was gloomy. But I shall not go back to that because now we are in the summer, in a bright country . . . Aldous . . is cured definitely cured, it seems since about a month. Work goes well and everything goes well.

Work goes madly as a matter of fact. He is finishing a novel already born when we were out to you so you see what it means: the strain was terrific. I am typing it out; some of it already, and that is always a sign that it nears completion. Apart from that we lead a peasant's life . . .

We have been reading chiefly easy or more difficult scientific books of interest to Aldous and which I read with great gusto . . .

I have done a lot of 'good-housekeeping' lately, I say with rather a sigh, for I do not like it and prefer weeding the garden, or mending fuses. We have had such an abundance of cherries that not with the help of all the friends and servants and neighbours have we been able to eat them, so they have been . . . made into jams . . This is all the harder work because my cook cannot read . . . so that I am often left with the boiling syrup literally in my hands. Last night we sat in the kitchen, I on a stool above the gas-range turning a lovely bubbling red juice in a copper saucepan reading aloud to Aldous who was sitting far below, a book on the history of philosophy . . . and the jam was not burnt.

. . But what is more comic still is that Aldous has decided to take violent exercise for the sake of his health and that that exercise is the most concisely found in the form of gardening. So he digs every spare inch of the ground and causes havoc all round him to the despair of the gardener . . . My despair is compensated by the fact that I believe it to be good for him . . . What a pity we cannot replace all that with some good riding in the cafetales.

. . We are going to South America in 1936, as surely as anything is sure . . .

I hope you will ask my boy one day to stay with you. He would adore it . . . But I wonder [if] with those wretched studies . . . he will ever have time to learn a bit about life.

Things were not quite as serene as Maria protested. Aldous's insomnia was at bay rather than cured, a matter of palliatives, of good weeks and bad. He was getting ahead—so many episodes to round off—the book was getting *long*. "I've been so busy with my bloody book that I've hardly painted at all." To Julian he wrote on 17th May,

> . . I have been dithering along with various downs as well as ups. At the moment, thank heaven, have an up in progress and am sleeping quite well with the aid of a wholly non-toxic mixture of calcium and magnesium, which, for some extraordinary reason, acts as a nervous sedative and mild hypnotic . . it's called *Calsédine* (made in France), does no harm, produces (so my doctor swears) no habituation, and leaves one perfectly fresh and cheerful in the morning. With its aid I do a fair amount of work—and about time too, as I have earned very little for a long time past. Have also taken to digging in the garden . . .
>
> . . I hope to get my book done by the end of the summer, if this beastly insomnia gives me the chance. It has been cold here and rainy, but pleasant . . . Mme de Béhague and the Noailles have gone—a relief, au fond: for, tho' nice, they have the rich persons' inability to conceive that other people have anything to do than eat lunches and teas in their houses.

The B.B.C., the previous autumn, had broadcast a series of talks on "The Causes of War", which, printed weekly in *The Listener*, attracted a good deal of attention and response. The speakers were Winston Churchill, Austen Chamberlain, Lord Beaverbrook, J. B. S. Haldane, W. R. Inge, then Dean of St Paul's, G. D. H. Cole, Aldous and some others, and most of them tried to come to grips with the acute question What Are We Going To Do About It NOW? Beaverbrook urged Isolationalism, Churchill said that Britain must be prepared to submit to Germany or resist, Professor Haldane proposed a League of Nations' curb on armament manufacture[1]; Aldous talked about the psychological phenomenon of war. Why do men and women make and accept war? "The causation of historical events is multiple . . .

And yet strictly speaking all the causes of war are psychological . . . Wars are not *fought* by climates or political or economic systems, they are fought by human beings . . . the question of psychology inevitably arises. . . .

[1] H. J. Stenning's introduction to the published edition of these talks, *The Causes of War*, The Telegraph Press, New York, Dec. 1935.

Now Aldous had already developed this theme in *Beyond the Mexique Bay* in 1933. What he had said then, in a sixty-thousand words digression on war,[1] was that the fundamental problem of international politics was psychological, and economic problems secondary. "Our so-called wars of interest are really wars of passion —'*La guerre naît des passions*'.

> Interests are always ready to compound, passions never. You can always discuss figures . . ask a hundred and accept eighty-five. But you cannot discuss hatred, nor haggle over . . vanities and prejudices . . .[2]

Aldous cited Alain, the French philosopher, of whom it is reported that when in the trenches, his fellow soldiers complained of the miseries of war, he would answer: "*Mais vous avez eu assez de plaisir; vous avez crié Vive l'Armée ou Vive l'Alsace-Lorraine. Il faut que cela se paye. Il faut mourir.*" And who is it, Aldous asked, who enjoys these passions, the people as a whole or only the rulers? *Both* he believed to be the correct answer.

> It is the rulers of course who declare war . . . But rulers cannot carry on a war unless the ruled are moved by the same passions . . . the mass of people must . . imagine that they want the war; that the war is in their interest or at least unavoidable . . .[3]

The ruled are sometimes actually more war-like than their rulers, who find themselves reluctantly propelled towards a war which they would like to avoid.

> At other times, the ruled are less the slaves of national passion and prejudice than the rulers. Thus, I think it would be true to say that, at present, the majority of French and English people are more pacific, less dangerously obsessed by the Moloch-theology of nationalism, readier to think of international politics in terms of reason, than their governments . . . When the French populace was imbued with nationalism the bourgeoisie was pacific. Now that it thinks of freedom, in terms not of nations, but classes, the rulers are nationalistic.[3]

Fortunately, periods of intense general excitement never last very long.

> The social organism does not seem to be able to tolerate more than about twenty years of abnormal agitation. Thus, the thrilling, heroic

---

[1] Published also separately in *Life and Letters*, April 1934, under the title "War and the Emotions".
[2] *Beyond the Mexique Bay*. Chatto & Windus, 1934.
[3] Ibid.

period of the religious revival, set going by St Francis of Assisi, was over in less than a quarter of a century. The great animal that was Europe could not stand the strain of sitting up on its hind legs and performing primitive-Christian tricks. Within a generation it had settled down once more to a comfortable doze. Every violently exciting religious or political movement of history has run much the same course. It will be interesting to see whether the revivalist enthusiasm worked up by Communists, Nazis and Fascists will last longer than the similar mass emotion aroused by the first Franciscans . . . St Francis had no printing press, no radio . . . Nevertheless, it may be doubted whether [Hitler, Stalin and Mussolini] . . will really do better. . . .[1]

Yet while they last, *Il faut que cela se paye.*

What Aldous proposed, in 1933, was the calling of an official World Psychological Conference with a view of finding means to secure international peace. If the delegates agreed on—"what, alas, is sadly improbable"—their governments' need to discourage manifestations of collective vanity and hatred, they would be faced with a great many problems. How to prohibit activities that give great satisfaction? What sort of emotional compensation must be devised? How much excitement do people need to keep them contented and in health?

. . . There is a possibility . . that dislike and fear of Hitlerian Germany may result in a movement towards the unification, or at least the rational co-operation, of the other nation states . . .

In his talk on the B.B.C. (recorded, it would seem, sometime in 1934) Aldous's argument was on similar lines. "War is a catastrophe . . . And yet for every hundred people who kill themselves in peace-time, only seventy kill themselves in war-time.[2]

. . Man is a profoundly social animal . . . nothing brings [men] together more effectively than a common dislike for someone else . . . War strengthens [this] sense of group consolidation to the pitch of intoxication . . . War produces a certain simplification of the social structure . . and men are on the whole happier in a simple than in a complicated society . . . War begets and justifies . . violence, delight in destruction . . all the anti-social tendencies we have been so carefully trained to repress . . . The Barbarian and the sadist are strong within us . . .[3]

[1] *Beyond the Mexique Bay.*
[2] This fall in the suicide rate was already observed during the Franco-Prussian war of 1870 and again, more markedly, during the 1914-1918 war.
[3] Text taken from *The Causes of War.* The Telegraph Press, New York, 1935.

And while the pleasures of hatred are certainly not greater than the pleasures of love . . . they are greater than the pleasures of abstract and impersonal benevolence.

> People can get more pleasure out of hating foreigners they have never seen than out of vaguely wishing them well . . . And governments foment nationalistic hatred and vanity. At school, children are taught to boast about their own nation . . . In dictatorial countries, this education . . . is continued by the State throughout adult life. In liberal countries, it is left to the voluntary labours of the Press . . .[1]

(Aldous did not love the Press and the Press did not love Aldous. The *Sunday Express*—under the editorship of James Douglas, he who said that he would rather give his child prussic acid than allow it to read *The Well of Loneliness*—once carried a two-page attack under the headline, Aldous Huxley—THE MAN WHO HATES GOD.)

Aldous's answer on the B.B.C. was no longer the World Conference but long-term research into the human mind. History had shown, he said, that madmen and neurotics have been responsible for an enormous amount of mischief; we run danger even in entrusting our destinies to men who may be suffering only from the milder forms of neurosis. Research then into the psychological causes of war was urgent, but we must not look for quick results. "Those who have explored the unconscious are pessimistic about the immediate prospects of abolishing war." Winding up, Aldous stuck to the temperate long-range view, refused to raise (false) hope, spoke of fifty years of intensive research. There was something very very discouraging about that talk, and about the analysis of the war-disease in *Beyond the Mexique Bay*.

> *The best lack all conviction while the worst*
> *Are full of passionate intensity. . . .*

There is one passage we must note, in view of what was to come. Some listeners, he said, "may feel surprised that I have not spoken of the need for . . religious and ethical preaching against war". Such preaching might be desirable and do a little good, but it was off the point because man was not entirely or even mainly a conscious being. "The psychological causes of war have root in the unconscious." And what was to happen in the interval, during those years of research into that unconscious?

> We must be content [he concluded] I suppose, to prescribe such political, economic and psychological sedatives as shall prevent the

[1] Text taken from *The Causes of War*. The Telegraph Press, New York, 1935.

patient from . . . committing suicide. If we can keep him alive long enough, the doctors may at last agree on the diagnosis and discover a cure.

The hungry sheep look up and are not fed. Aldous—inevitably perhaps —did not offer the listener anything he could feel or do. The paradox is that Aldous for his part at that stage was casting about for precisely that, for something to feel and do; he was holding the hero of his novel at a standstill for want of emotion and of action.

Meanwhile, on a day-to-day level, he would put in a small oar here and there. But the cool view still prevailed.

Old Henri Barbusse is trying to organize a mammoth congress in favour of peace [to Julian] . . His hobby is congresses . . . so he wants to have a really representative anti-war congress this time. His own left organization in France will of course be on tap . . . [he is also] going to try to get professional bodies—scientific, technical, legal . . This . . I very strongly urged him to go for . . if these congresses are any good at all they will only be good (because impressive) if they represent large numbers of respectable organizations. A peace demonstration would look serious if it were supported by the trade unions of doctors, engineers, lawyers . . and so forth in different countries . . . I am writing . . to ask you whether you think there'd be any hope of getting official representation from some important scientific body in England . .

Barbusse is "a dear old thing, indefatigable in verbiage and good works

. . droning interminably . . about the Social Consciousness and Russia —ignoring all facts and merely stating, again and again, what ought to be . . .

In June Aldous went to attend an international writers' congress in Paris. Among the ostensible sponsors were Gide, Priestley, Heinrich Mann. He came back indignant and disgusted.

I had hoped for serious, technical discussions . . [he put it to Victoria Ocampo]—but in fact the thing simply turned out to be a series of public meetings organized by the French Communist writers for their own glorification and the Russians as a piece of Soviet Propaganda. Amusing to observe, as a rather discreditable episode in the Comédie Humaine; but it made one angry when one thought of what might have been done and wasn't, when one saw the cynical indifference of the Communist organizers to the wretched little delegates from the Balkans etc., who had been hoping for some serious effort on the part of other writers to understand their problems, and who found only . . endless Communist demagogy in front of an audience of 2000 people. One finds on these occasions all the worst aspects of religion—the refusal of some to use their intelligence, because they need the consolation of faith; and the cynical ambition of others, who don't believe anything but are anxious to rise in the Communist hierarchy. And everywhere a complete indifference to truth and the common decencies of civilized existence.

In July Eugene Saxton with his wife came to stay; Drieu la Rochelle was in the neighbourhood, other guests proposed themselves. Sanary life kept on much as before, but when sleep and work went badly Aldous felt hemmed in—no talks with Gerald, no prospect of interesting news cures round the next street-corner, only *calsédine* to fall back on and the twice-dug garden.

> It was after two o'clock. Anthony lay on his back staring up into the darkness. Sleep, it seemed, deliberately refused to come, was being withheld by someone else, some malignant alien inhabiting his own body. Outside, in the pine trees the cicadas harped incessantly on the theme of their existence and at long intervals a sound of cock-crowing would swell up out of the darkness . . .[1]

He took against the place (this was hard on Maria); talked of selling the house. The money spent on running it; money spent on so much else: doctor's bills, Sophie's education, helping Jeanne through difficult years; helping friends—no one in trouble, and so many of us were, was turned down but given often before asking; money going to unknown refugees. And no money earned. At this point Aldous and Maria got into a state about Matthew's future —School Certificate—University Entrance . . . His Headmaster's view was that the boy was not doing badly at all, was overcoming the handicaps of an unsettled childhood and (oddly enough) too many languages (Matthew was tri-lingual as a child, having French —in which he had done his first lessons, English and Italian, with some German thrown in by his Fraülein Bella); it would be wise, they thought at Dartington, to give him and the school a chance. (Actually Matthew had been with them for only two years and a half, which was about one term more than Aldous had had when he was whisked away from Eton.) Aldous disagreed. So, quite strongly, did Maria. As a child she had been quick and clever at her lessons. And then, what with the convent and the governesses and the quickness, and her visual turn of mind—for example, she

---

[1] *Eyeless in Gaza.* Chatto & Windus, 1936.

could never get the words right in *Magic casements opening on the foam*—she *saw* sea and windows—she ended up with little education to speak of. She failed, we know, to get into Cambridge. Now history was *not* to repeat itself. If education was to Aldous what to most people is walking in the street *with* their clothes on, it was to Maria the personally unattainable ("he could never teach me to remember what I read in a book or spel") which one is jolly well going to make attainable to one's child. There was also this assumption: *Matthew is going to be a doctor.* (As Aldous had meant to.) This was never discussed; it was taken for granted.

Presently Aldous and Maria made a dash into Switzerland. They left in the Bugatti at 5 a.m. on a Saturday—500 kilometres in summer traffic—spent that afternoon and the whole of Sunday looking round Geneva and Lausanne, and were back by 9 p.m. on Monday night. The rush was an expression of their general state. They saw one school they liked very much, the Institut Rauch at Lausanne. Aldous informed Dartington that his son would not return next term. Dartington remonstrated and pointed out that the usual notice was required. There was correspondence. Aldous remained quite firm.

Matthew was not warned of the impending change. "Don't tell anyone, we don't want him to know," Maria wrote to Jeanne. Matthew left Dartington at the end of the summer term expecting to be back, not saying goodbye to his friends. His parents went to Geneva to meet him, another gruelling journey. The Bugatti started to boil—the radiator was ever its delicate point—and they had to limp home. Next morning at 6.30 they started again by train, twelve hours in a third-class carriage. They broke the news and introduced Matthew to the new school. He took it very well. On their return, fourteen hours, the train was packed and stank, they had to stand up in the corridor for half the way. Aldous went through his pockets but didn't have enough cash to change to second class.

Some weeks later Matthew came to Sanary for a long weekend, and they saw that he had adapted himself quickly. He seemed lively and was full of funny stories about the new place. "I am so relieved," Maria wrote to Jeanne. ". . What would we have done if he'd been unhappy or horrified?"

Maria's way now to keep things going was to live from day to day. When there was a good patch she made the most of it. At the heart of it all was still the novel; by then they rarely spoke about it to each other.

Ici les nouvelles sont bonnes [Maria wrote to Jeanne some time in September]. Aldous va bien et travaille assez bien. J'ai l'impression que ce roman se termine. Mais je n'en parle que très rarement. Il a

des raisons multiples pour ne me mettre qu'en face du "Roman"
accompli. Et je le comprends. Mais je m'en inquiète.

Toutefois nous sommes heureux, tranquilles et calmes.

And Aldous to Bob Nichols on 20th September:

Here I'm hard at work on a novel that won't get finished. Expect
to be in England in another month or so—unless of course we're
plunged into war by then. In which case we shall probably all be
dead. I wish I could see any remedy for the horrors of human beings
except religion or could see any religion that we could all believe in.

(That we should all be dead at once in case of war was pure Gerald
Heard—he was convinced that it would be incomparably more
ghastly than anything before.)

What was going on in Aldous's novel? What was going on in
Aldous's mind? We shall never be able to say. The perceptions,
pointers, flashes that shape a work of art or shape a man are
infinite and swift. All one can do is to attempt to trace some kind
of pattern. "The theme [of the novel], fundamentally, is liberty.
What happens to someone who becomes really very free . . . The
rather awful vacuum that such freedom turns out to be." For
Aldous the aloof observer, the *littérateur*, the so-called cynic, it was
in the day's work to write a novel about the vacuum, and leave it
at that. As he had done more or less in *Antic Hay*. For Aldous the
moralist, the man longing to make some sense of the world, the
man who had said at Oxford, "I think the good will win at the
end . . [if] the most persistent and tremendous efforts are made,"
for the Aldous who wanted to relieve the horrors besetting human
beings, it was not enough. The vacuum had to be filled. Deliberately
he renounced the winding up of the book in an artistically plausible
way, and looked instead for a *helpful*, one might say a didactic,
ending. Anthony Beavis would have to find something to feel and
do that "we can all believe in". That *I* can believe in. Because with
Anthony's predicament Aldous had built a model of his own.

I sometimes have the disquieting sense that I am being somehow
punished by so much good fortune [he had written earlier during
the crisis]—that it is a scheme to lead me deeper into my besetting
sin, the dread and avoidance of emotion, the escape from personal
responsibility, the substitution of aesthetic and intellectual values for
moral values—of art and thought for sanctity.

He was using the novel, using his *métier d'écrivain*, as a means of
getting through—finding a solution in the novel would be finding
a solution for his life. (At that point.) Maria was aware of this.

306

For a number of reasons Aldous wants to confront me with the finished novel, with the "fait accompli". Et je le comprends. Mais je m'en inquiète.

Aldous projected himself into Anthony Beavis. He was not Anthony Beavis though he made use of a great deal of autobiographical data. Aldous and Anthony shared a background, had been to the same schools, same places, read the same books; in fact they shared a mind. *La bêtise ne fut pas leur fort.* Both possessed intellectual freedom. Otherwise there were basic discrepancies. Anthony lacked the two essential factors in Aldous's life, Maria and that very *métier d'écrivain*; he has no central attachment, and he is a sociologist who is able to write fluently, one of those novelistic transpositions of profession which seldom really work, he was a sedentary intellectual and all the rest but with the talent left out; and whatever it may be worth, that talent, it makes the difference in kind (*and* carries its own compulsions and exemptions). In other respects too, Aldous was not free like Anthony who had no domestic duties and a comfortable private income; Aldous was indeed comparatively free, being able to go or live where he pleased; but it was, and well he knew it, a precarious freedom. Last not least, Aldous was simply a much nicer man, young man, boy, than Anthony. Nor had he driven his best friend to suicide. That story of the betrayal was based on one he heard; nothing like it or remotely like it occurred in Aldous's life. (Once more the exigencies of fiction, the need to coarsen and to dramatize the fable.) There *are* other, marked autobiographical undertones. Brian Foxe, the young man who killed himself, was an admitted portrait of Aldous's brother Trev; Anthony's emotional paralysis dates from his mother's early death. Perhaps it had best be left by saying that Anthony Beavis was a much distorted portrait of Aldous by Aldous. "The school now," as Gervas Huxley said, "there is quite a bit of Hillside in *Eyeless in Gaza*, Bullstrode is straight Hillside—but no straight Aldous, oh no, no!"

Now in this context—to set the record straight—Mr Beavis, Anthony's father, was not straight Leonard Huxley, in fact was hardly Leonard Huxley at all. Aldous had not intended Mr Beavis to be like his own father.

the character came from an autobiographical poem by Coventry Patmore, called "Tired Memory". [He wrote to his step-mother in November 1936] . . the element of philology . . was based upon descriptions given by Frieda Lawrence of her first husband . . . the character yet has a strong resemblance to the parson in D. H. Lawrence's *Virgin and the Gypsy*, a figure who was actually derived from the same source. After that it became necessary to fix the personage in time, as the inhabitant of a certain epoch. And here, I am afraid quite unjustifiably, I made use of mannerisms and phrases some of which were recognizably father's. I had not thought that they would prove recognizable to others and I am most distressed to find that they should have been.

Later Rosalind Huxley had a talk with Aldous on the subject. She spoke to him "about the excessive way he used traits of his father, and still more of Trev, then adding characteristics which were totally *alien*. To me he said how profoundly sorry he was ... He made the same mistakes about other people, seeming curiously unaware that these things hurt people ... but he was genuinely distressed and upset when they were mentioned. Yet he was the kindest and most considerate of people. I had a very great affection for him."[1]

Meanwhile it is still Sanary, September 1935. What is happening to Anthony as he lies sleepless in the Mediterranean night, listening to the cicadas who have ceased to charm? We do not know. Maria did not see the recent chapters (nor did anyone else). My guess, for what it's worth, is that Aldous had some intimation of where Anthony was going, but still could not see how to bring it off in terms of fiction—on that road to Damascus, whom was he to meet? The substance of this was getting ready to be tapped (had been tapped at other stages of Aldous's life—in *Antic Hay*, in *Those Barren Leaves*, that night in Spain). It was now, in this summer, that Aldous began to practice—with some difficulty—a kind of non-metaphysical meditation; what had started, at Gerald's instigation, as exercises in breathing and in mind control had led to this. It was his writing, however, which served him as the main discipline towards the break-through; at the same time, his writing, that is his circumstances and responsibilities, compelled him, unfortunately perhaps, to tap this thing in public and at once, when he was still not certain how to do it. Aldous had already gone a good way —on his own and with Gerald Heard, absorbing, using, at that point what Gerald had to offer—towards a "religious" solution. Now how to translate this into action? Aldous was yet to meet F. M. Alexander, Dr McDonagh and Dick Sheppard.

The Rev. H. R. L. Sheppard, Vicar of St Martin's-in-the-Field, Dean of Canterbury, Canon of St Paul's, a man overflowing with the love of his fellows, reckless in the expenditure of himself, orator, organizer, legend in his own life-time, a man who could make contact with every human being he met, the best known and most

1 Rosalind (Mrs Leonard Huxley), in a letter to S. B., February 1970.

loved priest in England whom when he died—early, suddenly, at his desk in 1937—the country mourned:

> his coffin was followed from St Martin's . . . through the streets of London to St Paul's by a great concourse of every kind and class of men and women . . . the streets were lined as though for royalty . . .[1]

this man who "had built his whole life on the concept 'love one another' ", who had been in the trenches in the first war and appalled by the suffering inflicted by man upon man, became convinced that Christianity was incompatible with war, and decided to make one great stand. In October 1934 he sent a letter to the Press.

> The main reason for this letter . . is the fresh urgency of the present international situation, and the almost universally acknowledged lunacy of the manner in which nations are pursuing peace.
>
> The situation is far graver than we allow ourselves to acknowledge . . .
>
> I represent no Church and no peace organization of any description . . .
>
> It seems essential to discover whether or not it be true . . that the majority of thoughtful men in this country are now convinced that war of every kind or for any cause, is not only a denial of Christianity, but a crime against humanity, which is no longer to be permitted by civilized people.
>
> Have we reached that state of belief?
>
> . . The idea behind this letter is not to form any fresh organization . . but to attempt to discover how strong the will to peace has grown.
>
> . . Would those of my sex who, so far, have been silent, but . . are willing to support a resolution as uncompromising as the following, send a postcard to me within the next fortnight:
>
> *We renounce war and never again, directly or indirectly, will we support or sanction another.*

Not a single postcard came for two days. On the third—the post office had had to organize delivery—van-loads of sacks, sacks crammed with postcards, postcards cascading over the floor. Over a hundred thousand. "The first thing was to get in touch with all those unknown people who had committed themselves . . .

> Thus it came about that an invitation to meet in the Albert Hall went out to every signatory . . . [in June 1935] Dick Sheppard was anxiously waiting in a room behind the platform . . wondering what was going to happen . . .

[1] Sybil Morrison, *I Renounce War: The Story of the Peace Pledge Union.* Sheppard Press Ltd., 1962.

Presently they began to arrive, old and young men, but mostly young, in the end they were packed so tightly that there was no more room. The sight of that vast gathering of men . . keyed Dick Sheppard to his best . . he caught, held and deeply involved everyone in the great hall that Sunday. With him on the platform were Edmund Blunden, Siegfried Sassoon, [the Rev.] Maude Royden and Frank [Brig.-General] Crozier. There were to be other Albert Hall meetings, but never again one like this.[1]

That was the beginning of what was first called H. R. L. Sheppard's Peace Movement and later The Peace Pledge Union. (The pledge was later altered to a simpler form; the P.P.U. exists today.) Local groups were formed; Dick Sheppard got a number of people to act as sponsors. (The first of these were, besides those already mentioned, Storm Jameson, Ellen Wilkinson, Donald Soper, Laurence Housman, Eric Gill, Vera Brittain, John Middleton Murry, George Lansbury, Arthur Ponsonby.) Postcards still came in at the rate of 200 a day.

The Huxleys went back to Albany in October. At once Aldous had to cope with a three weeks of dentist appointments; then they went over to Belgium for the marriage of Maria's little sister, which "from a quiet affair [M to Roy] became suddenly a ceremony with show and friends and therefore us". (Rose, a ravishing young creature, perhaps the most wayward and ebullient of the sisters, was marrying the poet Eric de Haulleville.) And after that Aldous and Maria settled down "to live in London like hermits . . until the novel, which is going well, is finished.

You can probably picture my life, a constant refusal at the telephone to see our best friends who think they have a right to see us and who instantly think it is me who will not allow Aldous to go to them.

They did see Gerald, who in the meantime had become interested in Dick Sheppard's Movement. And it was he who brought in Aldous. Dick Sheppard recommended absolutes; absolutes, in Dennis Gabor's words, "so simple that a child could grasp them but only an angel could follow them". Aldous's great forte was complexity, he had been wandering for so long in his contrapuntal maze, that at this moment there was something irresistible in that difficult, angelic, simplicity. He went for it as one might for a

---

[1] Sybil Morrison.

draught of spring water after a line of vintages. On 19th November he wrote those crucial words to Victoria Ocampo.

. . The thing finally resolves itself into a religious problem—an uncomfortable fact which one must be prepared to face and which I have come during the last year to find it easier to face.

"Meanwhile what an appalling situation we've all got ourselves into! Musso attacking Abyssinia: we using sanctions and so forcing the Italians to rally round Musso: the dictator's *amour propre* so . . inflamed . . that he can't admit any kind of defeat or make any compromise; and if he is forced into a corner he will act like Samson and pull the whole building down on his head—if he has to go, then let the whole of Europe go too!—It's the sort of behaviour one saw going on at one's preparatory school—and the whole world is threatened by it.

the only hope lies in the pacifists being better disciplined than the militarists and prepared to put up with as great hardships and dangers with a courage equal to theirs. Not easy. But I suppose nothing of any value is easy.

At the second big Albert Hall meeting on 27th November, Aldous *was* on the platform. He, like Gerald Heard, had become a sponsor of the Movement. On 3rd December Aldous gave the talk at the lunch hour meetings for Peace and Internationalism held weekly at Friends' House in the Euston Road.

. . Our end is peace. How do we propose to realize this end? . . If we want to be treated with trust and affection by others we must ourselves treat those others with trust and affection . . . We largely construct the ethical world in which we live. It is to a great extent a matter of choice whether we construct it as a world of fear and greed or as a world of trust and love . . . there is nothing inherently absurd about the idea that the world which we have so largely constructed can also, if we so desire, be reconstructed on other and better lines.
. . No end can be realized without appropriate means . . . No pacifist can permit himself to think in abstractions . . . war is a process of large-scale murder . . . hostile nations consist of individual men and women . . .

He went on to say—and *this was* the great turning point in Aldous's thinking—that the most propitious metaphysical environment for pacifism could not be humanism but a philosophy which recognized the existence of more than human spiritual realities. "Not, indeed

a belief in any exclusive deity attached to any particular community or place—such a belief inevitably makes for war—but in
a spiritual reality to which all men have access and in which they
are united:

> God .. regarded, and if possible experienced as a psychological
> fact, present at least potentially in every human being.

And Aldous ended this talk, "If enough people address themselves to living up to this belief, if enough people set out to experience
[this] spiritual reality .. then there will be peace; for peace .. is a
by-product of a certain way of life."

It is not certain who led Aldous to F. M. Alexander (Gerald?
Bernard Shaw?) Anyway to Alexander he went in that same
November and became his pupil. F. Matthias Alexander (1869-
1955) of Australia, ex-actor, therapist, discoverer and teacher of
the Alexander technique, author (*The Use of the Self, Creative
Conscious Control, The Universal Constant of Living*, etc., etc.), who
taught for some fifty years in England and the United States, of
whom Leonard Woolf has said that he was a quack but an honest
and inspired quack. G. B. S. and John Dewey had been his pupils.
Now Aldous went, every day, applying himself to the difficult task
of "kinesthetic" re-education, of learning how to walk, sit down,
reach for a book, open a door, in a new, but only very subtly
different, way. (As Shaw put it, "Alexander calls upon the world
to see a change so small and so subtle that only he can see it".[1]
Aldous became convinced that Alexander had made a very important, in fact an essential discovery.

> [He] discovered empirically [as Aldous put it in a nutshell 15 years
> later on in a letter to Dr Hubert Benoit] in experimentation on
> himself, that there is a correct or 'natural' relationship between the
> neck and the trunk and that normal functioning of the total organism
> cannot take place except when the neck and trunk are in the right
> relationship. His findings have been confirmed theoretically by
> various physiologists and, in practice, in the persons of the numerous
> pupils he has taught . . . for some obscure reason the great majority
> of those who have come in contact with urbanized, industrial
> civilization tend to lose the innate capacity for preserving the correct
> relation between neck and trunk, and consequently never enjoy
> completely normal organic functioning. Alexander and the teachers

[1] As quoted in *The Resurrection of the Body. The Writings of F. Matthias
Alexander*, edited by Edward Maisel. University Books, New York, 1969.

he has trained re-establish the correct relationship and teach their pupils to preserve it consciously. This, as I know by experience, is an exceedingly valuable technique. For not only does one have to become aware of the data of organic reality (to the exclusion of the insane life of phantasy); one also . . makes it possible for the physical organism to function as it ought to function, thus improving the general state of physical and mental health. (Incidentally, the "straight-spine" position so much insisted upon by the teachers of yoga is precisely the posture advocated by Alexander. The merit of A. consists in having analysed the essential factors in this posture and having developed a technique for teaching . . [it] . . .)

It was not at all easy to learn. Aldous—very willing, very patient —proved rather good at it. There he was practising away in Albany, how to place one's feet, how to get out of a chair. It became notice-able that he was holding himself differently—his movements looked deliberate and slow. Maria also went to Alexander, and they couldn't wait for Matthew to have a go at it. (He still dismisses it as "a rather expensive way to make a boy stand up straight". Alexander did not exactly run a charity institution.) Aldous even-tually got the hang of it, re-conditioned his habits as he would have put it—in the fluid, unnoticeable way it was supposed to be; and he kept it up for the rest of his life.

Meanwhile Alexander sent him to Dr McDonagh. J. E. R. McDonagh, "that odd fish," who had a theory that many or most disorders were caused by intoxication of the intestines. "No wonder you are a sceptic if you poison yourself with butcher's meat." Aldous (and in due course Maria and the children) submitted to his treatment by colonic lavages, vaccine injections and diet. Aldous's life became exceedingly active. Committee meetings with Dick Sheppard, discussions with Gerald as to ways and means, planning a pamphlet for the Peace Movement, writing letters to the Press. In the morning he sat in his goldfish-bowl working away with a will. This was the time when the missing chapters, the clinching chapters, at last, at last, were flowing—the encounter in Mexico with Miller and Anthony's post-"conversion" diary, broken up into seventeen chapters (quantitatively about one-seventh of that very long book) and inserted here and there like the clues in a treasure hunt; a labour which must have given Aldous a certain satisfaction. (Originally he meant to finish with fewer and shorter diary chapters; it was Maria who after much hesitation, urged him to extend Anthony's *journal intime*. And it is rather interesting to read this journal straight.)

Aldous and Maria did no longer live like hermits in London, but they stuck to early evenings and tried to see only people relevant to his present concerns. They also tried to live economically (Aldous having published no novel for four years and no book at all for twenty months). Maria never looked at a taxi and often walked instead of taking the bus. They became more social for a few weeks when Dr Charlotte Wolff came over from Paris, at their suggestion, to collect prints of some interesting hands. Dr Wolff stayed in Dalmeny Court across the road, and the Huxleys put themselves out in the way of introductions. In the early afternoon when Aldous had gone off to Alexander, Maria would open the door to T. S. Eliot or Virginia Woolf or Lady Ottoline, and then go out herself. Presently one could perceive the doctor by the tall window poring through a magnifying glass into a distinguished hand in the waning London winter light. (Albany became censorious but was also somewhat intrigued.) As well as taking prints, the doctor did a kind of—very remarkable—psychological reading. Soon there were queues. She was bidden to Mrs Simpson's.[1] Aldous introduced her to Julian under whom she later made her studies of the monkeys' hands at the Zoo. (All this led not only to an interesting collection of records but to Dr Wolff's decision to base her future work in England.)

News of Matthew was good. (He did not come home that Christmas holiday.) The sudden change of school had done him no harm and he had got through an immense amount of work. "Aussi un rapport excéllent sur le caractère," (Maria to Jeanne). "Heureusement qu'il ne perd pas cela en grandissant." As a young boy Matthew had been remarkable for his openness and niceness; now, rising sixteen, it became evident that he was not going to lose his warmth and generosity of nature, nor his marvellous talent for spontaneous contact. The "nice" boy ultimately became an even nicer man.

No New Year's Eve party—but in January Maria was able to write to Jeanne, "The book is approaching its end. Aldous's health is good without being brilliant; but he is working enormously and he is calm and quiet.

> J'espère que cette année sera aussi différente de la dernière que possible. Je crois que personne ne peut se rendre compte de ce que toute l'année dernière a eu d'horrible . . .

The further I get away from it, the more I realize how horrible it has been. . . ."

[1] The present Duchess of Windsor.

314

Chapter Three

Eyeless in Gaza: The Nobler Hypothesis

Dear Gene,

. . Aldous really thinks he is going to answer your letter but I know better . . .

We believe that certainly the manuscript will go to Chatto's in the first week of March.

No the old enemy insomnia is checked and by the man Alexander but more of that later as I am trying to answer your letter point by point as an efficient secretary should, I believe, do.

Aldous does not wish to see the proof.

Alexander . . . certainly has made a new and unrecognizable person of Aldous, not physically only but mentally and therefore morally. Or rather, he has brought out, actively, all we, Aldous's best friends, know never came out either in the novels or with strangers . . . Probably you will think we have gone cracky, so did I think of Aldous until I saw the results and particularly since I went myself. It comes in the novel too. Oh, how I hate that novel. Except that now that it is finished I really don't care any more; but I did hate it. Not meaning that it is not very good; when I say I hate it it is for very different and personal reasons. The misery it has caused us and so on.

E2 Albany W.1
21 February 1936

So Maria to Aldous's American publishers. But meanwhile Aldous had engaged himself to do a pamphlet for the Peace Movement (Chatto's were to publish it, price 3d., royalties to the P.P.U.). The idea was to get it out quickly so he wrote it when he was still in the final stages of the novel. (The material was of course related.) The pamphlet was finished by 21st March, and a week later the last batch of typescript of the novel went to Chatto's. Maria wrote at once to Jeanne.

Chère Janin,

Here is our latest news. The book is finished. Aldous is going away with Victor for three days while I'm getting ready for the children. Je commence à m'en réjouir follement . . .

With what relief Maria was returning to the sweet ordinariness of life. The Hutchinsons are coming to tea, en famille, because it

is their son Jeremy's twenty-first birthday . . . She is thinking of
going to Kew with Gerald—yesterday was so very fine—and taking
a picnic lunch . . . Tomorrow morning at ten Aldous will be off
with Victor Rothschild "to visit centres of industry and low homosexuality at Nottingham". Now plans for the Easter holidays. Such
an irresistible letter from Matthew yesterday. (I am translating
and compressing freely.) He's asked a friend to stay, thinking we'd
be in Sanary. May he bring him to London? What can I do? We
can't say no—the first time he's asked us. I don't think we should
ever say no. What about sending the two boys to Dalmeny Court—
Sophie can have the sitting-room sofa—they have rooms for five
shillings a night—*bain compris*—they might have their breakfast at
a Lyons, and afterwards come here where all will be right and
tight, and we can start the day. Matthew wants to show London
to his friend. I shall lose a certain intimacy with him, which we
renew at every holiday; but this is bound to happen one day, so
I'm resigned.

There's the expense . . . But I'm going to give up the idea of
hiring a car . . . It may all turn out cheaper in the end . . . Donc
je ne suis plus épouvantée. And Bessie (Bessie Simpkins who did
the housework) speaks such pretty English, because she's Irish, that
will be so nice for Sophie's accent. Adieu Janin et merci de me
prêter ta fille . . .

It all went very well (in spite of doctor's visits). Gerald had gone
to Greece, such a pity for Matthew, but Gerald needed a holiday
. . . They went to see a Chaplin and a film by H. G. Wells, and
spent Easter Monday Bank Holiday on Hampstead Heath. Sunday
they had Matthew's Dartington friend, Ivan Moffat, for lunch after
which they went to the Zoo, followed by tea at Juliette's. At the
Zoo, Aldous recited to the animals and teased the baboons with
his umbrella. It was a gusty day and he was wearing his floppy
overcoat and did look rather like a person out of Edward Lear. A
string of sneering capering little boys attached themselves to his
back, following him from cage to cage. Aldous appeared oblivious
to their existence. (This is Ivan Moffat's story.) "He must have had
eyes in his back—just as he was about to feed some monkeys, he
whipped round and proffered the carrot to the little boys. They
fled with shrieks."

The Huxleys had arranged to go to South America that summer,
on the suggestion of their Argentinian friend, Victoria Ocampo,
editor of the review *Sur*, literary and musical patron and a very
great beauty in her time. Dr McDonagh advised against it, and
in March Aldous cried off. ". . If the man weren't doing me so
much good, I wd ignore what he says . . . He says he can make a
complete job of the thing if I have another treatment this summer.
So I really have no alternative . . . for I have no intention of re-

lapsing into the condition I was in last year, if I can possibly help it." So in April, after the children were gone, Aldous and Maria went to Sanary for a short summer.

Eyeless in Gaza was published on 18th June. Ten days earlier Aldous had written to C. E. M. Joad to whom he had sent an advance copy,

> I'm very glad to know that you think the book's all right. I had lost all sense of what it was like—w'd have liked, if it had been possible, to put it aside and look at it again after two or three years. Wolves at the door imposed immediate publication and I let it go, feeling uncomfortably in the dark about the thing.

"We have no idea how it's doing," Maria wrote to Jeanne on 19th June, "but I'm almost certain it'll make enough to pay our debts [to Chatto's] and to keep us going for a year. At the moment we are still short, Aldous doesn't want to ask his publishers for anything before the accounts come in July, and we've given up the idea to fetch Matthew because of the expense." The book did better than that. The subscription (in England) was 4,000; with 26,700 copies sold by the end of the year. In other ways the reception, not unexpectedly, was very mixed. Readers often are disgruntled when their author ceases to provide expected fare. "Aldous," Harold Raymond once said, "shoots in front of his public flock. In a couple of years they have flown into his shot." Aldous's flock did increase after 1936, but some of it was a new and different flock. Then there were the critics . . . But that is literary history, not Aldous's. He had long given up reading anything about himself if he could help it.

What was the substance of *Eyeless in Gaza*? What, in essence, was it that Anthony at last believed in? The pacifist solution, certainly. The religious solution? Upon what ground or faith? What intellectual basis? Let us go to the book itself.

". . Swine will be swine." But may become human, I insisted. *Homo non nascitur, fit.*   [From Anthony's Diary, 1st June 1934]

"It begins," he answered, "with trying to cultivate the difficult art of loving people."
"But most people are detestable."
"They're detestable, because we detest them. If we liked them, they'd be likeable."
"Do you think that's true?"
"I'm sure it's true."

"And what do you do after that?"

"There's no after," he replied. "Because, of course, it's a lifetime's job."

[Last chapter, 23rd February 1935]

Empirical facts:

One. We are all capable of love for other human beings.

Two. We impose limitations on that love.

Three. We can transcend all these limitations—if *we choose to*. (It is a matter of observation that anyone who so desires can overcome personal dislike, class feeling, national hatred, colour prejudice. Not easy; but it can be done . . .)

Four. Love expressing itself in good treatment breeds love. Hate expressing itself in bad treatment breeds hate.

In the light of these facts, it's obvious what inter-personal, inter-class and international policies should be. But, again, knowledge cuts little ice. We all know; we almost all fail to do. It's a question, as usual, of the best methods of implementing intentions.

[Anthony's Diary, 26th May 1934]

Mark . . began to laugh. Foresaw the time when I'd preface every mention of a person or group with the adjective "dear". "The dear Communists," "the dear armament makers," "dear General Goering." [Anthony's Diary, 20th May 1934]

. . Helen asked if I were happy. I said, yes—though didn't know if happiness was the right word. More substantial, more complete, more interested, more aware . . . [Anthony's Diary, 1st June 1934]

God—a person or not a person? *Quien sabe?* Only revelation can decide such metaphysical questions. And revelation isn't playing the game—is equivalent to pulling three aces of trumps from up your sleeve. [Anthony's Diary, Christmas Day 1934]

God may or may not exist. But there is the empirical fact that contemplation of the divinity—of goodness in its most unqualified form—is a method of realizing that goodness in some slight degree is in one's own life . . .

[Anthony's Diary, 21st September 1934]

And how had Aldous led Anthony to these convictions? Anthony, aged forty-three, at the point of deadlock, is sent off on an apparently futile journey to Mexico in the wake of his Draconian friend Mark Staithes who is going to assist one Don Jorge, a coffee planter, in a private revolution. Mark and Anthony ride across

the Sierra Juarez as Aldous had with Maria and Don Roy. They
spend a night in a place where the bar of their hotel is a crypt-like
room propped by wooden pillars. A drunken young Mexican
appears, offers a drink, is turned down and starts shooting up the
place. (It was now that Roy Fenton got his answer as to why the
Ejutla incident was left out in *Beyond the Mexique Bay*—Aldous had
saved it for the novel.) But the *mauvais quart-d'heure* in a traveller's
day had become a merciless exposition of *timor mortis*; Anthony is
shown reduced to quivering terror. "Don't, don't!" he cries as he
darts to take shelter behind a pillar. (In life it had been Roy who
shouted to Aldous to take cover.)

. . Anthony imagined the revolver suddenly coming round the
pillar . . A fear so intense that it was like the most excruciating
physical pain . . . The noise of the revolver going off—that was
what he dreaded most . . . The pistol went off . . the report was
catastrophically loud. Anthony uttered a great cry . . shutting his
eyes, flattened himself again the pillar . . .

And so on. Going once more recently through the whole thing
with Roy, we rather agreed that here was another example of the
genesis of fiction. Roy heard no great cry; Aldous, he maintains,
behaved sensibly, kept calm, though there had been good cause
for fear (Roy's own terror had been the possibility of Maria's
suddenly appearing). And yet, *and yet*—"Of course I don't know
exactly *what* went on in Aldous's mind as he was hopping from pillar
to pillar."

Ejutla was in passing. Next day, Mark Staithes has a fall and
is hurt. Anthony rides on alone in an attempt to reach an habitation
and get help. After two hours' riding over desolate country, "the
miracle happened. Coming round a bend in the track he saw advancing towards him . . a white man . . ." The white man raises
his hat. They speak. Anthony has met the catalyst. James Miller,
M.D., Edinburgh. He loses no time, on their way back to Mark,
Miller takes Anthony to task.

"Well, Anthony Beavis . . what's your profession? Ever been married?
You ought to have been. How old are you?"
"Forty-three."
"And look younger. Though I don't like that sallow skin of yours.
Do you suffer much from constipation? . . and of course stiff neck
. . lumbago. I know, I know . . . And the irony, the scepticism, that
what-the-good-of-it-all attitude! . . Everything you think is nega-
tive . . .
"Oh, don't imagine I'm criticizing . . don't get it into your head
that I'm blaming you in any way." Stretching out his hand, [the

doctor] patted Anthony affectionately on the shoulder. "We're all of us what we are; and when it comes to turning ourselves into what we ought to be—well it isn't easy. No, it isn't easy, Anthony Beavis. [Miller speaks with the friendly directness of the Quakers; now we are getting some straight McDonagh–Alexander]. How do you expect to think in anything but a negative way, when you've got chronic intestinal poisoning? . . at the same time stooping as you do. Slumped down on your mule . . Pressing down on the vertebrae . . . And when the spine's in that state, what happens to the rest of the machine . . .

". . . You've got to change if you want to go on existing. And if it's a matter of changing—why, you need all the help you can get, from God's to the doctor's. . . .

Now, this passage in the novel is not sudden for the reader, the bait was laid already by Anthony's post-Miller journal which, due to the shuffled time sequence, begins before the Mexican meeting. In the journal Miller comes and goes—his connection with Anthony unexplained for the time being—organizing a peace movement in England, teaching an Alexander technique, preaching by example. Miller is a saintly man, elderly, friendly, humorous, wise and blunt —forerunner of the Scottish doctor of *Island*—combining the conduct and ideas of Dick Sheppard with the theories of McDonagh and of Alexander (though *very* far from Alexander's rather epicurean way of life) and a good many concepts of Gerald Heard.

"Speaking as a doctor [Miller concluded in the Mexican Sierra] . . I'd suggest a course of colonic irrigation to start with."
"And speaking for God," said Anthony . . "a course of prayer and fasting."
"No, not fasting," the doctor protested very seriously" . . only a proper diet . . As for prayer . . All that asking for special favours and guidances . . it tends to make one egotistical . . you're merely rubbing yourself into yourself . . . Whereas what we're all looking for is a way of getting beyond our own vomit."

And now we get a very characteristic passage:

Some way, Anthony was thinking, of getting beyond the books, beyond the perfumed and resilient flesh of women, beyond fear and sloth, beyond the painful but secretly flattering vision of the world as menagerie and asylum.

Anthony returns to London and the job of turning himself into what he ought to be. "It begins with the difficult art of loving people." He accepts help on *any* level: spiritual exercises, diet, physical training.

At today's lesson [Alexander] . . found myself suddenly a step forward in my grasp of the theory and practice . . . To learn proper use one must first inhibit all improper uses of the self . . . This process entails knowing good and bad use—knowing them apart . . . Increased awareness and power of control result . . trivialities take on a new significance . . Cleaning teeth, putting on shoes . . . Skill in getting to know the muscular aspect of mind-body can be carried over into the exploration of other aspects. There is increasing ability to detect one's motives for any given piece of behaviour . . . Also, one becomes more . . . conscious of what's going on in the outside world . . . Control also is transferred. Acquire the art of inhibiting muscular bad use and you acquire thereby the art of inhibiting more complicated trains of behaviour. Not only this: there is prevention as well as cure. . . There is an end, for example, of neurotic anxieties and depressions . . . In practice, neurosis is always associated with some kind of wrong use. (Note the typically bad physical posture of neurotics and lunatics . .) Re-educate. Give back correct physical use. You remove the keystone of the arch constituting the neurotic personality . . . Most of us are slightly neurotic. Even slight neurosis provides endless occasions for bad behaviour . . . Hitherto preventive ethics has been thought of as external to the individual social and economic reforms carried out with a view to eliminating occasions for bad behaviour. This is important. But not nearly enough . . . [We must find] a method of achieving progress from within as well as from without. Progress, not only as a citizen . . but also as a human being.

[Anthony's Diary, 3rd June 1934]

How hard though to achieve that progress—the vigilance, the patience, the continual saying No to habitual response.

Wouldn't it be nice, for a change, if there were another way out of our difficulties! A short cut. A method requiring no greater personal effort than recording a vote or ordering some "enemy of society" to be shot. A salvation from outside, like a dose of calomel.

[Anthony's Diary, 4th August 1934]

And what pitfalls. Meditation can become a bolt-hole from unpleasant reality, quietism mere self-indulgence.

"The contemplative life" It can be made a kind of high-brow substitute for Marlene Dietrich: a subject for erotic musing in the twilight. Meditation—valuable . . . only as a means of effecting desirable changes in the personality and mode of existence. To live contemplatively is not to live in some deliciously voluptuous or

flattering Poona; it is to live in London, but to live there in a non-
cockney style.   [Anthony's Diary, 17th September 1934]

Anthony has made a speech at a peace meeting . . . five hundred
people in a hall . . some invincibly ignorant . . Afterwards Mark
tells him,

> "Might as well go and talk to cows in a field." The temptation
> to agree with him was strong. All my old habits of thinking, living,
> feeling impel me towards agreement. A senseless world, where
> nothing whatever can be done—how satisfactory! . . I caught myself
> taking immense pleasure in commenting on the imbecility of my
> audience and human beings at large. Caught and checked myself.
>   [Anthony's Diary, 20th May 1934]

And what if they understand, if they *are* convinced?

> Very good meeting in Newcastle with Miller. Large and enthusiastic
> crowds—predominantly of the dispossessed. Note the significant fact
> that pacifism is in inverse ratio, generally, to prosperity. The greater
> the poverty, the longer the unemployment . . the more complete
> the scepticism about the conventional idols . . . A negative attitude . .
> Therefore not to be relied on. Negative pacifism and scepticism . .
> are just holes in the mind, emptinesses waiting to be filled. Fascism
> or communism have sufficient positive content to act as fillers.
> Someone with the talents of Hitler may suddenly appear. The
> negative void will be pumped full in a twinkling. These . . pacifist
> sceptics will be transformed overnight into drilled fanatics of national-
> ism, class war or whatever it may be. Question: have we time to
> fill the vacuum with positive pacifism? Or, having the time, have
> we the ability?   [Anthony's Diary, 4th November 1934]

We can only try. That, in the end, is Anthony's conclusion: We
have got to try.

> ". . if you treat other people well, they'll treat you well."
> "You're a bit optimistic, aren't you?"
> "No. In the long run they'll always treat you well."
> "In the long run," said Mark impatiently, "we shall all be dead.
> What about the short run?"
> "You've got to take a risk."
> "But Europeans aren't like your Sunday-school savages. It'll be an
> enormous risk."
> "Possibly. But always smaller than the risk you run by treating
> people badly and goading them into war."
>   [Mexico, 7th February 1934]

322

The book ends with Anthony by himself. In a few hours he is
to speak at a meeting in Battersea. He has had a nasty anonymous
letter—We're going to get you, you pacifist skunk. Anthony begins
by being very frightened—physical violence, they're going to beat
him up; how will he face it? (the point was made, we see now,
behind that pillar at Ejutla). He is tempted to funk it. Why not
go back to what nature meant him to do, "to looking on from a
private box and making comments". Ring them up, a small voice
says, tell them you've got flu. He checks this "baseness". Now he
goes into a long meditation.

> "Unity." He was committed . . as a hand is committed to the arm.
> Committed to his friends, committed even to those who had declared
> themselves his enemies. There was nothing he could do but would
> affect them all . . For good, if what he did were good, for evil if it
> were wrong. Unity, he repeated.
> Unity of mankind, unity of all life . . .

Unity—and separation, diversity—the conditions of our existence. *Born under one law, to another bound.* The evil of separation
bridged by the act of love and compassion:

> . . Constantly obstructed. But, oh, let them be made indefatigable,
> implacable to surmount all obstacles, the inner sloth, the distaste,
> the intellectual scorn . . . Affection, compassion . . . Peace . . .

The clock strikes seven. Anthony emerges into the present—calm,
resolved, serene.

Absolutes so simple . . . Never again was Aldous to appear so single-
minded, so confiding, so unqualifying . . . But the resolutions of
Eyeless in Gaza remained.

It is a curious book. Aldous himself found it hard to see it whole.
There is much that is very good (that scene of the two children
sailing their toy ship in the night) and some things that are awful
with the deliberate awfulness Aldous used to drag into his verse,
the awfulness, indeed, he perceived to be a part of human experience. (How unnerved Maria was by that dead dog dropping
on to the roof.) One obvious defect of the book is the comparative
brand-newness of the "solution" inserts, the use made, compelled
by those wolves at the door, of too recent experience. The tract, it
was said, had got into the novel. Many readers of my generation
and antecedents, myself included, were put off, resentful even; the
book's qualities tended to get overlooked. The story, I think now,
is extremely well-knit, the famous jumbled time sequence *is*

effective, adding rather than detracting from coherence, adding to perspective. There is also an unobtrusive sense of period: one knows that this is 1902 or 1911 or 1926. The book's major fault seems to me its length. Too many points are made more than twice; too much is over-insisted on in the "unregenerate" narrative parts. Perhaps it was because Aldous, unable for so long to find the ending, went on and on about the things he knew. The impact at two-thirds or less the length would have been greater.

As concerns Aldous, *Eyeless in Gaza* was the expression of a stage in a lifetime of development. Aldous did not so much change—he went on. One stage, but a crucial stage; a point of no return. Aldous never went back on the convictions he had come to. The belief in the existence of a spiritual reality underlying the phenomenal world, imparting to it whatever value or significance it possesses. The belief that this reality can be experienced by anyone who so chooses. The concern with the present and the future of mankind —"the world is to a great extent illusory . . it is none the less essential to improve the illusion." The belief that desirable social changes can be brought about by changing the individuals who compose society. The continued emphasis on the need for knowledge and intelligence (directed by a disinterested will)—"for insensitive stupidity is the root of all the other vices". These, in a more complex, subtle and wide-ranging way, became the constants of Aldous's life, thought and work. In 1936 they were in parts still intimations of what he had not yet himself fully experienced but already believed to be attainable; circumstances and the first fine flush of Dick Sheppard's radiantly virtuous absolutes impelled Aldous to preach early what from that point on he practised. *Eyeless in Gaza* was the blue-print, as it were, of what Aldous set out to discover and to be. It was the expression of the nobler hypothesis.

> For faith is not believing something which our intelligence denies. It is the choice of the nobler hypothesis. Faith is the resolve to place the highest meaning on the facts which we observe.[1]

The last words of *Eyeless in Gaza* are: "He thought of what was in store for him. Whatever it might be, he knew that all would be well."

[1] *Prayers and Meditations: A Monthly Cycle Arranged for Daily Use*, edited by Gerald Heard. Harper & Brothers, 1949. Seven out of thirty-one meditations were written by Aldous Huxley. His friend, Peggy (Mrs William) Kiskadden, has the typescript of these. *Faith*, meditation No 4, from which I quoted, is not by Aldous. (The ones by him are: *Being, Beauty, Love, Peace, Holiness, Grace* and *Joy*.)

Chapter Four

Striking Tents

As for our winter plans, Maria wrote to Jeanne from Sanary in June, "I cannot tell . . .

> Je me laisse vivre au jour le jour et profite de la tranquillité et de la chaleur et de la gaîté de ce pays qu'il est bien possible que nous n'habiterons plus pour longtemps.

I'm sure Aldous will sell the house at the first chance. "Although he is happy and in good spirits, I have sometimes the impression that he's bored. He won't admit it; but I have reason to believe I'm right. He's hardly interested in painting anymore and only does it because there's nothing else for him to do."

Boredom? Flatness? Accidie? Or a sense of having reached the end of what that calm Mediterranean country had to offer him? Of having done with old habits and old friends, of being held back by their modes of thinking, living? An instinct for the need of a new framework, other stimuli? Aldous's health was all right; he was sleeping well, he was writing. Odds and ends for the Peace Movement, and *The Olive Tree*, another collection of essays (off his hands in August, published in December), some of it had already appeared in print: the ten year old "Crébillon the Younger", very characteristic of his manner of the period; "In a Tunisian Oasis", also of the 'Twenties and first published in *Vogue*; some of his finest critical work, such as the lecture on T. H. Huxley, the introduction to *Lawrence's Letters* and the essay on the painter B. R. Haydon, one of

> those indomitable madmen who have made the British Empire and English literature, English politics and English science the extraordinary things they are. Haydon was one of those glorious lunatics . . .

For that not very homogeneous collection Aldous now wrote three or four new pieces: a long discussion, "Writers and Readers", about the effects if any of the written word ("The propagandists of the future will probably be chemists and psychologists as well as writers . . .") and, close to his present concerns, the essay on *Words and Behaviour* ("The most shocking thing about war is that its victims and its instruments are individual human beings").

It was particularly hot in Sanary that summer. The household was very quiet; Maria basking—she said—in laziness and peace. Actually she was struggling to acquire the alien skill of shorthand, and even found the time to type a chunk of a long novel I'd just finished. Alas she also passed the novel on to Aldous. It was a bad, empty novel, and he told me as much; on paper. Pages, hand-written, of analysis and good advice. I have them before me. He really did take trouble (though it was pretty shattering at the time). ". . lack of vital relationship between the characters . . . issues of little significance . . . the book needs to be simultaneously shortened and filled up . . ."

Matthew seemed to have taken a sudden step into grown-upness and he and Maria were pottering about a good deal on their own, making, she said, "an adorable companion". Then this nice quiet life was idiotically shattered.

> . . The earthly Paradise . . has been turned into a devilish hot turmoil. [Maria wrote to Eddy Sackville-West] One of my inter-ventions towards catastrophic friends has replaced the peace.
>
> We expected to lunch . . a whole very energetic family of French people [Jean Coutrot, ex-pupil of the Ecole Polytechnique, one of the new French technocrats who acted as a kind of unofficial brain trust to the Léon Blum government, whom Aldous had briefly met in June at the Abbaye de Pontigny] . . at a quarter to two arrives a telephone message from the hospital at Hyères that they cannot come because they have had a motor accident and are lying there. Which made me feel very guilty as I had spent the morning saying that he was a wild driver . . . Scirocco in full blast, 36 [centigrade] in the shade and no lunch was not an ideal way to travel . . wonder-ing as to the full horror of the accident . . .

They were taken to the bedside of a very badly injured woman whom they had never met before, after which the hospital sent them on to break the news to relatives further along the coast. The Bugatti seized up in the heat, Maria left it and Aldous in a field, and

> boarded the immense car of kind and stupid South Americans who I had stopped. Never have I been driven more slowly in my life . . .

Maria's letter goes on for some twelve pages; alas it is much too frank to quote. Enough to say that happily Coutrot was not badly hurt and that the woman recovered. For the Huxleys the turmoil did not let up for weeks to come; they were in for, Aldous ten, Maria ninety per cent, of hospital visiting, shopping, chauffeuring. Mme Coutrot and a son were put up at the Villa Huley.

When this subsided, in late July, time was almost up. There
was one last Sanary picnic, an apotheosis of a Huxley picnic. It
was a mid-day one and the site chosen by Renée Kisling an almost
inaccessible cove beyond Le Brusc. A vanguard consisting of Maria,
Renée, the two Kisling boys, tough little devils blackened by the
sun, Matthew and myself, went early to bathe and reconnoitre.
We left the cars on a promontory, Maria and the Kislings danced
down a precipitous goat track, Matthew did creditably; I shut my
eyes. Nobody expressed misgivings. Maria was in the kind of mood
in which she let Aldous fall off mules. At noon Edith Wharton,
Lalla Vandervelde, Paul Valéry and Mme Valéry, frail septua-
genarians, shepherded by Aldous, were seen approaching the edge
of the cliff. Led by the Kisling boys they undertook the descent.
Dislodged stones rolled. Aldous managed with surprising tactile
agility, the others seemed to do so by the force of the iron discipline
bred into their class and generation—they made it. Mrs Wharton
looked very flushed, the Valérys very white, but not by a word or
smile did they betray the fact that anything more out of the way
than walking from the garden into the dining-room had taken
place.

Presently Aldous left Sanary. First he went to Brussels where
Barbusse's big peace conference was now taking place, then, joined
by Matthew, on to St Trond and to Holland, visiting Joep and
Suzanne, re-visiting galleries (unadmitted, it was a farewell
round), thence to England where Matthew sat for an exam and
was put into the hands of Alexander and McDonagh, while Aldous
began on his second lot of treatments and did some active work
for the P.P.U. He gave a joint talk with Dick Sheppard at Friends'
House, and saw a good deal of Gerald Heard. Gerald's predictions
for the coming war were more than ever cataclysmic. There was
no defence against aerial attack. Battleships were obsolete. The
entire might of the British Home Fleet assembled in the Channel
could be rendered helpless within one hour (this I heard him say
with my own ears).

Maria, alone in the house in Sanary, began to go through her
papers, through clothes and books, giving away here and there.
"We *may* sell . . ." No offer had come, few people were confident
enough to buy a house. "We *may* go away . . ." Go away, was what
she said, not travel. "For long?" "Who can tell? We're Gypsies."
The American idea was already in the air. Maria always knew what
Aldous wanted before he knew himself. She brought out the box with
Aldous's letters, the letters he had written during their engagement

that had come to her day after day in Italy; Aldous's love letters. She would take these with her. Now in those hot afternoons she read them again, untying, re-tying the bundles one by one; moved, at times amused. "How young we were." "There's so much about books!"

Then out came her journal—one knew that she had been keeping one, great spates typed at night, not regularly but continuously since their early married days in London. This Maria let me have a glimpse of, that is she allowed me to read two or three pages about a dinner party we had been at, and one other page—"you must stop there"—about an episode I knew about. I was immensely struck. Like her letters, it was obviously dashed off, straight off the fire, but with what feeling, what acuteness, the journal was pure first reactions, pulling no punches about herself or anyone, and there was a candour, a sharpness, a ruthlessness of insight that took my breath away. This may have been the way in which Maria talked to Aldous about their friends. I am sure that she must have let him read, and use, the journal. How I regretted then not being able to read more; how bitterly I regret now that the journal is no longer there to read. With it, an incomparable record of Aldous's life and circle has been lost.

In September Maria joined Aldous and Matthew in London. Albany was still sub-let so they settled down quite happily at the Mount Royal at Marble Arch in three adjoining bed-sitters with kitchenettes and baths—anonymous, well-heated, functional. Maria fretted about the extravagance, although the novel was doing very well, they were still anxious about money. "Because we have to spend so much on doctors," (Maria to Jeanne) "but we're really very fortunate to be able to have the doctors and enjoy the luxury of our three rooms." They were very busy.

We have spent the whole winter [September to December] in London where we worked like slaves. [Maria to Roy] Aldous for the Peace Pledge Movement with Dick Sheppard and I as secretary and slavy to those two men. But we were happy and comfortable. [Weather] grey and grey and grey . . luckily I was too busy to think of it.

Aldous, besides editing *An Encyclopaedia of Pacifism*[1] for the Movement, drafted letters, answered the questions (some hard, some silly) that came pouring in, made speeches standing on P.P.U. platforms holding his notes within an inch of his eyes. Maria was

---

[1] Chatto & Windus, 1937.

busy with a thousand errands, helping to set up some of the practical work that members were undertaking such as looking after
destitute local families or released prisoners or guaranteeing main-
tenance to Jewish refugees. (Maria was not able to use the shorthand she had worked so hard at, Aldous had discouraged her—
"He calculates that I will never be able to do more than 60 words
a minute; he, speaking slowly, says 100 words a minute"—but she
got through a vast amount of typing.)

Aldous made the speeches he was asked to. Yet he had doubts
as to their effectiveness. Once he consulted Dr Charlotte Wolff.
"He told me he was worried about making contact with people.
That he didn't know—that he felt inadequate. How to make proper
contact with individual people? And more so with the many? He
wanted to be able to speak to the many. I tried what I could to
reassure him—one felt naive in front of him, that's obvious—I told
him that *his impulse was so strong* that it would be all right, that *some
day* he would be able to."[1]

Aldous's own peace pamphlet, *What Are You Going To Do About
It? The Case for Constructive Peace*, had come out six months ago. This
was the gist of his argument.

> War is a purely human phenomenon. Animals kill for food . . fight
> duels in the heat of sexual excitement . . Man is unique in organizing
> the mass murder of his own species. War is *not* a law of nature. The
> old saw about the survival of the fittest is obviously nonsensical—
> active warfare tends to eliminate the young and strong . .; aerial
> warfare kills indiscriminately.

War is not a law of nature. War is an absolute evil. Yet war is
made. What can we do about it?

> . . The Kingdom of God [cannot] be imposed on mankind from
> without, by means of change or organization (i.e. Marxian revolu-
> tion) . . [Man] himself must work for it, and work for it not only
> as a public figure, but also in private life.
> . . The whole philosophy of constructive pacifism is based on a
> consideration of the facts of personal relationship between man and
> man.
> There are men who profess to be pacifists in international politics,
> but who are tyrants in their families, bullying employers, or un-
> scrupulous competitors . . Such men are fools [to] suppose that it
> is possible for a government to behave as a pacifist when the
> individuals it represents conduct their affairs in an essentially mili-
> taristic way. Constructive peace must be first of all a personal ethic . . .

[1] From a recorded conversation with Dr C. Wolff.

. . Means determine ends . . the only right and practical policy is one based on truth and generosity.

How can such a policy be applied to the circumstances of the present? By the summoning at the earliest possible date of a world conference by the great monopolistic powers, England, France, the U.S.A. and Russia. "This, for instance, would constitute the only practical solution of the difficult problem of sanctions against Italy.

> People of goodwill are painfully perplexed because it seems to them that sanctionist countries are on the horns of a dilemma. Either sanctions must be intensified, in which case it is probable that Italy will, in desperation, precipitate a European war; or else Abyssinia must be sacrificed, in which case a wanton act of aggression will have been rewarded at the expense of the victim. In fact there is a third and better alternative . . .

The world conference, given intelligence and good will, could settle not only the justifiable claims of Italy but of all other dissatisfied countries . . . The peace of Versailles, economically speaking, was a thoroughly bad peace . . . The immediate application of pacifist principles offers the hope of a solution of problems which, if they are left to themselves, may become insoluble . . . There would have to be new agreements on markets, tropical raw materials, currencies and tariffs, migration and territorial adjustments.

> The greatest immediate sacrifices . . will have to come from those who possess the most. These sacrifices, however, will be negligible in comparison with the sacrifices demanded from us by another war. Negligible in comparison even with those which are at present being demanded by the mere preparations for war.
>
> What of the League of Nations? There is, unhappily, much truth in the Italian contention that the League in its present form is . . controlled by the two great monopolistic nations of Western Europe, England and France. These nations are unwilling to sacrifice their present superiority and, though this superiority was won by the use of violence in the past, they prefer to seem righteously indignant . . at the use of violence by unsatisfied countries at the present time . . . .

Pacifists in England now have one immediate task—"that time presses is, alas, only too true"—to persuade their government to apply the principles of preventive pacifism to the present international situation. Such a policy certainly has its risks. But anything else cannot fail to lead us into war:

. . We can break out of the circle. One generous gesture on the part of a great nation might be enough to set the whole world free. More than any other nation, Britain is in a position to make that gesture.

Which is better, to take a risk for a good cause, or to march to certain perdition for a bad one?

One generous gesture might be enough to set the whole world free. That was not an ignoble bugle call. The gesture, as we know, was not made. (Munich, whatever we shall decide that it has been, was not an act of constructive pacifism.) Men of good will fought or supported the war, that is, chose doing an evil thing that good might come of it, or worse be prevented. Some did so, pacifists of the previous war among them, because their abhorrence of Hitler's Germany was overriding (and that was something Aldous did not take explicitly into account), but for the majority the margin of choice, psychologically and materially, was very small indeed. Consequently, as again we know only too well, human beings everywhere were killed, maimed, bereaved; Czechoslovakia and Poland were *not* saved but underwent unspeakable suffering; the horrors of the torture camps and death camps continued and increased; when the German camps were put an end to—*one* war aim realized after what had been eleven years of possibly the greatest frightfulness of man to man in human history—Stalin's camps went on unliberated, unchallenged. The Allies dropped the Atomic Bomb on Hiroshima and Nagasaki. The H-Bomb did not take long to follow.

What might have been the course of events *if* the policies of the Peace Movement had prevailed? Would Hitler have been checked? Would he have been willing, even able, to call it a day? Is it conceivable that he and his hierarchy would have agreed to close Dachau, restore civil rights to Jews and dissolve the Gestapo, in effect to take steps to dismantle the dictatorial state?

And what if Britain had unilaterally disarmed, as was the stated policy of the Peace Movement? ("The political implications of pacifism may be briefly summed up as follows: . . . (5) Disarmament, unilateral if necessary."[1]) One obvious answer is that it was precisely because Hitler, misled by Ribbentrop and Co, believed that Britain would not fight that he advanced so freely towards war. Yet might there not have been a world of difference, of difference in kind, between not fighting out of self-interest or lassitude, and standing up against war actively, deliberately, courageously, risking the cost for the sole and professed reason that war is always

[1] *An Encyclopaedia of Pacifism*, edited by Aldous Huxley. Chatto & Windus, 1937.

evil? Might that not have been the generous gesture that set the whole world free? Or would it have been the suicidal and quixotic act that brought about our general enslavement? The question is unanswerable because the premise is not there: unilateral disarmament on the part of any Western country carried out in the spirit of the Peace Movement was inconceivable in the moral and political circumstances of the time.

And yet there was then an atmosphere of hope and purpose about the P.P.U. Membership increased; more eminent intellectuals, Bertrand Russell for one, joined the sponsors (he, with Professor Joad, Rose Macaulay and some others resigned after war broke out). Dick Sheppard stood for the Rectorship of the University of Glasgow as pacifist candidate with Winston Churchill as his chief opponent and, against all predictions, won the election. (He died before taking up the post.) Aldous's own work for the movement was at times quite down to earth. "For instance," wrote Gerald Heard,[1]

> he and I found out (it was easy to discover) how anxious the Nazi armament engineers were to get nickel, of which Germany was desperately short. The next thing was to see where the vital stocks lay—and that was in Canada. The price to corner the whole Canadian load was not much more than that of one of those floating steel anachronisms still then called Dreadnoughts. Through relatives we were able to get our brief but enormously important statement to the fatal Chamberlain. He sent back verbally the pet word of the purblind, "Impractical".

Naturally the Movement was attacked, and so was Aldous. Leonard Woolf argued personally; C. Day Lewis wrote a pamphlet (on current leftist lines) called *We're Not Going To Do NOTHING*.[2] Aldous answered some of their points in respective letters.[3] How out of tune he was with the political opinions of so many of his literary contemporaries! Take the Spanish Civil War. In the questionnaire published by Louis Aragon and Nancy Cunard, *Authors Take Sides* (1937), 127 out of the 149 writers polled were for the Republic; 5 for Franco; 16 either neutral or anti-war *per se*, Aldous among them.

In December Maria's father, Norbert Nys, broke his neck. He lived on, but in great pain. Maria went to him at Brussels. Back in

---

[1] *The Kenyon Review*, op. cit.
[2] Published by *The Left Review*, 1936.
[3] Nos. 393 and 404 in Professor Grover Smith's edition of the *Letters*.

London she went down with influenza, so did Aldous and Matthew though more lightly, and after this they decided on a break. Time, too, for Aldous to get back to his own work. Aldous and Maria returned to Sanary, Matthew to Switzerland (not to his strenuous school; after a successful exam he was to have a couple of months of rest and winter sports). Aldous, advised by Gerald, was thinking of continuing his son's education in the United States.

They found Sanary wind-still and quiet. ". . The avocado trees are so large and the sun is warm; mimosa and roses to welcome us. Alas, it will be to pack again as we are anxious to sell this house." (Maria to Roy.) They spent Christmas by themselves, all their friends, except Renée Kisling, wintering in the North. Maria was very run down indeed, to the point of admitting to a sense of perpetual exhaustion. Aldous was at the note collecting stage for a series of essays, *Ends and Means*, arising out of *Gaza* and the peace pamphlets, Maria reading to him for some hours daily. Their plans had crystallized.

> Now listen to our news. [To Roy on Christmas Eve] They are so exciting that I can hardly write about them. In March we go to the States; we mean to remain there some time. Perhaps nine months or a year and that is to include a visit to Mexico and to yourself if you will have us . . . We may be three or four of us so it will be a little more complicated than the first time we met . . The third may be Matthew who is a man of seventeen now and the fourth our very best and great friend Gerald Heard . . whom you would certainly like as much as we do. He, however, is a delicate man and we cannot expect to drive him as hard as we can drive ourselves.

On the same day Aldous wrote to Eugene Saxton:

> Thank you for the further information about colleges . . when we get across the Atlantic, I will have a good discussion and a look round. Meanwhile . . if Matthew is to have his educational visa and if, as seems likely, we ourselves stay for more than six months in America, it is necessary . . [to] have some kind of proof of my ability to support Matthew and myself while in the USA . . I think it would be best if Harper's were to write an official letter . . I expect that we shall be coming over in March.

And while they were away, the house might well get sold during their absence. Maria packed and stripped.

> Aldous spends his time tidying his cupboards and burning rubbish [Maria to Jeanne] We mix old M.S.s with rosemary and thyme and it burns with a scent of poetry even when it was nonsense or old.

What wasn't burnt was given away.

> Sophie aimerait-elle un beau Shakespeare et tous les romans de Jane Austen?
> Veux tu des dessins (3) indécents? Tu pourrais toujours les vendre.
> Veux tu des livres français . . dédicacés que tu pourrais vendre?

Maria's father did not recover. Pneumonia set it and in January he died. Maria went to Belgium for the funeral. Mme Nys came to Sanary for a long stay. This had never been easy and became less so. Maria's childhood devotion to her mother had long given place to censure, irritation and consequent self-reproach. Maria had adopted Aldous's values. The root of the trouble was probably a certain smugness, a remorseless self-sufficiency that was a characteristic of the old European bourgeoisie. To be educated and materially privileged was not something due to one's good luck for which one was grateful and a bit ashamed, but one's right and positively a merit. It was a refusal of humility that made them impermeable, politically and individually, to the needs of others. To Aldous, Mme Nys's mould of mind was fascinating; to Maria it was a source of grief and conflict. Her letters echo with, "I ought to be nice to her, *pauvre femme*, I want to be nice to her . . . I ought to *think* nicely of her." It was a resolution broken a hundred times. Her mother had only to come into the kitchen, open her mouth . . . She judged people, often harshly; was interested in her food. "And yet, I am her daughter . . . I don't say 'I told you so,' because ever since I heard her saying it to Père, I decided not to do it. And I don't shrug my shoulders saying, 'Oh, all right, *all right*'. And I don't fling out of a room in a rage not quite slamming the door . . . But now I'm learning to be in the wrong and not to blame anything that goes wrong on someone else." Mme Nys never ceased to adore, though she criticised; Maria remained her favourite. For Maria there was also a constant element of pity in the relationship.

> Pauvre femme. Elle a peur des cambrioleurs qui l'assassineront, elle a peur de la guerre, elle a peur d'être seule.

Mme Nys was getting very deaf.

> I think it is my moral duty to buy her a hearing machine. But a good one costs 2,000 frs.

By the middle of February Aldous had written the first 10,000 words of *Ends and Means*; Maria from one day to the next was feeling well again; travel plans had reached a further stage.

. . Gerald Heard . . will be crossing with us, and we expect to be travelling with him in the USA. [Aldous to Eugene Saxton] He is the trustee for a big estate out West and has to wind up the affair, and we shall make our way by easy stages with him across the continent and probably find some place in the mountains of Montana to stay at during the summer . . . Gerald is a very dear friend of ours and a most remarkable man; I hope very much you will be able to do something with his books . . .

. . practical details . . We don't want, on this occasion, to stay more than a week or so [in New York], as we have to go southwards for Matthew's affairs and then a very long way north-westwards for Gerald's—and incidentally our own pleasure and instruction . . . We'd be most grateful if you could find us . . a couple of single rooms for Matthew and Gerald Heard, and a bedroom and sitting room with kitchenette, if possible, for Maria and myself. The position needn't of course be elegant, so long as it's fairly quiet. Then . . I'd be glad of a little advice . . whether it's better to get, say, a new Ford or a second-hand specimen of some larger and more majestic vehicle. I expect we shall need a small trailer for luggage. Hints on this subject will be most welcome . . that's the reward of previous kindness—to be asked to be kind again!

And Maria to Jeanne:

. . Nous acheterons une grande voiture. Nous voyagerons pendant neuf semaines avant d'arriver ou nous passerons nos vacances d'été. Nous irons dans le désert . . .

. . Notre départ est presque fixé. Possiblement le 31 [mars] sur la troisième de la Queen Mary. Il parait que l'on y est mieux qu'en seconde sur d'autres bateaux. En tous les cas, maintenant que je suis si bien portante je voyagerais même à fond de cale. C'est trop bête de dépenser son argent pour un peu de comfort. Et comme je ne connais pas les secondes je me contenterai des troisièmes. Je ne me mêle pas de cette question. Qu'Aldous ou Gerald décident. Je pense qu'à ce point de vue là, décisions, le voyage sera agréable car Aldous et Gerald décideront tout.

On the last day Maria gave the Bugatti to Renée Kisling. On 19th February 1937, Aldous and Maria left the Villa Huley.

Aldous was supposed to make a speech in London on the 25th, but was held up in Paris—"I was in the pink . . when an undeveloped wisdom tooth brought me extremely low . . . [Aldous to Julian] I go into hospital tomorrow . . to have the thing hacked out."

Aldous arrived in London, still in pain. Once more they put up at their cherished Mount Royal. Albany was not let, they had as yet not found another tenant and had lent the flat to me; I had been living there since January, plying the typewriter in the goldfish-bowl. Now I didn't move out because Maria didn't think it sensible to start housekeeping for so short a time. This kindness had at least one fortunate result for them. Aldous's jaw was acting up again, and badly. A very pleasant young man who lived across the corridor in Mount Royal and to whom Maria in her way had spoken once or twice when taking in their milk, turned out to be a dentist. It was the weekend. He had one look at Aldous's Paris job, and did something effective then and there. On Monday morning Aldous went to his surgery. I wish I could recall his name because, as I repeat, he was a very pleasant man, but more to the point proved to be an extremely competent and up-to-date dentist. It was Tregar or something near it. He discovered abscesses at the roots and had to extract three more teeth. The whole job was done brilliantly; Aldous was very pleased and recovered quickly. T. and the Huxleys became more neighbourly than ever.

I remember Aldous being in a quiet, cheerful mood, going about his business with detached efficiency. He hadn't done any real travelling since Mexico in 1933 and he was looking forward to his nine weeks' motoring across a new continent. He did not give the impression of a man who was making a great decision. I don't think he thought about his going to America in that way. He was not attached to places—to suspend, at this point, such attachment as he had for family and friends, was a necessary, though almost certainly not conscious, step in his own development—there was little sense of parting. Move or Journey, whatever it might come to be, was in the lap of the gods, sufficient unto the day.

As for suspending his work for the Peace Movement, Aldous and Gerald, privately, were getting very very discouraged. They realized that in spite of so much present response there was no real chance of making the kind of impact that could push the government into action. There was plenty of fear of war but it was matched by fatalistic apathy. Not that Aldous was deserting the P.P.U. Gerald told him that he had shot his bolt and the most useful thing to do now was to re-state the case for peace by some sustained writing such as he was planning. Meanwhile Aldous was talking happily about the things he was going to see—National Parks, educational experiments, Professor J. B. Rhine's E.S.P. laboratory . . .

Matthew arrived (lodged in his own suite at Mount Royal), very pleased about it all, rather pleased with himself. He did not endear himself to Julian and Juliette by telling them in his elation that old Europe was finished.

10*a* Aldous and Gerald
Heard at Duke University,
Carolina U.S.A. 1937

b Aldous and Maria,
Berlin 1932

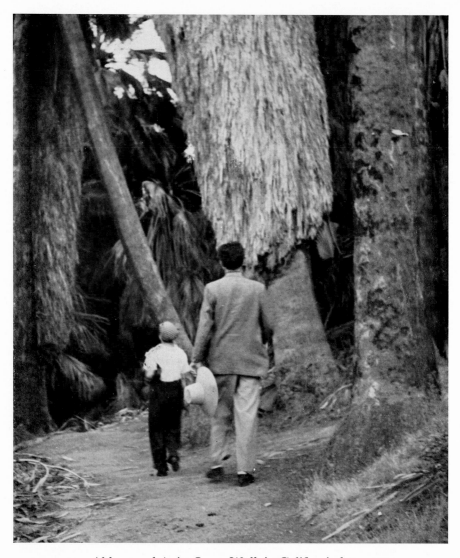

11   Aldous and Anita Loos. Walk in California late 1930s

If Aldous and Gerald did the planning—and went to the U.S. Embassy, the banks, the shipping offices—Maria carried out the detail. The packing. What to take? The minimum of clothes. Their own bedding. *Quite* a few books. What to leave behind? For Albany, too, was to be dismantled. (They were trying to get rid of the lease, with four and a half years still to run.) Maria had talked to a barrow man in Soho who not only would take their books away without charge but had promised her a pound or two for them. She asked me to be sure to stay in and answer the door-bell so as not to miss this golden opportunity. I implored her to let Percy Muir,[1] who happened to be a friend, have a look at the books first. Just odds and ends, Maria said, but consented because she didn't want to snub me. So Percy Muir appeared in Albany one morning. Aldous and Maria happened to be there. They watched him look at title pages, unhurriedly, concentratedly, one by one. There were 153 books in all. When Percy had finished he sat down and wrote a cheque. It was a handsome sum. Then he produced a folded sack—"just like a barrow man," said Maria. We helped him shove in the books and called a cab. Aldous and Maria remained gaping, though delighted, and a little doubtful if this hadn't been sharp practice—Are you sure your poor friend can afford it? Then Maria said, there was *one* thing off her mind now; I had shown such extra-ordinary business acumen that she would never have to worry about my future again. The 153 books were listed in Elkin Matthew's Catalogue of February 1937. The odds and ends in Albany included:

Matthew Arnold's Essays inscribed by his niece, Julia Huxley;
Clive Bell: some autographed copies, one signed by Jean Cocteau;
Russell Green's Newdigate poem "Venice";
Eric de Haulleville: Poems;
The Hay Diet, Maria's annotated copy;
Leonard Handley's novel, autographed;
Gerald Heard: one of his books with Aldous's notes;
Aldous Huxley: 1st editions of *Burning Wheel, Jonah, Leda*;
Aldous Huxley: sketch-book, described in the catalogue, ". . with two full-page pencil drawings, one of the interior of a railway coupé, the other of a landscape";
Julian Huxley's Newdigate poem;
Julian Huxley: several books, some with inscriptions;
Julian Huxley: a book inscribed to Matthew;
Leonard Huxley: *Life and Letters of Sir Joseph Dalton Hooker*, presentation copy inscribed to Aldous;
Robert Nichols: poems signed;
Sacheverell Sitwell: poems signed;

[1] The bibliographer, and a director of Elkin Matthew.

Paul Valéry: poems, signed;
H. G. Wells: a presentation copy.[1]

As Elinor told Philip Quarles in *Point Counter Point,* Aldous had no natural piety. At any rate, Percy Muir had known what he was doing; "I wish," he wrote the other day, "that I had many of the books now."

. . . The second week of March, the third, the fourth—last days. Everyone was being extremely busy in the day time and in the evening there were so many friends to see, but whoever came in first from their engagements made for Maria's room—I too went to Mount Royal every night whatever I had been doing and however late, it was not a time to be sensible or tired. There we talked. Later still, I would walk back to Albany across Mayfair, across Grosvenor, across Berkeley Square, thinking of what had been said and not been said, through the wind-blown London night.

Maria was very divided. She, too, was looking forward, was full of the car journey, the trailer, the new sights—they were gypsies! —then she still had that taste for living, that *goût de vivre.* There was also much anguish. (Gerald *had* alarmed them.) I saw her looking at people she was fond of, and she was fond of so many. There was Simpkins, the young Albany porter, who was saving to get married and exactly the right age to be called up. There was her own family. The guilt and misery of not being able to hand out passages to America to everyone. (This was no personal failure of nerve but a kind of rational conviction, reluctantly accepted— Aldous said that Gerald was a remarkable man, so Gerald knew what's what, and Gerald said that it was now possible to wipe out life in a modern city in a matter of hours.) I never quite put the question—Are you going for good? Matthew had been told that they were going to see him into an American college. Would *they* return? I don't think they quite knew, or wanted to know (although, if this is not too fanciful, I think Maria *had* some premonition). The point is that they were no more consistent than anybody else and the war was not the only factor in the complex impulses that prompted their going. ("Man is not an entirely or even mainly a conscious being.")

A few weeks before sailing they made a decision within a decision. Aldous wrote to his old employer Condé Nast in New York, and the same night Maria sent a cri de cœur to Jeanne: "*Puis que nous quittons l'Europe . . Je ne puis quitter tranquillement en vous laissant là.*

[1] The Elkin Matthew catalogue was kindly lent to me by a collector, Mr Paul C. Jones, of Chagrin Falls, Ohio.

I want to write you a long and very serious letter. It's about America.

Aldous and Gerald really think that the situation is getting worse and worse and that there may be a cataclysm before summer . . . This is something one should not talk about, there are so many people who cannot leave and it would be cruel to tell them about our fears. It's still possible that it won't happen, so why worry them pointlessly. Why worry Mère and Rose . . .

But as we are leaving Europe, I cannot go leaving you, you and Sophie, behind.

The letter to Condé Nast has gone off . . Aldous has asked him to find you a job in America . . if he does, you must come at once, Janin, without bothering about Sophie's school or the rent. If he doesn't, you must get ready all the same to leave at the end of term.

There followed instructions about ships, the quota, money, "We shall manage for you in one way or another.

If we were on our own, I don't think for a moment that we would leave. But we are not, anymore than you are; and wouldn't it be rather pointless to stay and risk so much when we happen to be among the very few free enough to be able to get away?

Don't tell Sophie. I don't talk war to Matthew. Remember what we thought of Mère when she did. I don't promise you an easy life, or a pleasant life, or riches, or anything. My one idea, and you must understand this, and give in, is to get you both into safety. Let me have your answer.

Aldous proposed that he should give me an interview, to be published the day after his departure. One afternoon we got down to it. Aldous perched on the arm of a chair with pad and pen. I was rather astonished when he started to forestall me. It was *he* who supplied the questions as well as took the note. There he was asking, scribbling, talking all in one, evidently an old hand at it; I had never seen him so efficient. He said a good deal more than he jotted down, but that's forgotten (I, too, possess no shorthand). The interview was never published for the silly and rather awful extraneous reason that someone pinched my typescript and tried to sell it to another paper. "Going to America?" Aldous said.

Q. Going to America? [Aldous wrote]
A. Yes.
Q. Lecture?
A. No. Learn. Not teach.
Q. Do you know US well?
A. Very little.

Q. What means of transport?
A. By car.
Q. Where going?
A. Across continent . . .
(I am transcribing a fraction only of Aldous's note.)

A. No very definite programme. But wish to see certain things. Esp. educational experiments.
Q. Are they more interesting than in Europe?
A. They are certainly more numerous . . .
Q. Do you intend to write while in US?
A. I hope that the material collected there may help me in completing a sociological book I am now writing.
Q. What about?
A. About the means which must be employed if desirable changes are to be realized. Certain of the American experiments in . . industrial organization etc. should throw considerable light on this problem. The causes of the wrong functioning of society are numerous and the means for remedying this wrong functioning will consequently have to be of many kinds—political, economic, educational, religious, psychological, philosophical. To employ one means—e.g. economic change—without the others is useless. The problem must be attacked simultaneously on a number of different fronts . . . I am hoping to learn a lot regarding this in America. . . .
Q. Do you propose to write another novel?
A. I hope so. But I find it impossible to make definite plans in advance. It depends on circumstances.

" 'Depends on circumstances', you want to end on that?" Aldous said he thought so.

Aldous, Maria and Matthew sailed from Southampton on the s.s. Normandie on 7th April 1937.
I went to see them off. The luggage had gone earlier, and they walked out of Mount Royal in mid-morning unencumbered. Maria was wearing her Florentine officer's cloak. T. had left his surgery to see them into their taxi. Aldous thanked him again warmly, Maria embraced him. At Waterloo the boat train was drawn up and we found the reserved compartment. Aldous seemed calm and cheerful. We were still waiting for Gerald. (Christopher Wood, their mutual friend, who was also sailing had made his own travel arrangements.) Minutes went. Gerald had told Maria that one should treat a thing like going overseas with perfect equanimity, it was not an occasion. She was sure that he was coming from

Bloomsbury by underground allowing neither more time nor less than he would for an everyday engagement. More minutes. There is nothing we can do, said Aldous. Maria spied a cluster of anxious looking elderly women on the platform. Below their overcoats they wore long skirts sweeping the ground. They must be some of Gerald's good women, said Maria. General anxiety increased. At last we saw him. The women stepped forward. Gerald, visibly put out, turned and got into the carriage. He sat down in a corner seat and pulled a curtain, his handsome inquisitorial profile stern and quiet. Maria went to the window with a conciliatory gesture, one of the women proffered a parcel. Maria signed to Gerald but the train pulled out. Luncheon presently arrived on trays. They had brought us pork chops in a greasy gravy which was as good an excuse as any not to eat. Thanks to Matthew, for whom naturally this was a great day, we got through the journey.

At Southampton we learnt that owing to some pettifogging squabble over harbour dues between the French and English the Normandie had not docked. She was lying in Southampton Water. Passengers were ferried by launch. It was a cold and longish ride on choppy waves. We were hauled on board. Aldous and Maria were at once escorted to a large and luxurious cabin (not the one they'd paid for: they were going tourist class) compliments of the French Line. They were also informed that they would have the freedom of the ship. Jeanne had sent champagne and some of this we drank now, Gerald reluctantly accepting a few drips. There was still an hour or more to go. Everything was entirely unreal. Gerald went to his own cabin. We wandered about the vast and brand-new ship, crossing and re-crossing public rooms, a gilded, throbbing, overheated limbo. Matthew drifted off. Every now and then Maria said, Eddy—you must give our messages to Eddy . . . Don't forget to give our messages to Moura . . . to Raymond . . . Don't forget our messages to Vera . . . To Naomi . . . to Marion . . . Give my messages to Bessie . . . She did not say what messages. It seemed clear enough. When the bell rang for visitors to leave ship, I said farewell to Aldous. Maria came up to the open deck—it was night-fall now—from where one took the launch. I was a symbol, the last of Europe, the last link. At the end she gave me the dispatch case she was carrying. I was just able to undo it and get out their passports and a clutch of papers. "Oh, Aldous would have been so cross," she said. I was already down the gang plank when Maria took off her officer's cloak, keep this, she called and let it fall.

PART SEVEN

Caesura: 1937-1939

Just tired and busy and amazed and
amused and charmed and horrified.
MARIA HUXLEY in a letter to the
Vicomte de Noailles

Chapter One

First Run Around

We have not had time to think about anything much. Just tired and busy and amazed and amused and charmed and horrified. No time to breathe and know what we think. That may come in some book some time.

THEY had had their days in New York (The Seabrooks, the Saxtons, strangers.) "You have no idea how *famous* Aldous is here," Maria to Jeanne, "perhaps I shall end by being impressed."

They bought their car. A Ford. The four of them set off on their first rush across country. They went south—through Virginia, Georgia, Florida, Louisiana.

> . . Have seen various seats of learning [Aldous's postcard to Julian, 7th May] from Charlottesville (mouldy) to Black Mountain (interesting), from Duke (a remarkable phenomenon) to Dillard, the negro coll at N Orleans (rather depressing) . . . Hope tomorrow to visit world's largest cavern—complete with elevator service . . and cafeteria.
>
> . . But soon, as we reached through the tobacco country and the cotton country [Maria to Roy] . . the many heat waves began . . . So we got on pretty fast, through the swamps of New Orléans . . . Then we began crossing Texas; at leisure first when the country was rolling and scrubby and alive with animals and tortoises crossing the roads. But soon the desert grew more desertic, the roads dustier and the sun more and more vicious till we became almost hysterical and drove from air-cooled cinemas to air-cooled hotel bedrooms . . .[1]

Maria took against the car. Wheel and seats were at wrong angles for her, it was tiring to drive. After some five weeks on the road they reached Frieda Lawrence's ranch in the mountains of New Mexico, San Christobal, 8,000 feet above the valley of the Rio Grande. Maria weighed herself on arrival in a drug store at Taos, her weight was down to 98 lbs. with her clothes on. Frieda asked them to stay the summer; they accepted. She lent them a log cabin by a rushing brook. The first weeks were rough, a pioneer's existence; at times Maria thought that she would have to give up. But on 23rd June she wrote to Eddy Sackville-West,

[1] *Letters of Aldous Huxley*, from one of Maria's few published letters.

344

. . Sybille told you the mad situation I have gone and put myself into. But now the worst is over, we are settled in, water flows, chimneys draw, cleanliness reigns and peace too . . . Nothing seems to matter much and I believe it is the terrific view from the hills that gives one that calmness and serenity.

Maria wrote to several friends about that first summer; her account to Eddy is the most candid. They understood each other very well; he was one of the rare people Maria could complain to and admit because she knew that he would not be too distressed. "Dearest and most faithful Eddy," this letter starts (faithful because *he* wrote regularly; some of their friends did not; there was a curious barrier), and it runs to some 3,000 words.

I am happy to think that you enjoy Sanary [They had lent him Villa Huley] . . That house and the walks were very precious to me; the memory of them still is, and even Aldous's grudge against it when he was ill has not spoiled it for me. You are right about thinking that I am not very pleased with all this—but this is a secret—for in reality I am always pleased enough with anything I get; not on principle, just because it is in my nature to be so adaptable that sometimes it shocks me. But we have been rushing too much and too fast until we settled here: then until last Monday there was such a terrific amount of work that I became very rattled underneath and so tired that I don't know how much longer I could have carried on. Now we are settled in a little mud-and-wooden house which has a paper roof . . .

. . The views are surely described in Lawrence's letters and our lives are going to be, I trust, monotonous. Aldous works in his bedroom which communicates with mine through an arch. Matthew sleeps in the sitting room which leads . . two steps down to the kitchen which is so small that one of us has to sit on the steps for meals . . . Gerald has a little hut on the other side of the stream and his ghostliness comes and goes . . . Our watches have suffered from the altitude so we do completely without and it is curious what a sense of time one has anyways . . . Matthew, as well as doing carpentry and plumbing, is doing algebra and American history; at night, while I wash dishes (no servants whatsoever, and I cannot say I realized what that meant, you would have to see me constantly with many brooms, I fear, and not mind—I have six different kinds of brooms but this does not help. They read aloud. We also have a bathroom [they had just built it themselves, with Matthew doing most of the skilled work] and Aldous insisted we have Butane, so now my life is comparatively grand. We did depend on a little kitchen range which needed feeding with wood constantly; not only heating us to a Dantesk degree but dirtying all

M*   345

our gloves and rags and hands, not to mention the times I used to burn my fingers.

. . Frieda's lover, Angiolino, is so Italian that of course we have to humour him a bit . . . Fundamentally he is very decent and honest. How much they care for one another, or rather in what way they care for one another I don't know. I long to write and tell you more but shall wait until we meet again. This place, I mean Taos, 20 miles off and where we never go, is a nest of scandal and quarrels. Frieda has been, and still is, so affectionate and generous and warm-hearted that I do not want anything to come back to her which could be misinterpreted. You know how things come back, even from Europe and however discreet one is. There is however no scandals, no complaints to amuse you with; just the quarrels with her and Mabel Luhan who wanted to steal Lawrence's ashes from a childish little chapel Frieda built over them here . . .

. . The desert . . begins four miles from us . . pink on the barren soil, grey with the sage-bush, bright green in the irrigated oasis and then black cracks which are the running banks of the Rio Grande . . .

Frieda's life is extraordinary. She lives in such a primitive way that we can hardly understand it. Angiolino built her a concrete house . . and the sitting room is hung by all Lawrence's pictures. But the heart of the house is a large kitchen which has only a wooden range which heats, or rather tepids, a little bath water and which must be lit for every cup of tea. The easiness might be called messiness, the milk which comes . . from a pretty jersey cow is around in all forms of creams, and butters, and sour creams, and milks and what not . . . there are also the pig-bowl and the cat-bowl and the dog-bowl; many things to horrify me and shock me; yet she is essentially clean if you can imagine that; perhaps because she is a blonde. My greatest horror is to be asked to meals; it is then taken for granted that I do the washing up—I arrive with my rubber gloves—but the mess is such that if there were a heaven I deserve a bit of it for every washing up I do. Meanwhile there she sits, talking of Montaigne or Buddha or Mabel Dodge and making us all feel happy and at home. There is an art of accepting things from people which I feel I shall never acquire. I suffer a great deal when Gerald tries, and succeeds, in doing my housework. He is very very precious to us all in a different way, and we miss him. [He had gone off to Hollywood to stay with Christopher Wood.] A changed Gerald too. Grows a little beard which had to come off when he went to Chris; looks rested, without stressed hands, silent on the whole and drinking wine and water with every meal . . .

We took some pictures . . . so badly developed . . and upon this might come a long string of complaints about the barbarousness of America, about the inefficiency, about the junkiness, the backwardness and above all the poverty. But—I would not have missed this life for anything . .

. . No American ever mends; they wear rags and holes; we stayed at a school where the headmaster went to a picnic with a hole in his trousers.

Frieda is continually visited out of the blue by vague friends or strangers; they want to see Mrs D. H. Lawrence, and though she complains she lets them. Then they bring her cakes . . and think they have paid her for her trouble. They are the most casual and tactless people I have ever known. Sometimes we suffer from it too. But I firmly say Aldous is working . . . and I have already learned to bear a stolid face . . But they don't mind finding me in blue jeans, or in shorts and with a handkerchief of Aldous over my head because I am dusting or going to my larder . . . My compromise is to keep my toes nicely painted because my finger-nails have had to go with so many other things. No housemaid's stockings, Eddy, because I wear none . . but large heavy boys boots with hooks when we go out for walks . . .

Please do not tire of writing again. At the moment you are the only link, with Sybille who writes very rarely; it is curious how distant and remote and unimportant Europe feels . . And yet I know I shall be Europe-sick . . Never London, never England, never Paris, never friends, I am afraid, but Mediterranean-sick, if you can understand that. I am too busy with my family to miss people. I am only by myself when I look out or wander round or drive to do the shopping. Just like at Sanary my only lonely hours are the very early ones; when the sun has risen over the plain which is brittle-clear, but we are in shade and pines are dark, I sit on the porch and feel that this is not my country. Unconquerable. Alien. Hating. The heat scorches, the water floods and carries away, I can see the dust whirlwinding in the plain . . .

Aldous, in the same month, was writing to Julian, "The country is most astonishing and beautiful—but I don't know if one cd stand it very long. I've never been in any place, except parts of Mexico, which gave such an impression of being alien, even hostile, to man."

While at the edges of the Mediterranean [Maria once more] the wildness is sufficient to make one appreciate the toil and architecture that goes into the terracing, the cypresses are signs of life . . the olives are pruned and there is a clemency on the air I love. Yet, we are told that "this country gets one." Yes, Matthew. But then he is young and very different. And he still has to learn that peace and not excitement are one's needs.

. . I had for two months about, no moment to my self nor no moments

347

which were not under severe physical strain . . . It was a curious sort of hunted feeling. I was looking for some time to think and instead I was being hunted by time to do. It gave me a feeling like a Kafka book and I, even now, have not had time to know exactly what it was I wanted to think about. You'll probably laugh. But then, I never mind being laughed at.

This is all. The letter is written and the love is sent.

About two months later, Aldous had as good as finished *Ends and Means*.

. . I finished the copying four days ago [Maria wrote again to Eddy in what must have been latish August] Against time and with the electricity of the storms in all my fingers every afternoon—but it is done . . I think [it] is excellent indeed and shall long to know what you think about it. Now he is revising it, and, of course, there is more to do. But not so much that I cannot breathe or write to thank you for a letter . . .

. . Matthew has come back from Chicago and Gerald arrived from Hollywood and we were once more all gay and busy and how they talk! But, also, the more I know Gerald the more remarkable and lovable I find him. We all laugh and say he should not this and he should not that; and I tease him and scold him. Then I am mostly very impressed. When he left us it was as if ten Geralds had left us . . . he is gone again to Chris and to who knows how many other of his 'penitenti' . . .

. . On the 10th about [September] we go to Denver and buy Matthew his school outfit. He goes to a very nice school at Colorado Springs [Fountain Valley] on the 15th. Then we return here for a short time. To pack up and leave for Hollywood and meet Gerald.

. . Aldous and Gerald are doing a lecture tour (I call it their Mutt and Jeff) . . . Aldous had consistently refused to do it until he was told by Gerald, quite rightly, that this was such a good opportunity to get his ideas of peace across. So with the help of Gerald he signed his contract. It was not as fearful as some contracts can be. It will be nice for them being together . . but it binds them to this country until early January. I shall not go with them because it would be expensive and because, seeing that Aldous will be admirably looked after by Gerald, I think I can have a little holiday . . . I should like to be in a comfortable hotel in a country place where I know nobody and can have books. But it may . . work out that I shall go to New York to settle my sister who has come over . . into a flat and look after the child a little. They will probably be lost and also very busy. American life, I have discovered is very hard on those who are not extremely rich. In spite of all electrical saving devices, work remains work and meals remain 4 meals a day. The life I have been leading here was a slight mistake; we none of us realized how much work there is going even at a minimum. But a good many women in America who are richer than we were when I first married work a good deal harder. I never had to do disgusting work; always in Europe we had at least a char.

. . Aldous and [G] must still prepare their lectures, they start in the West. I shall drive them about for the few, not too distant lectures. After the New Year, if they offer Aldous *tons* of money, he may work for the movies for a little while. Otherwise we shall travel . . .

I shall be glad to leave this place . . . I am rattled with the typing but it is not that either; nor doing most of Frieda's work. It is just that this place, in spite of the desert which is beautiful and the clouds . . is somehow empty and hollow . . . It did us all a lot of good. Until I started typing I had put on eight pounds . . . I often wish you were here; I have so little friends, sometimes ashamed of how I miss practically none of them, but I make up by caring very much about those I do care for. Being sad because you have stuck in your book. Knowing just what that means . . . I want to give you some advice about not squashing your sad thoughts under the novel, but coping with them. I always find I get over my sadness when I really look at it. But you are so far off . . . it is difficult enough to talk . . . those letters I rattle off with mistakes and bad grammar and so on; and when I think of how long Aldous takes to write a letter and of how many sheets he tears up I ought never to write at all. But what has one got friends for if it is not to expect them to like the news and overlook the rest.

In September the Huxleys loaded up the car again and left the ranch. They saw the Grand Canyon and what Maria called the view-places and arrived in California with a heat wave. They took a small flat in Hollywood. For the first couple of weeks they lived quietly, correcting the proof of *Ends and Means*. Then Matthew went off to his new school, and Aldous and Maria got into a whirl.

We have met here all the very eminent world of The Technical Institute of Pasadena [Maria to Roy], gone up Mount Wilson and looked at the sky with Professor Hubble, we visited the country and the prosperous ranches, we have met scholars on Bacon and novelists and sociologists and on the same day we have met Gary Cooper or Anita Loos or Charlie and the whole pattern becomes fantastic and improbable . . . We have seen . . the only Chinchilla farm in the world and the largest hogs, and the making of the Mickey Mouse films and working on orchids with mineral salts . . and oil drilling and hideous picture shows and the best and largest private collection

349

of French Modern pictures in the house of a nice mad-man . . .[1]
Yesterday we had a very *intellectual* dinner with Charlie Chaplin,
Paulette Goddard a very good and very handsome hostess and Upton
Sinclair one of the guests. Charlie . . did . . a mimic of Mussolini . . .
. . there are no buses or trams and distances so enormous taxis would
ruin us. But my chauffeur hours are not so bad as I get through a
good deal of reading. [When Aldous is at the dentist and so on] The
only misery can be the heat if I have to park in the sun . . .

The idea of making tons of money in the films had been started
by Jacob Zeitlin, the Los Angeles rare-books dealer, who had
written proposing himself as an intermediary. Aldous had answered
cautiously that he might be willing (later, they became friends).
Zeitlin suggested *Antic Hay*, *The Gioconda Smile*, *After the Fireworks*,
The World of Light and possibly *Point Counter Point* and *Gaza* as
suitable for cinematic adaptation. The studios would have none of
it. "The best they cd do in Hollywood was to ask me to adapt *The
Forsyte Saga* for the screen :[to Julian] but even the lure of enormous
lucre cd not reconcile me to remaining closeted for months with
the ghost of the late poor John Galsworthy."

Aldous, however, did a radio interview. The fee was $750 and
Maria spoke of the unfair enormity of the sum. After two agents'
commissions and State tax, it dwindled to an acceptable $190.

They went on a jaunt to San Francisco with Gerald and
Christopher Wood.

piled in the same old Ford which goes as well as ever and drives even
more tiringly but I have come to terms with it now. [Maria to faithful
Eddy] We had a beautiful drive up . . stopping at Carmel . . sparkling
white sand and green shores and eucalyptus groves. Like a Boudin
under blue skies. At San Francisco the bridges were in their full glory
. . and we drove over and over them and walked about the town,
with a centre and shops and Italian and French food and compact
so that one could walk and take taxis . . . While Gerald and Aldous
went to their Guru to improve their souls Chris and I wandered and
drove about . . .

Then at night, the fogs came like serpents along the bay . . and the
ships hooted and searchlights flashed . . .

We drove back slowly through the big redwood trees . . . I cannot
give an impression of the old large sequoias. They like to stand in
clusters and it must have something to do with their agedness that
gave one a curious feeling. They are very impressive and the stillness
in those forests very moving.

. . We also went to San Diego . . [it] was to be a mixture of La

1 John Davenport, I think.

Spezia and Toulon and a bit of Genoa (we have not yet learnt we are in America, it seems) and of course it was in fact the usual scattered untidy medley of wooden shanties with tin roofs and railways running in the street, then a large skyscraper, the best hotel and absolutely no centro della città to stroll in . . .

But the Zoo is the loveliest of all zoos—up and down a thickly planted sub-tropical park,

and the animals with fur healthy and shiny as that of a pet to a rich dowageress.

Aldous and Gerald had their first lecture in the Philharmonic Auditorium of Los Angeles in October. ("Aldous so slow and calm and passive, Gerald vehement and busy and coercive.") Presently the two men left for their tour "both in leather coats, small grey hats and umbrellas . . (at seven in the morning and chilly) . . They both promised not to die before I had joined them." Maria was to go east by bus as Gerald and Christopher Wood had terrified Aldous as to what would happen to her if she crossed the continent in the car by herself.

I would drown, starve in blizzards, be raped by hoboes . . . So now I have to sell the car here. I can't say I mind when I look at the map.

As for future plans. "Well, the Hollywood adventure is over. I loved it.

We were very amused, very interested and very cheerful and very well . . . Yet we are leaving it because it does not seem the place for us to settle down in . . . Now Marjorie [Seabrook] has come to the rescue as ever and it seems that Maryland, on the peninsula, would be . . perfect . . This here [California] is so far. So far, I suppose from Europe, or from New York or from I don't know what but it feels far . . . It will be Maryland probably and I like since ever that name. Only I do pronounce it like the French tobacco. Marylan. They don't understand me anyways. So I might as well have that pleasure to myself.

Mutt and Jeff came to an abrupt end. Poor Gerald slipped on snow in Iowa and broke his arm. Aldous took him to hospital and continued single-handed. "Very unpleasant for him . . very boring for me, as I find this process of lecturing extremely tedious. [to Julian] It was more tolerable when we were two and could throw the ball back and forth . . . I find myself often a bit overwhelmed by the curious rigidity and opacity of most human beings. There's

351

something dismally fixed, stony, sclerotic about most of them—a lack of sensibility and awareness and flexibility, which is most depressing. There seems to be nothing much to be done, beyond, of course, doing one's best to prevent the oncoming of mental sclerosis in oneself, to keep the mind open to the world and to that which transcends the world . . ."

Or as Maria put it, "Aldous tours the halls of America by himself and loathes human beings more and more in spite of all his theories and efforts. He, perhaps fortunately, is not so easily taken in." Whereas Gerald, "only wishes to see the good in people and then, when they say 'I am GOOD' he just believes it".

Aldous's lectures were on the lines of the book he had just finished and he was getting very bored with saying the same thing over and over again. There were compensations—in Chicago, he met Dr William Sheldon,[1] the man who evolved the psychological classification of individuals known as the Sheldonian Types, to whose work Aldous already then attached such great importance. "A very remarkable man . . ."

In this country I have associated—by an odd series of accidents—mainly with doctors and astronomers. Very nice professions, both of them; for the doctors can feel they're doing good, while the astronomers can be sure that they're not doing much harm. There are not many other people who can feel the same. And then the mere fun of those trades! The experimental work on a new cancer cure which I saw being done—fascinating and exciting.

Maria meanwhile, in spite of exhortations, had started east by car. She was heading for New York where Jeanne and Sophie had landed a few months ago. Christina Mills ("the wife of the handsome playwright who sent us roses when they had no food") came with her on the first lap. "After two days of exquisite desert we reached Taos." Frieda and Angiolino "were so lovingly welcome and the stoves and fireplace were soon roaring and beds made in my little house and the stillness seemed stiller than it had been all summer. Next morning there was thick soft snow.

There was no wind so Angiolino took me on a ride on the horses fattened and gay and when the sun came out and the distant desert was pink . . I felt this to be the most beautiful place I had seen. The snow was silent under the rapid horses and we came in as from a dream. [Maria to Eddy]

[1] Professor W. H. Sheldon, Ph.D., M.D., author of *The Varieties of Human Physique, The Varieties of Temperament, Varieties of Delinquent Youth,* etc.

"But the next day brought an air mail letter from my sister. A very disappointing letter and it said, with many good reasons and sad words, that, unless it were to please me, she was returning to Paris. By the time I had read it . . the distance to New York stretched beyond end and the cautions I had about weathers and hold-ups seemed more real." Nonetheless, Maria went on next day.

. . Except for some moments of lonely fears and one bad incident of sticking in snow and slush, I got to New York in 5 days from there. I was cold and I was sad . . but the continual beauty of the whole country was the uppermost feeling. I was dressed in Aldous's Tibetan sheepskin . . but it was dry and it was fine. I drove from before sunrise to after sunset and got both the lights of pink in the skies. The whole of this continent is golden.

But through Arkansas I was shocked at the houses, huts rather, in which people are expected to live.

Aldous and Gerald were lost because their addresses had blown out of the window of my car when I opened it one night to ask the way.

Washington was my first large town . . and my sister met me there and we talked and I was even more unhappy at her decision which I had made plans to change. I could not ask her to stay to please me, but I had hoped to make her wish to join, in parts, our life . . . The next day as I again flew out of the crowded streets of Washington, or was it Baltimore? I was arrested by a handsome star-like policeman for speeding (I was) . . a chewing judge in a stuffy smelly shack back of the road made [me] pay 26 dollars; upon which I wept bitterly and had no handkerchief and felt ashamed and wept for a whole hour until we both realized that I was not weeping about the fine but about the miserable news Jeanne had for me. So you see how comic we must have been; still in the sheepskin and we stopped and hugged and everything was a little better. But not much.

A depressing and unsettling stay in New York. Next step, finding a place for Aldous to come home to. In December Maria moved into a little grey house on a Hudson estate, Edith Wharton country, "as ugly as can be but comfortable and well-heated . . very near the Seabrooks who are better friends than ever". Presently Aldous arrived; Matthew, who had telegraphed that he couldn't afford to come for Christmas, had been sent the 100 dollars for the fare— "Now everything is really better. I am reconciled to Jeanne's going [to Eddy] because she seems so happy at the thought that she looks twenty years younger than when I arrived. She has taken the whole trip not as a bitter disappointment but as a marvellous holiday and appreciates all that Paris can give her much more than she ever did before."

Now once more Aldous and Maria put their heads together as

to their own plans. Maryland was dropped quietly. On 15th December Aldous wrote to Harold Raymond as follows, "For the moment I have a respite [from lecturing]; but after the new year shall have to set off on my travels again . . . After that I expect we shall be heading for Europe, unless in the interval I get any news about a scenario I wrote while out in Hollywood. If there was a prospect of somebody wanting to do something with it, I might go back there for a bit . . ."

And Maria: "I wish you would come, Eddy . . I wish you would. Why not before you go to St Anton . . Come, and return with—us. But this last decision is not yet quite certain so you had better keep it a secret as Guilia [their cook at Sanary] would be too disappointed if it did not materialize."

By the end of the year it was still in the balance. "I wish I could say we were returning to the . . life in Sanary but we don't know . . [Maria to Charles de Noailles, 30th Dec.] It will not be certain for a few weeks . . Then it may be Sanary, it may be Mexico, it may be Hollywood."

It was in fact as close as that. Aldous might easily not have settled in America, gone back to Europe and thus to England and the war. (On that score everything was simplified for them by the facts that Matthew *was* in America and would stay to complete his education, and that Jeanne and her child *had* gone back.)

Ten days later it had swung the other way (for the present: essentially the decision was still open-ended). Aldous heard that a studio *might* take his scenario. "Our plans," he wrote to Jacob Zeitlin on 10th January, "have crystallized more or less . . After my last lecture . . we shall aim at Los Angeles." Meanwhile he set off again to speak at Washington, Philadelphia and Toronto. "Your letter sounds most ironically commenting on our present mode of life," Maria wrote to Eddy.

Erring and Erring Jews, as well as gypsies as well as bohemians is what we seem to be more and more. But *I* even more than the others because all the packing and all the rushing about is always mine. I suppose I love travelling . . . But as gypsy princess . . whereas I am turned into a gypsy cinderella.

Now there was to be more packing and more rushing. They acquired a new Ford—the first one had done 18,000 miles. "You know how I hated it but I have not had a repair, nor was I in trouble on the road ever." Presently they set out again for California by way of Colorado and New Mexico.

Chapter Two

Ends and Means

*E*NDS AND MEANS had appeared in England and the U.S.A. It is a book in which Aldous attempted to relate all social problems, the problems of international politics, of economics and education, to ethics; and ethics to his conception of the ultimate nature of reality. Our world is in a bad way, he postulated, what can we do to rescue it from its present plight?

A desirable social order is one that delivers us from avoidable evils. The means to achieve such an order must be multiple, and they must be the right means, means *good* in themselves. The obstacles, unfortunately, are immense.

> Every road towards a better state of society is blocked, sooner or later, by war, by threats of war, by preparations for war.[1]

Yet war is not imposed on us by any kind of biological necessity.

> . . Man has now little to fear from competition with other species. His worst enemies . . are insects and bacteria . . . For man competition is now predominantly intra-specific . . entirely gratuitous and voluntary . . we are wantonly and deliberately pursuing a policy which we need not pursue and which we have the best scientific reason for supposing to be disastrous to the species as a whole . . .

Another formidable obstacle to desirable reform is built into the existing order of things. To bring about radical reforms we would have to change first our "machinery of government, our . . administration and industrial organization, our system of education and our metaphysical and ethical beliefs.

> . . Existing methods of government and . . industrial organization *are not likely to be changed except by people who have been educated to wish to change them.* [My italics] Conversely, it is unlikely that governments composed as they are today will change the existing system of education in such a way that there will be a demand for a complete overhaul of governmental methods. It is the usual vicious circle . . .

[1] All quotations in this chapter, unless indicated, are from *Ends and Means*. Chatto & Windus, 1937.

355

From which there is only one way of escape—"Through acts of free will on the part of morally enlightened, intelligent, well-informed and determined individuals, acting in concert."

Ends and Means became a kind of Bible to the Peace Pledge Union; unlike Hegel, *Mein Kampf* or Machiavelli, it had little influence on politicians or the masses; for the average sensual man it makes, like so much of Aldous's later work, disagreeable reading; it greatly affected some young men. Professor J. M. Tanner[1] speaks of the tremendous influence the book had on his generation (like *Crome Yellow* and *Antic Hay* on the one before)

> A tremendous influence on my actual life. I had been reading *Ends and Means* at Marlborough at the age of seventeen. Shortly afterwards I had an interview at Woolwich—I come from an Army family, my father had decided . . . Some elderly military gents were asking questions.
> "What do you read?"
> "*Ends and Means, Point Counter Point, Eyeless in Gaza* is more serious."
> "What, no Buchan?"
> "Oh yes. I enjoyed that very much at prep school—stuff for kids."
> I was flooded by the realization: this won't DO. Wrote to Daddy that night. Then began doing medicine and physics.[1]

What is this world of ours—? Aldous asked. What is the sense and point of the whole affair?

> . . Is there any reason for regarding this world as superior to the world of earlier geological epochs? In other words, can evolution be regarded as a genuine progress? These questions can be answered, with perfect justification, in the affirmative. Certain properties, which it is impossible not to regard as valuable, have been developed . . . The lower forms of life persist more or less unchanged; but among the higher forms there has been a definite trend towards greater control and greater independence of the physical environment. Beings belonging to the highest forms of life have increased their capacity for self-regulation, have created an internal environment capable of remaining stable throughout very great changes in the outer world, have equipped themselves with elaborate machinery for picking up knowledge of the outer world, as well as of the inner, and have developed a wonderfully effective instrument for dealing with that knowledge . . .

---

[1] J. M. Tanner, M.D., D.Sc., M.R.C.P., Professor of Child Health and Growth, University of London. Talking to S. B.

Now, does the world *as a whole* possess value and meaning? And if so what is the nature and value of that meaning?

This is a question which, a few years ago, I should never even have posed. For, like so many of my contemporaries, I took for granted that there was no meaning. This was partly due to the fact that I shared the common belief that the scientific picture of an abstraction from reality was a true picture of reality as a whole; partly also to other non-intellectual reasons. I had motives for not wanting the world to have a meaning; consequently assumed that it had none, and was able without any difficulty to find satisfying reasons for this assumption . . .

For myself, as, no doubt, for most of my contemporaries, the philosophy of meaninglessness was essentially an instrument of liberation. The liberation we desired was simultaneously liberation from a certain political and economic system and liberation from a certain system of morality. We objected to the morality because it interfered with our sexual freedom; we objected to the political and economic system because it was unjust. The supporters of these systems claimed that in some way they embodied the meaning (a Christian meaning, they insisted) of the world. There was one admirably simple method of confuting these people and at the same time justifying ourselves in our political and erotic revolt: we could deny that the world had any meaning whatsoever . . .

. . By the end of the 'twenties a reaction had begun to set in—away from the easy-going philosophy of general meaninglessness towards the hard ferocious theologies of nationalistic and revolutionary idolatry. Meaning was reintroduced into the world, but only in patches . . .

Is there a universal meaning? If so, can we reach cognizance of it? Aldous's present answer is affirmative. We can, if we choose, gain insight into the nature of ultimate reality. By Liberation. Liberation from the prevailing conventions of thought, feeling, behaviour—by the practice of disinterested virtue. In other words, by goodness. And intelligence. There must always be the cultivation of intelligence.

For insensitive stupidity is the main root of all the other vices.

. . Love, compassion and understanding or intelligence—these are the primary virtues in the ethical system, the virtues organically correlated with what may be called the scientific-mystical conception of the world. Ultimate reality is impersonal and non-ethical; but if we would realize our true relations with ultimate reality and our fellow-beings, *we must practice morality* . . .

357

Chapter Three

Hollywood, California

ALDOUS and Maria got there in mid-February. "We were very gay and meant to be happy here where we arrived .. in a California so green that it took one's breath away. We found a house the next day and moved in just for Aldous to be ill."[1] A mild but stubborn attack of bronchial pneumonia. Three weeks in hospital. "He came back yesterday .. still has to stay in bed ... They found it was not T.B., so we were patient and are going on to be patient and we read till we have nothing left to read."[2]

Their house was a small furnished one on N. Laurel Avenue. Aldous was slow in picking up. Gerald Heard was living on a hill six miles away.

> Today Gerald came with a little bunch of yellow flowers for Aldous and they were talking as passionately as ever and were happy with bread and honey for tea . . . [He] looks extraordinarily handsome with a neat and full red beard .. His arm still is painful .. he does stoop terribly but otherwise seems very happy .. But I may be all wrong . . . But then one knows the natural Gerald and forgets the 'become' Gerald.[2]

By April Aldous was doing a little painting and making notes for a future novel. He still had to lie down before dinner and was not allowed to go out at night. They saw a few friends, Edwin Hubble, the astronomer, and his wife Grace; Anita Loos, and through her some of the film world. "She is the doyenne of Hollywood, having started to write for the movies when she was seven," as Aldous had said, when he first met her in New York twelve years ago, in the letter that described her as so ravishing that one would like to keep her as a pet. Now she became one of their staunchest friends. They went for walks, with Gerald when possible, every afternoon.

> You see the simple life we lead and very much like London, Sanary or wherever we go.[2]
> Now it is spring . . . It was the time of year we were in Central America [Maria to Roy]. How many years ago? How old are we fast becoming!

[1] Maria to the Vicomte de Noailles, 6th March 1938.
[2] Maria to Eddy, 5th March 1938.

358

Plans were still fluid. ". . stay here till May. Go to the ranch [Frieda's] . . and when Matthew goes to College, return to Europe for a while. But that is not what my fortune teller tells me.[1]

Then came news that Maria's mother was ill in a Mexican hospital. Mme Nys had been travelling in Central America on her own all winter long with enjoyment and resource, "seeing everything plus all the things most people miss". Three days before returning to Belgium she was knocked down by a bus. Maria was on the point of going out to her, hesitated to leave Aldous, heard that she was out of danger. "But I may still have to go, and perhaps fetch her. The distance is that from London to Constantinople." (To Eddy.)

At Easter Lady Ottoline Morrell died in England. On 4th May, Maria wrote to Eddy. "Ottoline's death only reached us now and I daresay you don't know just how much she was to my life. In spite of the agonies of those young loves it was my greatest. And in those later years, in spite of a gap of coldness and distance, we had become devoted friends. I loved her dearly and am haunted by many thoughts. But they say she died peacefully, yet she did die suddenly. Is it to be wished for to die without a warning . . .? I hope she did not die of unhappiness. But none of these things we shall ever know. . . .

> . . . The doctor says [Aldous] is practically well. Yet I think he sometimes looks so tired. I hope all the tragedies for this year are over. Aldous's illness, Mother's accident and the irreparable death of Ottoline.

Then came a new prospect. Anita Loos rang up one evening asking if Aldous were approachable about doing the film script of Madame Curie for Metro-Goldwyn-Mayer. With Greta Garbo as Eva Curie. George Cukor, producer; Hyman, director—intelligent men whom Aldous had met at Anita's. (It was all due to her.) She now implored Maria to encourage Aldous to accept. "You will get enough to set you up for life, and I will protect you at the studio." Aldous was resting before dinner; receiver dangling, Maria went to talk to him.

"But *how* can I? And what can Garbo do in it? And anyhow I wouldn't be able to please them."

A moment later he caught fire. It *would* be interesting. One might do some scenes in the Belgian Congo, in Russia . . . show the use of radium in actual hospitals . . . Ideas flowed. They spent the rest of the evening talking. *And* it would be well paid, Anita

---

[1] Maria to Charles de Noailles.

had said so. No actual sum. It might be as much as a 1,000 dollars a month, perhaps he should hold out for that; then they could save half of it, he thought. More than half, Maria said. Next morning he slept an hour longer. "He's got a good reason at last to get well," Maria wrote to Jeanne.

Financial security would mean very very great peace for Aldous. Gerald doesn't understand this, he thinks the old books will always bring in enough to live on . . But if Aldous were ill, that wouldn't be enough and God knows how much these illnesses cost . . . Since the insomnia I am always thinking about his worry and distress when he was afraid that he mightn't be able to earn any more . . .

Anita Loos had raised first hopes in May; for the next weeks nothing happened (as nothing happened—or ever did—about Aldous's original scenario which had brought him there).

Now Aldous is taking it all so seriously that I'm afraid he'll suffer horribly if there is a disappointment . . . He wants to project the passion of scientific curiosity, and the nobility of such a life [Mme Curie's], the significance of the discovery of radium, the humility and courage of that woman. Aldous wants it to be done properly and nobly . . . The great advantage of having Garbo is that she passionately wants to play that part; she admires Aldous and would do a bit more under his direction . . .

He talked of going to Paris himself to interview the Joliot-Curies, although Maria was not even certain if the doctors would allow him to do the work at all. What they were advising was an air cure in the desert.

Meanwhile (late June) they moved again. "We are in a very large house [N. Linden Drive in Beverly Hills] with a cool ground-floor and three bedrooms and a green bathroom and a yellow one for Aldous and Matthew and all the bedrooms have two beds for us to choose from. We had to move because of Matthew [home from school]. So now we enjoy a garden and two fountains in a little patio . . Aldous is . . working away steadily at the novel. Under a large blue umbrella and wearing a summer suit which I think is indecently transparent but does not seem to bother him. [Maria to Eddy] Our latest fad is homeopathy and it works really well. Aldous seems to be cured definitely . . . Though he does not look strong; He looks sad sometimes which he never did.

Matthew is so grown-up that we spent the afternoon trying out cars for him. He starts a summer course at the university tomorrow and is well and tall with a Leica camera hanging around his neck. I try to spoil him a bit now. It is the age when one really passionately wants some things and might as well have them. When they come too late it is like not having them at all. As if I now had all the pearls I longed for when I lived in Italy . . . If you see a film with Hepburn (not good) called Holiday please notice that all the jewels are real. Her diamonds glitter hugely and are lovely; and the pearls the other woman wears are real too. That is Hollywood. If I could tell a story without ruining it I would embark on a few . . .

X. is well and . . gay in spite of some disease he caught bathing (he telephoned to say it was not syphilis while I was having Krishnamurti in to tea) . . .

Would you like America? . . in the end, after some sufferances, you would certainly come to like it and be able to live here. You see it is so large that in itself is a horror at first. Now I even wonder whether . . Europe would not feel a bit cramping. Then the people are extremely tolerant. But you can't get that for nothing; they are also careless. And they are kind . . . And here we have quite a few friends who are what I shall, ridiculously, call (for the lack of a better word) "civilized". But I would not like the East. The people are more like the English and freezing . . . But here we have some Mediterranean ease and kindness. We have some friends. Not mere acquaintances. That is much after such a short time.

Indeed Aldous and Maria had already met or were about to meet in the months that followed the eight or so men and women who became their friends for life—the Hubbles, Edwin and Grace . . . Anita Loos . . . Rosalind Rajagopal who was married to a Hindu and founded the Happy Valley community and school at Ojai . . . Krishnamurti . . . Peggy Bok, later Kiskadden . . . Beth Wendel . . . Christopher Isherwood . . .

. . I used to long for Sanary. But now all that is over. I could live here without going back to Europe. I have made my peace with it. Which does not mean that we are not going back . . . Aldous will want to go back and I shall go with him. That horrid feeling that I cannot leave him. Yet all the time he was lecturing without me he kept well and caught his pneumonia with me sitting next to him! Ironic. Yet I know I am right too.

The years of adjustment were harder than Maria let us believe. Living in America, living there with the Englishness and intellectuality of Aldous and Gerald—to whom the mind was still very much its own place—and with a rapidly assimilating Matthew, Maria was in many ways alone. She missed the companionship of a woman with a shared past. She missed her sister Jeanne.

I know, Jokes Chérie, that if you knew the country, if you knew my friends, if you could love and understand all this, I would feel less pain in being separated from you. Even your short stay in New York helps me a good deal when I write to you because I know that you know what I'm talking about . . . But it is as difficult to imagine the West as it would be for a Londoner to imagine cypresses and olive trees.

The consolations were the new landscapes—the night sky—the growing love for the desert.

One night walking home with Aldous, Maria was struck by the thought that seeing Jeanne was an actual possibility. "J'étais obligée de m'arrêter. Je tremblais et je pleurais." The letter was written the same night. Come . . . Now . . . For a holiday . . a few weeks. It is easy—we are able to pay the fare. The film makes it all right. Aldous is for it . . . Come! The appeal was propped by practical details—Bring light clothes, leave Sophie in Sanary with Sybille (I was spending the summer in the Villa Huley, still unsold), book a passage on the fast ship, the fastest inter-continental train, you could get here in eight days or nine . . . (The distance then, only some thirty years ago, between Paris and California was formidable, heart-breaking, more so possibly than at an earlier age when people thought nothing of taking three days to get from London to Bath.)

Jeanne, taking up life again in France, did not come. Perhaps the scheme, in Chamberlain's word, was impracticable. Maria answered generously, making light of disappointment. "But you must know that whenever you should want to come, *notre maison et notre cœur t'est ouvert*. You needn't give us notice; you needn't ask our advice. If you want to send Sophie, send Sophie. *Tu peux venir seule ou à deux, nues ou avec vos bagages* . . .

In July Madame Nys, convalescent, arrived from Mexico and stayed a month. Aldous's health was still much below par. M.G.M. at last made up their minds and a contract was signed. When the figures were out of the bag—$15,000 for eight weeks' work, Aldous and Maria were stunned. ". . $15,000—even with agents and taxes, it's enormous. But we're not celebrating or anything . . . I think that if destiny wants to present us with such a treasure it would be unreasonable to refuse. We have to envisage a long education for Matthew, and for Sophie too . . ."

So on the first Monday of August Aldous began his two months' stint at M.G.M. And what would they do after that? They would be rich enough to return, they might *like* to return, but—they had already cut themselves adrift—what would they be returning for? And was it worth it? Sanary for the winter? That would mean, Maria rationalized their thoughts to Jeanne, buying a car for three months' use. London?

What would we be doing and whom would we be seeing in London? So that journey would be a luxury and a caprice? It isn't as if Aldous could get a travel book out of it.

But what about returning for good?

At Sanary Aldous can only live part of the year, the working part; even so books are lacking. In London he can only live part of the year because of the climate . . . California—with its many disadvantages—combines some of the advantages of London and Sanary.

Anyway we can't go on like Lawrence, keep running off in search for the perfect place; it doesn't exist and it seems to me that at our age we ought at last to have found the tranquillity to stay where we are. I would understand a journey to an unknown country . . . where Aldous would find something new. In Europe there is nothing for him to do for I don't think he is going to start again losing his time preaching. If he wants to preach, let him publish his sermons . . .

So I've written to Sybille to find someone to buy [the Villa Huley] and at any price. [A week later she wrote to me again saying that Aldous and Matthew had decided to keep the house.]

At the end of his eight weeks Aldous turned in the finished script of Madame Curie (he thought it was rather good). The contract was not renewed. "They have followed their usual procedure [Aldous to Julian] and handed my treatment over to several other people . . By the time they are ready to shoot it may have passed through twenty pairs of hands. What will be left?" (Nothing. The film—new director, new script—was released five years later.)

Out of the blue, Maria, instead of the usual three or four closely typed pages, sent off a half sheet to Jeanne.

Aldous has absolutely no tuberculosis and it is true . . . It's some bronchial business . . . [the specialist] thinks it will be a matter of rest. He must lie down twelve hours a day. The climate here is all right. London or New York would be very bad.

I am so relieved that I realize [admit] how worried I was.

Whether they knew it or not, *this* determined their plans. The climate of Tucson, Arizona would have been even better. They would not have found there the other advantages they sought, libraries, intellectual stimulus, friends; the occasional chance to make some extra money in the movies. For the present they took a house on 1320 North Crescent Heights Boulevard. In 1925, Aldous had written to Bob Nichols, "when are you coming to Europe? I cannot believe that 622345678 Glen Av. Hollywood is a very salubrious address." *Tempora mutantur, et nos mutamur in illis.*

Chapter Four

1938/1939

DURING the Huxleys' first year and a half in America the news from Europe had been bad so steadily, had been so horrible, that, at a distance of some six thousand miles, it seemed too bad to be quite true. Until the Munich crisis.

This ghastly war came so close to being a reality . . . when it was over and we breathed again . . I thought of you, and all of you, as of ghosts. [Maria to Eddy] As of very ill people who had just escaped death . . . And how I did long to be with you and to know how it happened. How you stood it.

Gerald thought that they would close the frontiers and that no man could leave. And the fact that we "were safe" did not seem any comfort whatever . . Our thoughts and my wildest imagination strained to Europe. To Europe in general and to the face and moods of friends.

The radio spared us no . . details and no anxiety. On the worst day we went out . . to an Angricultural [*sic*] Fair. We had the radio . . on all the way and back and stopped to listen opposite the pigs. We were worn out by it. The distances made it worse I am sure.

Then I telephoned to my sister in Paris. It was marvellously clear and exciting and terribly sad. When it was over we both were (she wrote and told me) in despair. The distance seemed greater than ever . . . The child has not come. Had there been a war [Jeanne] would have waited too long. Now I know she will send her . . . I had a letter from Marion [Dorn] . . written while they waited in England for the first of October . . . And the letter from Paris from Charles de Noailles, waiting too . . And my mother's from Brussels and Sybille's from Sanary. No one taken in by words; no one wanting to fight. And now. What is the feeling? My sister writes from Paris that the detension was hysterically gay. As if there had been a war. Her concierge had just returned from a funeral; she explained that she could not feel sad. "Tout me semblait si beau, j'étais distraite, Madame. Les pavés gris me semblaient si beaux."

Meanwhile it is over. We are still ill with it. Aldous and Gerald would not admit it at the time. Gerald would hardly speak about it nor listen to the radio. He said we were mad. That was true, getting up all night and the real news coming in so early each morning . . . Then the disgusting pictures of gas masks; making people look like hogs. Now, this week, Aldous tells me, the pictures in *Life* are about the trenches in Hyde Park.

And then in California too life went on. The Huxleys had had to move in mid-crisis. Afterwards they discovered that they were in the ugliest house in Hollywood. It had a garden, though, "large and private like a Corot". Aldous at last was getting better. He was made to keep to his prescribed rest—ten hours at night, two in the afternoon. Rest without reading or talking. "He may listen to his radio in the afternoon, though technically he ought to sleep. I am rather annoyed with the doctors who were not at all precise about what they called taking it easy." All the same the week after Munich, because of their relief,

> the four of us went on a little trip. Chris always sits in front with me while Aldous and Gerald sit and talk in the back. Chris has bought me an altimeter and we measured all our whizzings up and down. [We] went leisurely through a golden campagna like country with the stubble of barley . . then up into high country that was like Devon, apple orchards and all . . then moors and lakes like Scotland and wild duck and Gerald loving it. They were all delightfully home-sick . . .

Aldous made up his mind. "He is going to start a short, easy, quick novel instead of going back to the big one he started . . . I think it is a good idea. So the other one can brew. [It never came to light] This one is about longevity, and is going to be comic too . . He is going to put in a lot about California life . . He is in a good mood." [To Eddy, 14th October]

Chapter Five

Private Miracle?

THERE had been for some time a great anxiety—submerged—
in Aldous's and Maria's life. His sight. Since 1913 he had lived
with it as a stationary affliction. This was no longer so. Such sight
as he had was, in his own words, "steadily and quite rapidly failing.
I was wondering quite apprehensively what on earth I should
do." During his first autumn in America he had heard of a method
of visual re-education, the Bates method in fact, and decided to
give it a try. The teacher, according to Maria was so paralysingly
stupid that Aldous did not go on, though he realized that there
might be a lot in it. Now he found another man in Los Angeles.
The first (extant) mention of the thing is a letter of Maria's dated
7th December 1938.

> Aldous goes on with his oculist and must be pleased with him. We
> don't discuss results every day; that would be agonizing. Especially
> as they vary so; but his theory is that what one can see once, one can
> see always. So now for the last three days Aldous has been able to
> see lines of "diamond type" which is so small that I have trouble
> reading it. He spends hours there, and at home he does exercises
> while he's resting; he looks at black. All this goes to show that there
> is hope . . .

Maria herself was none too well. "I've been so tired for the last
month that in the evening I sometimes cry in my bath; not out of
sadness but lassitude. My temperature is so low that it is ridiculous."
Her life *was* tiring. To begin with there was all that driving (Profession: *Chauffeur*, she put down in hotel registers). Gerald would
not permit himself to own or drive a car. "Out of humility . . . he
will not see that this is actually an extraordinary indulgence." Nor
does he "want to telephone or possess a telephone. So I not only
have to refuse for Aldous but for Gerald. I'm their secretary."
Now tomorrow, for instance,

> I shall drive Aldous to the oculist at 9.30. At 11.30 I pick up Gerald
> and leave him here; six miles each way. At 12.30 I fetch Aldous.
> He'll have lunch by himself and rest (because of the oculist he hardly
> works, *le pauvre*).

Meanwhile Gerald has to be driven to Pasadena because he wants
to see their friends the Hubbles. He can't go on his own because

366

he has no car, and he won't go with the Huxleys in the evening because he meditates from six to seven.

It takes us three quarters of an hour in the mid-day heat. We can't stay long because I have to take Aldous out again. Then I drive Gerald back because he must be home on the dot of six p.m. for his meditation. After dinner I read to Aldous as he is not allowed to read at all for the moment. I even read him the newspaper at breakfast.

Maria's letters throw some light on the contradictions in the life of that extraordinary man who was Aldous's best friend.

. . Tu sais combien j'aime Gerald et combien je le respecte et c'est autant plus triste de le voir rétrécir toute sa vie et toute sa philosophie comme il le fait . . .

. . You know how much I love Gerald and how much I respect him [still Maria to Jeanne] which makes it all the sadder to see him shrink his life the way he does, and his whole outlook. And then he criticises the life we lead (because he loves us). He thinks that we are seeing far too many people and are not confining ourselves to those who want to save their souls . . . He thinks that Aldous has the right to say, as Gerald does, I'm too busy, my work is too important for me to go and see you . . . But I think that this is absolutely inadmissible c'est orgeuilleux . . . Then he thinks that I spend too much time learning what others feel and suffer, and that we often see people we don't really want to see out of politeness. But as we, and specially Aldous, are sometimes interested in going out into the world, it seems to me that we owe a certain politeness to the world. Gerald tells me that's my Latin education . . . I tell him that politeness comes from the heart . . . But then perhaps I do bother too much about people . . . looking into their lives. I ought to shut my eyes, I waste so much time . . but as long as it isn't Aldous's time. Fortunately he has such a capacity for "withdrawing himself".

Now Matthew is with them for the Christmas holidays, thin and low in spirits. They rush him to their doctors. The lungs seem all right. After he left (on New Year's Eve, Aldous and Maria having gone to bed at nine), he sent his mother a charming, reassuring telegram.

Mathieu peut . . très finement me rassurer et me faire comprendre milles choses sans les expliquer définitivement; ce qu'Aldous ne peut ni faire ni comprendre.

In another letter Maria tells Jeanne never to misunderstand what may sound like criticism of Gerald. "I love and respect him and don't know what we should do without him and he is devoted to us to the extreme . . . He is impartial and just. Aldous *never* tires of seeing him and listening to him. He is able to be as silent or as chatty with Gerald as he is with me; and moreover Gerald stimulates him intellectually." Now look at the nice time they all had yesterday. After lunching at Anita's,

> we three went home for tea with toast and crumpets. Aldous *tout content*. Gerald reads till six, then meditates for an hour. At 7.15 he emerges and bakes, under my instructions, his first batch of bread. We heat up our supper and Gerald sets the table. Aldous comes down, all three of us in the best of humours. A & G discuss, always with the same interest, what they have been reading, while Gerald keeps an eye on his bread and doesn't burn it—at half past nine I drive him home. Aldous is already in bed, reading (he's been allowed to for the last few days). I still feel tired, but less than I did—anyway I think one has no right to be.

For Aldous's eyes *are* improving. Four weeks have passed—three hours at the "oculist" every morning—constant, watchful attention to right use.

> [8th January Maria to Jeanne] We have a definite improvement, though nothing spectacular as yet; what is certain is that even the right pupil is clearing up; the left looks quite cleared up but one must think that there is still some invisible opacity because he is still not able to read without fatigue. The *regard* is now that of his childhood photographs, and it moves me to see Aldous *looking at me* . . . Meanwhile he goes on with unbelievable patience . . . And its monstrously expensive . . .
>
> We are happier together than ever. I haven't written to you about this, but I think you must have guessed it from my letters. *Jamais en désaccord . . ni avec personne*—and he is becoming more and more patient.

Chapter Six

1938/1939 II—Eat and Drink and Read Books

BY mid-February Aldous is able to report to Chatto's that he is hard at work. On a short phantasy, "a wild extravaganza .. but built up of solidly realistic psychological elements .. a most serious parable". After which he hopes to write eight lectures on religion to be delivered in Calcutta (yes—they were planning to go to India) "for a thing appropriately called the Gosh Foundation". The letter—Aldous's first, it would seem, since 18th November—is written on a typewriter with outsize lettering.

Their life became less enclosed. In March, a European visitor (the last?) Jeremy,[1] the St John Hutchinsons' son—"an adorable boy .. very amusing and intelligent . . . I'd like to keep him here for ever. It made me realize how exciting it would be to see other friends." (It was he and his sister who as children had dubbed Aldous the Quangle Wangle.) Aldous and Maria took him to the sights, Disney's studio, Hubble's telescope, and Chaplin took them all out to dinner at Earl Carrol's restaurant—"un floor-show— jamais j'en ai vu d'aussi belles filles; toutes presque nues et le dîner mangeable".

> For a young man it was all pure delight. [Jeremy Hutchinson writes] Maria so down to earth, so poetical, so full of humour and teasing, and of course for the adolescent so sexy . . . Within an hour of arriving .. I was being conducted round Forest Lawn with Aldous caressing the marble pink bottoms of the statuary and pointing out the "staggering sensuality" as the eternal Wurlitzer sounds came out from behind the trees. . . .
>
> I had been bitterly disappointed with *Gaza* and unsympathetic to religious experiences, but of course it was Aldous of the Essays, Aldous of day to day social contact, Aldous the apparent Saint .. gentle, inquiring, fascinating, and fascinated too with every fact, every thought, hesitatingly brought out with the amazed inflection of his voice .. Aldous the same with everyone—the black cook, the Japanese gardener, Charlie, Hubble, Gerald Heard, me . . . For a young man (and for a boy) he aroused a deep response . . . I loved them both. My whole memory was one of gaiety and stimulation.

Summer plans now. They would like to go to Frieda's ranch but

---

[1] The present Q.C.

Matthew wants a change from mountains—"He likes the sea and girls."

But presently Aldous has a relapse—extreme fatigue, a probable spot on the lung. "How *can* we go to Calcutta in six months?"

In April they moved house; again. To Pacific Palisades, a farther suburb of Los Angeles, 701 South Amalfi Drive. It was a real horror, far and away their most extreme. They looked on it with affection. As they lived there for three years it is worth a description.

It is a paradise we have this time [Maria to Eddy] A large rambling house in wood inside and out and Angiolino calls it the *wagone di terza classe*. And the man was German and collected horrors in European "kitsch" and specialized in women's bosoms. Pictures of women . . all over the place . . and statues of bronze . . Some we hid and when I got tired of hiding I hoped to get used to it and we did. Aldous turned the statues around when he preferred bottoms to breasts. But there are three sitting-rooms and a study for Aldous and a little bed and bathroom separate for Matthew . . . Aldous's room is small and we had to hire a hospital bed as . . nothing in the house fitted him. As a table de nuit he has a large safe . . inside he keeps books and I always fear he may pinch his fingers.

Then there is a bar in the cellar . . Covered with more bozomed women and clocks which tick up and down a fan on a naked lady and luminous dogs as lamps and . . a full-sized painting of a gorilla carrying a woman in a chemise to a very easily guessed purpose; there also stands a harmonium next to the gorilla. But the house we can laugh at and it is the garden which is the paradise.

We stand on a sort of island; high over the sea, over-looking steeply a very green valley with trees and a polo field and all around are the hills. They were very green and now are turning slowly to that dry gold . . .

And the garden is a garden. About five acres and filled with flowers and citrus trees and large Avocados now ripe and roses and gladioli and many flowers we don't know . . . We live as peacefully as in Sanary and the telephone rings rarely . . they all know that Aldous is finishing a book. Work is understood here.

[He] is working with determination to get his novel finished for autumn publication.

Anita Loos, in Santa Monica, was by Los Angeles standards a near neighbour.

One reason why we walk often at night. When she works at the studio all day it is the only time she has for walking. And it is not safe for her to walk alone so she brings a ridiculous little dog . . . She and Aldous laugh a lot; we are very fond of her. Otherwise we see no-one except often Constance Collier the old English actress. She is pretty grand and ridiculous and yet also witty and pompous. She is a dear and so proud when Queen Mary sends her signed photographs and messages . . . The Chaplins we don't see often because Charlie is definitely working . . But we are good friends and Paulette is making quite a success . . . of her movie career. The other careers being brilliant right away. I mean business and love and so on.

. . Of course we . . see Gerald less because he still won't have a car or drive somebody else's so he has to come and stay when he wants to see us as it is fourteen miles to his canyon each way. He is very well indeed and happy in his little cell adjoining Chris's house . . .

To Jeanne, that same spring, Maria said about Gerald:

I think it's dangerous to live by oneself and with an *idée fixe* about continual meditation . . . And yesterday, when I was driving him home, I asked him if he didn't have to get anything. No, he had all he needed, fruit, bread etc . . and when I pointed out to him that all of it was eight days old and that he really could afford to buy himself a piece of bread . . . for him it's part of his Bovaristic image; part of the yogi and the saint etc . . . poor Gerald and he is profoundly unhappy and sometimes I torment him by asking monstrously precise questions. He never answers me with a lie, but I find that he lies by omission. And all this saddens me because he is as miserable, in his sphere, as Mère is in hers. Mère has neither principles nor morality . . . Gerald has them in abundance; Mère is lazy and allows herself to drift; Gerald works tenaciously at giving himself a positive direction; but they are both equally unhappy and I don't see that one of them does any more good than the other either for individuals or the world in general . . .

May 1939. ". . Tell me all about England, about Europe. Are you getting used to living under continual threat?" Aldous was signing or soliciting affidavits, Maria again implored her family to come while there was time. Jeanne was not the only target. The Nicolas's house in Holland was only a few miles from the German border: those letters also rained upon Suzanne. She would answer that Joep had just accepted another big commission, was doing stained-glass windows in yet another church or public building, wouldn't hear of leaving—they had no capital, were unknown in the U.S.A. Leave it all, Maria went on, better poor than dead. We'll help you. At least send the children. *Now.* Encourage Mère to come. Aldous made legal and financial arrangements to get two Jewish children out of Germany whose mother had been a pupil of his mother's at Prior's Field. For the rest the Huxleys, like so many others, led a divided existence, resigned to uncertainty, now aware of danger, now getting on with things, looking the other way . . .

. . In the past year I have worn myself out so completely twice with anticipation of what might happen that I am now callous. [Maria to Eddy] Callous for what *might*—I don't suppose I could be callous to what is reality. But as it has not happened, maybe it won't ever. Of course they talk about it constantly and follow the papers and the radio and they mind terribly. But having minded more and more intensely and pointlessly, because it helps nothing, I was worn-out and I just listen to them. I mean chiefly Aldous and Gerald.

. . There are so many interesting things going on in America. And [Aldous says] it seems that Europe can be looked at better from far away. And it is strange that one needs no roots really if one tries living without . . . So you see what I mean about roots and patriotism and so on. But I see how much Bertie Russell suffers from the trees here not looking like so much cooked spinach. And I am sorry for him . . . But we live on as if there were no nightmare, and I suppose that is what you all do. Eat and drink and read books.

Chapter Seven

Private Miracle

HIS teacher that winter had taken him quite a long way, Aldous found. Then he met a disciple of the late Dr Bates, a woman, Margaret D. Corbett,[1] a genius of inventiveness, patience, intelligence and sympathy, Maria said, and devoted to her work. She proved perfect for Aldous. To her now he went six times a week. The lessons were not boring—"You are taught to *use* your eyes, taught *how* to read, to look, to drive." And, Maria added, Mrs Corbett helped anyone who needed it; for those who could pay her fees were reasonable while Mrs Bates in New York charged twenty-five dollars an hour.

> Yesterday [4th May, Maria to Jeanne] he was able to read—not easily—the 15ft line at 15ft—that is normal, but hesitant, vision! It *is* a miracle!
>
> And our old friend Constance Collier, too, who was nearly blind with cataract is rapidly regaining her vision. Now I begin to dare talk about it; even Aldous talks about it. The left eye has altogether cleared up. The right eye is clearing rapidly and above all he is able to move it, it moves back: you remember that as he wasn't using the eye, there was a marked strabismus.

And to Eddy three weeks later.

> . . He has put on a lot of weight and with it a different air . . I cannot explain. If you saw Aldous you would understand—He is somehow smoothed out. His moods and his depressions have smoothed along with it . . . From having a vision of 15% he now has a vision of 50% and is making more rapid progress. So you see what that must mean to him. He can read even the paper without glasses, and above all he can read without fatigue. This is the great excitement of our life, and for me it will remain a miracle, and something to burn candles to the Virgin for.

And now Aldous, for his part, mentions it.

1 Author of *How to Improve Your Sight*, Los Angeles, 1938. Other literature on the subject: Dr W. H. Bates's own *Perfect Sight Without Glasses*, New York, 1920; *The Improvement of Sight by Natural Methods*, by C. S. Price, M.B.E., D.O. London, 1934.

.. I have been working on my eyes [he begins in a typical manner in a letter to his brother of 30th July] taking lessons in seeing from an admirable teacher here . . . Optometrists loathe the method, because it endangers a hundred-and-fifty-million-dollar-a-year spectacle industry. Most doctors oppose it, because Bates's experimental work established unquestionably, it seems to me after reading his papers —that the Helmholtz theory regarding accommodation and refractive error is wrong. Still, the more liberal doctors have now got to the point of saying that it can't do any harm. Meanwhile there are the empirical facts which are those in my own case.

Aldous now gives the technical assessment of his improved vision. As the subject is extremely controversial, I shall transcribe it in full. For clarity, it might be best to begin by repeating his summing-up of his case (in *The Art of Seeing*) as it stood when he had partially regained his sight in 1913.

[The attack of *keratitis punctata*] left me (after eighteen months of near-blindness . . .) with *one eye just capable of light perception,* and *the other with enough vision to permit of my detecting the two-hundred-foot letter on the Snellen chart at ten feet* [my italics].
[With spectacles, the good eye] was able to recognize the seventy-foot line at ten feet and to read tolerably well—provided always that I kept my better pupil dilated with atropine . . . A measure of strain and fatigue was always present, and there were occasions when I was overcome by that sense of complete physical and mental exhaustion which only eye-strain can produce.

And in his present letter to Julian, Aldous specified the strength of the spectacles he had been obliged to use.

bi-focals, first of six and-a-half diopters of magnification, then of eight and ten diopters [in 1938], plus special reading glasses of fifteen diopters.

The letter goes on.

I am now wearing no glasses, seeing much better at a distance, reading, and all without strain and with a general improvement in health and nervous condition. I have just done the whole of the revision of my typescript (a very trying job, as you doubtless know) without glasses and . . without fatigue.
Meanwhile, the vision of *the right eye* [the *bad eye,* that had been capable only of light perception] has increased in the last three months, so that, from seeing the big 200-foot letter on the chart at three feet, *I can now read the 70-foot line at six feet* and large nursery

print at the near point. The scar tissue is quite definitely clearing up, and I have good hopes that, if I persist, I may get back as much vision in the bad eye as I had in the good eye and that *the good eye may be pushed on from fifty per cent of normal vision (where it is now, having been raised from about fifteen per cent)* to something considerably nearer normal.

Meanwhile I have seen other cases responding in the same way. Constance Collier .. took the treatment for a cataract which had reduced one eye to a mere perception of light and darkness. After four months, she can now read normal print with this eye. Incipient cataracts clear up completely in as little as a month. Glaucoma is relieved very rapidly. I have seen several cases of children with squint completely cured . . .

And all through a perfectly rational and simple series of practices designed, first, to relax the eye and increase its circulation . . second, to train the mind to interpret what the eye sends it and not to interfere with the functioning of the eye by straining or staring.

What Aldous did not mention were the daily hours spent on learning those simple practices, the vigilance, the submission, the tough perseverance. *Not* to strain, *not* to stare, is as hard to learn for an urban adult as turning cart-wheels; harder. It needs a patience which, as Maria said, we would only understand if we ourselves had been half blind.

Chapter Eight

1938/1939 III

"**I** AM asking myself—are we really going to run off to India? I think for us that kind of thing is over. Why not stay where we are?" Aldous took the point. "We might travel inwardly," he said, "instead of outwardly."

In June they heard that "Mère is ruined . . . She has played the market. We always expected to have to help her one day . . . We shall do it *de bon cœur*." (Mme Nys was not then actually ruined, though soon after they substantially had to help her, and this Aldous did to his last day.)

Kingsley Martin, of the *New Statesman*, wrote to Aldous taking him to task no doubt about his politics or lack of them. Aldous replied.

. . I don't know where you got information about Gerald and myself being about to start a community; it doesn't happen to be true. I can't speak for Gerald; but certainly I don't know nearly enough about many things to be able to embark on such a venture . . . This doesn't diminish my interest in such ventures; for I become more and more firmly convinced that it is completely pointless to work in the field of politics . . first, because one can't achieve anything unless one is in a key position, and, second, because even if one were in a key position, all one could achieve would be, at the best, a deflection of evil into slightly different channels . . .

. . Religious people who think they can go into politics and transform the world always end by going into politics and being transformed by the world. (e.g. the Jesuits, Père Joseph, the Oxford Group.) Religion can have no politics except the creation of small-scale societies of chosen individuals outside and on the margin of the essentially unviable large-scale societies . . .

Christopher Isherwood first came to Hollywood that summer, under contract to a studio. As an old friend of Gerald's he soon met Aldous and Maria who quickly became very fond of him. They liked him, as the saying goes, for himself. Oh, they knew he was *a* writer. There is an entry in Virginia Woolf's Diary (November 1938) which goes:

Isherwood and I met on the doorstep. He is a slip of a wild boy: with quicksilver eyes: nipped: jockeylike. That young man, said W. Maugham, "holds the future of the English novel in his hands."

Of that aspect of their friend's identity the Huxleys had but little idea. They had not read then *Mr Norris*, didn't know of Issyvoo.

In his turn he now recorded his own first impression of Aldous. An Aldous in his forty-sixth year. After remarking on that "extraordinarily sinister house which was built and furnished in a style best described as log-cabin decadent", Isherwood went on:[1]

. . I had expected somebody resembling the skinny, thickly bespectacled, spider-like intellectual of the early photographs . . . Aldous . . in the flesh was slender but not at all skinny, and the insect-look . . now seemed to me to be more of a bird-look, benevolent and quick with interest in his surroundings. He no longer wore spectacles. When he talked, his beautifully sensitive features seemed literally to shine with enthusiasm . . .

Aldous's clothes were usually informal. But he wore everything well, and when he put on a suit he looked marvellously distinguished. It was not in his character to be consciously dressy; but he was never careless and I think he must have had a certain affection for some of the things he wore. For instance, he had kept a tie from Paris for more than twenty years and would remark that it was "like an early Rouault."

Aldous had given up . . spectacles because he had become a convert to the Bates Method . . I have neither the authority nor the inclination to express a personal opinion on this subject; I merely record that I have seen people who were discussing it become enraged to the point of incoherence and I can well believe that it has sometimes been the cause of fist-fights.

Aldous's novel, *After Many a Summer Dies the Swan*, was getting written with the speed almost of *Crome Yellow*. On 25th July, the eve of his birthday, copy was ready and revised. Maria, on Mrs Corbett's advice, had learnt to touch-type just in time. Aldous said he didn't mind the mistakes as long as the thing got done. He had a horror of sending out his work, and even the Madame Curie script, with M.G.M.'s typing pool standing by, had been copied at home by Maria.

I think we are pleased with it. [Maria to Jeanne about the novel] Matthew has been so nice. He finished reading it last night before going to bed. He said, "Well, I did enjoy that book, pop; very illuminating too!" What ease they have with each other.

Aldous hesitated to give it to me, he put it off as long as he could . . I think it's because he was afraid I might criticise the cynicism with which he described stupidity. I, who know him so well, can feel underneath all his impatience and horror of stupidity . . .

[1] *Mem. Vol.*

And to Eddy,

It's in his most excellent manner—the brilliant fiendish manner. Funny—Indecent—Horrifying. Yet it is also, thank God, placated with the other side that is Constructive.

> *The woods decay, the woods decay and fall,*
> *The vapours weep their burthen to the ground,*
> *Man comes and tills the field and lies beneath,*
> And after many a summer dies the swan.

The Tennysonian lines from *Tithonus*, Tithonus to whom the goddess granted immortality but forgot to add eternal youth. Aldous's theme was time: a parable about the illusion, if you will, of purely quantitative time. However, in *After Many a Summer*, Aldous really did apply his principle of mixing all the categories, the book slides from slapstick into philosophic dissertation, eroticism, pastiche, esoteric moralizing. If it was a return to Peacock, it is very far out Peacock indeed. The essential theme is immortality and time, and the locale is Southern California. The "finer shades of the American language" were vetted by no less an expert than Anita Loos. There is much straight description, Baedeker in his heyday would hardly have been more accurate about the ride westward from Los Angeles railway station, the Union Depot.

The first thing to present itself was a slum of Africans and Philipinos, Japanese and Mexicans. And what permutations and combinations of black, yellow and brown! What complex bastardies! And the girls —how beautiful in their artificial silk! . . . the car plunged into a tunnel and emerged into another world, a vast, untidy suburban world of filling-stations and bill-boards . . of vacant lots and waste-paper . . and churches—Primitive Methodist churches built . . in the style of the Cartuja at Granada, Catholic churches like Canterbury Cathedral, synagogues disguised as Hagia Sophia, Christian Science churches with pillars and pediments like banks . . .

EATS. COCKTAILS. OPEN NITES.

JUMBO MALTS.

DO THINGS, GO PLACES WITH CONSOL SUPER GAS!

. . The car sped onwards, and here in the middle of a vacant lot was a restaurant in the form of a seated bulldog, the entrance between the front-paws, the eyes illuminated . . .

ASTROLOGY, NUMEROLOGY, PSYCHIC READINGS.

DRIVE IN FOR NUTBURGERS.

. . Mile after mile . . interminably . . .

CLASSY EATS. MILE HIGH CONES.

JESUS SAVES.

FINE LIQUORS.

GO TO CHURCH AND FEEL BETTER ALL THE WEEK.

. . A real estate agent's office in the form of an Egyptian sphinx.

JESUS IS COMING SOON.

BEVERLY PANTHEON THE CEMETERY THAT IS *DIFFERENT*.

. . Past a Rosicrucian Temple, past two cat-and-dog hospitals, past a School for Drum-Majorettes . . . Sunset Boulevard . . . Beverly Hills. The surroundings changed. The road [was] flanked by the gardens of a rich residential quarter. Through trees . . the façades of houses all new, almost all in good taste—elegant and witty pastiches of Lutyens manor houses, of Little Trianons, of Monticellos; light-hearted parodies of Le Corbusier . . fantastic . . adaptations of Mexican haciendas and New England farms.

For Aldous this was no mere exotic travel, it was a description of what was to become his home-town.

. . The houses succeeded one another, like the pavilions of some endless international exhibition. Gloucestershire followed Andalusia . . .

"That's Harold Lloyd's place," said the chauffeur . . "And that's Charlie Chaplin's . . That's where Ginger Rogers lives. Yes, *sir*."

And then we have of course the passing evocation of the Beverly Pantheon—Forest Lawn, the Western necropolis immortalized a few years later by another English novelist Aldous did not read (though he's been heard to say that he enjoyed *Vile Bodies*). Nightmare Abbey, where the house party and most of the action of the book take place, is nightmare castle, an almost undisguised version of W. Randolph Hearst's aberration, where the Huxleys spent a fascinated weekend. (Domestic details, such as cotton sheets in a house with an old master in the lift, were imparted in Maria's letters.) In fact Aldous came as near to making use of living models as he ever did. His Mr Stoyte, the boorish owner of the castle, maintains a private laboratory researching ways of prolonging human life; Hearst's fear of death was notorious. Hearst's young woman friend, Marion Davis, was, at least to contemporary Californians,

as recognizable as she is in Orson Welles's film [*Citizen Kane*]. And the wicked Dr Obispo is said to have been modelled after a Hollywood physician. The novel also includes Huxley's composite of two of Southland's leading educators merged into an unctuous college

379

president named Dr Mulge, whose voice is a blend of vaseline and port wine. This did not endear the author to his models.[1]

On the "constructive" side, there is Mr Propter: Miller transmigrated from *Eyeless in Gaza* in the form of an American scholar. He holds forth on evil, time and liberation.

"I like the words I use to bear some relation to facts. [Mr Propter continued] That's why I'm interested in eternity—psychological eternity. Because it's a fact."

"For you perhaps," said Jeremy [the English high-brow].

"For anyone who chooses to fulfil the conditions under which it can be experienced."

"And why should anyone wish to fulfil them?"

"Why should anyone choose to go to Athens to see the Parthenon? Because it's worth the bother. And the same is true of eternity. The experience of timeless good is worth all the trouble it involved."

"Timeless good," Jeremy repeated with distaste. "I don't know what the words mean."

"Why should you?" said Mr Propter. ". . you've never bought your ticket for Athens."

From timeless good to longevitous wickedness—the Fifth Earl, a thorough-going autocrat with a nice turn of the pen and the tastes of the Marquis de Sade, the Fifth Earl of Gonnister who has succeeded in keeping himself alive and virile on a diet of raw carp gut into this two-hundred and second year.

(Carp gut? "Well, that was just a fantasy," Aldous said in the London interview twenty years later on. "Incidentally, long after I wrote it, I read in some medical paper a whole theory about cholesterol being the villain in the whole ageing process. So it wasn't an entirely fantastic picture—I mean if we would find something to inhibit the formation of cholesterol, you *would* do something to increase life . . .") At a price:

. . The shirt, which was his only garment, was torn and filthy. Knotted diagonally across the powerful chest was a broad silk ribbon that had evidently once been blue . . He sat hunched up, his head thrust forward and at the same time sunk between his shoulders. With one of his huge and strangely clumsy hands he was scratching a sore place . . between the hairs of his left calf . . .

1 From an article by Aldous's friend, Lawrence Clark Powell, then Librarian of the University of California, "California Classics Reread" in *Westways*, December 1970.

Deathless, Tithonus became a repulsive old man; the Fifth Earl has turned into a foetal ape that has had time to grow up— evolution's finest joke. Dr Obispo breaks into a Mephistophelian laugh. The Fifth Earl growls and lunges at his female, then

> smoothed the broad ribbon of his order with the palm of his hand . . making as he did so a curious humming noise that was like a simian memory of the serenade in Don Giovanni.

Mr Stoyte finds words. "Well . . once you get over the first shock —well, they look like they were having a pretty good time."

After Many a Summer, in Maria's words, is everybody's cup of tea in parts—but I can also see that it will be everybody's red rag in parts."

On the Sunday following Aldous's birthday and the completion of the novel, the Huxleys gave a big luncheon party. "Paulette [Goddard] brought a cake, a real birthday cake weighing 8 lbs., all white and inscribed '*Mon Coeur*,' that wasn't very explicit but charming in intention. And Charlot brought a case of Cordon Rouge, 12 bottles of Mum! Matthew said it was very good and dry. We had Helen Hayes and McArthur, her husband, the Charlies, the Hubbles . . Constance naturally and Chris and Gerald and the Rodakiewitz's (Peggy and her second husband). In the garden. Hazel [the negro maid Maria shared with Christopher Wood] came to help us and all that went admirably. They stayed till 7 o'clock and Charlie gave an exquisite performance; among other things a dance he is going to do with a balloon. They are going to start shooting next Monday. [Indeed, *The Great Dictator*] It will be the best thing he has ever done. Lilian Gish came later on and Orson Welles . . ."

As Christopher Isherwood put it, "One didn't think of Maria Huxley as being what is usually meant by a 'great' hostess; yet, in her charmingly haphazard way—by accident, almost—she created some historic parties."

There were a few more easy days. Aldous and Gerald do their spiritual exercises; Maria says she hasn't got the time so she is doing acrobatics instead. "Tell Sophie I can stand on my head now . . I think I was born acrobat." On Wednesday they are off to Santa Barbara where Rosalind Rajagopal and Krishnamurti are spending the summer. "He is charming and amusing and so simple. How he must suffer when he is treated as a prophet." Then Matthew needs a proper car. Maria proposes to buy him a new one—he ought to have the pleasure of a new car. "Aldous, curiously, turns a bit childish, he wants me to pass my car on to Matthew and get a new one for ourselves."

August, and everything overclouded once again by the one anxiety. Aldous had been offered another job by M.G.M., the adaptation of *Pride and Prejudice*; working again for a studio did not appeal to him at all and he meant to turn it down. But in the last week of the month, he accepted—to help even a few of those who would be needing help, he wanted all the money he was able to lay hands on.

Now it has happened, Maria wrote to Eddy after September 3rd. "It still seems unbelievable. Certainly unimaginable. For two days we were completely unexisting. I heard Chamberlain here in the middle of the night as he addressed you in London . .

"By the time my family got up I was just capable of telling them. Those hours had helped me to collect myself a bit. Though it is so much worse for all of you in the middle of it, yet you are obliged to do something—go or come or obey, whereas here we just listen and cannot believe. . . ."

CHRONOLOGY

1894
26th July — Birth of Aldous Leonard Huxley at Laleham, Godalming, Surrey

1895
29th June — Death of Thomas Henry Huxley

1899 — Birth of Aldous's sister Margaret

1901 — Aldous's parents, Leonard and Julia Huxley, leave Laleham and move to Prior's Field, Surrey

1902
23rd January — Julia Huxley's school for girls opens at Prior's Field

1903
Autumn — Aldous goes to Preparatory School at Hillside

1908
June — Aldous leaves Hillside
Autumn — Aldous goes to Eton
29th November — Aldous's mother, Julia Huxley, dies

1909 — Leonard Huxley moves to 27 Westbourne Square, London W2

1910
20th May — Aldous lines route of Edward VII's funeral as member of Eton C.O.T.C.

1911
Early Spring — Aldous leaves Eton because of serious eye trouble

Later — Diagnosis of *keratitis punctata*: near blindness lasting for some eighteen months

Summer — Aldous learns Braille
Autumn — Aldous tutored by (Sir) George Clark

1912
23rd February — Leonard Huxley married to Rosalind Bruce *aet.* 22

April — Aldous's sight beginning to improve. Writes his first novel on typewriter (T/S lost)

May/June — Aldous in Marburg, Germany

1913
April/May/June — Aldous staying with his brother Trevenen in Oxford, reading for Matriculation

July/August — At Grenoble with Lewis Gielgud
October — Aldous enters Balliol College, Oxford

383

1914
January/June   Balliol College
May   Aldous's paternal grandmother, T. H.
                                Huxley's widow, dies at Eastbourne
4th August   England at war with Germany
23rd August   Death of Aldous's brother Trevenen *aet*. 24
October   Aldous returns to Oxford, lives out of
                                college with the Haldanes at Cherwell
                                Edge

1915
January/June   Oxford, Cherwell Edge; competes for the
                                Newdigate with a long Byronic poem;
                                1st publication of verse in *Oxford Poetry*
Summer   Connel Ferry, Scotland; Westbourne
                                Square, London; Prior's Field
September   Westbourne Square
October/December   Return to Balliol College
5th December   First visit to Garsington
December   First meeting with D. H. Lawrence at
                                Hampstead

1916
January/June   Balliol College, Oxford
January   Aldous rejected by Army as totally unfit
February   1st issue of the *Palatine Review* founded and
                                edited by T. W. Earp and Aldous; 1st
                                publication of "Mole" and other poems
June   Acting assistant editor of *Oxford Poetry*.
                                Schools examination; Down from Ox-
                                ford with a First in English and the
                                Stanhope Historical Essay Prize
July/August   Temporary schoolmaster at Repton
August/September   Garsington; London; Prior's Field
September   Publ. *The Burning Wheel*
September/December   Aldous lives at Garsington, working on
                                Philip Morrell's farm

1917
January/April   Garsington, ibid.
April/July   Clerical job at the Air Board. Living with
                                his father and step-mother at 16 Brack-
                                nell Gardens, Hampstead
July/September   London; Oxford; Garsington
18th September   Aldous takes up post as schoolmaster at
                                Eton. Living at the Old Christopher (to
                                February 1919)
December   Publ. *Jonah*. Contributed, in course of
                                year, poems to *Wheels*, *Oxford Poetry*, the
                                Nation, *Form*

1918
January/December   Master at Eton
January/February   Working on *Leda*

Easter	Holidays London, Surrey, Garsington
Summer	Holidays Garsington, Prior's Field
November	Armistice. Working on "The Farcical History of Richard Greenow"
Christmas	Garsington

1919

January/April	Last Half at Eton. Aldous resigns
April	Easter Holidays. Aldous goes to Belgium to see Maria Nys at St Trond after a two and a half years' separation. Meets the Nys and Baltus families. Aldous officially engaged to Maria Nys
April	Starts editorial job on the *Athenaeum* under Middleton Murry (till October 1920)
June	Furnishes and moves into a flat at 18 Hampstead Hill Gardens N.W.3 (till December 1920)
10th July	Aldous married to Maria Nys at Bellem, Belgium
July/December	London. Miscellaneous journalism chiefly for the *Athenaeum*

1920

January/December	London
January	Brief stay with Drieu La Rochelle in Paris
February	Publ. *Limbo*
24th March	Death of Mrs Humphry Ward
19th April	Birth of son, Matthew Huxley
20th April	Starts additional job as dramatic critic on the *Westminster Gazette*
May	Publ. *Leda*. Takes on third job as assistant Chelsea Book Club (till August)
October	Resigns from the *Athenaeum*. Starts job on *House & Garden*
December	Aldous and Maria give up the Hampstead flat. Maria and child move to Belgium for the winter

1921

January/March	Aldous at 26 Regent Square, W.C.1 with Tommy Earp and Russell Green. Maria and Matthew at Brussels and Florence
April/May	Aldous and Maria's first stay in Florence. Villa Minucci
August	First visit to Rome (one week)
May/August	Aldous writes *Crome Yellow*
May/September	First stay at Forte dei Marmi (29 Viale Morin)
October	Aldous and Maria return to London. New job with Condé Nast (till late

	spring 1923). New flat: 155 Westbourne Terrace, W.2 (till December 1922)
November	Publ. *Crome Yellow*

1922

January/December	London. Office job with Condé Nast
May	Publ. *Mortal Coils*
June	Paris
August/September	Holiday at Forte dei Marmi, Villa Tacchella

1923

January	New flat: 44 Princess Gardens S.W.7 (till May or June)
8th January	First Three-Year Contract with Chatto & Windus at £500 a year
April	Holiday in Florence (2-3 weeks)
May	Publ. *On the Margin*
May or June	Sudden departure from England to live in Italy
Summer	Forte dei Marmi (Villa Fasola?). Writing *Antic Hay*
August	*Antic Hay* finished. Move to Florence, Castel a Montici, 15 Via Sta Margherita a Montici (till June 1925)
November	Publ. *Antic Hay*

1924

January/December	Castel a Montici, Florence
February	*Little Mexican* finished
March	Aldous starts writing *Those Barren Leaves*. Car travels in Italy
April	Maria's sister Suzanne marries Joep Nicolas. Joep and Suzanne spend part of their honeymoon with Aldous and Maria in Florence
May	Publ. *Little Mexican*
June	Publ. *The Discovery*, an adaptation of the play by Sheridan. Car travels in Italy
July/August	Forte
August	Aldous finishes *Those Barren Leaves* at Ambérieu, Savoie, France
September	Paris; London (King's Rd, Chelsea). Motor tour Holland and Belgium
October	Paris. Return to Florence (car journey through central and southern France. Starts *Along the Road*
November	Motor journey Rome and southern Italy

1925

January/June	Castel a Montici, Florence
January	Publ. *Those Barren Leaves. Along the Road* finished
March/April	Tunisia

June	Florence house searched by Fascisti
End June	Leave Castel a Montici for good
July	London. Aldous makes arrangements for round the world journey
August	Belgium. Aldous and Maria leave Matthew at St Trond for 11 months
September	Publ. *Along the Road*
15th September	Aldous and Maria sail from Genoa. Travel diary *Jesting Pilate* begun at sea
October	Bombay; Srinagar; Kashmir
November	Srinagar; Agra; Jaipur; Cawnpore for All India Congress. Encounters Gandhi and Nehru. Lahore
December	Lahore; Peshawar; Amritsar
1926	
January	Benares; Lucknow; Delhi; Calcutta
February	Aldous and Maria leave India for Burma. Rangoon. Up the Irrawaddy. Bhamo
March	Malaya: Penang; Singapore
5th March	Sail for Java. Stops at Batavia; Garoet; Buitenzorg; Miri; Sarawak; Labuan; Kudat; Sandakan
March	Change ship at Zamboanga in Southern Philippines to Manila
7th April	At Manila catch liner to San Francisco. Stop Hong Kong
April	Few days Japan. Cross Pacific
5th May	Arrive San Francisco. First visit U.S.A. Los Angeles.
May	By train to Chicago
17th May	New York for two weeks
May	Publ. *Two or Three Graces*
June	Sail for England. London. Aldous sits for his portrait to his uncle, the Hon. John Collier. 2nd Agreement with Chatto & Windus
July	London
August	St Trond. Aldous and Maria move to the Mountains for Matthew's health
August/December	Cortina d'Ampezzo (Villa Ino Colli)
October	Publ. *Jesting Pilate*. Aldous starts writing *Point Counter Point*. Aldous and Maria meet D. H. Lawrence in Florence: Aldous and D. H. L.'s first meeting since the single one in 1915
December	Publ. *Essays New and Old*
1927	
January/February	Cortina d'Ampezzo. Aldous breaks off work on *Point Counter Point* and starts *Proper Studies*

387

Mid-February	The Huxleys leave Cortina. Brief stay Florence (D. H. L.)
March/April/May	London
May	Aldous and Maria at St Trond for the death of Maria's grandfather, R. Baltus
June/November	Forte dei Marmi (Villa Majetta)
June	Rina Rontini, aged 15, enters the Huxley household. Brief visit of D. H. Lawrence.
July	*Proper Studies* finished. D. H. L. very ill in Florence: Aldous and Maria go to assist him until Frieda's return from Germany
August	Aldous takes up work again on *Point Counter Point*
November	Publ. *Proper Studies*
December	Christmas at Florence with D. H. L. and Frieda

1928

January/February	Les Diablerets, Vaud, Switzerland with Julian and Juliette and their boys; the D. H. L.'s join them
March/May	London (Onslow Mews, S.W.7). Getting Matthew off to his 1st school, Frensham Heights, Surrey
May	*Point Counter Point* finished
June	Paris. Aldous and Maria take a house near Paris, 3, rue du Bac, Suresnes
Late June/September	Forte dei Marmi (Villa Il Cannetto)
July	*Point Counter Point* selected by the Literary Guild in the U.S.A.
October	The Huxleys, Maria's sister, Jeanne Moulaert and her daughter, Sophie move into the house at Suresnes. Maria's grandmother, Emérence Baltus, dies.
November	Publ. *Point Counter Point*

1929

January/December	Suresnes, Paris
January	Aldous's first meeting with Gerald Heard in London at Raymond Mortimer's
Late January	Aldous and Maria stay for ten days with D. H. L. and Frieda at Bandol (Hotel Beaurivage)
February	Florence
March	D. H. L. very ill, stays with the Huxleys at Suresnes. D. H. L. sits for his portrait to Aldous's brother-in-law, Joep Nicolas
April	Aldous and Maria's first visit to Spain
May	Publ. *Arabia Infelix. Do What You Will* finished. London till mid-June

388

June/September	Aldous and Maria's last summer at Forte dei Marmi (Il Cannetto)
June	D. H. L. at Forte
July	Aldous takes the cure at Montecatini with Pino Orioli
August	A week in the Apuan mountains
15th September	Return to Suresnes
October	Publ. *Do What You Will*
October/November	Aldous and Maria go on a long motor tour through Spain.
December	Family Christmas at Suresnes

1930

January/April	Suresnes, Paris
January	London for production of play adapted from *Point Counter Point*, *This Way to Paradise*, at Daly's Theatre by Leon M. Lion
30th January	*This Way to Paradise* opens (Closes 1st March)
February	London; Suresnes; Venice where D. H. L. has entered the sanatorium Ad Astra
2nd March	Death of D. H. Lawrence at Venice (at the Villa Robermond)
March	Bandol. Aldous and Maria buy a house at Sanary
April	Aldous and Maria move into Villa Huley, La Gorguette, Sanary-sur-Mer
May	Publ. *Brief Candles*. Aldous in London in connection with D. H. L.'s letters
September/October	London. Journey with J. W. N. Sullivan to Paris and Berlin. London, Durham and Nottingham with Maria. London
October/December	Sanary
November	Publ. *Vulgarity in Literature*

1931

Mid-January/Mid-March	London (Dalmeny Court, Duke Street, St James's)
March	Aldous's first play, *The World of Light*, produced in London at the Royalty Theatre (closes after a brief run)
March/Late September	Sanary
May	Publ. *The Cicadas*
May/August	Aldous writes *Brave New World*
September	Publ. *Music at Night*
October/December	London (Dalmeny Court, later Rosa Lewis's old Cavendish Hotel in Jermyn Street)

1932

January/May	Sanary

February	Publ. *Brave New World*
May/June	Aldous and Maria dine with the King and Queen of the Belgians in Brussels. Travels in Germany with Raymond Mortimer
June/December	Sanary. Aldous writes unpublished play, *Now More Than Ever* (T/S believed to be lost)
September	Publ. *The Letters of D. H. Lawrence* edited by Aldous
October	Matthew enters Dartington School
November	Publ. *Texts and Pretexts*
December	London

1933
January	Sanary
January/May	Aldous and Maria travel in the West Indies, Guatemala, Mexico
3rd May	Death of Aldous's father, Leonard Huxley
June/December	Sanary. Aldous writes *Beyond the Mexique Bay*
November	Aldous and Maria's 3rd Spanish journey

1934
January/March	Sanary. Aldous working on *Eyeless in Gaza*
April	Publ. *Beyond the Mexique Bay*. Car journey in Italy
April/September	Sanary
June	Aldous briefly in London
October/December	London (18 St Albans Place, Regent Street, S.W.1)
December	Aldous and Maria take a seven year's lease on a flat in Albany
Mid-December	Move into E2 Albany, Piccadilly, W.1

1935
January/March	E2 Albany
January	Aldous in Paris (journalism), a few days
February	Few days Paris again
March/October	Sanary. At work on *Eyeless in Gaza*
October/December	E2 Albany. Aldous starts taking lessons with F. Matthias Alexander
October or November	Aldous joins Dick (The Rev. H. R. L.) Sheppard's Peace Pledge Union
3rd December	Aldous gives his first address on pacifism at Friends' House

1936
January/March	E2 Albany. Aldous working for Peace Pledge Union with Dick Sheppard and Gerald Heard
March	*Eyeless in Gaza* finished
April/September	Sanary

April	Publ. Peace Pamphlet *What Are You Going To Do About It?*
June	Publ. *Eyeless in Gaza*
September/October	Aldous and Matthew in Belgium and Holland
October/November	London (Mount Royal Hotel). Aldous and Maria work for the P.P.U.
December	Publ. *The Olive Tree*. Sanary

1937

January/February	Sanary. Aldous starts *Ends and Means*. Death of Maria's father, Norbert Nys
19th February	Aldous and Maria leave their Sanary house for good
March	London (Mount Royal Hotel)
7th April	Aldous, Maria and Matthew with Gerald Heard and Christopher Wood sail for New York on the s.s. Normandie
April	Brief stay in New York
April/May	Aldous, Maria, Matthew and Gerald Heard on a five weeks' car journey across the United States
May/September	The four spend the summer at Frieda Lawrence's Ranch, San Cristobal, Taos, New Mexico. Aldous finishes *Ends and Means*
October/November	Colorado; Hollywood
November	Publ. *Ends and Means*
November/December	Aldous and Gerald Heard lecture on peace throughout the United States. Gerald breaks his arm in Iowa, Aldous carried on
December	Maria takes a house on a Hudson Valley estate, Dairy Cottage, Foxhollow Farm, Rhinebeck, N.Y. Aldous and Matthew join her for Christmas

1938

January	Rhinebeck, N.Y. Aldous continues lecture tour. Aldous and Maria plan return to Europe
February	A scenario by Aldous apparently accepted by a film studio in Hollywood. Aldous and Maria change plans. Drive again across the continent. Stay at Frieda's Ranch. Arrive Hollywood. Take house on North Laurel Avenue. Aldous had severe bronchitis. Weeks in Hospital.
March	More or less acute aftermath lasting for over a year. Convalescence. Maria's

	mother injured by an accident in Mexico City
April	Death of Lady Ottoline Morrell
April/July	Aldous at work on a long novel (abandoned)
July	Move into house on North Linden Drive, Beverly Hills
August/September	Aldous works for Metro-Goldwyn-Mayer on a script of Madame Curie
September/October	House move in mid-Munich crisis to North Crescent Heights Boulevard, Hollywood. Matthew off to University of Colorado
October	Aldous decides to write a short phantasy with a Californian locale (*After Many a Summer Dies the Swan*)
November	Approximate beginning of Aldous's attempt to improve his sight by the Bates Method. Intensive training with a Bates Teacher. Aldous temporarily forbidden to read or write. Some improvement of sight noted by Maria

1939

January/February	At North Crescent Heights Boulevard, Hollywood
January	Further improvement in Aldous's sight. Allowed to read and write again.
February	Working on *After Many a Summer Dies the Swan*
April	Aldous and Maria move to a furnished house, 701 Amalfi Drive, Pacific Palisades (until February 1942)
May	Maria reports very definite improvement in Aldous's sight. Aldous does all his reading and writing without spectacles
June or July	First meeting with Christopher Isherwood
25th July	*After Many a Summer Dies the Swan* finished
26th July	Aldous's 45th birthday
July	Aldous describes his Bates training and precisely assesses his present sight in a letter to Julian
August	Aldous undertakes an adaptation of *Pride and Prejudice* for Metro-Goldwyn-Mayer
3rd September	England at war with Germany

SHORT LIST OF WORKS CONSULTED

BIBBY, Cyril: *T. H. Huxley: Scientist, Humanist and Educator.* C. A. Watts & Co. Ltd., 1959

CLARK, Ronald W.: *The Huxleys.* Wm. Heinemann Ltd. and McGraw-Hill Book Company, New York, 1968

DAVIS, Dennis Douglas: *Aldous Huxley's Pacificist Work: Death of a Sceptic.* A dissertation, available at the Library of the University of California at Los Angeles and Santa Barbara, and at the Detroit public libraries.

Aldous Huxley: A Bibliography, 1965-1971. To be published in 1974.

ESCHELBACH, Claire John and SHOBER, Joyce Lee: *Aldous Huxley: A Bibliography, 1916-1959,* and *A Supplementary Listing, 1914-1964.* University of California Press, 1961 and 1972.

FORD, Hugh, ed.: *Nancy Cunard: Brave Poet, Indomitable Rebel.* Chilton Book Company, Philadelphia, 1968

HUXLEY, Aldous: Complete Works
Collected Poems, ed. by Donald Watt with an Introduction by Richard Church. Chatto & Windus and Harper & Row, New York, 1971
The Letters of Aldous Huxley, ed. by Professor Grover Smith. Chatto & Windus, 1969 and Harper & Row, 1970

HUXLEY, Gervas: *Both Hands, An Autobiography.* Chatto & Windus, 1970

HUXLEY, Sir Julian: *Memories,* 2 vols. Allen & Unwin, 1970 and 1973. Vol. I, Harper & Row, 1971

HUXLEY, Leonard: *The Life and Letters of T. H. Huxley,* 2 vols. Macmillan, 1900

HUXLEY, Laura Archera: *This Timeless Moment: A Personal View of Aldous Huxley.* Farrar, Straus & Giroux, Inc., 1968 and Chatto & Windus, 1969

LAWRENCE, D. H., *Reminiscences and Correspondence.* (Letters to Earl H. and Aschsah Brewster, with reminiscences by them.) Martin Secker, 1934
The Letters of D. H. Lawrence, ed. and with an Introduction by Aldous Huxley. Wm. Heinemann Ltd. and The Viking Press, Inc., 1932
The Collected Letters of D. H. Lawrence, 2 vols., ed. by Harry T. Moore. Wm. Heinemann Ltd. and The Viking Press, Inc., 1962

MAISEL, Edward, ed.: *The Resurrection of the Body. The Writings of Frederick Matthias Alexander.* University Books, New York, 1969

MOORE, Harry T.: *The Intelligent Heart: The Story of D. H. Lawrence.* Wm. Heinemann Ltd. and Farrar, Straus, 1955

MORRISON, Sybil: *I Renounce War. The Story of the Peace Pledge Union.* Sheppard Press Ltd., 1962

NAHAL, Chaman, ed.: *Drugs and the Other Self.* Harper & Row, 1970

PLUMB, J. H. ed.: *Studies in Social History. A Tribute to G. M. Trevelyan.* Longmans, Green & Co., 1955

INDEX